German A. Duarte, Justin Michae
Reading »Black Mirror«

MW01048253

Media Studies | Volume 75

German A. Duarte is Assistant Professor of Film and Media Studies at the Free University of Bozen-Bolzano. His research interests include the history of media, film history, cognitive-cultural economy and philosophy.

Justin Michael Battin is Lecturer of Communication at RMIT University in Ho Chi Minh City, Vietnam. His research focuses on intersecting strands of Heidegger's philosophy with the everyday uses of mobile media technologies and mobile social media.

German A. Duarte, Justin Michael Battin (eds.)

Reading »Black Mirror«

Insights into Technology and the Post-Media Condition

[transcript]

The editors would like to extend their gratitude to the volume's language editor, Taylor Breckles, for her invaluable contribution.

Bibliographic information published by the Deutsche Nationalbibliothek
The Deutsche Nationalbibliothek lists this publication in the Deutsche National-bibliografie; detailed bibliographic data are available in the Internet at http://dnb.d-nb.de

© 2021 transcript Verlag, Bielefeld

Cover layout: Maria Arndt, Bielefeld
Typeset by Francisco Bragança, Bielefeld

Print-ISBN 978-3-8376-5232-1
PDF-ISBN 978-3-8394-5232-5
https://doi.org/10.14361/9783839452325

Contents

Imagining the Present Age

German A. Duarte & Justin Michael Battin

wat is this?

Almost a decade has passed since Charlie Brooker's seminal televisual program, *Black Mirror*, began populating the social imaginary with plausible scenarios deriving from the current post-media condition. The name of the program, as noted by Doug Hill, directly references the variety of digital screens that have, in his words, "proliferated in our daily lives, and all that too often seem to dominate them" (2017, p. 35). Although a wide range of digital technologies, particularly those permitting the generation, storage, and processing of data, are indeed pervasive in the current age, the general public has embraced their presence, viewing them as necessary to address societal issues related to energy, security, communication, transportation, health care, education, and food production. In part through the visible stewardship of public figures like Mark Zuckerberg, Elon Musk, and Jack Ma, these technologies have been widely adopted and integrated into everyday life, and thus rendered as ordinary (Williams, 2000 [1958]) and components of the everyday techno-scape (Appadurai, 1990).

It might be possible to understand the pervasiveness and taken-for-grantedness (Ling, 2012) of these new technologies as an analogous process. For Debray (1991), the development of technologies can be characterized by an unnoticeable character; human beings collectively accept these technological developments – mainly media technologies – as something natural since it is through these devices one perceives what is considered 'normal life' (1991, p. 202). Accompanying (and intertwined with) these technological developments is the radical cognitive transformation of everyday life, which likewise transpires seemingly without notice. For Heidegger (1977 [1962]), this transformation is best characterized by its technological character, *Das Gestell* (the framework/enframing). By organizing every form of human association and action (McLuhan 1994 [1964]), technologies and their corresponding essence, *Das Gestell*, exert forces that determine the way the subject encounters the world, and consequently discloses a particular worldly orientation (*Weltanschauung*). In Heidegger's words, "the need to ask about technology is presumably dying out to the same extent that technology more definitely characterizes and regulates the appearance of the totality of the world and the position of man in it" (1977 [1972], p. 376).

Such an orientation renders the subject unable to recognize and, by consequence, to comprehend the influence technologies have on its everyday existence, and the contemporary subject is thus obliged to develop "spaces of estrangement" from which it is possible to observe and account for its alienated condition. One of the most influential ways to exert these forces of estrangement on the subject was identified in Science Fiction, a genre that places technological concerns at its epicenter and organizes its narrative form as a dialectic between forces of estrangement and cognition (Suvin, 1972). In accordance with the Science Fiction genre, Brooker's *Black Mirror* addresses the aforementioned concern in a rather vivid manner, seemingly to ignite a critical lens and awaken viewers to their contemporary condition. Indeed, the series is "(...) notable for the potency in which it blends the disruptive powers of affect with the cohering powers of critique" (Conley & Burroughs, 2019, p. 140). Readings akin to these have inspired some authors to suggest that the program bears resemblance to Rod Sterling's *The Twilight Zone* (1959-1964), another classic anthology series that similarly entwined Science Fiction and social critique with shock and unexpected narrative twists. A notable difference, however, concerns the two program's thematic foci. Although thematic overlaps exist between the two programs, *The Twilight Zone* draws significantly more from the existentialist tradition to address the impact on human authenticity and identity wrought by the advent of consumer society and technological acceleration of the mid-20th century. *Black Mirror*, as a sort of successor, continues this exploration, albeit with more interest in depicting the apprehension that accompanies the colonization of human consciousness by technology's pervasive reach in the 21st century. Indeed, as noted by Cirucci & Vacker, "if *The Twilight Zone* reflected the existential angst and Cold War fears of the baby boomer generation, *Black Mirror* expresses the philosophical angst and technological fears for millennials in the twenty-first century" (2018, p. ix).

Continuing Science Fiction's storied tradition of promoting critical perspectives (see Freedman, 2000), *Black Mirror* constructs a fertile terrain for a social discussion on general concerns regarding these new technologies and their place in the construction of reality. As an anthology series utilizing an episodic format, *Black Mirror* inaugurated the second decade of the new millennium by generating a space of shared imaginary in which an inter-subjective need to more intently domesticate and reign in digital technologies emerged, lest they become too pervasive and entrenched in everyday life, beyond the point of any human regulation. It constructs this terrain on a strong particularity, which can be highlighted by the fact that generally the series is perceived as a dystopic vision of a (very near) future. However, as Sculos (2017) suggests, the program is perhaps more reflective of the present day than of a theoretical future, as it regularly provides commentary on the intersection between technology and contemporary thematic concerns such as the abjection of the other ("Men Against Fire"), social media addiction ("Smithereens"), and digitally enabled mob mentality ("The National Anthem" and "Hated in the Nation"). Moreover, the program presents common scenarios such as using currency to bypass digital advertisements ("Fifteen Million Merits") and malware-enabled hacking to commit digital blackmail ("Shut Up and Dance"). Additionally, the program features technologies that are already widely used, such as social media-based rating systems. These parallels between *Black Mirror* and the current reality have hardly gone unnoticed. For example, popular commercial publications such as *Wired* (Botsman, 2017; Kobie, 2019) have offered comparisons between "Nosedive" and China's Social Credit System, and Littmann (2019) demonstrates how "The Waldo Moment" highlights the politics of disrespect and disengagement that are widespread in our contemporary world, and of which technology has indeed played a significant role in propagating. Above all, however, the program depicts a different media condition strongly influenced by the force of dematerialization and coding of every human action that our present digital technology exerts. This last phenomenon, understood as symptomatic of a post-media condition, is conjugated by the television series under different plausible scenarios and popular concepts of interest to a variety of social fields and academic disciplines. As an example, consider the transformation of both cultural and collective memory if the event is primarily – and almost exclusively – technologically experienced, stored, and recalled ("The Entire History of You" and "Crocodile"). Within this framework, it is certainly legitimate to question the transformation of experience in the world, particularly one where numerous forms of surveillance omnipresent and human experience are codified into data at the moment of their happening. What becomes of human perception under this condition and how does it influence the contemporary construction of reality, as "Men Against Fire" so astutely interrogates?

The series ardently deals with symptoms we are witnessing in our current socio-technological context and invites us to consider how the culmination of the process initialized by the identification of the Enlightenment – mainly the Enlightenment that sees its maximal expression in the Leibnizian computational project – could represent an unimaginable, extreme techno-authoritarianism that goes even beyond our current notions of biopolitics and hegemonic forces of the dispositive (See Foucault, 2004 and Agamben, 2006). Two of the factors that strengthen and 'optimize' new expressions of social control are without doubt both the process of miniaturization and the popularization of technological devices. The mass production of mobile media technologies and their corresponding content as digital forms invaded and dissolved the formerly well-defined relationship between the private and the public spheres. As a corresponding result, the mass presence of these technological components occupied and fully shaped the whole social space, as depicted in "Hated in the Nation." This phenomenon represents a kind of leitmotif throughout the whole television series and serves as a conceptual gear for its plentiful depictions of techno-authoritarian scenarios. This could represent the framework through which the series analyses techno-authoritarianism as a force able to determine every form of value production within an economic system based on immaterial production ("Fifteen Million Merits"), the way this force determines every form of interaction and consumption with the object ("Playtest" and "Arkangel"), and every human-social relationship ("Hang The DJ"). Further, going beyond the invasion of the private sphere, and even beyond the traditional technological invasion of the body encapsulated in the figure of the cyborg, the series presents scenarios in which technological devices completely invade social spaces to the point of embracing all forms of human action. In fact, through the phenomenon of transhumanism, the series gives insights on a techno-authoritarian force embodied by a computational model able to determine people's most intimate memories ("San Junipero") while at the same time producing the center of the experience, that is to say, the body ("Be Right Back").

Despite the variance between the episodes in terms of story and content, the negative affordances of technology dominate (Singh, 2014). Like *The Twi-*

light Zone, the temporal proximity of the dystopian scenarios depicted in *Black Mirror* – those that could legitimately transpire in our present or not to distant reality – might be the precise feature that allowed the program to obtain such a presence in mainstream media, and consequently its ascension into the *Zeitgeist*. As noted by Chen, the techno-paranoia of the show seems to provide catharsis; "the concept of catharsis is one that wholly applies to the show's rapt audience. This desire to purge emotions, to experience the very horrors that we believe, in the recesses of our mind, *could* occur is what makes each episode of the show so alluring and somehow subsequently relieving" (2019). The series serves as a cathartic experience by means of the phenomenon of estrangement, which is generated by this precise narrative form. Further, as already noted, this television series seems to offer us the experience of a virtual present time, a present time that is directly derived from our daily lives and that seems to be the only existing temporal notion in our technological context. As suggested by Gillo Dorfles, in our digital technological context it seems that there is no longer space for the Bergsonian duration (*durée*), and consequently, unable to conceive an interval, the subject in our technological context seems to dwell a continuous present digital and hypertextual time bereft of future time (Dorfles, 2008). Nevertheless, the virtual present time generated in the series, which serves as a cathartic experience for the viewer (*viewer* in the case of *Bandersnatch*), is, maybe for its own cathartic nature, popularly perceived as a near future. This is a dystopian near future (Johnson, Márquez & Urueña 2020) which is no more than the present we live in, and that in its turn was constructed by the imaginary that Science Fiction developed during the second half of the last century. As remarked by James Ballard in an interview conducted in the late 90s,

> I feel myself that science fiction is now probably dead. It is a mid-20th-century movement and it is finished. I think it won. It achieved a great victory. It created the greatest popular literature of the 20th century. The science fiction imagery that we see in the cinema, on television, in advertising and so on, it's the most powerful imagery that the 20th century has produced. You could say that science fiction died because it succeeded (2019, p. 40).

Ballard's words are not only an strong statement that elucidates that, in our (former) mass media society, reality was the simple product of narratives that gave shape to the social imaginary, but these words also describe the way Science Fiction familiarized people with a perpetual and unique present time, as it constructed the social imagery on the assumption that in the technological context, in accordance with the thesis proposed in Heidegger's "The Age of the World Picture" (1977), the future is just a determined path that seems to erase any minority report. Unable to change the future, the subject of the post-media condition can only, from its eternal present, transform the perception of the past, a digital flexible past that forgets the fixity of history – granted by the materiality of the archive – and acquires the changeable nature of the digital immaterial object and the nature of memory.

To start the collection, German A. Duarte analyzes the way in which Science Fiction became a fertile terrain for philosophical reasoning as well as the way in which this genre became a popular space for the development of concepts able to populate the whole social imaginary by suturing a millenarian rupture in western philosophy. This chapter inquires about the notion of the concept, on the difference between the notions of *virtual* and *possible*, and on the way concepts – understood as complex and multidimensional images, – populate the social imaginary via Science Fiction narratives. By analyzing Shelley's *Frankenstein; or, The Modern Prometheus* (1818) as a foundational oeuvre, this chapter identifies Science Fiction as a clear symptom of an oncoming technological condition, one in which the irruption of electric technology began to exert a force of the externalization of being. Following this framework, this chapter analyses *Black Mirror* as a remarkable attempt to recover the inaugural spirit of the genre by mapping a series of various current social phenomena that features a post-media condition through an episodic format. It is to say, a human condition determined by the end of technologies as a simple prosthesis of humankind.

In the second chapter, Mazurek offers a (post)apocalyptic interpretation of two *Black Mirror* episodes, "Fifteen Million Merits" and "Metalhead," wherein the notion of the apocalypse is approached not so much in terms of its destructive potential, but as a powerful metaphor of paradigmatic transformation. Drawing from Jacques Derrida's discussion of the apocalyptic tone detectable across philosophical discourses, as well as Gilles Deleuze and Felix Guattari's view of the evolution of the natural environment into the industrial one, Mazurek identifies in both episodes a number of disappearing binaries hitherto considered formative for the development of western consciousness. These include oppositions such as nature-culture, nature-man, masculine-feminine, organic-technological, and conscious-unconscious.

This dismantling is further supported by the theories of Samuel Butler and René Descartes whose views concerning the (im)possibility of machine consciousness are also reflected in the show. Following the conviction of apocalypse's transformative rather than destructive power, the chapter concludes by offering a socio-philosophical reflection on the post-apocalyptic character of contemporary post-media western society.

In the third chapter of the volume, Joseph Macey and Brian McCauley analyze the episode "Playtest" with particular attention warranted to the ways in which digital games embody contemporary socio-economic realities of western life. While "Playtest" has been described as an episode that lacks a specific moral lesson or social commentary – indeed Charlie Brooker, the series creator, referred to it as simply "a romp ... good fun" (Hibberd, 2018) – it remains a cultural product which offers commentary on contemporary socio-cultural realities, both inviting and provoking discussion amongst fans, critics, and even academics. Central to their interpretation of this episode is the gamification of society and the wider cultural logic of Baumann's theory of liquid modernity. The episode functions as an allegory for liquid modernity, and one which can be further contextualized through the consideration of life in an increasingly gamified world. Furthermore, given the obvious significance of games in "Playtest," they examine the evolving role of video games in facilitating and promoting contemporary practices related to the economic, social, and cultural value systems of liquid modernity.

Continuing with the subject of games, Robbie Fordyce and Tom H. Apperley consider the series' interactive film, *Bandersnatch*, as an experimental hybrid of streaming video and digital game. Like all works in the *Black Mirror* series, it revolves its story around a commentary about everyday life. In their reading of this hybrid game, they argue that *Bandersnatch* is a mystery game in the sense that the combination of complexity and repetition of the various story paths presents a different exploration of *Black Mirror*'s science fiction world while still emphasizing the refrain of the danger of technology. From this, they observe that the social commentary provided by *Bandersnatch* focuses on the boredom of platformed entertainment. They derive this position from the way that its simple interface for play is functionally identical to the interface for browsing film choices on Netflix, and thus *Bandersnatch* comments on the mystery of possible choices amongst the shows we could choose to watch and the prospect of being bored to death by contemporary entertainment media.

In Chapter Five, Mauricio Molina-Delgado and Bértold Salas-Murillo propose that several *Black Mirror* episodes deal with one of the most problematic themes when studying the philosophy of the mind and cognitive sciences: *qualia*, i.e., the subjective qualities of experiences, *experimented on through technology*. The authors argue that most episodes occur in potential worlds wherein natural laws are compatible with the main thesis of functionalism. This viewpoint in philosophy of mind interprets mental states not as physical or non-physical functions, but rather as internal operations that mediate between the inputs and outputs of a system. Many of the arguments and counterarguments of functionalism have been proposed through thought experiments. Due to their fictional yet plausible nature, *Black Mirror* episodes play a similar role to these experiments: they propose imaginary situations in which the truthfulness of a specific thesis is verified or put into perspective. Episodes such as "White Christmas," "Playtest," "San Junipero," "USS Callister," "Crocodile," "Black Museum," and "Striking Vipers" contemplate the role of digital technology in reflections about *qualia* or problematizations of the relationship between mind and body, consciousness and brain. The authors assert that, in the *Black Mirror* universe, the self can be considered a disembodied concept. Some episodes take a position concerning this neuroscientific problem, while others imagine possibilities which defy contemporary science. In several episodes, the digitalization of sensations, feelings, or consciousness is enabled by a series of devices corresponding to interfaces that allow the input and output of information, as proposed by functionalism. Finally, the way the authors conceive of ethical issues in organic and non-organic beings face a contemporaneous problematic since *qualia* can be artificially generated.

In the sixth chapter, Justin Michael Battin analyzes the episode "Fifteen Million Merits" through a Heideggerian rendering of place and place-making practices. He suggests, in alignment with other texts in the Science Fiction genre, that the episode is duly concerned with presenting the virtues and hazards facilitated by a technology-as-power worldview; however, it is more fundamentally interested in elucidating what an ontological view of one's self (i.e. a self considered topologically) can reveal. While the short history of the genre consists of texts presenting dystopian visions of the world, they often conclude with an optimistic outlook. In contrast to these texts, the tale of "Fifteen Million Merits" eschews optimism by mirroring contemporary society's ubiquitous post-pessimistic malaise. He proposes that while such a condition endures and critical reflection seems destined for failure, as both the inhabitants of the episode's world and contemporary society seem to have accepted their fates in the current state of affairs, the notion of place and the role of the self as a catalyst for its founding seems to faintly endure. He concludes by proposing that through place and place-making practices, human beings, understood as *Dasein*, are capable of rediscovering and sustaining their ontological role as dwellers, interpreted by Heidegger as cultivators and preservers of existentially meaningful worlds.

The next chapter, written by Hatice Övgü Tüzün, considers the program's dystopian depictions of the world with emphasis on how technologies are transforming their makers and human relationships. The focus of the chapter, "Nosedive," is an episode that imagines a world in which the current climate of social media obsession escalates until all of society is engulfed by the pressure to maintain high ratings. "Nosedive" depicts an engineered society based on popularity, in which people desperately try to ascend the social hierarchy with fake kindness and carefully curated social media profiles. The episode also depicts an extremely 'mediated reality,' one primarily shaped by digital technology/social media and ruled by 'mediated desires,' often expressed through voyeurism and determined emotions. Within this framework, the author argues that "Nosedive" offers a memorable illustration of what Stjepan Mestrovic calls a "postemotional society" (1997, p. 38) wherein emotion has been "transformed into a quasi-intellectual phenomenon that makes it suitable for manipulation by self and others."

Continuing with "Nosedive," Santiago Giraldo-Luque, Ricardo Carniel Bugs, and Santiago Tejedor suggest that the episode raises three issues of interest for the fields of sociology and communication. Firstly, the episode represents the fictionalized and caricatured world of a reality that is real and current, but, in accordance with an "enframed" view of the world, goes mostly unrecognized by the users/viewers of the platform. Secondly, it describes the construction and self-reproduction of systemic power, which is fully sophisticated and functional, and is fed by the users/viewers themselves through the use of their devices and the emotional control exerted by the dynamics of social validation. Finally, the episode encourages viewers to reflect on the use of social networks not as spaces for conversation, meetings, or communication, but as stages for a passive, one-way exchange of automatic "likes" for emotional self-complacency. The episode, in the authors' view, prompts an urgent call for interdisciplinary action, specifically to raise awareness towards the fading prominence of communication, the power of screen-based platforms, and the need for a collaborative approach to media literacy and education.

Dealing with another expression of social control, the ninth chapter of this collection, written by Andrea Facchetti, presents an analysis on how "The Entire History of You" addresses and represents issues related to surveillance. This chapter focuses on the episode's ability to produce a fracture in the narrative framework by which discourses and visual imageries are nowadays formulated, represented, and enjoyed around the theme of surveillance. It argues that the critical potentialities of this episode lie in the ability to produce a new image of surveillance devices and of subjectivization. Specifically, this chapter draws a clear schema of contemporary surveillance, which is argued as being articulated into three main issues: the hedonistic matrix that characterizes our relationship with surveillance today, the fluid and mobile network of surveillance wherein elements can be reconfigured to occupy different positions and roles, and its normative character and the action of normalization operating in the society of control.

In Chapter 10, Ward also proposes that the issue of surveillance is a major theme in *Black Mirror* (which reflects contemporary social concerns around developments like data mining and increasingly sophisticated recognition technology), and one of the most novel ways in which it is addressed is in the episode "Crocodile." The episode was shot entirely in Iceland, during a period in which Reykjavik faced its heaviest snowfall in 70 years. The icy, mountainous backdrop jars with the British accents of the episode's characters, evoking the sense of rootlessness and disruption often familiar to *Black Mirror*'s dystopian imaginings of the near future. More than this, though, the setting clearly elicits the aesthetics of Nordic Noir, perhaps most notably referencing the transnational hybridity apparent in productions like *Lilyhammer* and *Fortitude*. In this chapter, Ward examines the ways in which "Crocodile" draws upon the conventions of Nordic Noir, not only in the foregrounding of the evocative landscape (an eminent factor in the episode's landscape from the moment the central characters take advantage of the isolation to cover up the initial crime), but also in exploring the familiar themes and concerns of the genre. While Nordic Noir's realist aesthetic perhaps jars with *Black Mirror*'s more surreal critique of a future not yet realized, this is another aspect of seemingly incongruent juxtaposition which renders the motif so powerful. The basis of this chapter's analysis is founded on the untenable tension between nature and technology, corporate outsourcing and public responsibility, and isolation and surveillance highlighted in the episode and grounded in the aesthetic.

The following chapter, by Artur de Matos Alves, explores the extremest form of a subject's surveillance and control through an analysis of "Men Against Fire," the fifth episode of the third season. In this episode, set in a post-apocalyptic time, a team of soldiers is sent to exterminate "roaches," ostensibly a mutant species of humans. After a mission, a soldier begins experiencing disruptions in his performance-enhancing neural implants (MASS device). The implants are revealed to be not enhancers, but rather perception-altering devices that make soldiers perceive a group of humans as monsters, therefore rendering the soldier more amenable to committing genocide. In this chapter, "Men Against Fire" is the point of departure for a reflection on media, propaganda, and ideology. Through Zizek's concept of hallucination as ideology, as well as Mark Fisher's concept of "verminization" as a rhetorical device in the justification of war, this chapter analyses the role of media and technology in accelerating the uptake of the ideological structuring of the social and political reality. The argument focuses on the use of the technological implant as a stand-in for a sociotechnical dispositive. Moreover, de Matos Alves argues that the figure of the MASS offers insights on the effects of media and the way contemporary media could represent tools for spreading and consolidating ideological representations of the Other.

In Chapter 12, the volume proposes an analysis on the way this television series sheds light on the fact that human beings and technology are intrinsically entangled and mutually constituted. As pointed out by Anna Caterina Dalmasso in her chapter, "Technicity and the Utopian Limits of the Body," technicity shall be thought of not as something that is merely added onto the natural core of embodied life, but as the very structure of the relationship between human beings and the environment. Thus, through "The Entire History of You," "Striking Vipers," and "San Junipero" this chapter analyzes the way digital prostheses contribute to informing and reconfiguring our bodily and embodied engagement with the world. This chapter also suggests an inquiry into the experience of inhabiting an avatar as acting like a prosthetic virtual body and analyzes the fantasies of disembodiment raised by the prospects of singularity and consciousness uploading as questioned by "San Junipero," in particular.

Alfredo Rizza continues the theme of communicative interactions between human and machine, albeit by considering the aesthetic and spiritual aspects of losing and reconnecting with loved ones. In particular, his chapter focuses on the episode "Be Right Back" and establishes, through the lens of Luigi Zoja's theory of the 'death of the neighbour' (2019), a comparison between that *Black Mirror* episode and *Solaris* (1972) by Andrei Tarkovsky. Through this comparison, the technology imagined in "Be Right Back" allows for the analysis of contemporary social media as phatic systems. As noted by Rizza, "Be Right Back" imagines that the technological reproduction of a deceased person works surprisingly well in linguistic-communicative terms, but only to the point when the deceased is actually reproduced in a material body, a 'body' whose behaviors show characteristics that recall certain kinds of textuality. The episode reveals that the bodily reproduction of the deceased does not show fundamental human features such as free will, rationality, or compassion.

After Rizza's introduction to the technological reproduction of a human being, Chapter 14, authored by Georgios Tsagdis, explores the ramifications of potentially digitizing consciousness, thereby preserving memory and subjectivity on the distinctive technological ground which enables and facilitates the utopia named San Junipero, the title of the fourth episode of the third season. This chapter re-signifies the Freudian analysis of the reality principle – which establishes an economy of desire and pleasure in the face of death – through Baudrillard's exposition of the articulation of the historical contingency that we call reality. It aims, therefore, to examine the significance of the place and function of death in our understanding and experience of the familiar reality of our human destiny, vis-à-vis a reality that promises to be without death, if not without pain and suffering. Accordingly, this chapter adopts the Platonic project of philosophy as a 'study of death' – as exigent in the post-simulated world as at the dawn of occidental thought.

In Chapter 15, Gabriela Galati explores the transhumanist optimism of mind uploading into a digital simulation, which the episode "San Junipero" openly presents as a virtual paradise. The episode's two subjects, having left their obsolete and transitory flesh behind, have their minds (consciousnesses? souls?) stored in a computer in an immense server room wherein they are finally able to live a liberated, flawless life. Subjectivity being located in the mind is a typical transhumanist perspective, a perspective which the final scenes of "San Junipero" seem to endorse. This chapter uses the concepts of complex subjectivities and the technological unconscious to show how the disembodiment illustrated by the episode is not only impossible, but above all undesirable: in a post-biological landscape an uploaded individual would cease to be a subject. Tracing the conceptualization of a technological unconscious through its genealogy from Sigmund Freud (1925; 1930) to Antonio Caronia (2006), among others, the concept suggests that a stratus exists in technology and the processes by which we interact with it that is not accessible to human thought, but that is nonetheless symbolically structured. This chapter therefore proposes that the technological unconscious is not meant to be analyzed as though it belonged to a subject, as it focuses on the apparatuses' autonomous actions and thus offers a key to uncovering certain collective symbolic clues.

One of the critically important issues facing mankind is climate change, and the media plays a critical role in the presentation and delivery of information to an audience. Gabor Sarlos closes the volume by proposing that dystopian portrayals produced in a contemporary context either implicitly or explicitly account for the effects of climate change. In the *Black Mirror* universe, never is this claim made clearer than in "Hated in the Nation." This episode depicts the human, technologically, and politically dominated view of nature, which is portrayed as wholly manipulatable and even replaceable with artificial systems. As one of the most pressing issues of the contemporary world, Sarlos suggests that the episode can be approached from four prominent angles, which provides not only the possibility for a focused analysis, but also permits placing the story into a wider context of interdisciplinary interpretation. Given that the impact of climate change can be widely felt across numerous arenas of contemporary life, approaching the issue, in addition to the thematic concerns *Black Mirror* addresses more broadly, requires a nuanced approach of interdisciplinarity.

Inspired by Brooker's seminal television series and the proposed notion that Science Fiction is a privileged genre for critical analysis, this volume therefore aims to address the aforementioned concerns of the post-media condition, particularly by drawing on innovative and interdisciplinary theoretical frameworks. As evidenced by the ascension of *Black Mirror* into the realm of pop culture and its anointment as a textual artifact worth exploring (see Johnson, 2020; Cirucci and Vacker, 2018), it is clear that the themes *Black Mirror* explores, as well as the contexts in which they have been presented, have resonated with viewers and academics alike. Indeed, very few contemporary television programs provoke spirited responses quite like *Black Mirror*. This timely collection therefore seeks to capitalize both on the show's enduring popularity as well as its topical relevance by presenting chapters that explore themes applicable to contemporary society.

Bibliography

Agamben, G. (2006) *Che cos'è un dispositivo?* Roma: Nottetempo.

Appadurai, A. (1990) "Disjuncture and Difference in the Global Cultural Economy" in *Theory Culture Society*, Vol. 7, pp. 295-310.

Ballard, J. G. (2019) *All That Mattered Was Sensation*. Brescia: Krisis Publishing.

Botsman, R. (2017) "Big Data Meets Big Brother as China Moves to Rate its Citizens" in Wired.com. Online Accessed 20/06/2020. Available from: https://www.wired.co.uk/article/chinese-government-social-credit-score-privacy-invasion

Chen, H. (2019) "Techno-Paranoia and the Allure of Black Mirror" in *The Liberator*. Online. Accessed 23/06/2020. Available from: https://theliber atormagazine.com/2019/10/26/techno-paranoia-and-the-allure-of-black-mirror/

Cirucci, A. and Vacker, B. (2018) *Black Mirror and Critical Media Theory*. London, UK: Lexington Books.

Conley, D. & Burroughs, B. (2019) "Black Mirror: Mediated Affect and the Political" in *Culture, Theory, and Critique*, Vol. 60, No. 2, pp. 139-153. DOI: 10.1080/14735784.2019.1583116

Debray, R. (1991) *Cours de médiologie générale*. Paris: Gallimard.

Dorfles, G. (2008) *Horror Pleni. La (in)civiltà del rumore*. Roma: Castelvecchi.

Foucault, M. (2004) *Naissance de la biopolitique. Cours au Collège de France. 1978-1979*, Paris: Gallimard/Seuil.

Freedman, C. (2000) *Critical Theory and Science Fiction*. Middletown, Connecticut: Wesleyan University Press.

Heidegger, M. (1977) "The Age of the World Picture" in Lovitt, W. (ed.) The Question Concerning Technology and Other Essays. New York, NY: Harper & Row Publishers, pp. 115-154.

Heidegger, M. (1977 [1962] "The Question Concerning Technology" in Krell, D. F. (ed.) *Martin Heidegger: Basic Writings*. San Francisco, CA: Harper San Francisco, pp. 287-317.

Heidegger, M. (1977 [1972] "The End of Philosophy and the Task of Thinking" in Krell, D. F. (ed.) *Martin Heidegger: Basic Writings*. San Francisco, CA: Harper San Francisco, pp. 373-392.

Hibberd J. (2018) "Black Mirror showrunner explains season 3 endings" in EW.com. Online. Accessed 20/06/2020. Available from: https://ew.com/article/2016/10/23/black-mirror-postmortem-interview-season-3/

Hill, D. (2017) "Black Mirror [Opinion]" in *IEEE Technology and Society Magazine*, Vol. 36, Issue 2, pp. 35-37.

Johnson, D.K., Márquez, L.P. & Urueña, S. (2020) "Black Mirror: What Science Fiction Does Best" In Johnson, D.K. (Ed.) *Black Mirror and Philosophy: Dark Reflections*. Hoboken, NJ: Wiley & Sons.

Kobie, N. (2019) "The Complicated Truth about China's Social Credit System" in Wired.com. Online. Accessed 20/06/2020. Available from: https://www.wired.co.uk/article/china-social-credit-system-explained

Ling, R. (2012) *Taken-for-Grantedness: The Embedding of Mobile Communications into Society*. Cambridge, MA: MIT Press.

Littman, G. (2020) "The Waldo Moment and Political Discourse: What's Wrong with Disrespect in Politics?" In Johnson, D.K., (Eds.) *Black Mirror and Philosophy: Dark Reflections*. Hoboken, NJ: Wiley & Sons, pp. 59-70.

McLuhan, M. (1994 [1964]) *Understanding Media: The Extension of Man*. Cambridge, MA: MIT Press.

Mestrovic, S. (1997) *Postemotional Society*. London, UK: SAGE.

Sculos, B. W. (2017) "Screen Savoir: How Black Mirror Reflects the Present More than the Future" in "Class, Race, and Corporate Power, Vol. 5, Issue 1, Issue 4. DOI: 10.25148/CRCP.5.1.001673

Singh, G. (2014) "Recognition and the image of mastery as themes in Black Mirror (Channel 4, 2011-present): in eco-Jungian approach to 'always-on' culture" in *International Journal of Jungian Studies*, Vol. 6, No. 2, pp. 120-132.

Suvin, D. (1972) "On the Poetics of the Science Fiction Genre" in *College English*, Vol. 34, No. 3, pp. 372-382. DOI: 10.2307/375141

Williams, R. (2000 [1958]) "Culture is Ordinary" in Levinson, B. A. U. et al. (eds.) *Schooling the Symbolic Animal: Social and Cultural Dimensions of Education*. London, UK: Rowman & Littlefield Publishers, Inc.

Black Mirror
Mapping the *Possible* in a Post-Media Condition

German A. Duarte

"Il y a, à tel moment, un monde calme et reposant. Surgit soudain un visage effrayé qui regarde quelque chose hors champ. Autrui n'apparaît ici ni comme un sujet ni comme un objet, mais, ce qui est très différent, comme un monde possible, comme la possibilité d'un monde effrayant. Ce monde possible n'est pas réel, ou ne l'est pas encore, et pourtant n'en existe pas moins : c'est un exprimé qui n'existe que dans son expression, le visage ou un équivalent de visage."[1]

---

[1] Gilles Deleuze – Félix Guattari, *Qu'est-ce que la philosophie?*, Les éditions de Minuit: Paris, 1991, p. 22.
"There is, at some moment, a calm and restful world. Suddenly a frightened face looms up that looks at something out of the field. The other person appears here as neither subject nor object but as something that is very different: a possible world, the possibility of a frightening world. This possible world is not real, or not yet, but it exists nonetheless: it is an expressed that exists only in its expression-the face, or an equivalent of the face." (1994, p. 17.)

Introduction

It has been almost a decade since *Black Mirror* started to populate social imaginary with a world not so different from ours. This might be the reason for its world-wide success, confirmed by an enormous number of prizes and nominations from all around the world. In fact, this television program is generally seen as a dystopian reflection of our current society since it is perceived as a near (too near) future of our present time (see, Johnson, Márquez & Urueña 2020). So far, every episode of the series has depicted a dystopian vision of plausible scenarios deriving from our current technological context. The series, which follows in a remarkable way the tropes of Science Fiction (henceforth referred to as SF), reformulates, in our technological context, the main concerns that occupied this genre during the last century, and in so doing, it highlights some profound differences from these 20th century nightmares. By representing different expressions of disciplinary and techno-authoritarian societies, this television series started to populate the social imaginary with new fears and concerns. Consider, for instance, new expressions of controlled societies in which the forms of surveillance have radically changed purpose, where even surveillance itself has become 'useless' since the subject represents a fully externalized entity (see Allard-Huver & Escurignan 2018; Zuboff 2019). Consider also the declensions of the forms of repugnant social punishment depicted in the series, punishments that sometimes imply the full alteration of the cognition of the punished subject. All of these terrifying scenarios are framed by the apparent technological possibility of replacing the human experience. In other words, all of these scenarios are produced by both the transhumanist hypothesis and the assumption of a technological singularity. This television series, therefore, identifies its major concerns as represented in these scenarios. In addition to the episodes in which the series deals directly and clearly with the transhumanist phenomenon,[2] every episode describes a technological context in which technology is no longer an extension of the human body, but is rather a clear coding and replacing force that changes human practice and human perceptions, including private memories and experiences.

---

2 For example, "Be Right Back," "San Junipero," "USS Callister," "Black Museum," "Striking Vipers," and "Rachel, Jack and Ashley Too."

As one can see, *Black Mirror* is producing a series of concepts based on a specific technological condition, which consistently differs from the mechanical or industrial technological condition that popularized SF as a genre during the last century (See Evans 2009). Furthermore, this television series describes a technological context similar to that which began this literary genre in its modern form, identified as Shelley's *Frankenstein; or, The Modern Prometheus* (1818). In fact, the foundation of SF resides in the identification of a different technological condition, one generated by electric power, a technology, following McLuhan, able to transform everything into information (see McLuhan 1994).

In this chapter, I analyze the ways in which SF became a fertile terrain for philosophical reasoning and, consequently, for the development of concepts destined to populate the social imaginary (Gomel 2011). Thus, in the first part of this chapter, I deal with the notion of the concept, its temporality, and the problematic popular belief that concepts are exclusively produced through traditional philosophical reasoning. I also focus on the relationship that concepts have within a technological context. Subsequently, I inquire into the way SF became an important tool for philosophical reasoning, and the way this genre sutured a millenarian rupture in western culture. This inquiry logically brings us to analyze the role Shelley's *Frankenstein; or, The Modern Prometheus* plays in the consolidation of SF as a narrative form able to articulate concepts through popular figures and popular understanding of technologies.

Through the analysis of Shelley's foundational oeuvre, this chapter identifies SF not only as a privileged philosophical tool, but also as a genre founded on the identification of a post-media condition. This notion describes the technological phenomenon in which technologies cease to exclusively represent extensions of the human body and start a process of the externalization of being. The post-media condition embraces and influences, consequently, the whole human experience and action. This phenomenon was specially identified within the field of artistic practice, above all by Krauss in her book, "*A Voyage on the North Sea" Art in the Age of the Post-Medium Condition*" (1999), and, considering digital technology, by Lev Manovich in his reflections of a post-media aesthetic. In addition, the concept of post-media is currently largely used within the field of media studies to describe the communicative structure deriving from social media. In other words, the concept is popularly understood as a communicative process that differs from the former mass media structure in which the subject represented a passive entity in social communication synergies. Post-media, within that framework, describes a differentiation between the former order of generalist media and the new forms of communication closer to a peer-to-peer (P2P) order. Nevertheless, in this chapter this notion describes – with full awareness that every technology is a technology of the body (Merleau-Ponty 1961) – a human condition in which technology, after the development of electrical power, went beyond the nature of a mediating entity. In other words, if technology was traditionally understood as a non-biological extension of the human body that mediates the relationship of object-subject[3], after the development of electric technology, and through the instance of the interoceanic telegraphic network, that status of technology declined. After this technological development, we started to face a different condition in which the entity that allowed us to supplant the natural weakness of our senses started to exert a force of externalization of the being to a global network of information. In McLuhan's words:

> Whereas all previous technology (save speech, itself) had, in effect, extended some parts of our bodies, electricity may be said to have outered the central nervous system itself, quite without segments. (1994, p. 247)

What McLuhan saw as an extension of the human central nervous system to the whole planet, represents, in this chapter, the foundational phenomenon of a post-media condition, that being a product of the irruption of a new technology, meaning at the same time a new form of human association and action, and even a new way of perceiving reality. The post-media condition, in this analysis, resents the separation from the traditional understanding of the 'extensions of man' that suddenly became externalizations of being. Through the lens of this phenomenon, I analyze different transformations, including communicational phenomena, from the disappearance

---

3 This sentence attempts to give a clear image of technology as a mediating entity placed in-between object and subject. I am aware that this relationship cannot be described in these terms. As remarked by Heidegger, this relation of the object-subject contains 'as much truth as vacuity' (1967, p. 60). Nevertheless, this figure allows us to give a consistent image in which a subject's existence is mediated through a body, which is, to a certain extent, produced by a technology. It would be possible to describe this relation as follows: Subject–Body/Technology–Object.

of the well-defined public and private spheres to the new figure of the cyborg, which no longer represents an invasion of the human body in order to adapt it to the physical world, but rather an invasion of the flesh to adapt the body to the cognition of an already externalized subject. This new human condition, that we define as post-media, entered the collective imaginary through the figure of Frankenstein's creature, since one identifies in that creature the creation, through electricity, of a new human being. Thus, in the chapter I identify SF as a genre inaugurated on the acknowledgment of this post-media phenomenon. And it is through this lens that I analyze *Black Mirror* as a popular attempt to map diverse declensions of the post-media condition.

The Notion of the Concept

In *Qu'est-ce que la philosophie?*, Gilles Deleuze and Félix Guattari introduce their text by dealing with the complex and rhizomatic nature of concepts. According to the authors, a concept is composed of fragments originated in – and through – many other concepts (Deleuze & Guattari, 1991, p. 23). They also noted that concepts are tightly related to a problem, but a not-yet-existing problem which, in its impossibility to appear at that moment, 'vibrates' to manifest its not-yet-accomplished-presence. Consequently, a concept does not define an existing problem since 'to exist' implies to be-out-side, as the etymological roots of the verb mean 'to stand-forth, to come forth.' In fact, the verb 'to exist' comprises the Latin '*ex*' (out) and '*sistere*' (to place). Nevertheless, through the concept one can identify the vibration of a not-yet-existing problem. Following this framework, the nature of the concept displays the being of another time, which is estranged from the Bergsonian *durée*. The concept develops a time which is replaced by forces of simultaneity (*simultanéité*) and permanence (see, Deleuze-Guattari 1991). Thus, concepts are generated through a deep rupture with the Bergsonian seriality, a rupture that diminishes duration through *tempora*, through territorialized plateaus that do not follow a succession. In other words, one could say, in a position close to Heidegger's, that concept's temporality (*Zeitlichkeit*) is a conjunction that is not built by states but by ecstasies (Heidegger, 1967, p. 350).

Deleuze and Guattari place the creative generation of concepts outside the objectivized time of the Bergsonian becoming (*devenir*), which is understood as objective states materialized into the series of past-present-future.

Through this temporal form of the concept, the subject generates a new distribution of both the object and the subject, and thus a new set of relationships, a new social space, a new reality. The concept is a pure form of estrangement (*Entfremdung*) that places the subject outside the succession of serialized states that are determined by the technological condition. Further, by exerting this force of estrangement, the concept represents the instrument to territorialize the space of the *Possible*, a space that is not a declension of the inscribed *virtual*, nor a figure produced by technological determinism, which, more than a deterministic view of social structures and cultural production, is the establishment of a World-View (*Weltanschauung*). In other words, to produce a concept means to place the subject in the space of the *Possible*, in the any-space-whatever (*space quelconque*) (Deleuze 1983). The space of the *Possible* is in fact a non-inscribed virtuality. The difference between the *Virtual* and the *Possible* is that the latter does not represent a declension of a determined present. As noted by Berardi, the *virtual* is a mere extension of the present, and thus of the realm in which reality is manifested (Bachelard 1931). Differently, the *Possible* is not an inscribed 'conjugation' of the duration. The concept of *Possible* does not imply any form of consequentiality, any form of need, nor of implication (Berardi, 2013, p. 61).

As one can see, it is from the present time, from this organized form, that the *Virtual* derives, which is nothing more than an already-inscribed becoming. Certainly, this determined becoming is strongly tied to a precise technological context and is established by what could be identified in the disclosive character of contemporary technology highlighted by Heidegger in his essay "Die Frage nach Technik" (1953). It is in that text where Heidegger describes the disclosive character of contemporary technology, which determines technology as a non-neutral entity (1953). Considering technology's disclosive character, and taking into account that Heidegger identifies, as the essence of technology, its force to allow everything to present[4]; a social context able to imagine a technological entity displaying autonomous features of cognitive functions is without doubt a society that intuits that it is facing great danger. Heidegger's reasoning warns us since, by analyzing technology as *Das Gestell*, it allows us not only to understand technology as

---

4 In Heidegger's words: "Das Ge-Stell stellt dann die Weise, wie jedes Anwesende jetzt anwest." (1949, p. 40.) "Enframing then sets the way that everything present now presences." (author's translation)

a force that disposes the way humankind encounters the world, but also as a reifying force that 'installs' humankind into the technological system, into the infinite net of ongoing complex processes that define being-in-the-world (see Mark Blitz 2014). In the words of Gunkel and Taylor,

> Enframing has two main aspects—things become situated as, and thereby reduced to the status of available objects [standing reserve] and human beings themselves become a part of this same process of objectification even as they are busy objectifying the world around them. The concepts of enframing and standing reserve therefore help to illuminate not only the manner in which entities are organized for technologically facilitated exploitation but also the mentality that both underlies and results from this calculable complex. Rather than encountering things as things, we come pre-conditioned to treat the world (and ourselves) as part of a standing reserve of preconditioned objects (2014, p. 129)

Following this framework, the concept, as a force of estrangement, enables the subject to dwell in the space of the *Possible*, to abstract the subject from the technological inscriptions that, through a *Weltanschauung*, exerts a force of subjectivization.[5] Through estrangement, the concept places the subject in the sphere of the Other Person (*Autrui*), thus exerting a redistribution of the whole, and one which is not visible from the present nor foreseen in the present's declensions or virtualities. In Deleuze and Guattari's words,

> The concept of the Other Person as expression of a possible world in a percep-tual field leads us to consider the components of this field for itself in a new way. No longer being either subject of the field or object in the field, the other person will become the condition under which not only subject and object are redistributed but also figure and ground, margins and center, moving object and reference point, transitive and substantial, length and depth. [6]
> (1994, p. 18)

---

5 This term is understood following Giorgio Agamben's meaning in which 'subjectivization' means 'producing the subject.' See Agamben 2006.

6 "Dans le cas du concept d'Autrui comme expression d'un monde possible dans un champ perceptif, nous sommes conduits à considérer d'une nouvelle façon les composantes de ce champ pour lui-même : autrui, n'étant plus ni un sujet de champ ni un objet dans le champ, va être la condition sous laquelle se redistribuent non seulement l'objet et le sujet, mais la

Being the expression of another world, *Autrui* represents the *Possible*, the tangent that brings outside from the inscribed virtual: the tangent that pushes the subject to wander in the fields of the undetermined. Hence, it is through the concept that it is possible to bring to the error the force of subjectivization, that it is possible to bring to fail the dispositive[7]. By releasing the subject from the *durée*, which imposes a temporal seriality of past-present-future, the concept places the subject in the condition to clearly observe that the future, in our technological context, is already determined; it is just a determined arborescent path that displays some virtual declensions. Such is the meaning of progress (strongly related to a technological condition), which is able to imagine the future as a conquest already visible on the horizon. Such is also the case of utopia (and, of course, also the case of dystopia), the maximal expression of the seriality of time that sees a terrible past, and an already inscribed salvation in the future. This is precisely the case of the revolutionary ideologies that, through a Hegelian imprint, conceive the present as a means to transform the already-inscribed future (thereby generating another defined and indelible inscription). The concept is alien to the technological inscription as it is estranged from the continuous reorganization of the perception of the past. In fact, Bergsonian *durée*, by generating a temporal seriality which finds its exemplification in the serialized past-present-future, imposes the understanding of present as the *momentum* that determines the future, and is, consequently, determined by the immediate past. Thus, it is through the perception of the past, generated from the present, that the definition of the already-inscribed virtualities of the future emerges.[8] Conversely, the concept displays its own *devenir*, its own becoming, which corresponds to the redistribution of the whole. That is to say, through the concept, the inscribed future dissolves from the present and allows us to feel the vibration, the problem, a not-yet-existing-problem that vibrates. Through the concept the subject is able to feel a 'there is' (*Il y a...*): "There is, at

---

figure et le fond, les marges et le centre, le mobile et le repère, le transitif et le substantiel, la longueur et la profondeur..." (1991, p.24.)

7   It is important to note that for Agamben the strategy to liberate things from the forces of the dispositive is through the profanation, understood in its literal meaning of restituting the thing to the use and property of mankind. See Agamben 2006, p. 27.

8   That was indeed Winston Smith's task at the Ministry of Truth in George Orwell's masterpiece.

some moment, a calm and restful world. Suddenly, a frightened face looms up that looks something out of the field." (1994, p. 17.)[9]

This frightened face needs to be recognized as a face; it needs to narrate and to be recognized as a frightened face in the narrative. It is in that face that one recognizes the vibration, the non-yet-existing problem that needs to become narrative, that needs to be an image in order to shape the social imaginary, and through it to be intelligible. Further, it is by watching that face that the subject is estranged and able to dwell in the space of the *Possible*, which means to escape from the virtuality already inscribed in the future. It is at that point that one can see Science Fiction as a privileged narrative form to develop concepts, to describe the frightened face, to map the space of the *Possible*.

Science Fiction: the narrative dimension of the concept

Darko Suvin suggested that Science Fiction is a literary genre that allows the author to describe and to imagine an alternative environment that does not correspond to her or his daily life. Further, according to him, this genre is able to reorganize synergies between cognition and estrangement. Within this framework, as noted by Freedman, the main problem with defining – or delimiting – Science Fiction as a genre resides in the connections or disconnections with the empirical world. Indeed, through them, the author generates a particular relationship between cognition and estrangement. The more the author is disconnected from her or his empirical world, the less realistic fiction becomes. This argument was developed based on the assertion that, on the one hand, estrangement differentiates SF narratives from the literary mainstream and, on the other, cognition differentiates SF from myth, fantasy, and folk tale (See, Suvin 1979 and Freedman 2000). SF, therefore, found its place in the traditional disciplines – and of course in the traditionally conservative field of literary studies – by displaying a particular balance between cognition and estrangement (See Todorov 2015). Notwithstanding, it might be possible to identify the phenomenon of the balance

---

9 "Il y a, à tel moment, un monde calme et reposant. Surgit soudain un visage effrayé qui regarde quelque chose hors champ." (Deleuze & Guattari, 1991, p. 22)

between estrangement and cognition in almost every narrative form.[10] Thus, the delimitation of SF as a genre through the relationship of cognition-estrangement becomes problematic and unclear. Nevertheless, this passionate and legitimate debate dealt with a millenarian concern regarding the phenomenon of artistic *pathos* (πάθος) and its relation to *logos* (λόγος). That is to say, by looking into the balance between cognition and estrangement within a narrative form that conjugates science, technology, and fiction, one is encouraging the analysis of the role of *pathos* – understood as a force of sufferance that brings the audience to ecstasy (ἔκστασις) – in the development of a rational analysis of a precise socio-technological context. In other words, one is analyzing, within the framework of literary studies, the presence of *pathos* in the generation of concepts, and, by extension, the presence of *pathos* within a philosophical reasoning that traditionally is exclusively related to *logos*.

Traditionally, as noted by Deleuze and Guattari in *Qu'est-ce que la philosophie?*, philosophy is focused on the generation of concepts (1991, p. 10). Yet, there is a traditional tendency to place philosophical reasoning as the complete opposite of any form of *pathos*. Indeed, *pathos* is understood as an appeal to emotion, as the force that awakens feelings, as the force of the irrational. The field in which concepts find their narratives, their shape in the imaginary, is a field devoid of *pathos*, because traditionally it is thought that complex concepts belong exclusively to the field of reason, to the realm of *logos*. Nevertheless, the passionate debate that defined SF as a literary genre allows us to see that by analyzing the particular relationship between cognition and estrangement in this genre, it becomes clear that SF is a particularly fertile narrative form in which concepts – and consequently philosophical reasoning – can be developed. In other words, SF would be the field in which concepts could be generated through alternative forms of traditional philosophical reasoning.

Beyond the fact that SF is no longer understood as a sub-genre belonging to a fanzine tradition, and that this genre found a place (even a polemic place)

---

10 It is also important to note that the concept of estrangement in narratives automatically brings us to the Brechtian process of *Verfremdung*. Nevertheless, both Suvin and Freedman clarify that the estrangement in SF is of another nature. In fact, Brechtian literary realism does not deal with technological forms of estrangement proper to SF. (See Freedman 2000, p. 22).

in the literary universe, what really emerged from the debate within the field of literary studies is that SF is able to become a philosophical tool that produces concepts through the form of the story, through the form of the tale, through the *mythos* (μῦθος). This characteristic of SF represents a radical rupture with a tradition that deeply influenced western culture. In fact, western philosophy progressively marginalized *mythos* (Curi 2009, pp. 18-19). *Logos*, as noted above, represents the sphere of the reason, and therefore of philosophical reasoning. In turn, *mythos* represents a tale, a story, a fable, a narrative that can be true or false. The one marginalizes the other since *mythos* revolves around the force of *pathos*, the natural opposite of *logos*. Yet, this dichotomy was absent in classical thought. As noted by Curi, in some texts of the Classical Age, *mythos* was also perceived as a way to develop a philosophical demonstration, as an instrument to bring forth a concept (Ibid, p. 17). A clear example of this is found in the Platonic dialog, *Protagoras*, in which the discussion turns around the fact that politics is an art and that it can be taught.

In this dialog, Protagoras introduces himself as somebody that teaches the art of politics. Thus, his statement presupposes the fact that he could teach a virtue. Socrates encourages him to better explain his argumentation, to demonstrate in a more explicit way that virtue is teachable, since his belief was contrary to Protagoras' assertion. At that point, Protagoras asks Socrates, as an old man speaking to his junior, if he

> (...) should put his demonstration in the form of a fable, or of a regular exposition?
> Many of the company sitting by him instantly bade him treat his subject whichever way he pleased.
> Well then, he said, I fancy the more agreeable way is for me to tell you a Fable (Plato, Protagoras, 320c.).[11]

As one can see, Protagoras is not only placing the process of demonstration in the sphere of *mythos* and not in the traditional way of conceiving it – that is to say, as a natural form of *logos* – but he is also, and above all, propos-

---

11 Plato, *Protagoras*. With the Commentary of Hermann Sauppe, Translated with additions by James A. Towle, Forgotten Books.

ing *mythos* as a tool of philosophical reasoning because it is "more agreeable" (χαριέστερον), it is joyful.

Western philosophy built its apparatus by distancing itself from the narrative forms belonging to the sphere of *mythos*. Nevertheless, it is possible to identify in another magnificent expression of Classical Thought a form of philosophical reasoning that generates *pathos*, a joyful narrative form traditionally placed in the sphere of *mythos*. In fact, antique tragedies are expressions of the Classical Greek Thought developed through *mythos* (Curi 2009, p. 19). Following this framework, it is possible to identify a complex philosophical reasoning in Aeschylus' *Prometheus Bound* and Sophocles' *Oedipus Rex* and *Antigone* that deeply analyses the Classical Age, and through them it is possible to study the Greek Thought of the Classical Age. In other words, antique tragedies are spaces for the materialization of concepts, and are the frame in which, through a tale, through a joyful narrative, the 'frightened face that looms up and looks something out of the field' becomes a figure, acquires a shape.

The tragedy is a narrative form that through *mythos* develops concepts. Yet, these tragedies witness, through the form of the *mythos*, a deeper transformation in the human condition. The Classical Greek tragedy represents the traumatic rupture with the ancient world of orality, a world that collectivized memory through both the form of the epopee and through the voice of the *aoidos*. The tragedy is therefore the element that witnesses the end of this form of memory (orality), which became progressively more obsolete with the introduction and assimilation of first the Phoenician Alphabet and then of the Greek one (See, Goody 1977). As one might suppose, Greece was the scene of a series of tribal wars, social inequalities, and human tragedies long before the emergence of the tragic expression. Nevertheless, these tragic events did not enact a profound transformation of humankind. As remarked by de Kerckhove, the only ferment likely to corrode the tribal mankind from inside is the development of the technology of the phonetic alphabet (De Kerckhove 2008, p. 105). Following de Kerckhove's analysis, the tragedy would be the product of the introduction of the written text in theatrical practice and, consequently, of the emergence of the actor, who at that point was able to recite a text and establish a different relationship with the audience. On the other hand, however, the tragedy would be a product of distancing from the epic narrative. That is to say, after the introduction of the written text, the epopee started to be fragmented into sequences pertaining to the action of the hero. Thus, the tragedy would be an 'analyzed' and 'slow' epopee (Ibid. p. 104), a sort of epopee able to express the sinister and terrifying reality in which we are involved.

Frankenstein: The Foundation of Science Fiction as the Reconciliation of *Logos* and *Mythos*

The tragedy represents the space in which concepts on the new alphabetic human condition developed – the space in which these concepts became image. Further, the tragedy was the space in which the concepts of a new human condition – a human condition deeply influenced by the emergence of a new technology – were constructed and shared. The tragedy is the scream of a humankind that analyses itself through the fragmentation and seriality of the alphabet. Not surprisingly, the novel that is generally considered to be the first expression of Science Fiction was built on a clear allegory to Aeschylus' tragedy. Mary Shelley's *Frankenstein; or, The Modern Prometheus* (1818) neither represents a shift away from the Gothic tradition (Aldiss 1995), nor a rupture from the criticism of the duplication of humankind – a phenomenon that find its roots in the myth of Narcissus. Additionally, it would be even possible to argue that Shelley's novel also does not represent an analogous concept to the kabbalistic Golem, which refers to a being created from clay, nor an analogous being to de Condillac's statue. *Frankenstein; or, The Modern Prometheus* goes beyond the identification of proto-industrial, and even beyond the identification of the industrial humankind, since Shelley's novel conceptualizes a being alien to mechanical duplication, and, consequently, a being that does not belong to the technological context of the writer, nor even to the First Industrial Revolution that succeeded the publication of the novel. Shelley's novel could be fully considered a modern tragedy, since it reconciles the *logos* and the *mythos*, and in so doing, it generates a series of concepts belonging to the space of the *Possible*.

By placing the scientific argumentation in the middle of the diegesis (Aldiss 1995), *Frankenstein; or, The Modern Prometheus* (1818) breaks with the alchemical tradition and elucidates an approaching technological context strongly influenced by the technology of electricity. Possibly influenced by Frank Mesmer's *Lebensmagnetismus* theories, Shelley's novel conceptualizes a human condition that belongs to the Second Industrial Revolution: a human condition that leaves the millenarian alphabetic fragmentation and seriality. In other words, Shelley's novel leaves the episteme of fragmentation and serialization, which finds its roots in the Phoenician Alphabet and whose maximal expression is Taylor's application of scientific management, Vickers machine gun, and even Lumière's *Cinématographe* (see Duarte 2018). Within the field of *mythos*, through a tale, Shelley's oeuvre allows us to see the way in which SF generates a space – in an analogous way with ancient tragedies – in which philosophical reasoning can be developed and can produce concepts. Thus, the first SF expression represents a narrative form in which, through the use of *mythos*, concepts are developed that elucidate the space of the *Possible*. Modern SF is indeed a precious tool for philosophical reasoning, since it proposes, within modernity, a narrative form that re-elaborates tragedy's function. Consequently, modern SF, by generating concepts through the *mythos*, sutured the millenarian dichotomy between *logos* and *mythos* that highly influences western philosophy.

Shelley's 'Modern Prometheus' is indeed the figure of a technological condition that does not belong to the industrial era. Thus, Frankenstein's creature could be considered as a concept rooted in the space of the *Possible*, alien to any sort of declension or virtuality inscribed in Shelley's time. Her concept is a real and concrete attempt to liberate humankind from mechanical philosophy and, consequently, from a mechanical conception of life. Indeed, Frankenstein's creature represents a deep rupture in a mechanical understanding of life, solidly rooted in Newton's *Philosophiae naturalis principia Mathematica* in which the image of a *Clockwork Universe* was concretized, an image that generated the understanding of life as a part of that divine clockwork. Conversely, Shelley's oeuvre identifies in electricity the *élan vital*, and in so doing she mapped the space of the *Possible*, a non-inscribed space in which the *élan vital* takes out our being from the physical condition and, consequently, from a mechanical vision of life. Further, Shelley demonstrates – as would be posited more than a century later by Merleau-Ponty – that every technology deeply transforms the body (See Merleau-Ponty 1961). Shelley's novel, through the identification of the *élan vital* in electric power, not only described a different body, but also a being able to dwell in the physical experiences of other flesh. Shelley describes a body that disappears together with both space and time (Heidegger 1950, p. 157). But above all, Shelley's oeuvre identifies the frightened face of the Second Industrial Revolution: the shape of a new human condition in which technology ceases to represent the 'extensions of man'. In fact, through the identification of electrical power as the primary element of life, it is possible to see that technology, after the introduction of electrical power, and throughout the instance of telegraphy, started to exert a force of externalization of being (McLuhan 1994, p. 248).

As one can note, through electrical power and, of course, through telegraphy, Merleau-Ponty's words find an image: "The world is wholly inside, and I am wholly outside my self."[12] These words encapsulate a new human condition in which technologies are no longer mere extensions of the human body, but rather they also exert a force of externalization upon the central nervous system (McLuhan 1994). Within this framework, it is also possible to remark that the force of externalization replaces fragmentation and serialization as episteme with a flux: an electrical flux able to dematerialize everything, able to reduce distances and eliminate time (Heidegger 1950), one that eliminates the episteme of serialization embodied by states within the serialized *durée* of past-present-future (Heidegger 1967, p. 350), and one that dissolves the verb 'to be' and finds its image not in states, not in sequences, not in fragments. The flux is the image of the rhizome, is the image of the fabric weaved by a ceaseless conjunction (Deleuze & Guattari 1980, p. 36).

As the first expression of SF, *Frankenstein* represents a clear statement of an approaching technological condition, a clear attempt to focus on the field of the *Possible* designed, on that occasion, by the coming irruption of electric power. Nevertheless, the awareness of being beyond a technological condition in which technologies are only extensions of human senses is even today still not fully assimilated. Today, in our digital social context in which digital technology has fully eliminated the traditional public and private spheres and even imposed a hyper-textual structure in which seriality and temporality completely differs from the former alphabetic serialization, there is not yet a full awareness of being far beyond the pre-electric age. As noted by McLuhan, in his pre-digital context, "(...) we continue to think in the old, fragmented space and time patters of the pre-electric age" (1994, p. 4).

---

12 "Le monde est tout au dedans et je suis tout hors de moi." (Merleau-Ponty 1945, p.467.)

Science Fiction: Concepts of a Post-Media Condition

Electric technology, representing the *élan vital* in Shelley's oeuvre, determined, as Frankenstein's creature shows, a new human condition that goes beyond the temporality of the flesh, and that goes even beyond the human-flesh that enters into the world of objects through non-biological extensions. Within this analysis, it would be possible to identify in the irruption of electric technology a force that determined the initialization of a post-media existence for our species. Frankenstein's creature is a well-defined image of that technological condition, no longer characterized by extending human bodies into space, but by the externalization of the being, even by the coding of the being into a new flesh. This new technology, that we suppose gave life to the creature in Shelley's oeuvre and that we identified in this chapter as the *élan vital*, also determined the beginning of a new human condition since it started to displace serialization and sequentiality as the primary episteme. This phenomenon was described by McLuhan in the first pages of his book, *Understanding Media: The Extensions of Man* as follows,

> After three thousand years of explosion, by means of fragmentary and mechanical technologies, the Western world is imploding. During the mechanical ages we had extended our bodies in space. Today, after more than a century of electric technology, we have extended our central nervous system itself in a global embrace, abolishing both space and time as far as our planet is concerned. Rapidly, we approached the final phase of the extensions of man-the technological simulation of consciousness, when the creative process of knowing will be collectively and corporately extended to the whole human society, much as we have already extended our senses and our nerves by the various media. (1994, pp. 3-4)

As one can note, more than a century after the publication of Shelley's *Frankenstein*, McLuhan highlighted the general impossibility to perceive the displacement of the old episteme, as well as the impossibility to be aware of being subject to a new form of technology that progressively determined the externalization of the being into a global and rhizomatic space of information. It is in this particular technological condition – when electric power shaped the form of production during the Second Industrial Revolution and when telegraphy embraced the whole planet – that the beginning of a progressive and arduous process that places humanity into our current post-media condition can be identified. Following this framework, one can identify the roots of the post-media condition in the complex articulation of two technological phenomena. The first is characterized by the fact that technology is no longer a purely physical force that, as a prosthesis, determines the ways of being in the world. The second is the force of displacement that this technology exerted on the episteme of fragmentation and seriality, an episteme on which western culture built its relationship with reality. It is from this second phenomenon that one can also note that humanity became subject to forces of dematerialization and codification that ended by dematerializing and codifying the being itself (Lyotard 1979). Further, it is from the same phenomenon of the replacement of fragmentation and serialization with a constant flux that one can also note that a different understanding of time emerges. One is no longer guided by the Bergsonian *durée*, materialized by a succession of past-present-future, but rather by an understanding of time guided by a total and incessant *hic et nunc* unable to even imagine an interval (Dorfles 2008).

As one can see, the post-media condition, which we defined in this chapter as an ongoing process triggered more than a century ago, is still unclear due to the fact that all of the theoretical apparatuses one uses to analyze human condition is a product of the obsolete episteme of alphabetic fragmentation and seriality. As already noted through McLuhan's words, "(...) we continue to think in the old, fragmented space and time patters of the pre-electric age" (1994 p. 4). The same, in my opinion, could be said in our technological context. Nevertheless, Science Fiction offers us a field in which, through the mechanism of *mythos*, one can identify some features of our post-media human condition. Unable to describe the future – since there is no future in the flux of an incessant *hic et nunc* in which the subject is unable to project its experience outside the incessant present time (Berardi 2013, p. 82) – SF, by means of its capacity to articulate *logos* and *mythos* in a fruitful generation of concepts, produces some fundamental insights on this particular human condition we identified as post-media. This is the case in regards to *Black Mirror*, which can be considered a popular television series that offers insights on the post-media condition.

Black Mirror: The Topology of the *Possible*

The first season of this popular anthology television series, broadcasted in 2011, is characterized by what can be considered the three main features of postmediality. In fact, in the three first episodes of the series – "The National Anthem", "Fifteen Million Merits," and "The Entire History of You" – the show delimitated a well-established conceptual framework that introduces the main phenomena of postmediality to the audience. The first episode, "The National Anthem," deals with a society mainly populated by mobile media and that constantly produces information, resulting in a kind of multimedia timeline that constitutes social ties (See Eugeni 2015). It is clear that the arborescent structure of mass media, in which one informs everybody, dissolves through the rhizomatic form of the P2P communicative structures (Duarte 2014). In this depicted society, social ties, formerly produced by generalist media (Stiegler 2009), are sporadically built by means of the spectacularization of an event. This society is clearly inherited from a former technological context that produced the condition of the so-defined 'society of the spectacle' – which does not represent a set of images or spectacles, but rather social relations mediated by images (Debord, 1992, p. 16)[13]. "The National Anthem" describes these phenomena by showing a media condition in which private and public spheres have vanished. However, what seems to be a society that has reached a higher form of freedom (e.g. in the episode, political power is unable to control information), in the end it is revealed to be a society guided by extreme forms of spectacular-pseudo-events, which displays a considerable reduction of freedom since even free will is subject to these hysterical forms of organizing the social space. Consequently, the episode also demonstrates a society in which the collective imaginary is alien to the former form of communication that required the private elaboration of information (Flusser 2008 and Berardi 2015). But above all, one can see in the episode a society that is alien to any social ties beside the irrational force of the spectacle. In this post-media society, the balance between cultural and collective memory disappears, since in the continuous *hic et nunc* there is no time to build an individual, or even an identity. It is not by chance that the episode uses the image of the royal family to show the way in which cultural

---

13   §4 "Le spectacle n'est pas un ensemble d'images, mais un rapport social entre personnes, médiatisé par des images." (Debord 1992, p.16.)

memory and collective memory crash in a great spectacle that extremely reduces the capacity of elaboration of information, and even the capacity to develop a collective reminiscence, in a post-media condition.

The first characteristic of postmediality could be thereby identified in the disappearance of public and private spheres, as well as in the drastic reduction of time to privately elaborate information. This phenomenon, as already noted, find its roots in the development of electric power and the introduction of telegraphy on a global scale (Barbier & Bertho Lavenir 1996 and Caronia 1996). It is, indeed, after these technological developments that one can begin to identify an externalized being. Further, electric power is pure information (McLuhan 1994), and consequently, is a technology able to exert a radical dematerialization of the whole. It is in this particularity of electric technology that one can identify the second characteristic of a post-media society. The force of dematerialization, initially perceived through the reduction and elimination of space and time (Heidegger 1950), became, in its current form, a force of dematerialization through the coding of everything. Consequently, it generates a society technologically able to exchange everything, even nature, for information (Lyotard 1979, p. 13). In this technological context, even all forms of praxis enter into a continuous circle of dematerialization, coding, and exchange (Baudrillard 1976, p. 23-24). It is for this reason that the post-media condition reveals that capitalism is far beyond just a force of material production. The continuous translation of everything, including any form of praxis and any human or cultural expression, clearly shows that capitalism is a force that produces human desires, the latter also codified and reified to then be placed into the info-sphere in which the subject dwells.

As noted in Shelley's oeuvre (the true foundation of SF) electric power represents the *élan vital* that deeply transformed the flesh, a flesh already modified by technologies such as prostheses, a flesh battered in its industrial production and battered by the cadence of the engine. Nevertheless, this flesh, which could find relief thanks to contemporaneous technological forms of production, is still battered for the sake of the production of value (See Marcuse 1964). In our post-media society – the society of symbolic exchange and death – one inherited the use of flesh in production, even in immaterial production. Like in a collective desire for the destruction of the body, immaterial forms of production spectacularizes the consumption of the flesh. This form of production of value – the immaterial production of cognitive capitalism – reifies and spectacularizes everything since, in the post-media condition, the form of production aims to produce abstraction and aims to generate emotions (See Berardi 2016). Even if in this technological context the use of the flesh could be spared, like in Aztec sacrifices, the flesh, as a surplus of the immaterial world, is squandered (see Duarte 2015). This phenomenon is clearly conceptualized in "Fifteen Million Merits," the second episode of the series, in which one can see the development of concepts about the contemporary use of flesh to produce nothing, to produce information and emotions. Can we be sure that the charters of the episode are pedaling to produce electricity? This remarkable episode analyzes how the use of flesh, as reminiscent of the old material *arbeitskraft*, in a post-media society is a mere exchange for reified information (See Baudrillard 1976 and Berardi 2016). Further, the form of production depicted in this second episode not only identifies new forms of reification, and consequently of alienation, but also depicts an extreme form of techno-rationalism in which the former well-defined moments of production and consumption, even consumption of mass produced culture (see Horkheimer & Adorno 1947), crash into an undefined non-sequential unique moment of production and consumption, the latter also transformed into a moment of production of data that are subsequently reified and consumed[14] (see Marcuse 1964).

Nevertheless, the battered flesh that leaves the line of production to produce immaterial abstraction displays a further modification in our post-media condition. Beyond the phenomenon of the cyborg, technology's invasion of the human body seems to happen exclusively in relation to an externalized being (Caronia 2008). The material invasion of the flesh, exemplified through the figure of the cyborg, in a post-media condition seems to act for the conciliation of the material world and the imperative world of information. That is to say, the invasion of the human body, formerly a phenomenon of the adaptation and improvement of the physical features of humans, in a post-media condition, is at the service of an externalized being still anchored to an apparently useless flesh. In the post-media condition, technological

---

14 In the episode, the moments of production could be identified in the characters pedaling or singing. In turn, the moments of consumption are defined by both the material consumption of goods and the consumption of TV shows. These moments are at the same time moments of production of data, a phenomenon that could be identified in the presence of the 3D avatars on which the TV show is built.

devices invade the body to make the physical reality intelligible. In fact, the human cognition is everyday closer to a non-linear continuous flux of information displaying a multidimensional and hypertextual character (Duarte 2014). This is the phenomenon conceptualized in the third and last episode of the first season: "The Entire History of You".

In this episode, the 'grains' implanted behind the ears of the subjects are devices that adapt the human body to the subjects' cognition, already extremely influenced by the incessant *hic et nunc* of the electrical flux. Unable to accept a material existence shaped by the obsolete Bergsonian *durée*, the 'grains' allow the subjects to experience a temporal form more in line with their cognition. Indeed, the externalized being, shaped by both the force of electrical power and the photochemical processes of pictorial representation, accepts cinematic narratives as the predominant form of reminiscence. That is to say, the subject's memory is mainly a construction of a technologically *re*presented event. To remember, in a post-media condition, is an act closer to navigating through a database of personal stored events than to relying on one's own mental faculties. Yet, this understanding of reminiscence corresponds to the phenomenon conceptualized in "The Entire History of You." Like the very nature of cinematographic images, unable to conceive a time outside the imperative and exclusive present time, the subject of the post-media condition perceives memory as a narrative effect that places her or him in front of the event, in front of the re-presented event (see Sontag 1973). In other words, the post-media subject comprehends the act of remembering as the construction of a narrative generated through the navigation of his or her personal database, which is no more than the experience of a cinematographic flashback, a narrative effect that allows the subject to perceive an actual image as a past event in the diegesis. In the episode in question, "The Entire History of You," the database is composed of all images and sounds recorded through the eyes of the subject. The database is stored and becomes accessible through the 'grains' implanted in the body of the subject. Unable to forget, since the entire life of the subject is recorded and stored in the 'grain,' the subject is only able to navigate the database of their experiences and perceives the images being screened on the retina as memories of past events. Thanks to the 'grains,' the subject acquires the cognitive capacity to deal with a temporality that corresponds to her or his cognition.

Black Mirror's first season deals with three major characteristics of the post-media condition, all of them directly in relation to the force of externalization exerted by electric technology. These three characteristics are the externalization of the human being depicted through the clash of the former private and public spheres: the externalization of human desires, and their subsequent reification in the immaterial space of the info-sphere (see Berardi 1995), and the externalization of the human experience, which is codified (or at least pretends to be codified) and store in the info-sphere. The successive seasons (to date, there have been five seasons) could be seen as declensions of these three main characteristics of the post-media condition. It is possible to understand *Black Mirror* as a map of the *virtualities* of our post-media technological context attempting to identify a *Possible*. These *virtualities* depict how technological devices are invading human bodies and the way these technologies conciliate material existence with the expansion of non-material realities, but above all it depicts the current human impossibility to grasp the object, which in its digital codification, becomes flexible, changeable, and intangible (see Hui 2016). Thus, the series depicts a subject unable to experience the world. In other words, it depicts a human being in a continuous attempt to reach an unreachable being-in-the-world. Above all, the post-media existence conceptualized by *Black Mirror* is the expression of a techno-totalitarian existence, the major goals of which reside in abandoning the human body in order to conciliate human existence to the previously mentioned characteristics of the object. One can identify in *Black Mirror* a criticism on a problematic generated by a great confusion based on the old, obsolete Cartesian belief in the well-established dichotomy: mind–body. In fact, under the lens of a post-media condition, *Black Mirror* deals, through the phenomenon of transhumanism, with an apparently human aspiration for the body to acquire the flexibility of the dematerialized object. The series sheds light upon an unclear will, upon a not-yet-existing-problem that can be described as the will to finally merge the subject with the (digital-flexible) object by eliminating from the equation the body, the center of the experience that connects the subject to the object and determines existence (See Esposito 2014, p. 91). As remarked by Ray Kurzweil, who believes in the technological possibility of 'uploading' human skills and human experiences, bio-technologies aim to reach such a transhuman scenario (see Kurzweil 2005). Whereas humanity reaches this dystopic utopia, society faces the transformation of its twentieth-century nightmares, masterly re-elaborated in this television series, with the hope of elucidating the fields of the *Possible*, of glimpsing the outlines of the frightened face, and of identifying the vibration, the non-yet-existing problem.

Bibliography

Agamben, G. (2006) *Che cos'è un dispositivo?* Roma: Nottetempo.

Aldiss, B. (1995) *The Detached Retina. Aspects of SF and Fantasy.* Liverpool: Liverpool University Press.

Allard-Huver, F. & Escurignan J. (2018) "Black Mirror's Nosedive as a new Panopticon: Interveillance and Digital Parrhesia in Alternative Realities" in A.M. Cirucci &B. Vacker (eds.) *Black Mirror and Critical Media Theory.* La ham, Maryland: Lexington Books, pp. 43-54.

Bachelard, G. (1931) *L'intuition de l'instant.* Paris: Stock.

Barbier, F. & Bertho Lavenir C. (1996) *Histoire des médias de Diderot à Internet.* Paris: Armand Colin.

Baudrillard, J. (1976) *L'échange symbolique et la mort.* Paris: Gallimard.

Berardi, (Bifo) F. (1995) *Neuromagma. Lavoro cognitivo e infoproduzione.* Roma: Castelvecchi.

Berardi, (Bifo) F. (2013) *Dopo il futuro. Dal Futurismo al Cyberpunk. L'esaurimento della Modernità.* Roma: DeriveApprodi.

Berardi, (Bifo) F. (2015) *Heroes. Suicidio e omicidi di massa.* Milano: Baldini & Castoldi.

Berardi, (Bifo) F. (2016) *L'anima al lavoro. Alienazione, estraneità, autonomia.* Roma: DeriveApprodi.

Blitz, M. (2014) "Understanding Heidegger on Technology" in *The New Atlantis: A journal on Technology and Society,* No 41. Online. (Consulted 15/05/2020) https://www.thenewatlantis.com/publications/understanding-heidegger-on-technology

Caronia, A. (1996) *Il corpo virtuale. Dal corpo robotizzato al corpo disseminato,* Padova: Franco Muzzio Editore.

Caronia, A. (2008) *Il Cyborg. Saggio sull'uomo artificiale.* Milano: Shake.

Curi, U. (2009) *L'immagine-pensiero. Tra Fellini, Wilder e Wenders: Un viaggio Filosofico.* Milano: Mimesis.

De Kerckhove, D. (2008) *Dall'alfabeto a Internet. L'homme « Littéré » : Alfabetizzazione, cultura, tecnologia.* Milano: Mimesis.

Deleuze, G. & Guattari, F. (1980) *Capitalisme et schizophrénie 2. Mille Plateux*. Paris: Les éditions de Minuit.

Deleuze, G. (1983) *Cinéma 1. L'immage-mouvement*. Paris: Les éditions de Minuit.

Deleuze, G. & Guattari, F. (1991) *Qu'est-ce que la philosophie?* Paris: Les éditions de Minuit, transl. *What Is Philosophy?* New York: Columbia University Press, 1994.

Dorfles, G. (2008) *Horror Pleni. La (in)civiltà del rumore*. Roma: Castelvecchi.

Duarte, G.A. (2014) *Fractal Narrative. About the Relationship Between Geometries and Technology and Its Impact on Narrative Spaces*. Bielefeld: transcript.

Duarte, G.A. (2015) *"La chose maudite*. The Concept of Reification in George Bataille's *The Accursed Share"*, in Human and Social Studies – Degruyter Open, Vol. IV, no. 1, (2015), pp. 91-110.

Duarte, G.A. (2018) "Introducing The Fractal Character of *Dasein* in The Digital Age", in Battin J.M. & Duarte G.A. (Eds.) *We Need To Talk About Heidegger. Essays Situating Martin Heidegger in Contemporary Media Studies*. Berlin: Peter Lang, pp. 21-52.

Esposito, R. (2014) *Le persone e le cose*. Torino: Einaudi.

Eugeni, R. (2015) *La condizione postmediale*. Milano: La Scuola.

Evans, A.B. (2009) "Nineteenth Century SF" in M. Bould, A. Butler, A. Roberts & S. Vint (eds.) *The Routledge Companion to Science Fiction*. London: Routledge, pp. 13-22.

Flusser, V. (2008) *Kommunikologie weiter denken. Die Bochumer Vorlesungen*. Frankfurt am Main: Fischer.

Freedman, C. (2000) *Critical Theory and Science Fiction*. Middletown, Connecticut: Wesleyan University Press.

Gomel, E. (2011) "Science (Fiction) and Posthuman Ethics: Redefining the Human" in *The European Legacy*, V. 16, Issue 3, pp. 339-354.

Goody, J. (1977) *The domestication of the Savage Mind*. Cambridge: Cambridge University Press.

Gunkel, D. & Taylor, P. (2014) *Heidegger and the Media*. Cambridge: Polity Press.

Heidegger, M. (1949) *Bremer und Freiburger Vorträge*. (In M. Heidegger, Gesamtausgabe III. Unveröffentliche Abhandlugen. Vorträge, Gedachtes Band 79. Frankfurt am Main: Vittorio Klostermann, 1994)

Heidegger, M. (1950) *Das Ding*, (In M. Heidegger, Gesamtausgabe. I. Abteilung: Veröffentliche Schriften 1910-1976, Band 7. Vortrage Und Aufsätze, Frankfurt am Main, Vittorio Klostermann, 2000)

Heidegger, M. (1953) *Die Frage nach der Technik.* (In M. Heidegger, Gesamtausgabe. I. Abteilung: Veröffentliche Schriften 1910-1976, Band 7. Vortrage Und Aufsätze, Frankfurt am Main, Vittorio Klostermann, 2000, pp. 165-188.)

Heidegger, M. (1967) *Sein und Zeit.* Tübingen: Max Niemeyer Verlag.

Horkheimer, M. & Adorno, T.W. (1947) *Dialektik der Aufklärung. Philosophische Fragmente.* Amsterdam: Querido Verlag.

Hui, Y. (2016) *On The Existence of Digital Objects.* Minneapolis: University of Minnesota Press.

Johnson, D.K, Márquez, L.P. & Urueña, S. (2020) "Black Mirror: What Science Fiction Does Best" in Johnson, D.K. (Ed.) *Black Mirror and Philosophy: Dark Reflections.* Hoboken, NJ: Wiley & Sons.

Krauss, R. (1999) *"A Voyage on the North Sea" Art in the Age of the Post-Medium Condition.* London: Thames & Hudson.

Kurzweil, R. (2005) *The Singularity Is Near. When Humans Transcend Biology.* New York: Penguin.

Lyotard, J.F. (1979) *La condition post-moderne.* Paris: Les éditions de Minuit.

Marcuse, H. (1964) *One Dimensional Man. Studies in the Ideology of Advanced Industrial Society.* Boston: Beacon Press.

McLuhan, M. (1994) *Understanding Media. The Extensions of Man.* Cambridge Massachusetts: MIT Press.

Merleau-Ponty, M. (1945) *Phénoménologie de la perception.* Paris: Gallimard.

Merleau-Ponty, M. (1961) *L'œil et l'esprit.* Paris: Gallimard.

Sontag, S. (1973) *On Photography.* New York: Picador.

Stiegler, B. (2009) "The Carnival of the New Screen: From Hegemony to Isonomy", in: P. Snickars & P. Vonderau (Eds.), *The YouTube Reader.* Stockholm; National Library of Sweden.

Suvin, D. (1979) *Metamorphoses of Science Fiction: On the Poetics and History of a Literary Genre.* New Haven: Yale University Press.

Todorov, T. (2015) *Introduction à la littérature fantastique.* Paris: Éditions du Seuil.

Zuboff, S. (2019) *The Age of Surveillance Capitalism: The Fight for a Human Future at the New Frontier of Power.* New York: Public Affairs.

It's the End of the World as We See It
A (Post)Apocalyptic Reading of *Fifteen Million Merits* and *Metalhead*

Marcin Mazurek

Framing (Post)Apocalypse

Much as it seems uncontroversial to locate "Metalhead" in the context of apocalyptic imagery, to place "Fifteen Million Merits" against the same background is likely to arouse intellectual suspicion, at least initially. After all, no detectable cataclysm seems to have taken place before the story unfolds, we are not exposed to the debris of human civilization and/or toxic wastelands resulting from warfare or nuclear holocaust, and we do not see any zombies threatening human survival, to mention just a few of the post-apocalyptic genre's favourite staples. On the contrary, the episode's world, along with its inhabitants, appear utterly advanced: unbothered by the mundanity of everyday problems, undisturbed by political chaos and social uncertainties, unruffled by health hazards, crime, pollution, or noisy neighbours – in other words, all the nightmares of risk society. Instead, its denizens seem to accept, if not thoroughly enjoy, their daily cycling routines, finding refuge in the ever-present screens radiating with stultifying tv-shows and hoping – to use Chuck Palahniuk's classic definition of latent consumerist desires – "that someday [they]'ll be millionaires and movie stars and rock stars." (2003, p. 166).

If anything, their universe is a satirical exaggeration of the paradoxes contouring the media-induced late capitalist society which, at the close of the second decade of the 21st century, we all know so well: oppressive but strangely rewarding, hyper-consumerist yet – through a plethora of talent and reality-shows – promising genuine emotions, feeding on our growing dependence on virtual modes of social existence and still offering the illu-sion of control. Interestingly enough, that illusion is executed not via the ubiquitous screens of our smartphones and tablets which we gently caress while giving them orders, but more and more often, just like the inhabitants of the episode's universe, through merely gesticulating our choices, suffice it to mention the gesture control option available in some of the high-spec Volkswagen automobiles. True, this sterile, post-button and post-touch-screen environment comes about as straightforwardly oppressive, resonat-ing with the echo of Aldous Huxley's *Brave New World* and its regime of uni-versal happiness, here replaced with universal celebrification. Yet, except for Bing the Savage, no one seems to complain.

Naturally, when looked at from this angle, this dark satire is a fairly obvi-ous comment on our contemporary obsession with instant fame and fortune achievable through glossy and shallow media pseudo-culture, which, as Tony McKenna put it, is "constantly trying to disguise the dull mechanics of economic exploitation with an authentic, popular veneer" (2019, p. 368). But does that bitter comment justify the use of apocalypse, even as an opera-tional metaphor?

In this respect, "Metalhead" does not raise such doubts. Although this episode has been habitually interpreted through a technophobic lens, often directly pointing to the disturbing question of "How Dangerous Will Robots Be?" (Midson and Donhauser, 2020, pp.177-186; Gurr, 2019, pp. 245-255), the overall setting of the plot clearly indicates an all-out catastrophe prior to the episode's main plot. Across a bleak and barren landscape, a group of weary survivors travel in a battered Skoda on a mission to retrieve an unspecified item from an abandoned warehouse, which is apparently a dying child's last hope. It is in this warehouse that the episode turns into a post-apocalyptic survival horror story, although careful viewers might spot a tell-tale warning a moment earlier as the group approaches the supposedly-abandoned build-ing. The signpost in front of it, underneath a big "To Let" caption, includes a subtle foreshadowing to what lies inside: hardware. Even though a signpost of this type is by no means unusual given the amount of subliminal hints permeating not only "Metalhead" (which features camouflaged references to "USS Callister" and "San Junipero") but also a number of other episodes; therefore, this hardly seems to be a coincidence. *Hardware* is actually the title of Richard Stanley's 1990 post-apocalyptic sci-fi horror movie (1990), which features a similar story related to a homicidal robot called Mark 13 on a deadly mission to wipe out as large a number of humans as possible, all part of a secret governmental population control programme. Again, just like in "Metalhead," one of the main protagonists, Moses (Dylan McDermott), does not survive the encounter. Mark 13 is ultimately destroyed by a mixture of feminine fury and ingenuity, but in one of the final scenes we hear DJ Angry Bob's (Iggy Pop) frantic voice announcing its mass production. This again echoes *Black Mirror*, specifically with the arrival of multiple robo-dogs at the house in which Bella, the episode's heroine, had died after having been "injected" with one of the robo-dog's deadly devices (in *Hardware* the robot manages to inject Moses with a lethal poison).

True, the overall tones of both films are entirely different – partly because of the semi-biblical framework of the *Hardware* story (the robot's name is a reference to Mark 13:20, which reads "no flesh shall be spared") and partly because of its toxic visual intensity – but the intertextual space which both pictures establish radiates with the same question, which exceeds the premises of a technophobic cautionary-tale and reaches further by accentuating the problem of human obsolescence. In terms of ultimate apocalyptic threats, few notions seem to deserve a higher rating on the list of end-of-the-world menaces.

But one may approach the notion of apocalypse in an altogether different manner. After all, an all-out annihilation of humankind – however natural and attractive in terms of the popular understanding of the concept – indicates a complete lack of survivors who could report the apocalyptic event(s) as well as a total absence of the audience who could contemplate it, thus rendering the whole of the apocalyptic discourse (and all other discourses, too) not only unnecessary but also impossible. What is more, mankind's obliteration questions the very notion of post-apocalypse which, by its prefix, implies apocalypse's incompleteness and hints at the presence of at least one survivor capable of re-living the end, even if only in a narrative form.

Hence, a different attitude appears necessary, one which would take the concept's inherent incompleteness as its non-negotiable departure point, thereby allowing for the understanding of apocalypse in discursive and metaphorical terms, as a genre rather than a means of exerting eschatological anxiety, religious concerns, or political pressure. Also, this new approach would have to highlight apocalypse's descriptive potential to embrace an all-encompassing and irreversible change, not only in terms of aesthetic contemplation of the end but also, if not in the first place, in terms of a radical paradigmatic and philosophical disruption of the ontological condition of the pre-apocalyptic gestalt. Finally, it should stress the emergence of a new order, this time a properly post-apocalyptic one; the prefix not so much offering a self-contradictory conundrum regarding whose voice we are listening to, but rather connoting the radical otherness of the emerging creation instead of a complete demise of the previous state. Simply put, the approach in question should expose apocalypse's revelatory potential, which in fact reaches back to its etymological roots. As David Robson observed,

> [...] apocalypse means revelation, and although apocalyptic discourse aims to define, contain, and domesticate otherness, it also serves to reveal the other. It is this revelatory or irreducibly prophetic dimension of apocalyptic discourse that prevents its perfect coalescence with any particular historical, political, or institutional manifestation. Apocalyptic discourse is usually profoundly hostile to the status quo. Its meanings and referents always exceed what 'is' and point toward what is 'other' than what is [...] (1995, p. 63).

In other words, Robson highlights the philosophical strength of the concept instead of its visual or religious appeal, and, indirectly, its metaphorical applicability whenever the "'other' than what is" emerges on the experiential and cognitive horizon of human actions. In this respect, apocalypse appears to be a radically ahistorical phenomenon: released from the obligation to serve as a fulfilment of religious prophecy, it reveals its double-coded potential, that of introducing an irreparable rupture in the old and an exposure of the new.

It is precisely the revelatory aspect of apocalypse which Jacques Derrida brings to the fore in his oft-cited essay, "Of an Apocalyptic Tone Recently Adopted in Philosophy." Again, reaching into the etymological origins of the term, he identifies the concept's self-prescribed mission as, "I disclose, I uncover, I unveil, I reveal the thing [...] that is neither shown nor said, signified perhaps but that cannot or *must* not first be delivered to up to self-evidence" (1984, p. 4). Interestingly enough, and again contrary to the concept's common denotations, Derrida stresses the invisibility of apocalyptic operations. No more spectacular earthquakes, biblical floods, alien invasions, or radioactive wastelands; once we treat apocalypse as an ultimate metaphor of a paradigmatic transformation, it will appear in a low-profile and discreet manner, detectable perhaps only by what Derrida refers to as "tone" and defines as, "a deviation in relation to the norm of philosophical discourse" (1984, p. 6). As he explains elsewhere in his essay,

> Conversely, we could even say that every discord or every tonal disorder, everything that detones and becomes inadmissible [*irrecevable*] in general collocution, everything that is no longer identifiable starting from established codes, from both sides of afront, will necessarily pass for [...] apocalyptic (Derrida, 1984, p. 30).

Thus, in the final analysis, apocalypse reveals itself as a twofold notion. On the one hand, it seems barely possible to ignore the idea's popular connotations of cataclysmic disasters and utter destruction, which, by the way, have evolved into separate literary and cinematic genres, going back to Mary Shelley's *The Last Man* (1826) and Felix E. Feist's *Deluge* (1933). What such representations seem to focus on, however, especially in post-apocalyptic films, is the spectacular and violent nature of the very apocalyptic act, habitually enhanced by special effects depicting crumbling cities (*Deep Impact* [1998], *The Day After Tomorrow* [2004], *2012* [2009]) or endless wastelands (*The Blood of Heroes* [1989], *The Book of Eli* [2010], *Mad Max: Fury Road* [2015]), rather than the less visible consequences of the rupture in the pre-apocalyptic condition – perhaps not as impressive aesthetically, but equally devastating once their outer layer is stripped and the true scope of the apocalyptic event is revealed.

In other words, we may identify two modes of representation of the post-apocalyptic condition relying on two seemingly contrasting imageries: one using visions more akin to cultural condensation, technological surplus, and uncontrolled urban growth – an invisible apocalypse of cultural-technological over-production, excess and exaggeration – the other highlighting the palpable effects of the apocalyptic event through the aesthetic of desolation, ruination, and decay. It is precisely these two aesthetic modes of representing the post-apocalyptic milieu that delineate the interpretative horizon of "Fifteen Million Merits" and "Metalhead."

Between Simulation and Desolation

Once we separate the post-catastrophic imagery from the post-apocalyptic discursive tone identified by Derrida, the ensuing perspective will allow for a post-apocalyptic reading of a number of *Black Mirror* episodes, of which "Fifteen Million Merits" remains probably the most radical, particularly in terms of announcing the number of ends which have habitually comprised the formative components of the apocalyptic discourse. Even a brief analysis of endism and its relation to a number of other postmodern discourses reaches beyond the scope of this chapter, but suffice it to mention that – once we concentrate on apocalypse's potential to announce the demise of the old – from a philosophical perspective its presence is clearly detectable in the form of the ever-so-popular prefix "post-" featuring in the names of at least a dozen or so contemporary discourses.[1]

The horizonless micro-verse of the episode, with all the routines of life (habitation, production, consumption, entertainment) crammed indoors, seems to open the list of the episode's ends with the end of nature, reduced to a simplistic screen visual meant to evoke the illusion of covering real miles while cycling. Naturally, bearing in mind the episode's peculiar mood, oscillating between dystopia and satire, we could read the ubiquitous artificiality and uniformity of, to use Marxist terms, both the base and the superstructure of the episode's environment as an ultimately ironic comment on contemporary Western society, which craves supposedly genuine emotions as long as they are properly mediated and neatly wrapped in a garish gift-paper of a glossy tv-show, one which "is always seeking to disguise the contrived

---

1 Whether the popularity of the prefix indicates a state of peculiar linguistic exhaustion and our inability to denominate a number of cultural conditions in a more precise manner, or simply highlights those conditions' provisional and transient nature is, of course, a subject of a different debate, especially in the light of such terms as post-postmodernism advocated, for instance, by English architect, Tom Turner (1995). One should also point out that among various post-discourses the prefix remains by no means universally compatible and signifies different contexts and approaches. But since its current presence is measured in decades now, it seems to have settled in for good and is here to stay, at least for the foreseeable future. *The Icon Critical Dictionary of Postmodern Thought*, for example, identifies as many as ten different "posts" to which we could add the prefix, including post-geography, post-history, and post-truth, to name but a few (Sim, ed., 1998, pp. 336–342). In this sense, the post-discourses seem to fulfil Derrida's condition of "tonal disorders" and hence acquire a somewhat apocalyptic quality.

nature of its cruelty behind the exhibition of the spontaneous, 'authentic' act" (McKenna, 2019, p. 367).

A closer look at the disappearance of nature, framing both the episode's aesthetics and its philosophical premise, may reveal an apocalyptic mechanism of a paradigmatic transition. True, on the one hand, nature is understood in its basic biological form as having been completely removed from the world of Bing and his fellow cyclists; even the perfectly green and round apples appear to be produced by vending machines rather than grown. On a different level though, nature has been replaced by a new form of "natural" environment; it is no longer organic but rather industrialized, mediated, and incorporated into a new cycle of production and consumption which fills up the whole of the episode's characters' cognitive horizon. An environment which is artificial, simulated, and commodifies every single gesture of spontaneous creativity, from a solitary song to an act of rebellion. The "natural" has thus not so much ended but evolved and been replaced; it is no longer biological but technological, and driven by the ultimate desire for ratings and popularity. Since even myths of the pre-mediated culture have been erased from collective memory, the change in question appears all-encompassing and irreversible.

As such, the underlying foundation of the episode's reality seems to almost precisely illustrate Gilles Deleuze and Felix Guattari's diagnosis of the contemporary Western condition which effectively blurs the boundary between nature and industry, and is heavily driven by the process of constant production, consumption, and, most importantly, the "recording processes," here represented by the capitalist ubiquity of media culture. As they note,

> [...] from one point of view, industry is the opposite of nature; from another, industry extracts its raw materials from nature; from yet another, it returns its refuse to nature; and so on. Even within society, this characteristic man-nature, industry-nature, society-nature relationship is responsible for the distinction of relatively autonomous spheres that are called production, distribution, consumption. [...] Hence everything is production: *production of productions*, of actions and of passions; *productions of recording processes*, of distributions and of co-ordinates that serve as points of reference; *productions of consumptions*, of sensual pleasures, of anxieties, and of pain. Everything is production, since the recording processes are immediately consumed,

immediately consummated, and these consumptions directly reproduced. (Deleuze and Guattari, 2000, pp. 3-4, emphasis in original).

One's compulsory participation in the life contoured by the social machinery of perpetual production becomes thus an unalterable existential condition, a *sine qua non* of being itself, taking place under persistent consumer pressures, round-the-clock surveillance, constant monitoring, and being given no chance to resign – even momentarily, by simply looking away – from the "natural" obligation to produce and consume. Mind-numbing cycling and the endlessly repeatable daily routines turn into ordinary responses to the requirements of the industrial environment, necessary for one's social survival and producing a cynical illusion of freedom reduced to a choice between a television channel, a virtual hairstyle, or a video game.

The consumers of this simulated reality, however, are also its producers; after all, it is their monotonous pedalling that powers the whole infrastructure and this particular connection in fact questions the possibility of classifying their society as purely oppressive since the oppression in question is executed by the system whose operational capability depends on the cycling routines of the masses, thereby rendering it, at least partly, self-imposed. Even Bing's rebellious gesture was provoked not so much by his political awareness of the system's vicious-circle characteristic, but by a quasi-erotic fascination with a female voice, a motif quite popular in the anti-utopian genre, from Yevgeny Zamiatin's *We*, to George Orwell's *1984*, to Ray Bradbury's *Fahrenheit 451*.

From a Deleuzian perspective, however, this ongoing feedback loop between production and consumption, or, to be more precise, between producers and consumers, translates into yet another end, this time that of human superiority over nature, understood both in terms of the long departed organic environment as well as in those of the industrial milieu. Gone is the illusion of the subject's dominance or even agency; lofty ideals of the enlightenment project are no match for the mediated industrial nature of unstoppable production, which turns the subject into a mere component in the machinery of simulated reproductions, in fact both producing it and being its product since, as Deleuze and Guattari have observed, it is no longer possible to make a, distinction between man and nature: the human essence of nature and the natural essence of man become one within nature in the form of production or industry, just as they do within the life of man as a species. Industry is then no longer considered from the extrinsic point of view of utility, but rather from the point of view of its fundamental identity with nature as production of man and by man. Not man as the king of creation, but rather as the being who is in intimate contact with the profound life of all forms or all types of beings [...] (2000, p. 4).

This evaporation of the hierarchical relation between the subject and his or her now-industrialized natural environment produces a particular sense of human dethronement resulting from the disappearance of one of the West's formative binarities, namely the one between culture and nature. The former, understood as the implementation of the sum of mankind's creative efforts, no longer holds the upper hand when confronted with the determining power of nature redefined along industrial, capitalist, and technological lines, even though, historically speaking, the industrial milieu is a product of cultural-technological development. As Deleuze and Guattari sum up, "man and nature are not like two opposite terms confronting each other – not even in the sense of bipolar opposites within a relationship of causation, ideation, or expression (cause and effect, subject and object, etc.); rather, they are one and the same essential reality, the producer-product" (2000, pp. 4-5).

What happens when a subject is thrown into such an industrialized environment, deprived of its humanist pedestal erected by enlightenment philosophy, and reduced to a cog in the machinery of production? Predictably, it becomes a component of the production-consumption system, a human machine of sorts, a term to which Deleuze and Guattari add the adjective "desiring." Desiring to produce, process, and exchange, adopting technological extensions of its body, turning its own limbs and organs into smaller mechanical units, rods and levers connecting it with other machines, organic and otherwise, and turning itself into an "ultimate residue of a deterritorialized socius," (Deleuze and Guattari, 2000, p. 281) which the authors of *Anti-Oedipus* refer to as body-without-organs.

Interestingly enough, the concept of desiring machines was partly inspired by Samuel Butler, a 19th century English writer, today mostly remembered for his 1872 novel, *Erewhon*, a utopian satire on Victorian society, in which disease and crime are reversed resulting in criminal persecution of people unlucky enough to catch a cold and a semi-medical treatment of anyone malicious enough to, for instance, steal something. But the Erewhonian society is characterised by yet another feature, surprisingly useful in the analysis of "Metalhead:" a total lack of machines which the Erewhonians believe pose a serious threat to humanity because – given the pace of their expansion combined with Darwinian evolutionary logic – the question of their developing some form of consciousness is only a matter of time.

In 1863, Butler wrote an article titled "Darwin among the Machines" which he later reproduced in the three chapters of *Erewhon* as "The Book of the Machines." In this essay he outlines the seemingly logical possibility of the emergence of artificial intelligence. Of course, Butler never used that name, but considering the contemporary popularity of the AI theme, especially among cinematic representations – suffice it to mention such Hollywood blockbuster franchises as *The Terminator* series or *The Matrix Trilogy*, among others – Butler's personal techno-anxiety appears truly prophetic. As if following the basic storylines in the aforementioned films (let alone *Hardware* and "Metalhead"), he reaches a rather present-day conclusion that, at a not yet identified point, humans will pose a serious threat to machines' "life" and therefore the machines are likely to seriously consider the possibility of human elimination.

It must be noted, however, that Butler's argument is not technophobic from the start, even though he quickly begins to sketch morbid visions of masterful machines using humans as slaves:

> [...] they will rule us with a rod of iron, but they will not eat us; they will not only require our services in the reproduction and education of their young, but also in waiting upon them as servants; in gathering food for them, and feeding them; in restoring them to health when they are sick; and in either burying their dead or working up their deceased members into new forms of mechanical existence (2002, p. 135).

His initial observations, however, concern the very nature of consciousness, which he sees in a manner akin to Deleuze and Guattari, that is, in terms of universal connectivity and through exposing the mechanical nature of biological entities, which for Butler are not that different from the mechanical ones, even though the most sophisticated machine he mentions is a "vapour-engine." Stressing the mechanical nature of human body, which in itself consists of smaller mechanical units ("Is it man's eyes, or is it the big seeing-engine which has revealed to us the existence of worlds beyond worlds into infinity?" [Butler, 2002, p. 123]), he proceeds to conclude that a "great deal of action that has been called purely mechanical and unconscious must be admitted to contain more elements of consciousness than has been allowed hitherto (and in this case germs of consciousness will be found in many actions of the higher machines) [...]" (ibid p. 121), and finally sums up his contemplations with an almost rhetorical question: "Are we not ourselves creating our successors in the supremacy of the earth?" (ibid p. 126).

If we tried to reply to Butler's question using the conceptual assumption behind "Metalhead," the answer would obviously have to be entirely affirmative. Not only are the remaining humans tracked and hunted, but they are obliterated. The precise motives behind the robo-dogs' deadly mission, however, remain obscure.[2] In this respect, "Metalhead" is doubly post-apocalyptic; the apocalypse has already taken place and yet another is occurring as we follow Bella's desperate attempts to survive. From the opening shots, we gather that human culture and civilisation, as well as all its flaws – like the myth of equal society as subtly hinted at in the car conversation echoing Orwell's *Animal Farm* – are gone. The pigs, an ironic Orwellian symbol of social equality, are all dead since, as one of the characters puts it, "dogs took care of them." In terms of the representational imagery – comprised of a black-and-white depiction of the Scottish landscape, barren and bleak – we are clearly exposed to the aforementioned aesthetic of post-apocalyptic desolation.

But the apocalyptic act is still taking place as the rupture is not complete; Bella is still fighting for the lost cause that is her life after having failed in her final mission to seize the mysterious item from the abandoned warehouse. Her struggle, however, extends beyond a simple faceoff between the human and the mechanical, as it also narrates a dismantling of more than one binarity. First of all, she is a woman; this immediately locates her among the cinematic portrayals of ingenious and determined females who are the only ones capable of confronting the monstrous or mechanical other after all of the men have failed, resigned, or died. Even though Bella's victory over

---

2 For the sake of contextual accuracy, we should note, however, that in the first draft of the script the robo-dogs were controlled by a human operator (Brooker, Jones, Arnopp, 2018, p. 415).

the robo-dog results in her death, within the intertextual context of similar-ly-themed cinematic representations, she ranks alongside symbols of femi-nine power and competence such as Sergeant Ripley (Sigourney Weaver) of the *Alien* series, Sarah Connor (Linda Hamilton) of the *Terminator* franchise, and Jill (Stacey Travis) from *Hardware*.

In "Metalhead," men are not even able to help; they all die before the proper struggle begins. They have strength and skills, but they seem to lack the abil-ity to improvise which turns out to be Bella's greatest advantage. Tricking the robo-dog into following the tracking device in the bottle, wearing out its battery by waking it up all night long, and blinding its sensors with paint all demonstrate her ability to take over traditionally masculine traits without – as revealed in the final scene – losing her sense of sympathy and compassion. Unfortunately, in this post-gender world, that is not enough.

In their article "*Metalhead* and Technophobia. How Dangerous Will Robots Be?" (2020, pp. 177-186), Scott Midson and Justin Donhauser point to another dismantled binarity by suggesting that the robo-dogs "exemplify the Cartesian linking of animal and mechanical against the uniqueness of the human" (2020, p. 178). For Descartes, obviously, the uniqueness of the human lies in the capacity for self-doubt as a logical conclusion which the subject (or, more likely for Descartes, "the man") reaches after having ques-tioned the reliability of sensory perception. In Descartes's view, our senses are deceitful but do not deprive us of "the power of judging well and of dis-tinguishing the true from the false (which is, properly speaking, what people call 'good sense' or 'reason') [...]" (1998, p. 1). This power facilitates our critical self-reflection, an act which in itself can only be performed by a "thinking thing," which Descartes refers to as *res cogitans*. Against *res cogitans* he places *res extensa*, the "extended thing," the realm of matter and substance includ-ing our own body, which thus completes our material existence while at the same time introducing a mind-body dualism, one of the most profound and formative binary oppositions, instrumental in shaping the Western mind-set at least up until the mid-20th century. As Descartes himself explains,

> I have a body that is very closely joined to me, nevertheless, because on the one hand I have a clear and distinct idea of myself, insofar as I am merely a thinking thing and not an extended thing, and because on the other hand I have a distinct idea of a body, insofar as it is merely an extended thing and

not a thinking thing, it is certain that I am really distinct from my body, and can exist without it (1998, p. 96).

However, as Midson and Donhauser notice, Descartes's seemingly unshakable binarity is challenged by the robo-dogs which possess "advanced learning and problem-solving capabilities" (2020, p. 178), thus displaying some form of mechanical consciousness, at least in Butler's understanding of the term. Unsurprisingly, Descartes remained highly sceptical of the very idea of mechanical self-awareness, which on the one hand is only expected given his pre-industrial surroundings, but on the other clearly demonstrates that most of his neat binarities lost much of their credibility when confronted with the late 20th/early 21st century advances in science, technology, and social matters. Today however, his arguments concerning inanimate autonomy of machines evoke little more than reflectional nostalgia:

> For one can well conceive of a machine being so made that it utters words, and even that it utters words appropriate to the bodily actions that will cause some change in its organs (such as, if one touches it in a certain place, it asks what one wants to say to it, or, if in another place, it cries out that one is hurting it, and the like). But it could not arrange its words differently so as to respond to the sense of all that will be said in its presence, as even the dullest men can do. [...] For while reason is a universal instrument that can be of help in all sorts of circumstances, these organs require some particular disposition for each particular action; consequently, it is for all practical purposes impossible for there to be enough different organs in a machine to make it act in all the contingencies of life in the same way as our reason makes us act (Descartes, 1998, p. 32).

Like many of his binary presumptions – including Eurocentric and patriarchal convictions – the distinction into *res extensa*, perceived as the sphere of the inanimate and the immaterial, and *res cogitans*, understood as a uniquely human feature, loses its relevance when confronted with the skills and abilities of the apocalyptic robots. Reasoning is no longer a solely human domain, which until recently placed us on the top rung of the evolutionary and existential ladder, high above other creatures, animate or otherwise. The exclusivity of *res cogitans* for humans is thus disturbed by the robo-dogs' presence which (who?) are capable of drawing rational conclusions on the basis of verifiable observations, and then act accordingly. Yet it gets even worse. Not only are they capable of self-reparation, but also of improvising, which includes the abilities to drive a van and pick locks, both of which derive from a seemingly autonomous decision-making process enclosed within the broader framework of their deadly mission. That mission, paradoxically, appears not only to rely on their superior operational capability ("Are we not ourselves creating our successors in the supremacy of the earth?" [Butler, 2002, p. 126]), but also epitomises an ultimate version of reason seen as a collection of rational procedures, unclouded by emotions, moments of weakness, hesitations, or bodily harm, and applied with deadly effectiveness and precision. In other words, they become a morbid embodiment of enlightenment ideals only filtered through a technophobic-Darwinian logic and executing an irreversible evolutionary change which, needless to say, triggers the apocalyptic wheel of human (mis)fortune.

Concluding Remarks

Described as the "*The Twilight Zone* of the twenty-first century [which confronts] the existential conditions of modern technological civilization and the truly radical philosophical challenges [...]" (Cirucci, Vacker, 2018, p. vii), *Black Mirror* as a whole does much more than simply comment on the ubiquity of media culture in our lives. By offering a succession of gloomy technological predictions, "slices of dystopia; a future – clearly not too far away from our present [...]" (McKenna, 2019, p. 366), it exposes its viewers to a new landscape of cognitive experience, which is no longer a reflection of reality but its extension. What unfolds is a new territory for which, to paraphrase the title of Mark Neale's documentary on William Gibson, there are no maps (Neale, 2000); perhaps because, as Jean Baudrillard, another prophet of the post-media condition, famously declared, "[i]t is [...] the map that precedes the territory" (1994, p. 1). Additionally, with this peculiar reversal of reality and representation in the background, if one dared identify the underlying spirit of the show, one could probably do worse than call it apocalyptic. Again, not only in terms of literal desolation, although the depressing landscapes of "Metalhead" and the episode's general sense of doom might be read metaphorically as indicators of the scope of changes in our thinking of technology in general (and of ourselves) that the series has grasped.

In terms of the rupture in the tone of discourses concerning various embodiments of our post-media condition, *Black Mirror* is a voice of change that echoes the postmodern sensation so aptly expressed by Fredric Jameson that,

> something has changed, that things are different, that we have gone through a transformation of the life world which is somehow decisive but incomparable with the older convulsions of modernization and industrialization, less perceptible and dramatic, somehow, but more permanent precisely because more thoroughgoing and all-pervasive (1999, p. xxi).

Applying Jameson's observation to the emergence of the post-media society, it seems only logical that the subtle monumentality of the transformation in question can be best expressed only in visual terms. In this respect, *Black Mirror* does indeed depict the end of the world as we see it through multiple scenarios of ever more dystopian futures including those in which our social identities depend on the amount of stars we collect ("Nosedive"), our enemies are conveniently uglified and are hence easier to kill ("Men Against Fire"), and personal happiness is achievable only as a utopian illusion ("San Junipero").

By drawing these (and many other) dystopian pictures, *Black Mirror* in general (and "Fifteen Million Merits" in particular), enforces a critical reflection on the media-induced "natural" environment of the contemporary Western condition. Offering at times only slightly exaggerated visions of the future that in many cases are already here – such as those relocated to the realm of social media, perpetually mediated and constantly self-monitored by our consumerist mind-sets – it alerts us to both collective and personal consequences of our more and more intimate relationships with our machines and the visions of the world they inspire (and also control), including the relationships we are a part of, our political preferences, and our often embarrassing desires. What it does in the first place is *reveal* to us, in a truly apocalyptic manner, that we have already entered that territory of the map, only it is drawn in a larger-than-life scale and therefore overwhelms us with its intricate details, life-style obsessions, and other existential options, most of which blur the boundary between our role as spectators and as participants. Furthermore, it also demonstrates that, as of today, we tread upon this map even though we do not seem to have a map to guide us. The only two questions that remain are whether we are ever going to find one and, more importantly, if we really need it.

Bibliography

Baudrillard, J. (1994) [1981] *Simulacra and Simulation*. Ann Arbor, MI: University of Michigan Press.

Brooker, Ch., Jones, A., and Arnopp, J. (2018) *Inside Black Mirror*. London: Ebury Press. E-book.

Butler, S. (2002) [1872] *Erewhon*. Mineola: Dover Publlications Inc.

Cirucci, A. M. and Vacker, B. (2018) 'Introduction', in Cirucci, A. M., Vacker, B. (eds.) *Black Mirror and Critical Media Theory*. Lanham: Lexington Books.

Deleuze, G. and Guattari, F. (2000) [1972] *Anti-Edipus. Capitalism and Schizophrenia*. Minneapolis: University of Minnesota Press.

Derrida, J. (1984) 'Of an Apocalyptic Tone Recently Adopted in Philosophy', *The Oxford Literary Review*, Volume 6, No. 2 [online]. Available at: https://www.jstor.org/stable/43973661 (Accessed: 31 May 2020)

Descartes, R. (1998) [1637] *Discourse on Method* and *Meditations on First Philosophy*. Indianapolis: Hackett Publishing Company.

Gurr, B. (2019) 'Killing the Creator in 'Metalhead'' in McSweeney T., Joy, S. (eds.) *Through the Black Mirror. Deconstructing the Side Effects of the Digital Age*. Palgrave Macmillan, pp. 245-255. E-book.

Hardware (1990) Directed by Richard Stanley [Film]. UK: British Satellite Broadcasting.

Jameson, F. (1999) [1991] *Postmodernism, or, the Cultural Logic of Late Capitalism*. Durham: Duke University Press.

McKenna, T. 'Behind the Black Mirror: The Limits of Orwellian Dystopia', *Critique*, Volume 47(2) [online]. Available at: https://doi.org/10.1080/030 17605.2019.1601887 (Accessed: 25 May 2020)

Midson, S. and Donhauser, J. (2020) '*Metalhead* and Technophobia. How Dangerous Will Robots Be?', in Johnson, D. K. (ed.) *Black Mirror and Philosophy. Dark Reflections*. Hoboken, NJ.: Wiley Blackwell, pp. 177-186.

No Maps for These Territories (2000) Directed by Mark Neale [Documentary]. Docurama.

Palahniuk, Ch. (2003) *Fight Club*. London: Vintage

Robson, D. 'Frye, Derrida, Pynchon, and the Apocalyptic Space of Postmodern Fiction', in Dellamora, R. (ed.) *Postmodern Apocalypse. Theory and Cultural Practice at the End*. Philadelphia: University of Pennsylvania Press.

Sim, S. (ed.) (1998) *The Icon Critical Dictionary of Postmodern Thought*. Cambridge: Icon Books.

Turner, T. (1995) *City as Landscape: A Post-Postmodern View of Design and Planning*. London: Taylor & Francis.

Mind Games
Playtest as an Allegory for Liquid Modernity

Joseph Macey & Brian McCauley

> "Configurations, constellations, patterns of dependency and interaction were all thrown into the melting pot, to be subsequently recast and refashioned; this was the 'breaking the mould' phase in the history of the inherently transgressive, boundary-breaking, all eroding modernity. As for the individuals, however- they could be excused for failing to notice; they came to be confronted by patterns and figurations which, albeit 'new and improved', were as stiff and indomitable as ever."
> *(Bauman, 2000 p. 6)*

Episode Summary

"Playtest" tells the story of Cooper, an American taking the trip of a lifetime in order to escape the pain of his father's death from Alzheimer's. Cooper leaves behind his grieving mother, to whom he feels he cannot connect after the loss of his father, and continually ignores her calls throughout his travels. In London he connects with Sonja, a technology journalist, before financial problems force him to take a short-term job with a cutting-edge video game company.

At the offices of the game company, Cooper is seated in a white room and is implanted with experimental augmented reality technology used to run a new game. After the implanted device has been setup, Cooper experiences an augmented reality version of *Whack a Mole*. He is then taken to meet the head of the company who informs him that the implanted technology will access his neural activity in order to generate a personalised game experience and 3D graphics that only he can see. He will be testing the most personalised, immersive survival horror game possible.

Following the meeting, Cooper is taken to an empty mansion where he is left alone, although he is connected via an earpiece to those who are administering the playtest. Cooper is tasked with staying in the mansion as long as possible while the augmented reality technology taps into his deepest fears. Despite the assurances that the game is harmless, the ensuing experience is highly traumatic, culminating in the realisation of his worst fears: the implanted technology begins to dig into his brain and, in a cruel parody of his father's fate, Cooper loses all memory and sense of self.

After the implant is removed, Cooper recovers and is able to travel home. Upon arrival, his grieving mother is unable to see Cooper, and when she dials his phone number the ringing of the phone takes Cooper back to the original white room and he has a seizure. We see that the equipment is still being calibrated, the playtest has not yet begun. It is revealed that the telephone call interfered with the testing of the implant and Cooper died as a result, shouting for his mother in his final moments.

Liquid Modernity

Bauman's theory of liquid modernity is communicated in the final book of a trilogy exploring the effects of globalization on economic, political, and social structures (1998), and the decline of the public sphere and the resultant lack of collective influence, outlining the need for global political reconstruction (1999). The final book, *Liquid Modernity* (Bauman, 2000), concludes the trilogy, representing an increasingly relevant work that examines how we have moved away from the solid social structures of the past and towards a more fluid modern existence, highlighting the need to question the notion of what it means to be human.

For Bauman, modernity can be defined as many things and measured by many different markers, but in the case of liquid modernity it is defined and measured as pertaining to the individual. Liquid, meaning fluid, refers to the ever-shifting roles of individuals within modern society; "indeed, in our contemporary age the relationship between the individual and society is changing because the concepts of identity, individual and individuality are becoming meaningless" (Palese, 2013 p. 1). Bauman identifies a phenomenon where we can view Man as a tourist in his own life, where he exists as a consumer in a consumer-driven society, adapting to changes in a fluid manner that allows him to maintain a modern identity characterised by consumption. Bauman points to Orwell's *Nineteen Eighty-Four* and Huxley's *Brave New World* as two diametrically-opposed dystopian visions that share the common foreboding of a tightly-controlled world. In his own words, "Orwell and Huxley did not disagree on the world's destination; they merely envisaged differently the road which would take us there were we to stay ignorant, obtuse, placid or indolent enough to allow things to go their natural way" (Bauman, 2000 p. 54). The concept of liquid modernity itself points to a tightly-controlled world, albeit not with an overarching political nemesis but, rather, wholehearted devotion to the cult of modern consumerism.

In the condition of liquid modernity, individuals are required to renegotiate concepts of identity and self-image as they navigate a world in which they are presented with a seemingly endless number of options. It is an existence in which the stability of previously defined roles and boundaries have dissolved, as can also be seen in the work of Sennett (1999). This dissolution of the established norms of modernity is particularly evident in the growing influence of digital games in contemporary society. Games have always been a significant part of the socio-cultural fabric, even offering opportunities for transgression of existing social boundaries, albeit in restricted circumstances (Hill and Clark, 2001; Geertz, 1973; Wilson, 1986). However, the ever-expanding influence and availability of digital games in contemporary society sets them apart from the games and play of earlier periods. Originally an entertainment media like any other, they have evolved into a prominent means for the construction of both personal and cultural identities (Raessens, 2006), one which, arguably, exceeds that of other cultural products. In the contemporary condition of liquidity, or Sennett's "flexibility," traditional social structures used as reference points for personal identity have been weakened; a space has been created in which concepts of identity are being constructed in a more experiential, playful manner. We are defining ourselves according to our fandoms, our experiences – such as travel, our hobbies (such as gaming), and our sexual preferences, not because they are more important than previous frameworks, but because they are all that is left to us.

Gamification/Ludification

Bauman's views on the modern world as a consumer-driven game can be best encapsulated by the rise of gamification within contemporary society. The technique of gamification is one which provides added value to consumers by increasing motivational affordances to services, thereby engendering more gameful experiences (Hamari, Koivisto and Sarsa, 2014)[1]. Gamification has also been proposed as constituting a phenomenon, rather than simply a process; one which is a constituent part of our contemporary culture (McGonigal, 2011; Koivisto and Hamari, 2019; Hamari, Koiovisto and Parvinen, 2019). However, both of these approaches have attracted criticism, indeed the last decade has seen a sustained debate within game studies concerning the nature, and relevance, of gamification (McGonigal, 2011; Seaborn and Fels, 2015; Bogost, 2015). While some have critiqued the very concept of gamification, others have attempted to distinguish between the promotion of gameful experiences in non-game contexts and the wider cultural significance of games and play.

Consequently, the concept of ludification has been employed as a means of describing the rise of play in different areas of culture and society. Proponents of ludification distinguish it from gamification in that the latter term refers solely to the application of game elements in non-entertainment spheres while ludification is concerned with the spread of play as a practice in our everyday lives (Mäyrä, 2017). In this way, gamification is a specific example of the wider, more far-reaching, process of ludification (Raessens, 2014). No matter the theoretical positioning, that which is beyond doubt is the evolution in cultural significance of games, and of play from predomi-

---

1   Note 1: Gameful design is a concept intimately linked to gamification, the two can be hard to distinguish as it is argued that the primary difference lies in the designer's intentions, for the purposes of this work we will use the more commonly used term "gamification" as an umbrella term.

nantly leisure activities into a near hegemony. The dominant view of play as being a luxury, a wasteful and unproductive use of time, is receding, with games being employed as educational tools, as economic drivers, and as art (Dillon, 2016; Thibault, 2016; Egenfeldt-Nielsen, Smith, and Tosca, 2019). Indeed, games are emblematic of the ways in which liquid modernity is characterised by transient concepts of self within social systems, of previously solid distinctions becoming mutable. Bauman has previously identified that playfulness has moved beyond childhood and that adults in the condition of liquid modernity embrace the concepts of play throughout their lives: "the mark of postmodern adulthood is the willingness to embrace the game whole-heartedly, as children do" (Bauman, 1995 p. 99).

Analysis

> "But if you never err, you can never be sure of being in the right either. If there are no wrong moves, there is nothing to distinguish a move as a better one, and so nothing to recognise the right move among its many alternatives – neither before nor after the move has been made."
>
> *(Bauman, 2000 p. 63)*

The uncertainty of choice highlighted by Bauman (2000) is reflected in the loss of stability and increasingly fluid nature of society. This is a theme that is present in the majority of *Black Mirror* episodes, which show us the potential of technology to disrupt our experiences in the world around us. But it is Cooper's experiences, as envisaged by the creators, that truly encapsulate Bauman's vision of the changing world. We must note that the narrative arc of the "Playtest" episode is one in which time is not strictly linear, and the final scenes return to earlier points in the story. However, for the purposes of this interpretation of the episode we will discuss events as they are presented to the viewer.

Life in liquid modernity

As stated above, Bauman envisages life in the condition of liquid modernity as being characterised by the transition from a solid modernity to a more fluid and transient form of existence. As we are introduced to Cooper, we see his initial experiences in an increasingly ludified world as undeniably positive; he is able to negotiate a path through the world according to his desires and is able to overcome setbacks.

A brief slide-show of Cooper's travels across the world further re-enforces this ever-shifting modern experience; he is accumulating quintessential experiences and accruing cultural capital, from the beaches of Thailand to running with the bulls in Pamplona. This montage illustrates the fact that "instagrammability" functions as a means of assigning value to a destination based on the potential to create attractive imagery for social media sharing (Hosie, 2017) and that, increasingly, social media has become a space for users to relate to themselves and others in a playful manner (Deumert, 2014). We can see, therefore, how the value systems of liquid modernity have become more ephemeral in nature, they have moved away from the established, fixed, reference points of earlier society and are open to renegotiation.

This can be seen when, having left Sonja, Cooper finds out that his credit card has been cancelled. Instead of approaching the problem as could rationally be expected, for example by contacting his family, he seeks help from Sonja, a transitory acquaintance. In this way we can see that social intimacy is being negotiated and redefined through developing online practices (David and Cambre, 2016). It is gamer girl Sonja who helps him make the fateful decision to accept the job at SaitoGemu. Sonja then ups the ante by convincing Cooper that taking a photo of any new technology will be worth a lot more than any payment he receives for the job. Bauman's vision of a functioning society is one wherein the individual questions their reality, but here Cooper fails to question the ethics of his choices in deference to a pretty girl whom he has only just met. A society that doesn't question itself is one that Bauman views as ill in that individuals becomes enslaved to the narratives created around them (Kutarna, 2018). Cooper here has made the decision to unquestioningly defer to his fluid reality, with the questionable ethical implications of his choices reflecting the challenging situations which arise when ethical responsibility is shifted from the structure of society to the individual (Bauman, 1993).

Love in liquid modernity

The final leg of Cooper's world tour finds him in London where, despite being alone in a foreign country, he is easily able to satisfy his desires, his need for pleasure and stimulation, by using the dating app Tinder to find and contact a potential partner. Tinder has been described as fulfilling a host of needs including a sense of excitement and fun (Sumter, Vandenbosch and Ligtenberg, 2017), and as one of a host of emergent technologies actively changing the development of interpersonal relationships (LeFebvre, 2018). The traditional structures that once anchored how we develop relationships continue to shift and have been deemed responsible for the 'dating apocalypse' (Sales, 2015) where traditional relationships have lost to a casual hook-up culture. While many celebrate the freedom and choice inherent in this development, it may reflect Bauman's belief that the prevailing ideas of our day actively limit us through restricting awareness of the wider society; we are presented with options selected by others, or by algorithms. As David and Cambre (2016) point out, Tinder actively excludes users from freely defining their interactions with others through the swipe logic that shapes users' social dynamics; indeed Bauman specifically identified 'computer-dating' as symptomatic of the erosion of the solidity and security offered by romantic relationships which he termed 'liquid love' (Bauman, 2003). Hobbs, Owen, and Gerber (2017) argue that apps such as Tinder are not necessarily as toxic as Bauman predicted, but for Cooper his Tinder liaison with Sonja represents the high point of his journey yet also the beginning of his demise.

The themes of sexuality and inter-personal relationships continue with a brief interaction between Cooper and Sonja in which he discovers that she plays games. Although not explicitly stated, it is evident that Cooper's interest in Sonja increases after she acknowledges that she is a keen game player. This interest speaks to the trope of the 'gamer girl' in which female gamers are notable by their existence in the masculine space of gaming, accordingly they are presented as objects of fascination and are eroticised. It is a process of fetishizing the other akin to that of orientalism, with all the inherent power relationships replicated (Said, 2014).

Given that games have been presented as a means of negotiating identities, and of providing experiences which allow players to experiment (Waggoner, 2009), the dominant socio-cultural values and images of mainstream gaming are overwhelmingly young, white, and male despite the reality having been proven to be different (Shaw, 2012). As with the opportunities afforded in liquid modernity, the apparent breadth of roles and experiences offered by games is something of a chimera. The very presence of the gamer girl highlights the lack of visibility of females in the prevailing culture of gaming, despite the number of females playing contemporary games, for she reveals the clearly-defined expectations of what a 'real gamer' should be, and those who do not accord to this idealised construction are dismissed, relegated to the margins. At the same time, the gamer girl affirms the masculinity and heterosexuality of the gamer, replicating and reaffirming the socio-cultural norms of wider society (Butt and Apperley, 2016; Dowling, Goetz, and Lathrop, 2019). Indeed, the wider cultural significance of the hyper-sexualised gamer girl can be recognised in the growing body of gamer girl pornography (Cole, 2018).

Despite the apparent positivity of the gamer girl within the episode, signified on the one hand by Cooper's elevated interest in Sonja and on the other by the implicit celebration of the idea that girls can be gamers, it is in fact a trope which highlights existing power structures and cultural assumptions. Thereby illustrating the underlying conflict that exists in the condition of liquid modernity: that the apparent freedoms offered to individuals are predominantly illusory, as they are those which have been created by existing hegemonies. As such, individuals cannot truly become free without questioning the power structures of society and those "opportunities" which are provided to them. If an individual is simply consuming these opportunities, they are in fact reinforcing the status quo and accepting those roles which have been selected for them.

Play in liquid modernity

When Cooper initially embarks upon his journey, he is able to overcome the boredom of a long-distance flight by immersing himself in a game played on his mobile phone. When asked to turn his device off he continues to use play to insulate himself from a potentially troubling experience, and to ease the anxiety of a fearful child, by pretending that the increasing turbulence is actually the bumps and shakes of a roller-coaster. In these scenes we are easily able to understand the positive aspects of play which can both insulate us from potential unpleasant situations and also offer us the ability to reframe experiences in order to make them more manageable. Play, and games, in this sense are undeniably positive.

This theme continues later in the episode with the commencement of the playtest, after which the episode is named, wherein Cooper is introduced to the experimental augmented reality technology used in the new game. This scene presents games as being at the cutting-edge of technological development, legitimizing their status in a society in which innovation and invention are venerated. For Bauman, the human condition in the stage of fluid modernity is one where progress is no longer a temporary measure towards a finished state but a perpetual, never ending challenge and necessity, that is in effect what it means to stay alive and well. Cooper's reaction to this augmented reality game is one of extreme positivity, the game is pure, unbridled fun. Following this initial test, there follows a discussion between Cooper and Shou Saitu, the enigmatic genius behind the games company, concerning the nature of games and the experiences they afford to players. The game designer states that games are "safe spaces" in which fears can be both confronted and overcome. In this statement we can easily recognise the conceptualisation of play as a social contract, an activity which occurs within a delimited and known context; the "Magic Circle" of play (Huizinga, 2014 [1938], Salen and Zimmerman, 2004; Stenros, 2014).

This point marks a change in the narrative arc, one in which the dramatic atmosphere of the episode, and the game experience communicated to the viewer, becomes significantly darker and more traumatic. If the first segment can be seen to communicate the contemporary realities of life in liquid modernity, the second represents a future in which the potential consequences of this existence are realised.

After the meeting with Shou Saitu, Cooper is taken to an old manor house in the grounds of the company estate. Recognising the building, he is told that the house was 3D-scanned and replicated in the company's most famous survival horror game *Harlech Shadow*, a game Cooper played previously. Bauman (2000) identifies non-spaces, such as airports, public transport, and hotel rooms as those which are un-colonised; they are free of all identity markers and discourage settling in, functioning as places where what needs to be done should be done. The Harlech House, here as a physical embodiment of a previous construction of computer code, represents a non-space for Cooper in that he is now alone in a space that exists only for the task at hand. It is a space which foreshadows the experiences yet to come as it transgresses boundaries between virtual and real, it is simultaneously one and the other.

This blending of real and virtual, both in respect to the house and to the nature of augmented reality, has implications for how play is both experienced by the player, and how it is communicated to the non-player. The work of Huizinga, which gave rise to the concept of the magic circle, describes play as occurring inside an imagined space apart from normal life where rules operate differently and we are allowed to experience things not allowed in our regular lives (Huizinga, 2014/1938; Salen and Zimmerman, 2004). The use of digital technology to create personalised games and gameful experiences – the digital gamification of the physical environment – is already a reality with games like *Pokemon Go* functioning as training grounds in which people are beginning to evolve ludic literacies within the wider public space (Mäyrä, 2017). Consalvo (2009) goes somewhat further in arguing that games can no longer be seen to occur within a bounded space, that play and games have spread throughout our lives to such an extent that they are defined solely by context.

The potential future of play presented in "Playtest" is one which expressly questions the notion of the designated and defined play space as the direct interface with the subject's brain, and results in an experience which is deeply personal, one which cannot be observed or understood by others. The already negotiable, context-specific, boundaries of play have been completely dissolved as even the player is unable to distinguish between the game and reality. There is no social contract, there is no way of identifying what is, or is not, a safe space. This is the culmination of liquid modernity, all boundaries between reality and fantasy have been dissolved, and the player/subject has lost all agency.

No matter the context of play, the presence or otherwise of a mutually-negotiated magic circle, participating in play has tangible real-world effects, both positive and negative (Sublette and Mullan, 2012). Indeed, the lack of player agency described above speaks to a redefinition of what it means to play games and the real-world consequences of play in virtual worlds. As new spaces and opportunities for play are realised and made available for consumption, predominantly via online and/or digital technologies, it is natural that players experiment with the new possibilities afforded to them. Given its ability to function as a liminal space, the online environment is a fertile ground for transgressive play (Waskul, 2005; Sicart, 2015), whether that be griefing in MMOs (Chesney et al., 2009) or trolling in discussion forums and message boards (Phillips, 2015). Those indulging in such behaviours often frame them in terms of a game, as entertainment, however, in such a game only one of the participants is aware of the rules of play while the other(s) have been reduced to the status of game pieces. Griefing also serves to transcend the immediate context of "play", with such behaviour having wider socio-cultural and economic effects (Bakioglu, 2009). A more consensual re-imagining of what constitutes a game can be found in the practice of "abusive game design" in which the presence of the designer is made obvious through elements which seek to frustrate the player, thereby creating a form of dialogue between the two parties (Wilson and Sicart, 2010). The practice of abusive game design is a direct challenge to the established orthodoxy of the contemporary games industry which players are simply consumers, and games are judged in terms of usability (Kultima, 2015).

Abusive game design is distinguished from "dark design" in that it actively reveals the power and influence of the designer, thereby encouraging players to recognise, and to question, existing norms. Dark design, however, is coercive in that it uses game mechanics to drive behaviours which may not conform to the value systems of the players, behaviours which may even be to their detriment (Zagal, Björk and Lewis, 2013). In the vast majority of situations, dark design patters are employed to drive player monetisation, to further drive increased consumption and financial expenditure.

For Bauman, it is the notion of consumerism which best illustrates how a person can consider themselves free yet, in reality, remain shackled within postmodern society. Indeed, most activity within liquid modernity is presented as a form of shopping within a society and culture defined as consumerist (Bauman, 2000). A such, it can be argued that these alternative conceptualisations of games are models for negotiating the context of liquid modernity in that they actively, and aggressively, question the established cultural narratives with which they have been presented.

We see here a reflection of discussions concerning the nature, and function, of enjoyment in contemporary life: in his recent work, Bown describes how our culture trumpets the right, even the requirement, to enjoy ourselves while at the same time prescribing that which is to be enjoyed. A consequence of this perspective, this lionising of individual enjoyment at the expense of responsibility to others, is that it reinforces the dominant socio-economic and cultural structures of our society, and it provides willing capitalist sub-

"Jouissance"

jects (Bown, 2015). Yet, enjoyment also offers a way to transcend these pre-scribed roles, these designed interactions, through the exploration of "jou-issance" (Lacan, 2005), the pleasure beyond pleasure. Jouissance is a form of enjoyment which lies beyond socially-accepted definitions of pleasure and can take many forms, but at heart it is transgressive in that it allows enjoy-ment of experiences beyond those that are constructed for us while, at the same time, revealing the nature of those constructed experiences. Through enjoyment, through games and play, we can explore the boundaries placed upon us, we can seek to become more active participants in the construction of our identities.

Conclusion

> "...by asking questions about our own soci-ety, we become freer. 'An autonomous society, a truly democratic society, is a society which questions everything that is pre-given and by the same token lib-erates the creation of new meanings. In such a society, all individuals are free to create for their lives the meanings they will (and can).' ... 'Society is ill if it stops questioning itself.' We become enslaved to the narratives being manufactured all around us, and we lose touch with our own subjective experiences."
> (Kutarna, 2018).

The arrative arc of "Playtest" can be seen as an allegory for life in the contem-porary age, one in which notions around games and play serve to highlight both contemporary realities and also potential futures. The episode opens with Cooper leaving his family home in order to escape his relationship with his mother, one that has become unbearable since the death of his father; here we see the emergence of liquid modernity as a reaction to the previous, solid modernity – it is a means of coping with the shifting responsibilities and relationships which linger on in a changed world. The apparent freedoms of liquid modernity, its ephemeral nature, are demonstrated in the photo montage of Cooper travelling the world, living a transient and self-gratifying life, moving from one pleasure to the next according to his own desires. Finally, we observe the consequences of liquid modernity: human suffering, political and economic instability, and the dominance of transnational, moneyed elite. This is communicated in the need for Cooper to use an app in order to have enough money to survive, resulting in him signing up for the play test run by a Japanese company in an English country home – one decorated in a blend of hi-tech and orientalist aesthetics – effectively giving himself to this unbounded elite. This, in turn, leads to his traumatic final experiences and death.

In the first half of this episode Cooper appears to be liberated in that he travels the world free of the burdens of home life. However, this is illusory as he does not seem to be questioning the world, merely moving within well-established tropes: the character even dismisses the notion of "self-discovery" with a casual shake of the head when talking with Sonja in the bar. In the second half of the episode, he is very literally a slave to a narrative which is manufactured around him, although the narrative is constructed from his subjective experiences. Furthermore, at no point does he question the societal structures around him, or even those who are inserting experimental technology into his brain: he is a willing and acquiescent member of society and, most chillingly, a test subject.

"Playtest," then, is not simply a body horror tale concerning the potentially dehumanising effects of technological advancement, but neither is it merely "a romp." It is, instead, a means of understanding contemporary socio-economic realities and a possible future that awaits a compliant and unquestioning population. More significantly, however, the episode highlights the evolution of the socio-cultural and economic importance of digital games in the condition of liquid modernity. As a consequence, we can see that contemporary practices surrounding the consumption of digital games offer an avenue through which we can confront, and overcome, manufactured narratives. We are not limited to the role of consumer as prescribed by dominant forces; by questioning how and what we consume we can create new forms of interaction which expose the previously obscured boundaries, thereby establishing a dialogue between societal stakeholders.

Bibliography

Bakioglu, B.S. (2009) "Spectacular interventions of second life: Goon culture, griefing, and disruption in virtual spaces." *Journal For Virtual Worlds Research*, 1(3), pp. 4-21.

Bauman, Z. (1993) Postmodern ethics. Blackwell Publishing Limited

Bauman, Z. (1995) *Life in Fragments. Essays in Postmodern Morality*. Oxford: Blackwell

Bauman, Z. (2000) *Liquid Modernity*. Polity Press.

Bauman, Z. (2003) *Liquid Love: On the Frailty of Human Bonds*. Cambridge: Polity

Bogost, I. (2015) "Why gamification is bullshit." *The gameful world: Approaches, Issues, Applications*, pp. 65-79.

Bown, A. (2015) *Enjoying It: Candy Crush and Capitalism*. John Hunt Publishing.

Brooker, C. (Writer), and Trachtenberg, D. (Director). 2016. *Playtest*. [Television series episode] In L. Borg (Producer). *Black Mirror*. Los Gatos: Netflix.

Butt, M. A. R., and Apperley, T. (2016, August). Vivian James–The politics of# Gamergate's Avatar. In *1st International Joint Conference of DiGRA and FDG, Dundee, Scotland* (pp. 1-6).

Chesney, T., Coyne, I., Logan, B. and Madden, N. (2009) "Griefing in virtual worlds: causes, casualties and coping strategies." *Information Systems Journal*, 19(6), pp.525-548.

Cole, S. (2018) https://www.vice.com/en_us/article/43835d/gamer-girl-porn-rule-34

Consalvo, M. (2009) "There is no magic circle." *Games and Culture*,(4), pp.408-417.

David, G. and Cambre, C. (2016) "Screened intimacies: Tinder and the swipe logic." *Social media+ society*, 2(2), pp. 1-11.

Deumert, A. (2014) "The performance of a ludic self on social network (ing) sites." In *The language of social media*. Palgrave Macmillan, London, pp. 23-45

Dillon, R.(2016) The golden age of video games: The birth of a multibillion dollar industry. AK Peters/CRC Press.

Dowling, D.O., Goetz, C. and Lathrop, D. (2019) One Year of# GamerGate: The Shared Twitter Link as Emblem of Masculinist Gamer Identity. *Games and Culture*, p.1555412019864857.

Egenfeldt-Nielsen, S., Smith, J. H., and Tosca, S. P. (2019) *Understanding video games: The essential introduction*. Routledge.

Geertz, C. (1973) *The interpretation of cultures* (Vol. 5019). Basic Books.

Hamari, J., Koivisto, J., and Parvinen, P. (2019) January. Introduction to the Minitrack on Gamification. In *Proceedings of the 52nd Hawaii International Conference on System Sciences*.

Hamari, J., Koivisto, J. and Sarsa, H. (2014) January. Does gamification work? A literature review of empirical studies on gamification. In *2014 47th Hawaii international conference on system sciences* (pp. 3025-3034). IEEE.

Hibberd, J. (2018) https://ew.com/article/2016/10/23/black-mirror-postmortem-interview-season-3/

Hill, W.D. and Clark, J.E. (2001) Sports, gambling, and government: America's first social compact?. *American Anthropologist, 103*(2), pp.331-345.

Hobbs, M., Owen, S. and Gerber, L. (2017) Liquid love? Dating apps, sex, relationships and the digital transformation of intimacy. *Journal of Sociology, 53*(2), pp.271-284.

Hosie, R. (2017) Instagrammability: Most Important Factor For Millennials on Choosing Holiday Destination. *The Independent*, 24.

Huizinga, J. (2014). *Homo Ludens*. Routledge.

Koivisto, J. and Hamari, J. (2019). The rise of motivational information systems: A review of gamification research. *International Journal of Information Management, 45*, pp.191-210.

Kultima, A. (2015) September. Game design research. In *Proceedings of the 19th International Academic Mindtrek Conference* (pp. 18-25).

Kutarna, C. (2018) https://www.psychologytoday.com/us/blog/age-discovery/201801/living-in-liquid-modernity

Lacan, J. (2005) The tokyo discourse. *Journal for Lacanian Studies, 3*(1), pp.129-44.

LeFebvre, L.E. (2018) Swiping me off my feet: Explicating relationship initiation on Tinder. *Journal of Social and Personal Relationships, 35*(9), pp.1205-1229.

Mäyrä, F. (2017) Pokémon GO: Entering the ludic society. *Mobile Media & Communication, 5*(1), pp.47-50.

McGonigal, J. 2011. *Reality is broken: Why games make us better and how they can change the world*. Penguin.

Muriel, D. and Crawford, G. (2018) *Video games as culture: considering the role and importance of video games in contemporary society*. Routledge.

Palese, E. (2013) Zygmunt Bauman. Individual and society in the liquid modernity. *SpringerPlus*, 2(1), p.191.

Phillips, W. (2015) *This is why we can't have nice things: Mapping the relationship between online trolling and mainstream culture*. MIT Press.

Raessens, J. (2006) Playful identities, or the ludification of culture. *Games and Culture*, 1(1), pp.52-57.

Raessens, J. (2014) "The Ludification of Culture." In: M. Fuchs, S. Fizek, N. Schrape, P. Ruffino, eds. Rethinking Gamification. Lüneburg: Meson Press.

Said, E. 2014. Orientalism. In *Geopolitics* (pp. 75-79). Routledge.

Salen, K. and Zimmerman, E. 2004. Rules of Play. MIT Press; Cambridge, MA.

Sales, N.J. 2015. Tinder and the dawn of the "Dating Apocalypse". *Vanity Fair, 6*.

Seaborn, K. and Fels, D.I. 2015. Gamification in theory and action: A survey. *International Journal of human-computer studies*, 74, pp.14-31.

Sennett, R. 1998. *The corrosion of character: The personal consequences of work in the new capitalism*. WW Norton & Company.

Shaw, A. 2012. Do you identify as a gamer? Gender, race, sexuality, and gamer identity. *new media & society*, 14(1), pp.28-44.

Sicart, M. 2015. Darkly playing others. In *The Dark Side of Game Play* (pp. 100-116). Routledge.

Stenros, J. 2014. In defence of a magic circle: the social, mental and cultural boundaries of play. *Transactions of the Digital Games Research Association*, 1(2).

Sublette, V.A. and Mullan, B. 2012. Consequences of play: A systematic review of the effects of online gaming. *International Journal of Mental Health and Addiction*, 10(1), pp.3-23.

Sumter, S.R., Vandenbosch, L. and Ligtenberg, L. 2017. Love me Tinder: Untangling emerging adults' motivations for using the dating application Tinder. *Telematics and Informatics*, 34(1), pp.67-78.

Thibault, M. 2016. Lotman and play: For a theory of playfulness based on semiotics of culture. *Σημειωτκή-Sign Systems Studies*, 44(3), pp.295-325.

Waggoner, Z. 2009. *My avatar, my self: Identity in video role-playing games.* McFarland.

Waskul, D.D. 2005. Ekstasis and the Internet: Liminality and computer-me diated communication. *New Media & Society*, 7(1), pp.47-63.

Wilson, R.R. 1986. Play, Transgression and Carnival: Bakhtin and Derrida on" Scriptor Ludens". *Mosaic: A Journal for the Interdisciplinary Study of Literature*, 19(1), pp.73-89.

Wilson, D. and Sicart, M. 2010, May. Now it's personal: on abusive game design. In *Proceedings of the International Academic Conference on the Future of Game Design and Technology* (pp. 40-47).

Zagal, J.P., Björk, S. and Lewis, C. 2013. Dark patterns in the design of games. In *Foundations of Digital Games 2013*.

Exhausting Choices
Bandersnatch and the Future of Our Entertainment Platforms

Robbie Fordyce & Thomas H. Apperley

This chapter interrogates the Netflix 'film' *Black Mirror: Bandersnatch* (2018), written by Charlie Brooker and directed by David Slade, using a close reading approach informed by metaphorical and allegorical analysis of videogames (Begy, 2013; Bogost, 2006; Murray, 1997; Wark, 2007), and seeks to draw out how the film explores the gamified choice-driven systems of the purchase screens of entertainment platforms. We argue that *Black Mirror: Bandersnatch* (*Bandersnatch*, hereafter) engages in a well-crafted reference to its conditions of distribution by finding similarities between the branching nature of selection-based play in hypertext games and the selection-based mechanisms of contemporary streaming video services, such as Netflix. In order to engage in this analysis, this study will examine both formalist ludological and visual themes within *Bandersnatch* and explore how these elements draw out themes of entertainment, exhaustion, and boredom in a manner that approximates entertainment platforms.

Bandersnatch is an out-of-season production for the *Black Mirror* (2011-) series. Released on December 28th, 2018 via Netflix's digital distribution platform, the film contributes to the themes explored across the *Black Mirror* series through the presentation of anxiety, fears of new devices, paranoid inability to determine reality, and technology evolving beyond control. *Bandersnatch* is distinct from the rest of the series in terms of its interactivity: it is presented as a 'game.' In the game, you watch short sequences of filmed video about a young computer programmer, Stefan, and make a choice between two options about what happens in his life. Sometimes you issue commands for Stefan, sometimes you have control over the circumstances around him. As you play through, you unlock different options and get caught in causal loops that you must escape, à la *La Jetée* (Marker, 1962), *Groundhog Day* (Ramis, 1993), and *Legend of Zelda: Majora's Mask* (Nintendo, 2000). Alongside this, Stefan gains increasing awareness of his lack of control, until he recognises the viewer as his antagonist. *Bandersnatch* doesn't operate like TV because it demands a different type of interactivity than Netflix usually provides. During the game, it remains unclear as what or whose side the player is on. Accordingly, goals are ambiguous: is Stefan's survival optimal, should he be directed into murder or to succeed in his game? Or were we happy with him living a pretty normal life with a non-successful game release? *Bandersnatch* doesn't offer much choice to the player, as most games go, and if we leave it alone it will just make choices for us. But it does offer the ability to decide things, and this is what makes it unique from the other episodes that Netflix offers.

Bandersnatch is both a game and a film; it can be played, but it can also be left to proceed by itself. While in contemporary terms it is not much like the familiar games of the current era, such as action-packed *God of War* (Sony, 2018), multiplayer games such as *Apex Legends* (Respawn Entertainment, 2019), or frenetic games like *Candy Crush Saga* (King, 2015), it does harken back to earlier forms of gameplay. Its restricted multi-choice system of branching narrative moments directly recalls non-digital games and early videogaming, including 'gamebooks' such as Puffin Book's *Fighting Fantasy* (1982-1995) series, Scholastic's *Twistaplot* series, or Bantam Book's *Choose Your Own Adventure* (c.f. McSweeney and Joy, 2019, p. 271), and the late-70s, early-80s text-based adventure games such as the *Zork* (1977-1982) series and *Wizard and the Princess* (1980).[1] Indeed, the story of *Bandersnatch* is the story of the transmediation of a fictional gamebook adventure, titled 'Bandersnatch,' into a game for 1980s home computers, also 'Bandersnatch.' As with all parts of the *Black Mirror* series, the episode engages in a Science Fiction critique of our present moment. However, while the rest of *Black Mirror* looks to the future to model its critiques, *Bandersnatch* is mostly set in the past. Rather than acting as an attempt at a prophecy about future developments from present conditions, *Bandersnatch* instead draws a connection from the past to the present and critiques the limited set of predetermined choices we have in digital entertainment media.

---

1 The trademark holders of Choose Your Own Adventure filed a lawsuit against Netflix (Gardner, 2019).

From the perspective of trends in contemporary videogaming, *Bandersnatch* is highly conventional as videogames go, given its relatively simple game mechanic of having players choose between a few limited options. Yet *Bandersnatch* is worth singling out for its debut on Netflix; it is unique for a game to be released on a major international content delivery platform that is otherwise dedicated to television and film. It blurs the line between film and television. *Bandersnatch* allows for limited interactivity where users/viewers can select from a set of options about how to respond to a problem or crisis, and a time limit within which a choice must be made or else the game autonomously continues with one of the options. These limitations exist because the platform, Netflix, has an interface for users that is tightly controlled so that the platform can reliably operate across mobile, desktop, and television contexts. *Bandersnatch*'s interface works within this framework, hence the restricted parameters for play. Following *Black Mirror* logic, *Bandersnatch*'s reflexive commentary of civil society drives the plot; yet critics have suggested that this reflexivity is perhaps merely an extension of the limited nature of *Bandersnatch*'s interface (Hills 2019). The narrative conceit of *Bandersnatch* is that the plot revolves around the development of an interactive fiction game, also titled 'Bandersnatch,' which presents a recursive loop between the narrative and the form of play. The protagonist, Stefan, struggles both psychologically and metaphysically to convert the 'Bandersnatch' gamebook into a playable videogame. During *Bandersnatch*'s story, Stefan pursues the development of his game with substantial dedication before the structure of play overtakes the narrative of the world and begins to affect the protagonist's reality. Stefan becomes partly aware of the emerging game-like nature of his reality and seeks escape. In some cases, he escapes through suicide, while in other cases 'Bandersnatch' consumes him instead.

Bandersnatch's plot is branching; somewhat unlike other games, the individual explorations of the plot (sans repetitions) do not reconcile with the exploration of a single personal experience, instead they become increasingly divergent in their mapping of Stefan's reality. This can be explored through the various repetitions, deaths, and loops that occur within the plot. The core of the story that develops through different threads is the development of 'Bandersnatch,' in which it takes on a life of its own and starts to infect the world around it. As is standard with the *Black Mirror* series, the metareflexive aspects of the techno-plot start to overtake the reality of the world in which the protagonist lives. Stefan becomes infected by the paranoia of the development of the game and, in several endings, he dies, consumed by demons both real and imagined.

By teasing out the allegorical dimensions of *Bandersnatch* we identify two critical and related issues. Firstly, it provides an insight into the way that the breakdown of 'reality' suggests an allegorical connection between digital games and the mystery genre that highlights the epistemological status of games. Secondly, as with all *Black Mirror* titles, there is commentary on contemporary society, and we argue that the commentary in *Bandersnatch* is allegorical and presents a parable of the nature of boredom in contemporary commercial media in which Netflix is exemplary.

Bandersnatch as interactive fiction

Bandersnatch has its roots in a gaming genre called 'interactive fiction,' a form of gameplay that is narrated through second or third person address, with players being able to guide the direction of the story.[2] Players make selections from a limited range of pre-given options that progress the story, potentially leading to success or death, and often involving loops or dead ends that the characters may have to escape from, tropes which *Bandersnatch* also employs.

The interactive fiction genre is comparatively old in terms of videogame genres. The genre's early development in the history of computer games is at least partly due to the computational overheads being relatively low; interactive fiction as a text-based genre with no complex programming requirements was also only a modest departure from existing media forms. The genre of interactive fiction is defined by narrative text formatted as a novel and few, if any, images; in those games that used any sort of spatial exploration system, movement was generally limited to the cardinal directions, and the games were often plagued by a lack of clarity about how to progress at any given moment. The shift from reading static digital works to reading interactive digital works was not nearly as radical as the first 3D worlds and did not require a new hermeneutics of interactivity beyond what computers already required. Indeed, Janet Murray argues that the existing framework

---

2 In their essay on *Bandersnatch*, McSweeny and Joy (2019, p. 272) locate it in a history of interactive film.

of interaction had already been developed within tabletop roleplaying con-texts, and that interactive fiction games acted as the 'dungeon master' for a single-player game (1997, pp. 74-75; c.f. Apperley, 2006, pp. 17-19).

One of the earliest successes in the interactive fiction genre was the game *Zork*.[3] Despite a fairly generic fantasy plot, *Zork* would set the standards for interactive fiction by providing users with information, characters, and nar-rative that could be interacted with through a simple command line. Players would input commands into the command line and these would be parsed by an interpreter. Commands would be simple verb/noun combinations, such as "pull switch," "hit troll," "push button," and so on, with the interpreter capable of managing a few synonyms. Because this system historically allowed the pairing of incongruous verb/noun pairings, the genre has also developed a reputation for absurdist humour, due to the possibility of attempting to "pull dragon." Other works in the genre would simply provide the player with a few choices to decide between, as in a multichoice exam, and it is this second form of interactive fiction that *Bandersnatch* builds upon.

One of the benefits of interactive fiction is that development is highly plat-form-independent; i.e. the code for an interactive fiction game can be con-verted to other platforms relatively easily. This is because both the interface and the story are presented almost entirely through text alone, thus games had relatively low demands in terms of porting the title from one hardware context to another. This is unlike graphically-intensive videogames wherein incidental decisions by operating system developers can affect how software must be programmed in order to make use of graphics cards and other com-puter hardware. This issue is compounded in desktop computing, where the software drivers for graphics cards can vary wildly. Interactive fiction can be developed in ways that are platform-interoperable, and we see the same technique developing in the way that *Bandersnatch* operates across a number of distribution contexts – TV, console, computer, mobile – all allowing effec-tively the same interaction.

Interactive fiction as a genre has subsequently influenced the develop-ment of the 'point and click genre,' which includes well-known titles such as *Monkey Island*, *Day of the Tentacle*, *The Dig*, *Discworld*, an *Indiana Jones* series

---

3 *Zork* was written by students at MIT in the late 70s and published commercially from 1980. It remains freely playable at TextAdventures.co.uk. See Montfort (2003) for an extensive discussion of the development of *Zork* and 'electronic literature.'

of games, the *Leisure Suit Larry* series, *Broken Sword*, and many others (see: Reed et al., 2020). These games tend to have a mystery or crime theme and, like interactive fiction more generally, have included humour as a strong influence. These games have in turn influenced the development of other contemporary games in the exploration and mystery genres, including *Kentucky Route Zero* (Cardboard Computer, 2013) and *What Remains of Edith Finch* (Giant Sparrow, 2018).

While interactive fiction titles modelled on the original form have reduced in visibility in recent years, its core functionality remains in the dialogue trees of many high-profile narrative games such as *The Witcher III* (CD Projekt Red, 2015), *The Elder Scrolls V: Skyrim* (Bethesda Game Studios, 2011), the *Mass Effect* series (BioWare, 2007-2017), *The Outer Worlds* (Obsidian Entertainment, 2019), *Walking Dead: The Game* (Telltale Games, 2012), *Game of Thrones* (Telltale Games, 2014), and many others.[4] Game development within the interactive fiction genre continues to be developed in amateur and community contexts; modern interpreters such as the Inform, ADRIFT, and TADS programming environments represent simplistic programming contexts that allow online communities to make and share verb/noun command line parsing games at a low cost. The application Twine allows for players to develop choice-based interactive fiction that can be loaded by modern HTML browsers, with one relatively high-profile game being "You are Jeff Bezos" (2018), the aim of which is to spend all of Jeff Bezos' billions of dollars.

Bandersnatch, in turn, is a step in the progression of the genre, presenting a different kind of interactivity in a different kind of context and, notably, a different category of spectatorship. *Bandersnatch* is played in a context that comes with a different type of shared experience than games usually do, with the prospect of being played in spaces with an audience of others. Because *Bandersnatch* is distributed on Netflix, it can be played in contexts that already have shared social experiences: namely Netflix's other film and television serials, as well as other platforms. This is different from an individual playing games on a mainframe in the late 1970s or reading gamebooks. Alongside this spectatorial approach to gameplay, it is intriguing that the player is not in direct control of Stefan; instead, the player subtly intervenes in the world around Stefan in a way that disestablishes a direct avatar-type

---

4 Dialogue trees are discussed at length in Wardrip-Fruin (2009, 51-69).

relationship in the game. *Bandersnatch* presents a new kind of experience play for interactive fiction, departing from prior forms.

The mystery genre

The *Black Mirror* series uses a Science Fiction frame to explore horrors born from technology, bringing with it themes such as the unknown, and an idiosyncratic idea of human folly. At its core, *Black Mirror* presents an idea of a reality that exceeds the conventional, and this exceptional reality breaks through into the everyday through complex technology. The *Black Mirror* thesis of technology is that social reliance on increasingly complex technical devices leads to a point in which the techno-social system is so complex in its interactions that social reality can no longer be properly grasped by people. Within this complexity, some sort of 'evil' (a deliberately vague term) enters into the world leading to individual ruin but, crucially, the evil techno-social system remains in operation, presumably to consume more individuals in the future. This evil might take the form of robots with terrifying predatory intelligence, or it might be an irreversible upload of one's brain into a simulation, or an absurdist scopophilic punishment on live television, or the misery of a technological solution being worse than the problem. As such, the series has an overwhelmingly paranoid feeling, not dissimilar to Cold War era spy films. For *Bandersnatch*, the narrative complexity of the various paths that one can go down creates a system of reasonable complexity, and it is in Stefan's attempt to understand and produce a meaningful game experience that leads us to the evil technology. In *Bandersnatch*, however, this complexity is exacerbated because not only is Stefan struggling to understand the mystery of both the book he is transmediating and the game he is creating, he is also wrapped up in a crisis about the real. Stefan's exploration of his world is one that can be understood through reference to the mystery genre; in particular *Bandersnatch* parallels the experiences of the author turned private investigator in Paul Auster's "City of Glass" (1990). Both stories present a character exploring their reality, with a conflicted relationship between the author/character in "City of Glass" that mimics the player/character in *Bandersnatch*. Both stories begin with a conceit (investigation/programming) that eventually disappears as the terms of reference or borders of reality crumble away.

Gilles Deleuze and Luc Boltanski have both presented accounts of the nature of the mystery/detective genre. Deleuze's "The Philosophy of Crime Novels" (2004), originally published in 1966, explores the way that such mystery stories represent a form of fiction that focuses on the discovery of the truth independent from any individual – i.e. a scientific truth that exists independent of any perspective that is founded in an exploration of the world rather than relying on hearsay or interpretation. This truth cannot be immediately known however, it must be arrived at. Deleuze describes the detective novel as a device that can have two sides or perspectives. The first is the side of the detective who hunts a criminal, and by mirroring it we come to the second, the criminal who eludes the detective. Neither, Deleuze suggests, are especially remarkable relative to the other – or at least the genre works best when there is a relatively even pairing. Yet *Bandersnatch* loses sense of a proper antagonist part-way through the story with the exception, perhaps, of the player themselves. For Deleuze, the 'philosophy' of crime novels is that the detective in the story themselves (as distinct from the police of the real world) is a philosopher of sorts, who explores the world and tries to capture all its dynamics. The truth that they seek isn't a truth of relations between objects and events that can be found in the world, but rather a desire to understand the rules of the reality that they occupy. This is experienced in a profound way by Stefan, as some paths lead to him becoming aware of the nature of his loop and the influence of the player. What Delezue's observation makes clear is that both Stefan and the player's relationship to traditional narrative is opaque but also that the search for truth is constantly frustrated, producing an anxious paranoia in Stefan. In *Bandersnatch*, however, the exploration of the world would appear to not be about discovering the rules that order the diegesis, but about discovering how quickly the rules fall away. As the episode progresses, the simple choices offered to the player lead to a dissolution of structure rather than its establishment. Because he lives in the world of *Black Mirror*, all Stefan can do is progressively develop a more paranoid knowledge that reality is more complex that he can comprehend, and begin to grasp the horror of the evil that lies behind it.

Boltanski, too, describes a similar account to Deleuze's detective in the mystery novel. Boltanski's *Mysteries & Conspiracies* (2014) outlines another theory related to the genre of mystery. Within the mystery genre we find the thriller, the war story, the conspiracy/spy story, and the crime/police detective story. The mystery is distinguished from genres such as Science Fiction and fantasy in the way that they ground themselves in a real – or at least with regards to the genres that Boltanski focuses on. Mystery sits on a continuum between the real and the impossible, being very much concerned with unusual events. Mysteries are couched within a commitment to a real world, but continue by revealing unusual, complex, inexplicable, exotic, monstrous, or otherwise less-than-apparent aspects of the world in which the story takes place. To understand the nature of mysteries, Boltanski argues that a mystery suggests that there is a distinction between the perceived state of affairs and the real state of affairs, but that crucially this gap between perception and reality must be signaled in order to generate the process of discovery or unravelling that comprises the nature of the genre. Boltanski argues that the various genres can be identified not by the nature of their hero, or aesthetic tropes, or even the general uncovering of the plot, but rather by the thing that is unsettled in the course of examination. For instance, the spy film is often centred on identifying exactly how contingent and precarious the otherwise colossal edifice of the late-20th Century nation state is. So too is the detective novel often defined by the legal system, where without its heroes, criminals would pervert the order of capitalist property rights. Under what he calls the "reality of reality" (2014, p. 15), Boltanski suggests that what is being uncovered or unsettled is not a shared reality, but rather a complex account of "what is at stake" (2014, p. 18). 'Reality' in this context is a presentation of the world that we occupy, in the sense that the representations are, or at least describe, phenomena in our world that might conceivably exist in a way that we would accept it, and where the boundaries between the possible, the impossible, and the unlikely are all managed and known through their correspondence to the world around us. The extent to which we accept these representations as representations of reality come down, apparently, to the degree to which we are prepared to accept the backdrop of reality as the frame under which events take place. In this sense, Boltanski's account of reality as a frame shares some key characteristics that Johan Huizinga (1949) attributes to play. Huizinga's 'magic circle' is a much-maligned cliché in game studies, but it does convey the important notion that play is a lesser reality or world of its own, with its clearly constructed and arbitrary rules.

However, Huizinga's (1949, p. 10) bounded play-world creates order. Just as for Boltanski 'the real' is not equivalent to reality because the real operates with its own set of rules that are independent from the rules and order of reality. For instance, the way that fantasy envisions an array of fantastic peoples, magic, and dragons, but conventionally avoids the inclusion of laser rifles and space ships; for Boltanski, this is situation wherein a set of events and actors are "attached to the particular events through which they manifest themselves and to the situations that these events bring about" (2014, p. 9). It is this sensibility that is being 'detected' in the model of detective fiction, which is why fantasy-crime works such as Jean-Luc Godard's (1965) *Alphaville*, and Phillip K. Dick's (1968) *Do Androids Dream of Electric Sheep?* can incorporate detective fiction so seamlessly into novels about fictional worlds. The process of detection is about exploring the parameters of the world itself, not solely the nature of the truth of a singular crime. Thus, the process of detection evaluates the internal consistency of reality, in a similar way that the rules of the game – for Huizinga – create and order the world.

Allegories of boredom

In *Gamer Theory*, McKenzie Wark details what she sees as the particular mediatory quality of digital games, in terms of how digital games present their allegorical relationship to meaning. Inasmuch as the plot of a novel presents allegory through text, the game presents its allegories through its algorithmic processes (2007. p. 59). It is no accident that *Bandersnatch* is controlled by the very means that one scrolls through the apparently infinite but very much circulatory experience of Netflix (Fordyce, 2019). The act is very familiar, sorting through line upon line of familiar titles. Each line presents a familiar line-up of thumbnails, but as the descriptions and covers bleed into a unified aesthetic grammar the ability to distinguish each visual experience from what you've already seen before becomes difficult. The variation and repetition of the line-ups complicates this further. Scrolling vertically and horizontally, you can search through a range of experiences, hoping to find one that is unique or different, or at the very least is perhaps forgotten. The algorithmic allegory of *Bandersnatch* is the repetition of Netflix with a small range of choices.

In *Bandersnatch* choice and boredom intertwine. The Netflix user is caught between boredom and the possibility of finding something to watch that alleviates their boredom. Netflix always has something to watch, it is just a question of finding the right series that staves off the boredom just enough to prevent the user from opening Amazon Prime, Disney+, or HBO apps (or even worse, leaving the app space completely). The narrative of *Bandersnatch* offers both trivial and significant choices: what tape should Stefan listen to on the bus? Should he murder his father? But the mode of playing through *Bandersnatch*, which encourages Netflix users to explore every pathway, makes these choices banal. The morality of the choices is not significant as users are expected to choose all options during the course of playing, in stark contrast to the 'dialogue trees' mentioned earlier, where choices are made once and then impact the rest of the game (and in the case of Bioware's *Mass Effect* (2007-) series, cascade over the remaining games in the series, should the player import their character into subsequent games). *Bandersnatch* requires an exhaustion of possibilities, but it differs from Netflix in that there is no 'hidden gems' to find which may distract users from the search. It stages the search itself with the possibility of fruitful discovery, only to tell the user explicitly with meta-reflexive irony that, like Stefan, they are trapped in Netflix. In this sense, the film follows the typical *Black Mirror* dystopian commentary: imagine a Netflix that you could not simply leave. A media world of the infinite scroll wherein the user is always *almost* one click ahead of boredom.

Netflix appears to infinitely defer boredom through its constantly updated and expansive library with customized suggestions offered based on viewing history and likes. In this deferral it captures attention, and by adding 'games' to its stable of content it gestures towards a possibility of absorbing and integrating a threat to that attention, the digital game. *Bandersnatch* was not the first interactive programming that Netflix published, just weeks earlier on November 18th, 2018 they had republished a simplified version of Telltale Games' *Minecraft: Story Mode* customized for the platform.[5] The five chapters of content followed Telltale's critically acclaimed and commercially successful formula of elaborate 'point-and-click' decisions with significant moral choices that impacted later choices. They ended up on Netflix despite Telltales' acrimonious closure during 2018 (Lanier, 2018). It transpired that Telltale Games' winning formula could not overcome problems caused by "nonstop crunch culture, toxic management, and ... creative stagnation" (Farokhmanesh, 2018). In this respect, although ambitious, *Bandersnatch* is

---

5   The Netflix edition was customized to be played using a TV remote and thus many of the interactive situations were reduced to a yes/no, while other versions made full use of the range of options available with complex hand-held controllers.

much smaller in scale than *Minecraft: Story Mode*, and simulates a translation of mediums from book to computer to Netflix, rather than being a literal translation of the original *Minecraft* (Mojang, 2011) into the Telltale Games engine, into the Netflix app. Subsequently, Netflix has released a couple of other pieces of interactive programming, but has mainly relied on traditional programming, even in later seasons of *Black Mirror*. Again, in the dystopian visions of *Black Mirror*, *Bandersnatch* gestures towards a future wherein all media has been translated into a single platform.

Wark (2007, 70) argues that the role of digital games is to capture boredom. Play was captured by the rise of the digital game, which responds to the boredom of the player with endless rounds of repetition, level after level of difference as more of the same (2007, p. 16). Her analysis of the game *State of Emergency* (VIS Games 2002) describes how games operate to displace boredom by constantly 'making-over' the game (2007, p. 161). The game changes the terms of play constantly, by opening up new spaces to the player and changing the level of control the player has over that space. The exploration of videogames is an alignment with the exploration of Plato's cave. The argument is thus: upon realizing that one is stuck in the cave – perhaps like the protagonist, Stefan – one's goal becomes to account for the cave itself (Wark, 2007, pp. 6-8, 59-61, 210). The hope is that there is some threshold to the system of play, a new order to be found, or at least some sense of escape. This threshold is explored by a process Wark describes as 'trifling.' In the process of finding the limits of a game, the player tests those limits. Trifling with games can often lead to programmed novelty, described by Aarseth (1999) as epiphanies, which allow players to access a new area or engage differently with one they are already familiar with. But it can also lead to counterplay (Apperley, 2010; Meades, 2013) where elements of the game are recombined in unexpected ways by players, the classic example being rocket jumping in *Quake III Arena* (Lederle-Ensign & Wardrip-Fruin, 2016). In this respect, contemporary games offer players a great deal of space and control over that space, which gives it a quantitatively different capacity to alleviate boredom. However, for Wark, boredom has a critical capacity, as it is the starting point for understanding the game as an algorithm (2007, p.33). She uses the concept of 'trifling' to conceptualize this new relationship with the algorithm (see: Suits, 1978); the trifler 'struggles to escape boredom and produce difference' (Wark 2007, p. 40). The interactive fiction of *Bandersnatch* on the Netflix platform creates a game wherein the difference between playing and trifling is erased as there is no end point that can be reached. Or at least there may be an endpoint to *Bandersnatch*, but there is no conceivable end to Netflix, which on the completion of *Bandersnatch* is already offering players links to new content.

Conclusion

In *Bandersnatch* what is 'at stake' is not the resolution of a mystery, but the form of entertainment. Netflix as a platform is both questioned and reestablished in the form of an interactive story-game that incorporates, but confuses, the protagonist and the viewer, while also emptying out the structure or meaning of the form of the game. The experience of playing *Bandersnatch* is much less about the following of a particularly special plot, but rather the uncovering of a set of rules that organize the world. These rules cannot be simply explained but must be personally experienced through mediated but physically-initiated feedback between person and software platform. There is something of a mystery of play to any game that cannot be prefigured prior to the moment of engagement: a game can be described, strategies can be detailed, a narrative recounted, and a difficulty outlined, but the actual experience of gameplay remains elusive and not readily transmediated into other contexts. All games hold within them an element of mystery that exceeds simple description.

Acknowledgements

The authors would like to kindly thank the Overland Literary Journal (Melbourne) for publishing an shorter version of this work. Tom Apperley's participation was funded by the Academy of Finland funded Centre of Excellence in Game Culture Studies [grant No 312395].

Bibliography

Apperley, T. (2006). Genre and Game Studies: Towards a Critical Approach to Vide Game Genres. *Simulation & Gaming* 37(1), 6-23. DOI: 10.1177/1046878105282278

Apperley, T. (2010). *Gaming Rhythms: Play and Counterplay from the Local to the Global*. Amsterdam: Institute of Network Cultures.

Auster, P. (1990) "The City of Glass" in *The New York Trilogy*. New York: Penguin Books.

Begy, J. (2013). Experiential Metaphors in Abstract Games. *ToDiGRA: Transactions of the Digital Games Research Association* 1 (1), http://todigra.org/index.php/todigra/article/download/3/96

Bogost, I. (2006). *Unit Operations: An Approach to Videogame Criticism*. Cambridge: MIT Press.

Boltanski, L. (2014) *Mysteries & Conspiracies*. Cambridge: Polity Press.

Deleuze, G. (2004) "The Philosophy of Crime Novels". In *Desert Islands and Other Texts: 1953-1974*. New York: Semiotext(e).

Dick, P. K. (1968) *Do Androids Dream of Electric Sheep*. New York: Del Rey Books.

Farokhmanesh, M. (4 October, 2018). The Tragic End of Telltale Games. *The Verge*. Accessed 6 March, 2020, from: https://www.theverge.com/2018/10/4/17934166/telltale-games-studio-closed-layoffs-end-the-walking-dead

Fordyce, R. (2019) 'Bandersnatch': that game we all played. *Overland*. Accessed 5 February, 2019 from: https://overland.org.au/2019/02/bandersnatch-that-game-we-all-played/

Godard, J-L. (1965) *Alphaville*. Athos Films.

Hills, M. (2019) 'Black Mirror: Bandersnatch' and 'The Affair' of Re-Narration In (Gendered TV) Taste Cultures. CST Online. Accessed 9 February, 2020 from: https://cstonline.net/black-mirror-bandersnatch-and-the-affair-of-re-narration-in-gendered-tv-taste-cultures-by-matt-hills/

Lanier, L. (21 September, 2018). 'The Walking Dead' Game Developer Hit With 90% Staff Layoffs as 225 Are Let Go. *Variety*. Accessed 6 March 2020, from: https://variety.com/2018/gaming/news/walking-dead-game-developer-hit-staff-layoffs-1202952915/

Lederle-Ensign, D. & Wardrip-Fruin, N. (2016). What is Strafe Jumping? idTech3 and the Game Engine as Software Platform. *ToDiGRA: Transactions of the Digital Games Research Association* 2(2) http://todigra.org/index.php/todigra/article/view/35

McSweeney, T. & Joy, S. (2019). Change Your Past, Your Present, Your Future? Interactive Narratives and Trauma in Bandersnatch. In T. McSweeney & S. Joy (eds.). *Through the Black Mirror: Deconstructing the Side Effects of the Digital Age* (271-284). London: Palgrave.

Meades, A. (2013). *Understanding Counterplay in Video Games*. London: Routledge.

Montfort, N. (2003). *Twisty Little Passages: An Approach to Interactive Fiction*. Cambridge: MIT Press.

Murray, J. (1997). *Hamlet on the Holodeck: The Future of Narrative in Cyberspace*. Cambridge: MIT Press.

Reed, A., Murray, J. & Salter, A. (2020). *Adventure Games: Playing the Outsider*. New York: Bloomsbury.

Slade, D. (2018) *Bandersnatch*. Netflix.

Suits, B. (1978). *The Grasshopper: Games, Life and Utopia*. Peterborough: Broadview Press.

Wardrup-Fruin, N. (2009). *Expressive Processing: Digital Fictions, Computer Games, and Software Studies*. Cambridge: MIT Press.

Wark, M. (2007). *Gamer Theory*. Cambridge: Harvard University Press.

Games Cited:

Apex Legends (2019) Electronic Arts.

Broken Sword: The Shadow of the Templars (1996) Virgin Interactive Entertainment.

Candy Crush Saga (2015) King.

Day of the Tentacle (1993) LucasArts.

Discworld (1995) Psygnosis.

God of War (2018) Sony Entertainment.

Indiana Jones and the Last Crusade (1989) Lucasfilm Games.

Kentucky Route Zero (2020) Steam.

Leisure Suit Larry series (1987-2009) Sierra Entertainment.

Mass Effect series (2007-2017) Bioware.

Minecraft Story Mode (2015-2016) Telltale Games.

Monkey Island series (1990-2010) LucasArts.

Quake III Arena (1999) Activision.

State of Emergency (2002) Vis Games.

The Dig (1995) LucasArts.

The Elder Scrolls V: Skyrim (2011) Bethseda Softworks.

The Outer Worlds (2019) Obsidian Entertainment.

What Remains of Edith Finch (2017) Annapurna Interactive.

The Witcher III: Wild Hunt (2015) CD Projekt Red
Wizard and the Princess (1980) On-Line Systems.
You are Jeff Bezos (2018) - https://direkris.itch.io/you-are-jeff-bezos
Zork (1977) Infocom.

Qualia Inside the Mirror
The Technification of the Subjective Experience in *Black Mirror*

Mauricio Molina-Delgado & Bértold Salas-Murillo[1]

Introduction

Old university friends Danny and Karl, having bumped into to each other after a long time, sit down to play *Striking Vipers*, a fighting game that reunited them often when they were younger, and Danny was still single. It is certainly a different game, a virtual-reality one, in which they feel the avatars' bodies and blows. Just like eleven years ago, Danny chooses a fighter called Lance and Karl casts a deadly woman named Roxette. But this time the fight is brief because, surprisingly, they start kissing each other. It seems that, in this virtual-reality world, they feel, move, and desire differently than in the real world.

This is the premise of *Black Mirror*'s "Striking Vipers:" in a video game, two friends find the possibility of experiencing their bodies and sexualities differently, including from a woman's perspective. In this way, the episode deals with one of the most problematic themes when studying Philosophy of Mind and Cognitive Sciences: *qualia* mental states (the subjective qualities of experiences) experimented on through virtual-reality technology. Danny and Karl's story takes a stance regarding the functioning of the mind and offers a *mise-en-scène* of its subjective and social consequences, which includes inviting the viewer to reimagine gender roles.

---

1 We would like to thank Andrea Cuadra for checking the preliminary draft of this paper as well as for her valuable comments.

"Striking Vipers" supposes a distinct slant around the debate of *qualia*. This episode assumes, as the functionalist approach in Philosophy of Mind does, that our perceptions are but information fully explained in terms of computational representations. In spite of this assumption, stances that pretend to reduce those phenomenal experiences to the level of information or to neural activations have faced multiple criticisms. Many of the counter-arguments have been proposed through *thought experiments*, like those proposed by Nagel (1974) and Jackson (1986).

Due to its fictional and plausible nature, "Striking Vipers," as well as other *Black Mirror* episodes, plays a similar role to these experiments: it proposes imaginary situations in which the truthfulness of a specific thesis is verified or put into perspective. This has been one of Science Fiction's goals since its origins in the nineteenth century: to explore the possibilities hinted at in science findings. *Black Mirror* contemplates the role of digital technology in reflections about *qualia* or problematizations of the relationship between mind and body, consciousness and brain, in episodes such as "White Christmas," "Playtest," "San Junipero," "USS Callister," "Crocodile," and "Black Museum." In this chapter, we will not elaborate on cognitive nor epistemological theories, but rather on the discussions that these episodes provoke.

Quest for *qualia*

In another paper (Molina, in press), we argue that most of the first four seasons of *Black Mirror* occur in possible worlds[2] whose natural laws are compatible with the main thesis of functionalism, as understood in Philosophy of Mind. With the episode "Striking Vipers," the fifth season confirms that stake.

Functionalism understands mental states as functions which cannot be properly seen as physical or non-physical, but as internal operations that

---

2 In spite of the fact that the notion of possible worlds has been used at least after Leibnitz, the contemporary use of the term is strongly connected to modal logic. According to this concept, our actual world even if it would be special as the unique real one, is part of a group of worlds, including another world that even having no real existence are merely possible (Divers, 2002).

mediate between the inputs and outputs of a system. As Elugardo posits, it "is the view that each type of mental state is identical with a state that is a causal consequent of certain kinds of inputs and other mental states and which, in turn, causally brings about certain kinds of outputs and other mental states" (p. 161). According to functionalism, the mind is not identical to the brain and mental states cannot be reduced to brain states. However, the mind does not properly represent a substance or entity independent of the brain.

In general, functionalists accept some form of materialism despite rejecting the possibility of reducing mental states to brain activity, since they claim that the same mental state could be generated from several different physical states. In other words, for functionalists the same mental state can be performed in multiple brain configurations. This seems compatible with current neuroscientific knowledge regarding brain plasticity, but it can also be extended to the case of possible instantiation of mental states on various material bases, such as well-known biological entities (as is the case of the neurological systems of animals, humans, and not humans), in unknown beings such as possible inhabitants of planets other than Earth, or non-biological entities such as a computer or an android (psycho-functionalism).

According to functionalism, mental states would be specified not by a certain material configuration, but by the functional relationships between inputs external to the system (such as perceptions), system outputs (such as acts), and other internal functional states (such as propositional attitudes like beliefs and wishes). Those relations could be codified in a formal language (a *language of thought*) using rules linking internal states to external inputs and outputs (behaviors) (Fodor, 1975), giving rise to a kind of functional-rule language to define various states. For example, we can define the wishes of a subject in terms of the actions that s/he would perform if s/he had certain beliefs. Thus, a subject who wishes to be a professional athlete should have certain habits such as training hard and taking care of her diet – of course, assuming that s/he believes that training and diet have an impact on his/her chances of success.

The description above refers to the functionalist description of an individual mind. To analyze a good part of the arguments of Science Fiction works, as well as the particular case of the *Black Mirror* series, it is essential to consider what this philosophical position has to say concerning the relations between two or more minds. At least from Descartes' proposal, it has been a great challenge for the philosophy of mind to explain how it is possible for different minds to communicate with each other. While it seems clear that each mental entity has access only to its external states and to the behavior of other entities, access to the internal states of other subjects seems impenetrable. In appearance, we have a privileged path to our inner world but not to that of others. To solve this, the so-called *theory-theory* has been postulated, according to which we have, in our mind, a *theory of mind* describing our own and others' mental states. This theory would link the behaviors of the subjects with their internal states in the way we described previously, probably encoded in the language of the mind. Thus, the laws that, according to functionalism, govern our behaviors and mental states would also be reflected in our personal theories, which would allow each one to make predictions and interpretations of the mental states that govern the behavior of others.

The functionalist position, however, must face several objections, two of the most important coming from the problems of intentionality and *qualia*. The first group of objections indicates that a system described in terms of the interrelationships between inputs, internal states, and outputs is not capable of generating intentionality. Intentionality is understood as the characteristic of mental states of referring or being about other objects or states of affairs (*aboutness*). Searle, in his famous "Chinese room argument" *thought experiment* (introduced in the 1980's article "Minds, Brains, and Programs"), imagines a situation in which a person in a closed room receives a text written in Chinese as well as some questions (also written in Chinese characters) from people outside. Though the person in the room does not understand Chinese and has no grammatical or lexical knowledge of this language, he or she has a list of instructions (rules associated to Chinese characters) that shows how to respond to the questions. In this way, people outside the room receive the answers and believe that the person in the room speaks Chinese language. However, according to Searle, rather than having a real understanding of this language, the person in the room only has operated formal symbols with no intentionality. In a similar way, it would be possible to imagine a machine interacting with people but totally lacking comprehension or intelligence.

A second group of objections comes from the apparent inability of functionalism to explain the qualitative character of experiences. This argument claims that, in the functionalist explanation, an important part of the consciousness and the mind, such as the phenomenal qualitative character of the experiences, is largely absent. Following one of Jackson's arguments, let's

consider Mary, a scientist who specialized in the neural and physical basis of color perception, and who nonetheless lives in a black-and-white environment. According to Jackson, if she were to experience the color red for the first time in her life, she really would acquire a totally new knowledge.

In another *thought experiment*, Nagel remarks the fact that knowledge of a bat's neurophysiology does not allow us to know what it's like to be a bat. Thus, physical theories of mind, including not only functionalism but different forms of psycho-physical reductionism seem to fail in explaining the subjective character of experience.

Mirrored *qualia*

Black Mirror's episodes enact elements from these debates. The conversion of mental states into digital data is frequently a main element in their narratives: mental states as sensations (pain in "Black Museum"), cognitions (believing or understanding in "White Christmas"), emotions (enjoyment in "San Junipero"), quasi-perceptual states (hallucinating in "Playtest"), and conative states (wanting and trying in "U.S.S. Callister"), among others. We can consider that most of these mental states also bear qualitative states or *qualia*. Emotions and perceptions, for instance, clearly have a phenomenal character, but other cognitive states are likely to be directly or indirectly linked to *qualia*. Thus, informational aspects of mental states are central in most of the episodes of *Black Mirror* but only a few of them, such as "Striking Vipers", show an explicit stance about the matter (in this case, in favor of a functionalist interpretation of *qualia*). Generally, however, episodes convey a fictional story that assumes the subject presence of phenomenal experiences associated to other mental states. We will examine the specific questions these episodes submit.

"A photocopy of you"

"White Christmas" is an episode made up of three stories, all of which revolve around Matt, a charismatic and apparently confident middle-aged man. First, he guides Harry in his quest for meeting women through *Z-Eyes*, a device which transmits vision and hearing. In the second story, Matt explains to Joe how he trains *cookies* of people, i.e. a consciousness' digital clone stored in an egg-shaped container. In order to explain the training, he recalls the process of Greta's *cookie*. Finally, while keeping Joe company in a cabin, Matt incites him to confess how he killed his former father-in-law and provoked the death of his ex-wife's daughter.

The three stories deal with identity and consciousness: body, sensations, feelings, and memories, all of them turned into computerized information. The first one revolves around the collaboration between two conscious entities, Matt and Harry, in a single body, Harry's. In the second story, Matt trains *cookies*. What is a *cookie*? As explained to Joe: "a photocopy of you". The *cookie* doesn't have a real body, but a digitally simulated one. She is just the duplicate of one real person's consciousness (Greta) with no flesh. In some way, she is in the same situation as Matt in the first story, when he had Harry's eyes and ears, even will and affections, but no body. Furthermore, Greta's *cookie* has a perception of time, not a physical one, but digitally-built one: Matt turns the knob and six months go by. Time passes without any event, and Greta's *cookie* feels bored and suffers because of it.

Finally, the third story tells, by way of Joe's memories, how his fiancée, Beth, breaks up with him just after becoming pregnant, and blocks him through *Z-Eyes*. Years later, Beth dies in a train crash, and the blockage disappears. Joe is then able to see the child he supposes is his, and realizes, because of the girl's Asian features, that she is not his. Deeply affected by the discovery, he kills his former father-in-law with a toy, a crystal ball, and leaves the child abandoned in the grandfather's residence, so far from other people that she finally dies of cold and hunger. Joe confides all this to Matt unaware of the fact that he is not Joe himself, but a *cookie* manipulated by Matt to confess, because the real Joe is not talking to the police. The weapon used by Joe to kill his former father-in-law, a crystal ball, works, then, as a metaphor: it materializes the duplicated world, miniaturized, of Greta's and Joe's *cookies*.

As we can assume according to the perspective of the camera, Matt hears and watches through Harry's ears and eyes. This is possible only if those perceptual experiences are codifiable as any kind of information. Similarly, we should assume that, in order to block images from a given person–as it occurs in this episode when precautionary measures are imposed–a programming code that generates perceptions can be partially modified. As we said above, in the case of artificial entities such as the *cookies*, programming codes can produce consciousness-bearing phenomenal states. Remarkably, the experience of the flow of time seems computationally manipulated. It is therefore possible to assume that, in the universe of "White Christmas," the technological developments can produce phenomenal states both in living organisms as well as in artificial entities.

"Black Museum" is another episode composed by multiple storylines, all of them linked to Rollo Haynes' *Black Museum*. A former neurological research recruiter, Haynes, introduces a young girl, Nish, to the story behind the museum's main attractions. The first one concerns Doctor Dawson, who has accepted an implant (a *receiver*) allowing him, through a wire linked to another person, to feel their experiences: pain–so he can diagnose more precisely–, pleasure–he can feel his partner's orgasm, besides his–and even death. Dawson's device is a technology developed from a real experience: a rat was accidentally hurt with hot coffee and another rat felt the pain, which remains the situation that caused the discovery of mirror neurons (Rizzolatti, Fogassi & Gallese, 2006; Rizzolatti & Fogassi, 2014). As in "Striking Vipers," a device in the episode answers the question: How does intercourse feel for the opposite sex? What about other people's pain? For Dawson, this connection has a consequence: he eventually becomes addicted to the many active synapses in suffering and dying.

The second story is less obscure, but even sadder: Carrie and Jack are a happily married, until an accident puts her in a coma. Jack then accepts Haynes' offer to install Carrie's consciousness in his brain. Thus, Carrie can see and hear through Jack's senses, and he can hear her. It is a coexistence of two conscious entities, like that of Matt and Joe in "White Christmas." But this link to Carrie became too tight for Jack. Haynes then gives him other options: first, Jack can put his own senses on hold for Carrie, leaving her in darkness for hours, and even days. Later, Haynes takes Carrie's digitalized consciousness off of Jack's brain and installs it in a stuffed monkey. There, she cannot move or be heard but, as in Jack's brain, or for Greta's *cookie* in "White Christmas," she feels the passing of time.

Black Museum's main attraction is a hologram of Clayton Leigh, a convicted murderer or, more accurately, a digital version of himself, which he ceded before his execution. This digital self retains memories and affections, and feels pain, a similar situation to the one described in the "USS Callister" episode, as detailed below. This is an important detail, as it allows Haynes to offer a perfect recreation of his execution to the museum's visitors: any tourist can be his executioner and receive a souvenir: a capsule with Leigh's face in eternal agony. The enthusiasm of the museum's attendees is reminiscent of Milgram's famous experiment (1974); however, he concluded that obedience rather than sadism explains the behavior of participants in the study when they accepted to enforced punishment to other people. In contrast, the behavior of the *Black Museum's* visitors is clearly driven by sadism. Finally, Haynes explains to Nish, there has been a decline of the digital self: after thousands of executions, the digital synapses have deteriorated, and Leigh's hologram is now the figure of an almost dead man.

A Second World

"San Junipero" presents the successive encounters between Yorkie and Kelly, two girls in their early twenties who meet in a nightclub in 1987. They seem very different: the former is shy, while the latter is pretty vivacious, and they have such good chemistry that Kelly, afraid of commitments, runs away just after they have had sex. The other girl then begins a search that carries her through the 1990s and into 2002, wherein she finally finds her friend.

The episode's screenplay finally presents this world's logic: their encounters occur in a virtual world called San Junipero. The real Yorkie and Kelly are two old women, connected to machines, in two nursing homes separated by many kilometers. They "live" in San Junipero just a few hours every week, and abandon that world at midnight, just like digital Cinderellas. The time restriction, it is explained, is there to prevent dissociation between the real and virtual worlds. But there are *full-timers*, people whose body is already dead, who inhabit this festive (and evasive) world permanently.

Despite the treatment of *qualia* being a real challenge for functionalism and artificial intelligence, Science Fiction usually simply assumes that computational systems are capable of producing qualitative experiences. That is the case in "San Junipero" as well as in multiple chapters of *Black Mirror*. Besides, this episode shows that real and digital bodies are very different: in "Striking Vipers," a man can be a woman; in this one, an old lady can be a girl.

"USS Callister" deploys different levels of Science Fiction: space opera, virtual reality, genetic experimentation, and, finally, on-line video reality. This episode presents the adventures of Captain Robert Daly and his loyal crew, who travel across the galaxy searching for new planets and civilizations. This world, a virtual one, has been conceived by the real Daly, a talented but shy and resentful programmer, co-owner of Callister Inc. He has created a universe inspired by *Space Fleet*, a *Star Trek*-style TV show, wherein he is a leader and a ladies' man, and his colleagues and employees, who do not respect him or even talk to him in the real world, are either his devoted subordinates or harmless foes. The crew are forced to accept Captain Daly's authority: if they refuse to follow his orders, he tortures them or transforms them into awful monsters.

The new programmer in Callister Inc., Nanette, enters this virtual world without noticing. Yet again, and like all her colleagues aboard the *USS Callister*, this is not Nanette but a digital self, created from a DNA sample. Daly has taken the sample from a coffee cup in order to introduce her to this world shaped to his will. According to functionalism, "the mind is a program" and, in this *Black Mirror* episode, this "program" can be encoded in a saliva sample and replicated in a virtual world. This is theoretically problematic. Even if we accept that genetic information is equivalent to computational data, as the functionalist approach does, it is usually assumed that DNA code bears information about the nature rather than nurture aspects of individuals. It seems to be even more difficult to accept that these data encode memories from the individual's life, as it is proposed in "USS Callister."

Like in the "San Junipero" episode, the inhabitants of *Space Fleet*'s virtual world own their experiences, but not their bodies. Also, the crew has the memories from their real existence up until the moment Daly took the sample; onwards, they are a different self, with new desires and pain. This means that virtual characters, not only robots or androids, have *qualia*. Nanette and her colleagues have the will—which is different from that of the original self, like the real Nanette—but not the agency, because Daly can make them suffer, take their mouth and eyes off, and even change their shape. He can even destroy them and, with the DNA conserved in his fridge, create a new digital version of the crew who will continue suffering.

Digitalized experiences

Another kind of digitally-built experience appears in "Playtest." This episode introduces the audience to Cooper, a typical millennial connected permanently to social media. Later, it is explained that his father has recently died from Alzheimer's disease. Cooper arrives in London, where he participates in a test for SaitoGemu, a successful and secretive videogame company. For the test, SaitoGemu's technician implants a miniature device called *mush-room* into the back of Cooper's neck, close to his visual cortex. Through the *mushroom*, his brain "downloads the game" and receives mental images, seen only by Cooper. As in "Striking Vipers," "Playtest" presents a virtual reality world, that of the game, wherein the player has a digital body. Diodato points out that a virtual body is an apparition of a grammar, "an interactive digital image, the self-phenomenalization of an algorithm in binary format arising in its interaction with a user-consumer" (Diodato, p. 1). Cooper goes inside a horrific mansion. There, even though he knows that it is a video game, he experiences fear (close to a heart attack) and pain (a stab wound).

This episode's achievement is the uncertainty of the viewer about what is virtual and what is real. As in those of "White Christmas" and "San Junipero," the screenplay of "Playtest" toys with spectators' awareness of reality. At some point, the software seems to start failing, and Cooper's –and the audience's –question become: Is this part of the test? Furthermore, Cooper is afraid of losing his mind, like his father. In this way, a neurodegenerative disease, Alzheimer's, is made equivalent to a software problem.

Two storylines cross in "Crocodile." The main one is Mia's, a wife, mother, and successful architect, who witnesses and helps to hide the accidental killing of a man a decade before, and now tries to cover the event by killing the culprit, an old friend. The problem for Mia is that, minutes after the murder, she is witness to a traffic accident, currently being investigated by an insurance company. This leads to the second storyline, that of Shazia, the insurance investigator, who uses a machine, the *recaller*, to recover memories, sometimes, through *stimuli* such as smells or sounds, in order to define an accident's responsible party. Obviously, both lines finally converge.

As in "White Christmas" or "USS Callister," "Crocodile" presents the digitalization of sensations and memories, now as a resource to investigate accidents and crimes. In this episode, it is possible to translate subjective perceptions in a way that allows other human beings to understand the information associated with those perceptions. This is not limited to human beings: Mia's last crime is "witnessed" by a guinea pig, and police are able to recover the animal´s memories. This is a daring position: a guinea pig distinguish human figures and their actions, the way humans do? Can human beings recognize information codified in a different format used by a non-human animal? Can it be used as proof to indict a person? These kinds of questions remind us of Nagel's aforementioned article about the bat.

Finally, "Striking Vipers" presents two heterosexual friends having sexual encounters in a videogame's virtual world, wherein the former is a man and the latter a woman. As in "San Junipero," with an old woman becoming a younger one, or in "USS Callister," with people being transformed into space monsters as a punishment, this episode goes further with the possibility of feeling as another being: an athletic and sensual woman, for example.

In addition, the storyline questions who the experiences' owners are. Through a first-person shot, the *mise-en-scène* puts the spectators in Danny's shoes. Danny is amazed because he feels his avatar's muscles. There is a link between both bodies, the real and the virtual: the real one seems affected by actions in the game, as we find in a sequence that matches Lances and Roxette's movements in the game and the reflex action of Danny's body on the couch where he lies. Conversely, Lance feels a bump in the virtual world, when Danny's son kicks his father.

The real surprise arrives with the kiss and, in a second fight between Lance and Roxette, the sexual intercourse: "[I] Guess we are gay now", says Karl in the form of Roxette, after having sex. But they enjoy these encounters only in the video game world and remain heterosexual outside. Paradoxically, it is also something "exclusive": Karl tries to have intercourse with other male players, and even with a polar bear, and he fails to feel the same pleasure. After several encounters, he wants to explain to his friend: How does it feel to be a woman during sex? He suggests an "impressive" experience: "A fucking orchestra."

Conclusions

This chapter proposes that several *Black Mirror* episodes lead to the analysis of *qualia*, subjective and objective experiences, digital consciousness and body, among other issues. Some episodes, such as "Striking Vipers," take a position about a neuroscientific problem; others imagine some possibilities which defy contemporary science (e.g., genetic self in "USS Callister").

Black Mirror conveys this reflection in a coherent way. Even when it is an anthology series and every episode is autonomous, we find a shared universe and homogenous pessimism concerning technology in most of the episodes; among the few exceptions are "San Junipero" and "Striking Vipers." Evidence of this shared universe can be found, for example, in the fact that the device which enables the entrance to San Junipero is identical to that of "Striking Vipers." Yorkie and Kelly meet for the first time in a nightclub called *Tucker*. Later, it is explained that TCKR Systems is the neural research and technology company that created San Junipero, which in turn is Haynes' employer in "Black Museum," and the game's manufacturer in "Striking Vipers." Besides, *Tucker*'s logo appears in "Playtest" and "Metalhead." This homogeneity allows a discussion about "densification," a notion coined by Jean-Pierre Esquenazi describing the process of gradually generating of a fictional world, which is, according to this author, the TV series' aesthetic originality (Esquenazi, 2017).

Among the distinguishing elements that give coherence to this universe, we found a series of devices that enable the digitalization of the sensations, feelings, or consciousness. These artifacts correspond to interfaces that allow the entry and exit of information, as proposed by functionalism; for example, the *receiver* in "Black Museum," a device that allows the transfer of information from one system to another: from a person (a sick or dying one) to Dr. Dawson. It is interesting that a woman's orgasm can be transmitted as an information package.

Similarly, the *mushroom* in "Playtest," a device employed in a virtual reality video game, might enable the informational transfer of pain or pleasure, just like we find through another device and in another video game, in "Striking Vipers." While in *Black Mirror* episodes this occurs without any questioning, Ned Block maintains that the experience of an orgasm exceeds the informational content: this experience would be impressive and other orgasm's information would not. Or, as Block asserts, "I vastly prefer my own orgasms to those of others" (Block, p. 33).

Pain is also an impressive experience. In the *Black Mirror* world, pain can be transferred like other pieces of information. Evidently, we can retake Block's criticism about the transference of an orgasm. It is also possible to soften pain through the software, in an operation analogous to that of adjusting an image on a screen, making it clearer or darker. However, what is modified in that example is the *stimulus*, which can be computationally represented, while in *Black Mirror* what it is adjusted is the qualitative experience. According to Block or Nagel, this seems to be impossible but in the functionalist world of *Black Mirror* experiences are but information and data that can be modified. We discover this computational adjustment in the *pain sensors* mentioned in "San Junipero." Similarly, the *Z-Eyes* in "White Christmas" allowed not to mitigate but to eliminate the access to some senses' information.

In "USS Callister," it is proposed that an ADN sample can nourish a computational program in order to create a digital self. That means that the genetic code entails digital information and that the material basis (proteins) is not relevant. Functionalism has also proposed this kind of argument (Gutiérrez, 2006).

We could assert that, in the *Black Mirror* universe, the self is a disembodied concept. For some characters, personality is embodied in the shape of a living creature which processes information, but this incarnated condition is rather accidental, and an identical self could be replicated using a storage device, such as a *cookie* (a "photocopy of you") in "White Christmas." Similarly, the *full-timers*, permanent inhabitants of San Junipero, are completely disembodied entities, even if they seem indistinguishable from people made of flesh and bone, such as Yorkie and Kelly, who use external information in order to operate in the virtual world.

The *recaller*, the device to recover memories in "Crocodile," refers to the *long-term memory* proposed by contemporary cognitive psychology (Baddeley, Eysenk & Anderson, 2015). According to this position, the memory's contents are representationally stored in an associative device, even if the chain to recover these contents is frequently weak. The informational condition of these memories makes it possible to put them in a visual code on the screen. It is even possible for the perceptions stored in a guinea pig's memory. From Nagel's perspective, we can question whether this code is universal, such that human beings could recognize images from the qualitative experience of a non-human being. Again, we can adopt some of the points of view of anti-functionalist positions (embodied, situated cognition, etc.) and criticize the philosophical bases of the series, but *Black Mirror* is certainly coherent with functionalist theses and reflects the disembodied and formalist vision of the universe that this approach proposes. Even if we consider this philosophical approach as misleading, it is important to emphasize that functionalism has fostered research programs in AI, Data Science, and other disciplines, as well as technological developments. Thus, functionalism has had effects in our contemporary societies and, in consequence, also ethical implications.

In the *Black Mirror* world, where *qualia* can be generated artificially, the way we conceive ethical issues in organic and non-organic beings becomes problematic; for example, in the ability to provoke pain (the torture of the crew in "USS Callister") or suffering (the boredom of Greta's *cookie* in "White Christmas") in a digital self. Besides, technology enables new forms of social control: in episodes such as "White Christmas" and "Crocodile," the digital recreation of memories and selves has become a resource for police investigation, to the point of proposing that the digital self can confess a crime perpetrated by its human counterpart. In addition, in "White Christmas" and "The Entire Story of You," wives can block fathers' access to children or to themselves, as Matt's and Joe's wives do. The contents of an individual's perception and projection become the object of public jurisdiction, as we find in the epilogue of "White Christmas," where a convicted criminal is sentenced to appear to other people as a gray shadow for the rest of his life, or in "Men Against Fire," where the army can control the perception of its soldiers. Finally, as we have mentioned, this technology of the self invites the audience to reimagine the gender roles in "Striking Vipers" and to reconfigure their relationships, as we find in the episode's epilogue.

As analyzed by Ierardo (2018), social control is a recurring theme in *Black Mirror*. There, the subject is framed within the possible consequences of developing technologies in the loss of the private lives of individuals. We consider, however, that in the case dealt with in the present chapter, social control goes a step further. In fact, it would not only consist of social control but also of a radical authority over the individual's being: an ontological control. The scenario depicted here is not simply the possibility of modifying the conditions external to the subject to control him or her. In other words, there is a fundamental difference between imposing a prohibition of approaching a given person and preventing the very possibility of seeing her or him by interfering within his or her cognitive structure, and convicting a person in prison for a long period of time and modifying his very perception of time. It is not a question of modifying the world in which individuals move, but of modifying the very way they *are* in the world, the way they perceive it, *feel*, and *live* in it. *Black Mirror* gives us a hint of this kind of control.

Bibliography

Baddeley, A. Eysenk, M.W. & Anderson, M.C. (2009). *Memory*. New York: Psychology Press.

Block, Ned (1996). "Mental Paint and Mental Latex". *Philosophical Issues*, 7, pp. 19-49. doi:10.2307/1522889

Diodato, Roberto (2012). *Aesthetics of the Virtual*. Nueva York, State University of New York Press.

Divers, John (2002). *Possible worlds*. London, Routledge.

Elugardo, Reinaldo (1983). "Functionalism and the Absent Qualia Argument". *Canadian Journal of Philosophy*, 13 (2), pp. 161-179. URL: https://www.jstor.org/stable/40231311. Accessed: 11-07-2019.

Fodor, Jerry A. (1975). *The Language of Thought*, New York: Thomas Y. Crowell.

Gutiérrez, Claudio (2006). *Ensayos sobre un nuevo humanismo: genes y memes en la era planetaria*. San José, Costa Rica: UNED.

Ierardo, Esteban (2018). "Sociedad pantalla". *Black Mirror y la tecnodependencia*. Buenos Aires: Continente.

Jackson, Frank (1986). "What Mary didn't know". *Journal of Philosophy*, 83, pp. 291-295.

Milgram, Stanley (1974). *Obedience to Authority: An Experimental View*. London: Tavistock.

Molina, Mauricio (In press) "Para cuando el Golem no sea hecho de barro: apuntes sobre los mundos posibles de *Black Mirror*". En María Lourdes Cortés y Camilo Retana (eds). *Locos por las teleseries*. San José, Costa Rica: Universidad de Costa Rica.

Nagel, Thomas (1974). "What Is It Like to Be a Bat?". *The Philosophical Review*, vol. 83, no 4, pp. 435-450. URL: http://www.jstor.org/stable/2183914. Accessed: 04/02/2014 15:52.

Rizzolatti, G., Fogassi, L., & Gallese, V. (2006). "Mirrors in the mind". *Scientific American*, 295(5), 54-61. Retrieved from www.jstor.org/stable/26069039

Rizzolatti, G., & Fogassi, L. (2014). "The mirror mechanism: Recent findings and perspectives". *Philosophical Transactions: Biological Sciences*, 369 (1644), pp. 1-12. Retrieved from www.jstor.org/stable/24500753

Technology and Place in Science Fiction
Exploring the Post-Pessimism of *Black Mirror*

Justin Michael Battin

Introduction

Any mentioning of the *Black Mirror* televisual program is likely to conjure images of a technological dystopia to those familiar with it. According to Johnson, Marquez, and Ureña, the experience of *Black Mirror* is akin to "watching a dark reflection of society – one that is just slightly cracked – that depicts our flaws, our fears, and our possible future" (2020, p. 3). Based on the range of discourses circulating about the program, there is little doubt that its predictions of society's current state and trajectory have triggered uneasiness. This anxiety, even if fleeting, suggests a need to consider the ontological conditions that have given rise to such prognostications. Granting consideration to these ontological conditions will not only account for how the program addresses thematic content relevant to contemporary society, but also locate it within the current trajectory of the Science Fiction genre. This genre, particularly its rendition since the Industrial Revolution, has frequently explored the human understanding of *technology-as-power* by drawing attention to its ramifications on the broader social world. Although these explorations tend to be dark and dystopian, the Science Fiction genre is, at its core, unapologetically optimistic by way of its invitation to read humanity's understanding of technology through matters of place and place-making practices, which, if fathomed topologically, is fundamental to the manner in which the unity of the world manifests as mattering and worth safeguarding (see Malpas, 2017 [2012], pp. 23-41). Through a careful textual reading of "Fifteen Million Merits," this chapter argues that a Heideggerian account of place is demonstrative of the foundation on which the

Science Fiction genre rests, and invites a perspective through which we can better understand and address not only the world *Black Mirror* so vividly displays, but also its ontological underpinnings.

Science Fiction: A Brief Reflection

Science Fiction is a genre with a remarkably rich tradition. The genre has, thus far, spanned numerous media formats, from the literary to the cinematic, and is one with a quality ranging from the pulp to the prestige. Despite the enormous oeuvre falling under the categorical designation of Science Fiction throughout the occidental epochs, this chapter draws inspiration from the genre's relatively short history, primarily the texts originating from the Industrial Revolution. This specific period is novel and worth emphasizing as this is precisely when the Science Fiction genre obtained its current identity in the social imaginary and established distinctions between the didactic and fantastic, and when prophecies of scientific discovery and exploration juxtaposed with utopian and dystopian futures, with each respectively depicting mankind's social progress or destruction.

To comprehend the genre's emergence, and correlatively its exploration of the technology-as-power motif, requires framing it within its historical context and the transformative social changes that accompanied it (Evans, 2009, p. 13). The Industrial Revolution and early 20th century signify the triumph of modernity in the occidental world; it is the period when individual pragmatism and technological capacity, rather than religion and community, became regarded as more plausible vehicles to address social concerns and as more reliable for providing a secure, safe, efficient, and egalitarian world. As Giddens suggests, those people populating this period, unlike any preceding them, lived in the future rather than the past (1998, p. 94), and aimed to embark upon a bold new trajectory through their knowledge and implementation of science and technology.

Drawing on the archetypical Enlightenment figure capable of transcending societal constraints, such as a scientist deciphering the mysteries of the natural world or a world-travelling explorer, the Science Fiction genre of this period showcased how a singular person can achieve exceptional feats through their vast scientific knowledge and with the aid of technological devices. Given the incredible changes to society that accompanied the

Industrial Revolution, such as mass migrations to urban centers, new social organizational structures, efficiency-driven modes of production, the wide proliferation of new consumer goods, and faith being placed in technology rather than religion and community, it is inevitable that pertinent discourses would emerge to address them. These discourses frequently manifested through numerous fictional media channels and forms, among them being the Science Fiction genre. Considering the vast scale and frenetic pace of these changes, it is unsurprising that not all texts outwardly endorsed an optimistic vision. Although numerous stories aligned with Verne's *romans scientifiques* – hopeful stories grounded in hard science that emphasized explorations, adventure, and an altruistic uses of technology (Alkon, 2002, p. 19) – prognostications of dystopian futures were prevalent. Murphy (2009, p. 472) notes that E.M Forster's "The Machine Stops" from 1909 has the strongest claim of being the original dystopian text. In this short story, the author portrays,

> ...a totalizing administration that 'mechanizes' every dimension of daily life (from the organization of nature and industry to the standardization of the person). He develops abstract yet critical account of the new social spacetime of the [early] twentieth century. Yet, even has he foregrounds his apocalyptic horror at the unraveling of the world he knows, he clings ... to the prophetic possibility that one day humanity will again prevail (Moylan, 2000, p. 111).

Forster's text is pertinent to acknowledge because, while it ardently offers critical commentary on the numerous changes ushered by the Industrial Revolution, it equally provides a glimmer of optimism. The widespread dependency on technology, suffocation of ideas, and de-humanizing alienation exhibited in this tale are presented in such a manner as to demonstrate that they can be countered. Murphy, however, astutely suggests the hope that this dystopian tale offers does not necessarily reside in the fictional characters enduring the nightmare, but rather in the *readers* themselves (2009, p. 474).

Delany (1984) suggests that Science Fiction is, in fact, quite unique because of its capacity to present stark disparities between a reader's lived universe and what is presented in the diegesis. Alkon, taking this notion further, argues that Science Fiction has an exceptional propensity to de-familiarize aspects of the reader's ordinary world, but in such a way that stimulates cognition, awakening them to the "*principles* governing those features of life that we are invited to regard as unfamiliar" (2002, p. 11). Freedman echoes this sentiment, stating that "the science-fictional world is not only one different in time or place from our own, but one whose chief interest is precisely the difference that such difference makes (2000, p. xvi). Freedman also astutely proposes that the Science Fiction genre and the tradition of critical theory share a special affinity with one another, as it is the nature of both to draw on contemporary issues and concepts and speculate about the future (2000, p. 181). In his own words, "science fiction, like critical theory, insists upon historical mutability, material reducibility, and utopian possibility. Of all genres, science fiction is thus the one most devoted to the historical concreteness and rigorous self-reflectiveness of critical theory" (ibid, p. xvi). This distinct form of reader engagement is precisely what separates Science Fiction from other forms of storytelling like myths, folk tales, and fantasy, as none of these "so insistently calls into question our sense of the world as it is nor by doing so invite readers to adopt a critical outlook with strong affinities to scientific method" (ibid, p. 13). Science Fiction, therefore, appears to be a suitable genre to not simply illuminate critical notions facing contemporary society, but to suitably engage with them by both emphasizing the need to grapple with the matters raised via a range of perspectives, as well as by pursuing utopian-inspired alternatives.

Our current societal imaginary, whether critically distinguished as a secular age (Taylor, 2007), the Anthropocene (Davies, 2016), liquid modernity (Bauman, 2000), a global village (McLuhan, 1962; 1964), an age of disruption (Stiegler, 2019), or the fourth Industrial Revolution (Schwab, 2015), is indeed a linear consequence of the ideologies embedded within and propagated by the Industrial Revolution and modernity, all of which resonate in the present day. Although these epochal distinctions carry their own concerns and reaches, as they stem from different academic disciplines, each advocate that these ideologies are sustained and propelled by a key constant: *technology*. The Science Fiction genre of the industrial era onward has repeatedly addressed the multifaceted connection between human beings and technology. Frequent consideration, in particular, is warranted towards technology's alluring character: it recurrently shows itself as the key component for which one can defy their own biological limitations, assert their will, and/or achieve a desired outcome. In what seems like a subtle reference to Nietzsche, Susan Sontag notes that this alluring quality is driven by something deeper – *power as value*; "things, rather than the helpless humans, are the locus of values because we experience them, rather than people, as the sources of power. According to science fiction ... man is naked without his artifacts" (1966, p. 216). Shelley's *Frankenstein*, for instance, is a narrative centered on a single man's desire to replicate God by using technology to assemble and reanimate a human body (Murray & Heumann, 2016). Fritz Lang's German Expressionist masterwork, *Metropolis* (1927), articulates the use of technology as an expression of power through the Taylorist mechanization of workers by a bourgeois elite (Minden & Bachmann, 2000, p. x). Further evoking the technology-as-power motif expressed in *Metropolis*, Science Fiction satires such as Huxley's *Brave New World* (1932) and Orwell's *Nineteen Eighty-Four* (1949) act as warnings for a creeping technocratic modernism (Posner, 2000). More recently, Pixar's *WALL-E* (2008), while offering a scathing critique of consumerist culture and contemporary capitalism (McNauhtan, 2012), is more deeply demonstrative of the perils wrought by the Baconian ambition for technology to be a wieldable tool capable of relieving humanity of its burdens (Mattie, 2014, p. 13). Irrespective of their story content, these texts have placed engagement with technology-as-power at their thematic epicenter, a tradition *Black Mirror* has fervently continued.

To better understand the presence and impact of technology-as-power in contemporary society, its role in shaping the current epoch as exhibited through *Black Mirror*, and its role regarding Science Fiction more generally, it is first key to ardently jettison definitions that restrict technology to its purely instrumental, anthropological, and materialist conditions, and instead adopt an approach that permits technology to unveil itself in its most intimate manner – by focusing on its presence in matters of place, broadly understood as "locations imbued with meaning that are sites of everyday practice" (Cresswell, 2009, p. 177).

Technology and the Happening of Place

Approaching technology through the lens of place first requires a careful consideration of the term. Drawing from Cresswell's interpretation mentioned above and Jeff Malpas' reading of Heidegger, place will be regarded as an open region in which a world coalesces or, for a lack of better term, *happens* (2006, p. 29). Three points demand attention with respect to this interpretation of place. First, the happening of place metaphorically mirrors the unveiling of a horizon. According to Colomina, "a horizon defines an enclosure ... it marks a limit to the space of what can be seen, which is to say, it organizes this visual space into an interior" (1996, p. 51). A horizon temporally gathers the world around an inhabitant, slowly demarcating where one *is* through the contents permitted into and arranged within its perceivable boundary. Malpas echoes this notion, yet cautions against consigning too much emphasis on place as a harmonious enclosure. Although the gathering of place into a unified whole suggests a sense of boundedness, since unity and wholeness imply fruition, Malpas advises that this "is a form of boundedness tied to the idea of that which something begins in its unfolding as what it is, rather than that at which it comes to a stop; a concept of boundary as *origin* rather than as *terminus*" (2006, p. 29). As the happening of place transpires, this ostensible boundary is where the constituting elements of place are admitted and installed into the gathering realm. Similar to how a horizon permits the manifestation of world into view, the boundary of place is where such elements announce themselves. A horizon is by its very essence temporal, and is therefore in perpetual flux, avoiding any stasis; new elements continuously enter, reside, and become reconstituted within its permeable bounds. Heidegger himself also relied upon this word to elucidate this notion, proclaiming that "a boundary is not that at which something stops but, as the Greeks recognized, the boundary is that from which something *begins its presencing*. That is why the concept is that of *horismos*, that is, the horizon, the boundary" (1977 [1954], p. 332).

The second point concerns the individual components that facilitate and constitute the gathering – those seemingly ordinary *things* that show themselves as available for use in a given place. According to Malpas, "what is extraordinary about these ordinary things is the manner in which they provide the focus for the opening of world, which includes, of course, their own opening as things, their own appearing and coming to presence" (2017 [2012], p. 15). In accordance with Heideggerian thought, these things are not objects-in-themselves, but are rather "mutually defined only through the way in which they are gathered together within the place they constitute" (Malpas, 2006, p. 29). The nature of things and their relationship to place has been, from the onset, pervasive across Heidegger's writings. In *Being and Time*, for instance, Heidegger argues that things acquire meaning not through any ontic or abstract property, such as size, weight, or color, but rather through their place in a referential nexus; "each object is defined by a network of practices in which it is employed, the result toward which it is directed, and the other objects with which it is used" (Wrathall, 2011, p. 200). While this form of intelligibility stitches the fabric of one's practical world, it ultimately fails to indicate how things can be existentially meaningful. Those things comprehended purely through their referential character typically make few demands on a person and therefore are not critical for one's self-realization. In contrast, things which manifest as existentially important genuinely matter for the self and its world by way of soliciation, revealing themselves as *necessary* to engage with in the moment (White, 2005, p. 125). While each plays a role in the manifesation of place, those with recognizable existential importance are particularly crucial for the third point, the topology of place.

Topology, if broken down into its Greek root words, *topos* and *logos*, suggests "the saying of place" (Malpas, 2006, p. 33). This particular component of place seems to be of special focus for Heidegger, especially in his later thinking, as it fruitfully allows for the tripartite recognition of the happening of world, the embroidering one performs to stimulate and sustain its manifestation, and a situatedness and belonging within that unfolding world. As proposed by Malpas, "Heideggerian topology can be understood as an attempt to evoke and illuminate that placed abode ... topology is an attempt to illuminate a place in which we already find ourselves and in which other things are also disclosed to us" (ibid, p. 34). This illumination is articulated through the concepts of *poiēsis* (ποίησις) and *dwelling* (wohnen), the latter of which alludes to the threshold moment of one thing transforming into another, a sort of *ekstasis* (ἔκστασις), and the former, in Heidegger's view, is the basic character of a human being (1977 [1954], p. 326). The unison of these two concepts, Heidegger proposes, permits a human being to recognize the manifestation of place as an appropriating event (*Ereignis*). Through this event, place and one's involvement within it occurs with a sense of urgency and owndom (see Grant, 2015, pp. 213-229). According to Malpas, "the happening that is at issue here is not some abstract 'occurrence,' but a happening in which we are gathered in to the concreteness and particularity of the world and to our own lives" (2006, p. 221). This understanding emerges, for Heidegger, through his etymological analysis of the word *wohnen* (dwelling), as he identifies that the word originally meant to cherish and protect, to preserve and care for (Heidegger, 1977 [1954] p. 325). If understood essentially, being-in-place permits a distinguishable opening to acknowledge the sense of at-homeness that is, to echo the aforementioned horizon, temporally unveiled (or brought-forth) when a person involves the self with things in an existentially-binding manner. The place to which that human being belongs thereby transforms; it becomes remarkably enriching, compelling, and, perhaps most importantly, necessary to protect and preserve, particularly those very conditions that permit a sense of place to emerge at all (see also Dreyfus, 2017 [2003], Prince, 2018). Through such a perspective, a person is more attentive to that which poetically emerges in their experiential horizon and is thus better able to trust his or her own role as a cultivator and preserver of existentially-meaningful worlds. As the philosopher writes, "to dwell, to be set at peace, means to remain at peace within the free, the preserve, the free sphere that safeguards each thing in its essence" (Heidegger, 1977 [1954], p. 327).

Equally important to Heidegger's ruminations on place is technology, and particularly contemporary technology, as it is seemingly a danger that hinders a person's ability to experience things *as they are* and the world *as it is*. The inability of people to fathom the intimacy of place and account for their role in nurturing its manifestation has seemingly sparked widespread rootlessness and a feeling of homelessness; people no longer authentically dwell (ibid, p. 323-339). This is, in Heidegger's estimation, technology's *essence*. Before proceeding, it is critical to clarify that Heidegger is no Luddite. He is not vehemently opposed to technology nor is he aiming to uncover some enigmatic, undiscovered strategy for bringing technology under human dominion. Rather, as elucidated by Dreyfus, "Heidegger's concern is the human *distress* caused by the *technological understanding of being*, rather than the *destruction* caused by specific technologies" (2017 [1992] p. 188).

Throughout the history of the occidental west, it has been customary to define technology as-novelty, as-industrialization, and as-instrumentality (McOmber, 1999). Although each proposes a different stance for how technology develops, the notion of a tool-like character exists as a common thread between them. Technology, therefore, is regularly comprehended as that which can be wielded or implemented to resolve an identifiable issue in a given time or place (the aforementioned technology-as-power motif). This interpretation of technology has endured because, over the previous two centuries of western thought, technology has been grounded predominantly through only one of Aristotle's four causes – *causa efficiens*, the source that brings something into existence – and this lone cause has set the standard for all causality (Heidegger, (1977 [1962]), p. 290). This persistent prioritization of technology solely as the means by which results can be obtained, and the concurrent disregarding of the remaining three causes (*materialis, formalis,* and *finalis*), has contributed to a widespread narrowing of how technology is defined and comprehended. Contemporarily, technology is too often regarded as a means to an end or as a human activity, and rarely is its essence warranted much attention. This essence is by no means technological, and lies well beyond anthropological and instrumental views on technology (ibid, p. 289). Rather, the essence of technology is a mode of being, of revealing and manifesting. However, as Blitz suggests, "technological things have their own novel kind of presence, endurance, and connections among parts and wholes." (2014, p. 71). Technology, especially from the Industrial Revolution onwards, promotes a peculiar type of revealing of and gathering of place, one where everything encountered manifests as exploitable for some technical utilization.

In his seminal essay, "The Question Concerning Technology," Heidegger specifically uses the neologisms *challenging-forth* and a *setting-in-order* to illustrate how, through a technological understanding of the world, all things manifest as *bestand* (standing-reserve), as pure resources or replaceable stock that exist solely to be efficiently manipulated and optimized for means-end purposes. Albert Borgmann (2009 [1984]) notes that this view of the world shows itself with the most clarity through humanity's contemporary engagement with nature, which consistently appears as an available resource for domination and consumption, whether for the extraction of raw materials or as an ideal site to replenish one's physical and mental energies (see also Heidegger, 1966, p. 50). This form of revealing seems to be omnipresent in all realms of contemporary life, as people have, for a lack of better term, become *enframed* by technology. According to Taylor and Gunkel,

Enframing has two main aspects—things become situated as, and thereby reduced to the status of available objects [standing reserve] and human beings themselves become a part of this same process of objectification even as they are busy objectifying the world around them. The concepts of enframing and standing reserve therefore help to illuminate not only the manner in which entities are organized for technologically facilitated exploitation but also the mentality that both underlies and results from this calculable complex. Rather than encountering things as things, we come preconditioned to treat world (and ourselves) as part of a standing reserve of preconditioned objects (2014, p. 129).

Hubert Dreyfus, drawing from Kuhn, suggests that the science paradigm of the Enlightenment tradition is an ideal comparison to illustrate Heidegger's notions of enframing and standing reserve. He posits:

> A science becomes normal when all practitioners in a certain area all agree that a particular piece of work identifies the important problems in a field and demonstrates how certain of these problems can be successfully solved. Thus, a modern scientific paradigm sets up normal science as an activity of puzzle solving. It is the job of normal science to eliminate anomalies by showing how they fit into the total theory the paradigm sketches out in advance. In a similar way, the technological paradigm embodies and furthers our technological understanding of being according to which what does not fit in with our current paradigm ... that is, that which is not yet at our disposal to use efficiently ... will finally be brought under our control and turned into a resource (2017 [1992], p. 185).

This comparison clarifies how the essence of technology is both encompassing and systemic, bringing more and more objects into its paradigm of total mobilization, where everything, including one's individual self, becomes repositioned into an exploitable resource. As Heidegger himself laments, "everywhere everything is ordered to stand by, to be immediately at hand, indeed to stand there just so that it may be called upon for further ordering" (1977 [1962], p. 298).

Borgmann's device paradigm, which in itself is a response to Heidegger's reading of technology, offers a practical account of the impact of *enframing* and *standing-reserve* in our contemporary world. Specifically, Borgmann's paradigm speaks to the loss of meaning of things and places, and the transformation of culture at the hands of technology (Tijmes, 2001, p. 11). Borgmann is particularly interested in addressing the notion that technology allows for the aforementioned Baconian desire of liberation and enrichment through the utilization of resources – freeing people from painstaking physical labor or the frustrating amount of time one waits for something to be produced. All things in existence today are technologically *available*, and seem to harbor the following characteristics: *instantaneous, ubiquitous, safe,* and *easy* (Borgmann, 2009 [1984], p. 41). In the globally-connected world, there is no shortage of available artifacts to illuminate this phenomenon, whether they are media texts available for instantaneous download from an Internet connection irrespective of place, or edible fruits resting on a supermarket shelf far removed from their place of origin. These examples, in Borgmann's view, were made possible, yet also rendered existentially vacuous, through devices. Like Heidegger, Borgmann draws on the use of the word *thing*, proclaiming that a thing "is inseparable from its context, namely, its world, and from our commerce with the thing and its world, namely, engagement. The experience of a thing is always and also a bodily and social engagement with the thing's world" (ibid). Borgmann notes how a stove, as a thing, provides far more than mere warmth; as an existentially important part of one's life, it becomes a focal point for a house, coalescing the work and leisure of the family into one congruent place. Devices, in contrast, which are representative of the "pattern or paradigm of modern technology" (ibid, p. 3), conceal the critical components that permit whatever they deliver *to be*. The processes and individual components that make the device's output possible are rendered invisible by the device itself. As Borgmann writes, "what distinguishes a device is its sharp internal division into a machinery and a commodity procured by that machinery" (ibid, p. 33). Thus, a society *enframed* by technology's essence prioritizes the output (and the efficiency of its production and delivery) above all else; any transcendental source of value is lost and a person, rather than contributor to the establishment of place, is simply another cog ushered into the ordering of technology.

Mattie's reading of Pixar's *WALL-E* noted above is particularly insightful for elucidating why this ontological condition is so troubling; he writes,

> Machines and other technical means liberate us from necessities and likewise remove us, or allow us to remove ourselves, from attachment to particular families, traditions, communities, and locations. Yet our ease and freedom come with new burdens: the painful "boredom" and "anxious restlessness" of isolation and "uncultivated leisure." The mass desire for ever-new forms of diversion and escape from any settled state, physical or mental, suggests that our advances in technology have caused us not to feel at home, or at rest (2014, p. 13).

This restlessness and lack of feeling-at-home are among the most precarious characteristics of the technological understanding of being. In addition to turning everything into a resource, "what technology does ... is hide its own place-bound character while also obscuring place as such" (Malpas, 2006, p. 293). A technological understanding of being morphs one's place into acting as nothing more than a mere position. One becomes understood as located in neutral, vapid space, with the ability to act established as extension (*extensio*); "the world just is the spatial, and things are nothing other than they are given in and through such spatiality" (ibid, p. 294). If place is reduced to mere space, one loses a sense of place, or sense of belonging, and experiences a disruption to the recognition of where one *is* as well as what grounds and supports that place – their involvement, *understood topologically*.

For Heidegger, in addition to a number of his commentators (see Dreyfus and Spinoza, 2017 [1996]), a renewed attention to technology's disclosive character, returning it to the realm of *poiēsis*, is necessary if humanity is to grasp what technology essentially *is*, to resist its most harmful attributes, and to catalyze the renewal of utopian energies in order to recover confidence and embark upon lives worth living. Dreyfus, in particular, suggests that to appropriately account for the essence of technology, one must first recognize "this threat is not a problem for which we must find a solution, but an *ontological condition* that requires a transformation in our understanding of being" (2017, p. 188). Engagement with technology manifests place in a way that can reveal truths about the underlying conditions of a human being's world; "to consider technology essentially is to see it as an event to which we belong: the structuring, ordering, and requisitioning of everything around us, and ourselves" (Blitz, 2014, p. 71). Thus, attentiveness to technology as establishing and revealing place permits the capacity to better preserve what is meaningful for people as they dwell in their everyday world, and to better recover an original interpretation of themselves (i.e. as Dasein). Despite the omnipresence of *enframing*, Heidegger did optimistically note that it was possible to turn away from this danger, specifically as one recognizes what has been forgotten. In the philosopher's own words, "the closer we come to the danger, the more brightly do the ways in to the saving power begin to shine and the more questioning we become" (1977 [1962], p. 317).

Technology, Science Fiction, and *Black Mirror*

The acknowledgement and questioning of one's ontological condition, while rarely addressed through the above-mentioned terms, is of significant concern to the Science Fiction genre. In the examples provided, the genre's diegetic-bound characters mosey through their everyday routines, typically without concern, until they encounter a scenario that instills them with varying degrees of anxiety and distress. They are suddenly perplexed at the immediate loss of meaning, a withdrawing of world, yet, through reflection, captivated by the possibilities unveiled by their being-in-place. The Science Fiction genre does aim to display the virtues or damages technology has wrought, but in accordance with its position as a critically reflective genre aiming to produce utopian-inspired futures, it is fundamentally more concerned with elucidating the ontological view of what one's self, guided by an understanding of being-in-place, can portend.

Lang's *Metropolis*, for instance, presents a world picture that is utterly inhospitable to the bulk of the populace within it – the workers in the city's depths are somnambulant, existing as mechanical cogs uncritically serving a machinist paradigm. According to Telotte, "the futuristic city of *Metropolis* suffers from a debilitating 'world picture,' a dominant philosophy that has fashioned a glittering and grimly efficient society, but one that seems fundamentally at odds with itself, in which workers and managers rarely even glimpse each other" (1999, p. 55). Upon witnessing the plight of the workers for the first time, the story's main character, Freder, questions the sustainability of this shared world, one built on unrestrained capitalism enabled by a technology-as-power worldview. Machines have assumed a god-like status, workers have become slaves, and symbols of hope can be easily manipulated to further strengthen this world's technological paradigm (Wosk, 2010, p. 403). Freder's concern, however, appears to be inspired less by empathy towards the workers and appall over their dire conditions, but more because of a suffocating uneasiness. Freder comprehends that the divide between the proletariat and bourgeois in this society is utterly untenable; the foundation of his potential *to be* is destined to collapse, and his place in the world and ability to proceed confidently within it is threatened by this totalitarian technological paradigm. Through the character of Maria and the authentic meaning she stimulates, *as a thing*, Freder realizes the potential to bridge the gap between the workers below and the elites above, and to forge a new world picture in which technology still has a vital role to play, but one free of an unsustainable incongruence.

WALL-E likewise presents a debilitating world picture – one so uninhabitable that human beings were forced to abandon it in favor of a Baconian paradise aboard a space-yacht, at least until Earth is again suitable for settlement. This paradise, however, proves to be more devastating to the human condition than life on a terribly polluted Earth. Mattie observes how, after many years away from home, "human beings have conformed to the mechanical processes of the ship, accepting axiomatically that all the artificial conveniences and sensations the ship offers are the sum of reality" (2014, p. 12). Primarily through the adventures of WALL-E, a robot with humanoid instincts and feelings, audiences witness how the passengers live fleeting lives void of any existential substance. It is a society based on little but diversion and consumption and, while the passengers do possess choice, such as which games to play or color of clothes to wear, they are, as Mattie notes, ultimately "subject to the ship's grand control. As technology has conquered outer space, it has apparently mastered or remade human nature, reducing to an artificial simplicity the complex problem of how human beings are to live" (ibid).

What unites these extraordinary texts are not only their critical interpretations of technology-as-power, but also how these interpretations are tied to matters of *place*. *Metropolis* was developed during a period of social upheaval and chaos in the Weimar Republic, wherein society's view of modernity shifted away from fascination and towards its apparent dehumanizing effects (Hayward, 2018 [1996], p. 171). *WALL-E*, roughly 80 years later, was created during a period in which climate change was finally accepted by society as a legitimate threat to human life. With both, the need to start anew drives the narratives, albeit not by dissolving civilization and beginning from scratch, so to speak, but rather by reviving a perspective that has been lost. In *Metropolis*, the end titles propose that society's successful future lies in reconciling the hand (*technē*) and the head (*epistēmē*) with the heart, which can be read loosely as caring (Heidegger's *Sorge*) for where one is and that which populates it, but in a mode that permits its nourishment and long term sustainability (*Wohnen*)[1]. *WALL-E*, likewise, according to Mattie, show-

---

1   The Platonic and Aristotelian distinctions between *technē* (τέχνη) and *epistēmē* (ἐπιστήμη), or the definitive split between the practical and the theoretical, was, in conjunction with

cases how "each living generation must take responsibility for perpetuating the community and its way of life, no matter how providential its founding" (2014, p. 19). The captain of the space-yacht, comparable to Freder in *Metropolis*, comes to see himself as responsible for restoring place (and thereby the place of others, considering his position as a figure of authority) to its ontological origins, as a cultivatable venture. The captain finds himself utterly bored with the monotony on the ship and eager to explore the vast possibilities beyond its technologically-ordered confines, particularly those possibilities imbued with existential purpose, which, in the context of the story, can be found exclusively on Earth. As Mattie identifies, the captain is exposed to earthy processes such as photosynthesis, the distinctions between earth, sea, and sky, and how these are all uniquely connected to the development of human civilization; "in learning about the Earth, the Captain discovers that work is necessary, not only to revive the planet but also to fulfill human nature" (ibid). These characters, in Heideggerian vernacular, have responded to the call of being, which, although remaining as a mere whisper, is still comprehensible. While a technological understanding of being might be our destiny, if we take Heidegger's proclamation as truth that this condition is the natural trajectory of the metaphysical tradition, it is certainly not our fate. As exhibited by *Metropolis* and *WALL-E*, alternative views beyond the technological understanding of being can be cleared into view and nurtured into existence by individuals compelled by its call. The Science Fiction genre, particularly in these two examples, reveals its optimism, as it draws upon topical material to stimulate in viewers an urgency to preserve that which seems to be fading – a human being's ability to reconstitute a sense of being in place, particularly in times of evident turmoil.

---

the prioritization of *causa efficiens*, a central reason for why technology became widely understood with means-end reasoning, and consequently manufacturing and manipulating. Heidegger references the pre-Socratic philosopher, Xenophon, who considered *technē* and *epistēmē* as indistinguishable terms, and "names for knowing in the widest sense" (Heidegger 1977 [1962], p. 294). Both were suitable vehicles for the bringing-forth of *alētheia* (ἀλήθεια), truth understood as unconcealment. Indeed, for Heidegger, to consider *technē* (the etymological root of technology) solely through a human act or as means undermines its true scope; "what is decisive about *technē* does not lie at all in making and manipulating nor in the using of means, but rather in the aforementioned revealing. It is as revealing, and not as manufacturing, that *technē* is a bringing-forth" (ibid).

The bulk of the episodes in *Black Mirror*, however, in contrast to the two texts discussed above, rarely appear to share this optimistic perspective. A hint of the show's bleakness can, in fact, be read in its title sequence. Glancing into a mirror offers a moment to reflect upon the self and where it immediately *is*. A cracked mirror, however, impedes that reflection by obscuring clarity and distorting perspective, particularly by diverting one's attention away from the full picture and towards specific fragments of the mirror. Furthermore, the color of the mirror infers a sense of opaqueness. In his later work, Heidegger referenced how the happening of *Ereignis* metaphorically aligned with one's arrival to a clearing in a forest, the word for which in German is *Lichtung*. Appropriately, the adjective *licht*, which translates to open, is the same word for light. Considering the opaqueness of the mirror in question, it is fair to suggest that in the context of the program, any light stimulating an opening for meaningful reflection is, ultimately, destined to dim and close. While the program's characters often find themselves reeling from a withdrawn world and able to recognize the anxiety of their epoch, they ultimately lack the ability to respond to it essentially or have their ability to respond subsumed by the technological machinations of their world.

Never does this scenario play out more uncompromisingly than in "Fifteen Million Merits," an episode showcasing a society subdued by technologically-enabled spectacle. Echoing the plot of *Metropolis*, the workers of "Fifteen Million Merits" are Taylorist cogs powering a machine-like social system, generating energy through daily cycling duties. For their efforts, merits are awarded to exchange for a range of consumable items: necessities (toothpaste), pleasures (video games/skins for their digital avatars), conveniences (bypassing commercials), and sustenance (food, the bulk of which is referred to as being synthetically produced – it is fuel rather than food). Similar to the populace aboard the space-yacht in *WALL-E*, the workers are delivered an endless stream of entertainment options, ranging from gratuitous pornography to humiliation-oriented reality televisual programs, all to ensure complacent behavior. While the system's highest echelon of elites are not seen, a clearly demarcated division of labor exists. Janitors fitted with yellow attire tend to the workers' area, removing their discarded debris. These janitors appear to occupy the lowest position on the social ladder, given the harsh treatment they receive by some of the workers and, additionally, how they are depicted as disposable villains in the purchasable first-person-shooter video games. Those cycling, while seemingly low in terms of stature in the society as well, are at least afforded opportunities to transcend their social position by exchanging the titular (and rather difficult to obtain) fifteen million merits for a chance to achieve celebrity status through a televised talent show, where a panel of judges ultimately decides their fate. The main character of the episode, Bing Madsen, otherwise known as Cycle 6-324, cares little for it all; it is evident that he is plagued by existential dissatisfaction, and bored with what he designates as stuff and confetti. He exhibits minimal enthusiasm and, despite being perpetually surrounded by people, feels no sense of community or sense of place, at least until he encounters Abi, a fellow cyclist blessed with the ability to sing. He proclaims quite unabashedly that he has yearned for something far more substantial than what his world currently offers, and that Abi's aspirations to be a singer have filled him with inspiration and purpose; moreover, he suggests that others would equally benefit from her gift. Altruistically, he donates his entire lot of merits to her so that she may be given a chance to compete, as she is, in his words, "something real...more than anything that's happened all year." While the harsh realities of this world are made quite clear from the onset, it is not until Abi's trial performance and the judges' subsequent response, however, that the technological foundations of this world are more lucidly revealed.

This society, as a definitive representation of the technological understanding of being, considers all things through an exploitable and malleable lens. Abi, despite seemingly winning the audience's approval with her performance, sees her potential as an inspirational source for communally-enriched meaning instantly repackaged into a purely consumable commodity, specifically as a pornographic superstar. The judges' responses indicate that she was not worthwhile enough of a commodity as a singer, and was therefore forced to abandon her ambition for a different reality of fame. The in-episode audience members themselves are scantly able to respond to this repackaging as a collective, as they are in attendance via avatars, thus nullifying their ability to suitably measure and respond to the reactions of their peers. Rather, they simply accept the repackaging, guided by the panel's recommendation. Furthermore, although in attendance via telepresence, the audience is, in reality, isolated in their in-home quarters, watching the program from afar and being delivered the performance through a *device*, which, following Borgmann's understanding, reduces the performance to nothing more than a mere consumable output. *Hot Shot*, the title of the competition program, particularly through its processes of celebrity production and delivery, shows itself to be utterly in service of this society's technological understanding of being.

The influence that the judges hold is important to note here. In the society depicted in "Fifteen Million Merits," individuals, isolated in their homes and cut off from existentially-meaningful communal engagements, not only overwhelmingly rely on celebrities for entertainment but, also, locate themselves within the celebrity/idol paradigm, echoing concerns of Adorno and Horkheimer, who warned that celebrity figures encourage the celebration of the society that enables their production (1997 [1944]). Immediately prior to Abi's performance, for instance, she is instructed to declare to the viewing audience that she would like to be "as big as Selma one day," an oft-referenced singing sensation who has apparently achieved notable success. Although Abi fakes the aspiration behind the declaration, the mere instruction to state it demonstrates how, in this system, the masses have been rendered "psychologically immature and ... drawn to the magic of these larger-than-life personalities in the same way children identify with and implicitly trust their parents. Mass society has produced a people peculiarly susceptible to these forms of manipulation" (Marshall, 1997, p. 9). Those living in this world view the celebrity-journey as one they themselves can embark upon to escape their proletariat burdens, an observation that particularly resonates as Bing and Abi traverse through the populated green room, and again when viewers are introduced to one of the deciders of Abi's fate, the aptly-named Judge Hope. For those competing in this competition, it's clear that, referencing Marcuse's *One-Dimensional Man*, the promise of celebrity exists as a site of false value and "serves to placate the individual into an acceptance of the modern (unsatisfactory) condition" (ibid, p. 10).

Bing, however, is able to see beyond this ruse and recognize it for what it *is*. While he has been able to overlook this world's existential deficiencies and establish a sort of equilibrium with it, albeit in an unfulfilling fashion, it is only once he observes the complete commodification of his friend, and is subsequently taunted by it, that he finally experiences the aforementioned withdrawing of world and corresponding rejuvenation of place. During an advert documenting Abi's journey from possible singing sensation to pornographic superstar, one which Bing cannot skip due to his (now) insufficient funds, he experiences a complete breakdown, destroying the televisual screens in his living quarters before collapsing in enervating grief. At what is unmistakably Bing's lowest moment, he experiences, similar to Freder in

Metropolis and the captain in *WALL-E*, a moment that provides an opening for *Ereignis*. In particular, while on the floor, he takes note of a shard of glass from his broken televisual screen resting in front of him. At this junction he takes the shard, cuts his hand a bit, but suddenly recognizes a discarded box with the label *cuppliance*. This box, formerly Abi's, contains a liquid substance contestants are required to consume prior to their on-stage performance. The name, no doubt, implies the act of compliance – consuming this beverage seemingly nullifies a contestant's ability to dispute the judges' decision. Although Bing says nothing, the combination of the camera work and shot emphasis, such as the shard and crumbled *cuppliance* box, indicate that Bing has recognized something; the world suddenly appears different. The next scene, as illustrative of this new perspective, opens in darkness before illuminating with incandescent light – it is early morning and Bing is the first one to arrive at the cycling workstation. After logging in and commencing his morning cycling routine, the audience is presented with a brief montage depicting a mishmash of scenes: Bing practicing a dance routine alone in his quarters, Bing cycling with determination, and a series of sacrifices: Bing rations his toothpaste allotment, forgoes spending merits on entertainment, and rather than spend his own merits on food, he instead eats the scraps left behind by his cycling colleagues. It is evident that Bing has a plan and, therefore, a renewed sense of purpose.

Curiously, one image frequently repeats: Bing's avatar continually progressing into a digital horizon as he cycles for merits. Although this repetition is seemingly intended to narratively showcase the merits he compiles over the passage of time, it equally demonstrates a more fundamental phenomenon – *the gathering of place*. Based on the character's earlier utterances and exhibited malaise, he clearly feels detached from this world. Throughout the montage, however, which by its very cinematic nature is predicated on temporality, the audience is able to fathom how a sense of place is gradually forming and being nurtured. Suddenly the tired repetition, monotony, and complete lack of genuine involvement that encapsulated his world have seemingly vanished. Rather, a world of commitment and belonging coalesces around Bing and, while the audience is not yet privileged to his understanding of that place, nor its ultimate endgame, it is clear based on the recurring horizon imagery that this developing sense of place continues to manifest through his own motivated efforts. Both the bike and the merits are of particular note throughout this montage sequence, as they too come to take on newfound significance. The use of these technologies prior to the montage was founded on pure instrumentalism – the bike was employed solely to generate merits, which were subsequently utilized for the reasons aforementioned above (fuel, entertainment, and so on). Although the bike and digital currency have certainly contributed to the fabric of Bing's world, in the referential sense described in the chapter's previous section, only now have they been instilled with existential importance. The merits and bike are now critical components for the fostering and sustaining of his developing sense of place. Whatever he is working towards is evidently driven by his own recognizable ability to use these technologies and to cultivate his own inspired reality by anticipating beyond the horizon. As he pedals the bike, accumulates merits, and ardently pursues the horizon, he showcases a pre-reflective attentiveness to the connection between dwelling, *poiēsis*, and the unveiling of world. Given Bing's tenacious spirit, one could state that he is experiencing *Ereignis* and therefore recovering his true self; "this does not mean returning to some fixed nature, but [rather] accepting our role as the beings to whom our own being, and being in general, makes a difference. This can happen only if we enter into "owndom" that is, there as the realm in which being is an urgent issue for a community" (Polt, 2005, p. 383). Ignited by the tragedy of Abi's potential for community-enriched meaning being stripped away and repackaged into an exploitable commodity, Bing experiences a revival of topological understanding, and has identified a pathway to suitably confront the debilitating nihilism of his world. This nihilism, which one may contend is omnipresent in our own contemporary reality, is argued by Malpas as,

> a denial of the very *topos* in which thinking itself comes to pass; and the possibility of finding a way to think in the face of a such as denial (a denial that refuses to even recognize its character as denial) is thus essentially dependent on maintaining a proper sense of the topological character of thinking, and so of thinking's proper *place*, as well as our orientation within it (2012, p. 97).

This montage is demonstrative of how Bing's understanding of Abi's existential importance, for both himself and his community, acted as a necessary catalyst to revive a topological consideration of place.

Following Bing's eventual accrual of fifteen million merits, he trades them for a slot to compete on *Hot Shot*. Prior to entering the stage for his performance, he informs the show's assistant that he has already consumed his compulsory *cuppliance*, using Abi's crumbled box as evidence. This moment provides the audience insight into Bing's intention and likewise prompts a question: whereas Abi was obedient, acquiescing to the judges' ruling, will Bing triumph by following through on his ambition, whatever that may be? It would seem based on the motivation exhibited throughout the montage sequence that Bing possesses the resilience to follow his culti-vated path. Similar to Abi, Bing also receives the crowd's adoration, at least until he shockingly retrieves the glass shard and points it towards his carotid artery, demanding the attention of the judges and the crowd, refusing to leave until he "says his peace." Once given the blessing of the judges to speak, Bing unleashes a flood of repressed emotions. He asserts that the panel of judges should feel rather than process, creating an overt distinction between humanity and technology, and that they should treat the contestants as peo-ple rather than fodder (or, one might say, resources to be optimized). In his emotion-fueled declaration he laments that nothing in this society is real; the entire world of the workers is nothing more than a simulation, and any-thing considered real is doled out in meager portions, of which Bing notes may actually be necessary, as at this point anything grounded with truth or substance might be too difficult for the populace to handle. He continues by questioning the legitimacy of the system; why are the bikers exerting so much effort for a meaningless existence? It is at this moment that his rant becomes personal – he references Abi, whose tragic situation inspires him to verbally assault the judges, badgering them for their role in promoting such a hollow world. The crowd, either stunned or confused, says nothing. After a few moments of silence, Judge Hope emphatically declares that Bing's per-formance was the most worthwhile moment on the reality program's history. While it may initially appear like a moment of triumph, Bing, like Abi, finds himself enduring a similar repackaging scenario, as Judge Hope states that he would like to offer Bing a slot on one of his streams, which will allow him to rant, rave, and espouse his views twice a week. Through the guidance of Judge Hope, the audience begins to cheer for Bing, pressuring him into accepting the offer.

In accordance with the technological understanding of being, this soci-ety, driven by instrumental reasoning, has, in a rather expedient fashion, systematically engulfed Bing's act of dissent. This society, with its emphasis on spectacle and organized control, mirrors Marcuse's interpretation of the culture industry, which, as John Storey notes, "in its search for profits and cultural homogeneity, deprives 'authentic' culture of its critical function, its mode of negation" (2012 [1997], p. 147). According to Marcuse, any authentic, insoluble core capable of grounding society with limits placed on organization and manipulation, "in an industrial society ... is progressively whittled down by technological rationality" (1991 [1964] p. 66). The process of whittling down, of stripping away anything imbued with authentic meaning occurs by "turning it into yet another saleable commodity" (Storey, 2012 [1997], p. 147). Whereas *Metropolis* and *WALL-E* demonstrate a renewed appreciation for place and place-making practices, and conclude by indicating that this appreciation will continue, this episode of *Black Mirror* denies its prolongation immediately upon its presence being publicly felt. The scene closes, for instance, with Bing standing before an audience cheering for his acceptance of the offer, demanding he conform to the hegemony of this society. As he stares out towards the avatars and absorbs their calls for acquiescence, one judge proclaims, "it beats the bike," to which Judge Hope, replies, "certainly does." This shot of Judge Hope is especially noteworthy, as he displays the expression of an apex predator, one prepared to pounce on its cornered prey. The judges know they have coerced him; despite all his motivations and efforts to recover a sense of meaning in the world, he can do nothing to stem the tide of this technological paradigm, and thus succumbs to its systematic mobilization.

The final scene of the episode depicts Bing, alone, concluding a televised rendition of his earlier performance, now delivered via a device (and thus stripped of authentic meaning) to all those remaining on the bicycles. He makes light of the situation with satire, although satire now unmistakably in service of that paradigm, demonstrating again how, as Marcuse proclaims, works of resistance become "deprived of their antagonistic force, of the estrangement which was the very dimension of their truth. The intent and function of these works have fundamentally changed. If they once stood in contradiction to the status quo, this contradiction is now flattened out" (1991 [1954], p. 64). To conclude his program, Bing announces that he will finally complete the deed he proposed on the stage; he will slash his throat due to the unbearable situation of their shared world. He once again holds the shard towards his neck and declares, "farewell forever ... 'till the same time next week." After the stream has gone offline and Bing is truly alone, he takes the shard of glass, that *thing* which so directly attuned him to a world of effervescent meaning and fervently ignited *Ereignis*, and places it in a protective black case. It is now nothing more than a mere prop for his commodified dissent, a resource-commodity. The episode closes with Bing standing in front of a window in his new, posh apartment, gazing towards a horizon once again. The main difference between the two horizons concerns the latter's eerie stillness. Aside from two birds zipping along, no constituting elements seemingly enter, nor does Bing demonstrate any active motion. He simply stands alone, looking into the still world before him, while the song Abi sang earlier plays non-diegetically before the narrative fades into darkness.

Although this somber ending may invite considerations of *Black Mirror* as a pessimistic program, particularly if compared to the optimistic conclusions of the other two texts explored, *Metropolis* and *WALL-E*, it should rather be situated differently: as reflective of a post-pessimistic perspective, "the understanding that neither an optimistic nor pessimistic attitude is justified due to the lack of alternatives" (Gonnermann, 2019, p. 27). In both the world of *Black Mirror* and the contemporary post-media condition, the omnipresence of the technological understanding of being has seemingly prevailed. This is not a world defined by its darkness and oppression, but rather its despondency and resignation. The truly terrifying conclusion one could draw from *Black Mirror* is not the dystopian world it so astutely predicts, but rather the manner in which this world has already been accepted as inevitable. Echoing Mark Fisher's notion of capitalist realism (2009), the world of *Black Mirror* repeatedly expresses not only how the technological state of being – the ontological foundation of contemporary capitalist societies – eradicates any potential alternatives, but also that both optimism and pessimism are futile positions. The characters, many of which believe they can truly make a difference in this world, eventually realize the ineffectiveness of their ventures and accept their fates. Rather than challenge social hegemony and engage in the meaningful enactment of social change, individuals accommodate themselves within the system, accepting an unsatisfying equilibrium within it. The post-pessimistic perspective of *Black Mirror* echoes two other dystopian works of fiction in the twenty-first century, Kazuo Ishiguro's *Never Let Me Go* and M.T. Anderson's *Feed* (2002), both of which have protagonists who, like Bing, "make themselves comfortable within the conceptual limits offered by the system" (Gonnermann, 2019, p. 37). Considering that the Science Fiction genre is predicated on facilitating the reader's critical faculties, one must question whether this post-pessimistic depiction is paralleled on an extratextual level. Gonnermann proposes that while such texts do cultivate a rather bleak view of society, the genre still has the potential to manifest optimism beyond the diegetic narrative. In particular, she references Iser's notion of "the ideal reader," a term for someone so shocked by the depiction of the dystopian paradigm that they find themselves inspired to participate in the political process. She notes, however, that an alternative response is possible; in accordance with a post-pessimistic outlook, the depicted dystopian future might defeat the reader into further accepting the capitalist-realist paradigm (ibid, p. 38).

If *Black Mirror* is, as stated in the opening lines of this chapter, a broad reflection of contemporary society and its possible trajectory, what responses could one expect? Any reading of the program must acknowledge that technology-as-power is its epicenter, particularly as a systemic paradigm. The program also shows how a revival of *topological thinking* and attentiveness to place-making practices through the motivated use of *things* can instill confidence and purpose, particularly in instances to challenge hegemonically-enabled injustices. However, *Black Mirror* equally inquires whether such a perspective is sustainable in the contemporary age, particularly when faced with totalizing systematic domination.

In Heidegger's late thought, he used the word *Gelassenheit* (releasement) to express openness towards being – a manner in which human beings could suitably use technology in place-bound purposes, yet somehow rebuff its essence and the system it produced and perpetuated. Heidegger proposed that as one gains an understanding of the technological understanding of being and moves to gain a free relation from it, one neither fully embraces it nor resists it (see Heidegger, 1966). Through this approach, the danger of technological thinking is resisted, albeit not in the form of rejection, but rather through acknowledgement; "such a comportment would certainly not relinquish technology ... but would allow the technological to appear as itself a mode of revealing, and yet without things being thereby reviewed only as a resource" (Malpas, 2006, p. 301). Malpas subsequently advises that such a situation is increasingly hard to sustain, particularly as technology-as-power pervades more and more aspects of daily life. Yet, it must be remembered that moments appear that not only invite, but also encourage such releasement (art and tradition being perhaps among the most prominent in contemporary life). Indeed, the reconfiguration of the world through the technological must always include the topological, as "all revealing occurs in and through place" (ibid, p. 302). The manifestation of the world, regardless of whether through a technological paradigm or otherwise, is always topological. Although an outlook of post-pessimism seemingly reigns, it cannot endure forever, as the technological understanding of being is destined to undermine itself via its own inherent tensions; as Malpas states,

> The more the technological covers its own character as a mode of revealing, and so as itself constitutive of a certain place and placing, the more it misunderstands and misrepresents its own character and the more it opens up the possibility of its own breakdown. The technological impulse toward a complete ordering of the world is thus at odds with the very character of the technological as a mode of revealing, as a form of the *Event*, as a happening of place ... so far as the comportment that goes with releasement is concerned, it must itself be a comportment attentive, not only to the *Event*, but also to the *Event* as a happening of place—perhaps as the maintaining of a certain "sense of place." Even in the face of technological ordering, then, place endures—both individually and "historically"—and so, in that endurance, does the possibility for another mode of revealing to come forth endure also (2006, p. 302).

Regardless of whether society is depicted and interpreted through Science Fiction as enduring a dystopian, utopian, or post-pessimistic trajectory, the possibility for phenomenological seeing via *Ereignis* can never remain concealed for too long. The contemporary succumbing to post-pessimism, inspired by the essence of technology, will inevitably endure its own questioning, no doubt inspired by an impromptu awakening to place and place-making practices. To sufficiently address and counter the technological understanding of being, one must therefore attune one's self to a perspective that can account for the *thingly* character of technology in the happening of place, and, concurrently, the happening and saying of being. Such a phenomenological perspective is key for how the world and our place within it can manifest as mattering to us, and therefore be discerned as worth safeguarding and, ultimately, preserving and prolonging.

Bibliography

Adorno, T. & Horkheimer, M. (1997 [1944] *Dialect of Enlightenment*. London, UK: Verso.

Alkon, P. (2002) *Science Fiction Before 1900: Imagination Discovers Technology*. London and New York: Routledge.

Bauman, Z. (2000) *Liquid Modernity*. Cambridge, CA: Polity Press.

Blitz, M. (2014) "Understanding Heidegger on Technology" in *The New Atlantis: A Journal on Technology and Society*, No. 41. Online. Accessed 20/02/2020. Available from: https://www.thenewatlantis.com/publications/under standing-heidegger-on-technology

Borgmann, A. (2009 [1984]) *Technology and the Character of Contemporary Life: A Philosophical Inquiry*. Chicago, IL: University of Chicago Press.

Colomina, B. (1996) "Battle Lines" in Welschman, J. C. (ed.) *Rethinking Borders*. Basingstoke, Hampshire: Macmillan Press LTD.

Cresswell, T. (2009) "Place" in Thrift, N. & Kitchen, R. (eds.) *International Encyclopedia of Human Geography*, Vol. 8, Oxford, UK: Elsevier, pp. 169-177.

Davies, J. (2016) *The Birth of the Anthropocene*. Berkeley, CA: University of California Press.

Delany, S. (1984) *Starboard Wine: More Notes on the Language of Science Fiction*. Pleasantville, NY: Dragon Press.

Dreyfus, H. (2017 [1992]) "Heidegger on the Connection Between Nihilism, Technology, Art, and Politics" in Wrathall, M. (ed.) *Background Practices: Essays on the Understanding of Being*. Oxford, UK: Oxford University Press, pp. 173-197.

Dreyfus, H. (2017 [2003]) "Christianity without Onto-Theology: Kierkegaard's Account of the Self's Movement From Despair to Bliss" in Wrathall, M. (ed.) *Background Practices: Essays on the Understanding of Being*. Oxford, UK: Oxford University Press, pp. 231-246.

Dreyfus, H. & Spinoza, C. (2017 [1997]) "Highway Bridges and Feasts: Heidegger and Borgmann on How to Affirm Technology" in Wrathall, M. (ed.) *Background Practices: Essays on the Understanding of Being*. Oxford, UK: Oxford University Press, p. 198-217.

Evans, A. B. (2009) "Nineteenth Centurty SF" in Bould, M., Butler, A., Roberts, A. & Vint, S. (eds.) *The Routledge Companion to Science Fiction*. London and New York, Routledge, pp. 13 – 22).

Fisher, M. (2009). *Capitalist Realism: Is There No Alternative?* Winchester, UK: Zero Books.

Freedman, C. (2000) *Critical Theory and Science Fiction*. Middletown, Connecticut: Wesleyan University Press.

Giddens, A. (1998) *Conversations with Anthony Giddens: Making Sense of Modernity*. Stanford, CA: Stanford University Press.

Gonnermann, A. (2019) "The Concept of Post-Pessimism in 21st Cenutry Dystopian Fiction" in *The Comparatist*, Vol. 43, pp. 26-40.

Grant S. (2015) "Heidegger's *Augenblick* as the Moment of the Performance" in: Grant S., McNeilly J., Veerapen M. (eds) *Performance and Temporalisation*. London, UK: Palgrave Macmillan.

Hayward, S. (2018 [1996]) *Cinema Studies: the Key Concepts*. Abingdon, Oxon: Routledge.

Heidegger, M. (1996) *Discourse on Thinking*. New York, NY: Harper & Row.

Heidegger, M. (1977 [1962] "The Question Concerning Technology" in Krell, D. F. (ed.) *Martin Heidegger: Basic Writings*. San Francisco, CA: Harper San Francisco, pp. 287-317.

Heidegger, M. (1977 [1954] "Building Dwelling Thinking" in Krell, D. F. (ed.) *Martin Heidegger: Basic Writings*. San Francisco, CA: Harper San Francisco, pp. 323—339.

Johnson, D. K., Marquez, L. P., & Urueña, S. (2020) "Black Mirror: What Science Fiction Does Best" in Johnson, D. K (ed.) *Black Mirror and Philosophy: Dark Reflections*. Hoboken, NJ: Wiley & Sons.

Malpas, J. (2006) *Heidegger's Topology*. Cambridge, MA: MIT University Press.

Malpas, J. (2017 [2012]) *Heidegger and the Thinking of Place: Explorations in the Topology of Being*. Cambridge, MA: MIT University Press.

Marcuse, H. (1991 [1964]) *One-Dimensional Man*. Boston, MA: Beacon Press.

Marshall, P.D. (1997) Celebrity and Cultural Power: Fame in Contemproary Culture. Minneapolis, MN: University of Minnesota Press.

Mattie, S. (2014) "WALL-E on the Problem of Technology" in *Perspectives on Political Science*, Vol. 43, No. 1, p. 12-20.

McLuhan, M. (1994 [1964]) *Understanding Media: The Extension of Man*. Cambridge, MA: MIT Press.

McLuhan, M. (2011 [1962]) *The Gutenberg Galaxy: The Making of Typographic Man*. Toronto, Canada: University of Toronto Press.

McNaughtan, H. (2012) "Distinctive consumption and popular anti-consumerism: The case of Wall*E" in *Continuum: Journal of Media & Cultural Stud-*

ies, Vol 26. No. 5: Wising Up: Revising Mobile Media in an Age of Smartphones, pp. 753-766.

McOmber, J.B. (1999) "Technological Autonomy and Three Definitions of Technology" in *Journal of Communication*, Vol 49. No. 3, pp. 137-153.

Minden, M. & Bachmann, H. (2000) *Fritz Lang's Metropolis: Cinematic Visions of Technology and Fear*. Camden House.

Murphy, G. J. (2009) "Dystopia" in Bould, M., Butler, A., Roberts, A. & Vint, S. (eds.) *The Routledge Companion to Science Fiction*. London and New York, Routledge, pp. 473-477).

Murray, R. L. & Heumann, J. K. (2016) *Monstrous Nature: Environment and Horror on the Big Screen*. Lincoln, NE: University of Nebraska Press.

Polt, R. (2005) "Ereignis" in Dreyfus, H. & Wrathall, M. (eds.) *A Companion to Heidegger*. Malden, MA: Blackwell Publishing.

Posner, R. (2000) "Orwell Versus Huxley: Economics, Technology, Privacy, and Satire" in *Philosophy and Literature*, Vol. 24, No. 1, pp. 1-33.

Prince, C. (2018) "Self-Understanding in the Age of the Selfie: Kierkegaard, Dreyfus, and Heidegger on Social Networks" in Battin, J. M. & Duarte, G. (eds.) *We Need to Talk About Heidegger: Essays Situating Martin Heidegger in Contemporary Media Studies*. Berlin: Peter Lang Verlag.

Schwab, K. (2015) "The Fourth Industrial Revolution: what it means and how to respond" in *Foreign Affairs*. Online. Accessed 20/02/2020. Available from: https://www.foreignaffairs.com/articles/2015-12-12/fourth-industrial-revolution

Sontag, S. (1966) *Against Interpretation and Other Essays*. New York, NY: Picador

Stiegler, B. (2019) *The Age of Disruption: Technology and Madness in Computational Capitalism*. Cambridge, UK: Polity Press.

Storey, J. (2012 [1997]) *Cultural Theory and Popular Culture: An Introduction*, Sixth Edition. Abingdon, Oxon: Routledge.

Taylor, C. (2007) *A Secular Age*. Cambridge, MA: The Belknap Press of Harvard University Press.

Taylor, P. A. & Gunkel, D. (2014) *Heidegger and the Media*. Cambridge, UK: Polity Press.

Telotte, J. P. (1999) *A Distant Technology: Science Fiction Film and the Machine Age*. Hanover, NH: Wesleyan University Press.

Tijmes, P. (2001) "Albert Borgmann: Technology and the Character of Everyday Life" in Achterhuis, H. (ed.) *American Philosophy of Technology: The
Empirical Turn*. Bloomington, IL: Indiana University Press.

Wosk, J. (2010) "Metropolis" in *Technology and Culture*, Vol. 51, No. 2, pp. 403-
408.

Wrathall, M. (2011) *Heidegger and Unconcealment: Truth, Language, and History*.
New York, NY: Cambridge University Press.

White, C. (2005) "Heidegger and the Greeks in Wrathall, M. & Dreyfus, H.
(eds.) *A Companion to Heidegger*. Malden, MA: Blackwell Publishing, pp.
141-155.

Mediated Subjectivities in Postemotional Society
Black Mirror's Nosedive

Hatice Övgü Tüzün

> Loss of conscience due to the satisfactory liberties granted by an unfree society makes for a *happy consciousness* which facilitates acceptance of the misdeeds of this society. It is the token of declining autonomy and comprehension
> (*Marcuse, One-dimensional Man, p. 76*).

Already a cult classic of 21st century TV, *Black Mirror* depicts, in each standalone episode, how modern technology not only disrupts but also circumscribes human life (Martin, p. 16): "the central premise of a *Black Mirror* episode often provides a small – but telling – exaggeration of a trend or phenomenon in contemporary life, usually connected to technological innovation, and usually set not terribly far into the future." In fact, a very striking element in almost every episode is how eerily familiar the world presented on the screen seems. Presumably set in the near future, *Black Mirror* presents dystopian depictions of the world, with emphasis on how man-made technologies are transforming their makers and human relationships. In brief, the series (Sola and Lucena 2016, p.5) "describes how the screen (black mirror) or screens of new technologies have invaded our daily life, modifying us, transforming us, changing us, posing new problems that seem to portend, according to Brooker, black horizons."

Black Mirror's "Nosedive" imagines a world in which our current climate of social media obsession escalates until all of society is engulfed in the pressure to maintain high ratings.[1] In this deceptively utopian world drenched in pastel colors, society is engineered into a new hierarchical system based on popularity, which people desperately try to attain with fake kindness and their carefully curated social media profiles. Thus, the frenzied pursuit of social approval on social media has become a desperate drive to be liked at all costs. Living in a world of 'mediated reality' primarily shaped by digital technology/social media and ruled by 'mediated desires,' the vast majority of people have become voyeuristic consumers of second-hand emotions since almost all emotional phenomena is automized, rehearsed, and planned. Although these people assume they are choosing their lives, it is all staged and the system of control is represented as one which is programmed and controlled without them knowing it. In this chapter, I argue that "Nosedive" offers a memorable illustration of what Stjepan Mestrovic calls "postemotional society" (1997, p. 38) where emotion has been "transformed into a quasi-intellectual phenomenon that makes it suitable for manipulation by self and others." According to Mestrovic (1997, p. xi), "contemporary Western societies are entering a new phase of development in which synthetic, quasi-emotions become the basis for widespread manipulation by self, others, and the culture industry as a whole." As Mestrovic further suggests (1997, p. 57), a postemotional society introduces a new form of bondage to carefully crafted emotions and "values insincere sincerity, synthetic candor, feigned frankness, and affected openness."

The main qualities of this kind of society were presented and critically examined in Herbert Marcuse's seminal *One-Dimentional Man* (1964) which raised (Kellner 1991, p. 15) "the specter of the closing off or "atrophying," of the very possibilities of radical social change and human anticipation." Offering a total critique of contemporary advanced industrial societies, "Marcuse was one of the theorists to analyze the consumer society through analyzing how consumerism, advertising, mass culture, and ideology integrate individuals into and stabilize the capitalist system" (ibid, p. 16). Once they are integrated

---

1   Since 2014, the Chinese Communist Party has been testing a Social Credit System that is quite similar to the one depicted in "Nosedive". This national reputation system monitors citizens' behaviour and trustworthiness; a citizen who is caught breaking the law loses certain rights such as booking a flight and might even be blacklisted. As of 2019 (Kobie), "there is no single nationally coordinated system... and the pilots that do exist don't all work in the same way. So far, taking part in both the private and government versions is technically voluntary; in the future the official social credit system will be mandatory."

into this system, individuals can no longer function as authentic agents in charge of their own destiny, but rather simply become cogs in an omnipresent system that continues to thrive at their own cost. As Kellner further remarks, *One-Dimentional Man* continues to be relevant

> because of its grasp of the underlying structures and tendencies of contemporary socio-economic and political development. The scientific and technological rationalities that Marcuse describes are even more powerful today with the emergence of computerization, the proliferation of media and information, and the development of new techniques and forms of social control (ibid).

A person can only 'choose' when they are in control of herself whereas in this kind of society the vast majority of people are co-opted into the system and seem to be placidly content with, what Marcuse would call, their "democratic unfreedom."

As early as 1964, Marcuse made the astute observation that "[o]ur society distinguishes itself by conquering the centrifugal social forces with Technology rather than by Terror, on the dual basis of an overwhelming efficiency and an increasing standard of living" (p. 40), adding that the containment of social change "is perhaps the most singular achievement of advanced industrial society" (p. 42). Within this framework, widespread affluence runs parallel to the repression of consciousness in society:

> as the project unfolds, it shapes the entire universe of discourse and action, intellectual and material culture. In the medium of technology, culture, politics and the economy merge into an omnipresent system which swallows up or repulses all alternatives. The productivity and growth potential of this system stabilize the society and contain technical progress within the framework of domination. Technological rationality has become political rationality (p. 44).

Marcuse did not live to see the rise of Internet, digital technologies, or social media, yet his critical thought and concepts (Fuchs 2016, p. 116) "are still well-suited to be one of the methodological foundations for a critical theory of the Internet, digital and social media." The continuing relevance of Marcuse's analysis is aptly illustrated in "Nosedive" where a new type of order has seemingly absorbed all opposition and exerted near-complete control over the thoughts and actions of people. Since dynamics of change and renewal are stifled in this society, people seem to be stuck in a rut, unable to open up to different and/or critical points of view. With the rise of digital technologies, the degree of control seems to have intensified rather than weakened. Thus, the "postemotional type" is ironically the captive of their own technological affluence which she cannot control.

The "postemotional type" of this era can also be considered an extension of David Riesman's "other-directed type," described as (Mestrovic 1997, p. xi) "a powerless inside-dopester whose emotional life has been reduced mostly to curdled indignation and being 'nice'." The other-directed types subject themselves "to the jury of their peers" (ibid, p. 44); they are cosmopolitan yet "at home everywhere and nowhere, capable of a rapid if sometimes superficial intimacy with and response to everyone" (ibid, p. 47). The central character of "Nosedive," Lacie Pound, is a perfect example of the postemotional/ other-directed type who "takes cues from peers and the media as to when he or she should rationally choose to exhibit a vicarious indignation, niceness or other pre-packaged emotions" (ibid, pp. xii-xii). Lacie is initially introduced as an ambitious young woman who derives her sense of personal value and self-worth from her smartphone, like almost everyone else she interacts with. Seemingly at home and content with living in a "climate of affected, feigned emotion, as if it were rehearsed and planned ahead of time" (ibid, p. 13), she is overly nice to people who all appear to be blissfully ignorant of the fact that they are caught up in a system that has destroyed their individuality. In an environment where relationships are mediated by screens and apps, nobody is free to be their authentic selves. Lacie's greatest desire in life is to increase her overall rating so that she can have enough credits to move into her 'dream' home. Although she enthusiastically seizes the unexpected opportunity to give a speech as Maid of Honor at her top-rated friend Naomi's wedding, she takes a 'nosedive' and hits rock bottom when she encounters a series of unfortunate events on her way there. In the final scene, Lacie is locked up in a cell, opposite another detainee with whom she starts trading insults. Ironically, it is only after she is forcefully removed from the 'system' and thrown in jail that she seems to find some semblance of authenticity.

Mestrovic (ibid, p. 4) argues that postemotionalism occurred during a time in Western history "that most social forecasters thought would be characterized by the end of ideology, the end of history, the triumph of democratic ideals, post-industrialization, and the end of racism, sexism, and other forms of oppression." Mestrovic (ibid, p. 13) also observes that several things are new in this era:

> (1) The camera is now ubiquitous and therefore makes all these emotional phenomena potentially staged, artificial, and second-hand. (2) What David Reisman called other-directed 'inside-dopesterism' is also a ubiquitous mode of consuming information nowadays, thereby transforming most persons into voyeuristic consumers of these second-hand emotions. (3) Even twenty years ago, there were no full-time, professional 'opinion-makers' or 'newsmakers.' (...) By contrast, the 1990s is the age of live newsmaking created by persons designed as *newsmakers* whose impact is gauged almost as quickly by opinion polls, which are immediately refracted by designated opinion-makers and whose impact is gauged almost as quickly by opinion polls, which are broadcast back to the inside-dopesters. It is difficult to conceive of the possibility of feeling a genuine, spontaneous emotion in such a social structure. (4) Finally, in all of the illustrations that have been examined, and others that the reader can supply, one cannot help suspecting a climate of affected, feigned emotion, as if it were rehearsed and planned ahead of time.

"Nosedive" presents a perfect illustration (as well as extension) of postemotional society as defined by Mestrovic. The omnipresent social media platform has infiltrated all realms of life and all interactions are mediated through its filter; all people wear a digital contact lens connected to their phone's rating app. It is a world wherein every action and interaction, be it online or offline, is ranked. The interface this society is using resembles apps like Facebook and Instagram, but it has a rating system of one to five stars instead of a 'heart' or a 'like.' No one is allowed to avoid rating and being rated, and one's 'score' determines their social position. In this modern cast system, a high score provides better access to all kinds of services and, by extension, lifestyles whereas a lower score leads to marginalization and sometimes even ostracization.

As Francois Allard-Huver and Julie Escurignan maintain (2018, p. 115), this world is a panopticon in which "mobile devices and social media serve as 'disciplinary' tools to normalize people's behavior. Citizens experience a new relationship with the media and the ensuing social order, theorized by Jansson as 'interveillance.'" Thus, the logic of surveillance is substituted with a culture of interveillance (ibid, p. 122): "As mediated social interaction and the instantaneous circulation of images and opinions collapse into reined participatory techniques for consumer monitoring, the classical Big Brother model of top-down surveillance is intertwined with a number of other, increasingly interactive forms of mediated control, some of which are marked by a high degree of social complicity even pleasurable and/or empowering engagement". In "Nosedive," interveillance has become systematic and hierarchical since the place of all individuals in society is entirely determined by this score. Consequently, everyone has become compliant with surveillance culture based on peer-rating (ibid, p. 122).

Representing the average person, Lacie too spends most of her time engaging in 'socially appropriate' performative acts such as taking, posting, and liking pictures. In the opening scene, we see her jogging and exercising while she obsessively rates other people with five stars. She lives in a suburban neighborhood wherein all the houses look the same. She habitually 'likes' everybody else's stuff, hoping that they will like hers in return. Next, she takes selfies and posts content that will get her more attention and 'likes.' Lacie wants so badly for everyone to up vote her that she is always giving out a five-star rating. She lives in a neat little flat with her brother, Ryan, who acts like an anchor point for her since he shows almost no concern with the rating system and constantly mocks Lacie's obsession with it. Yet even the cynical Ryan needs some ratings to 'exist' within the system and he gets them from his gaming friends. Ryan is clearly portrayed as the antithesis of Lacie and challenges the way she sees the world.

Throughout "Nosedive," we are presented with several incidents which illustrate that Lacie's perception of the world and herself in it is deeply skewed. For instance, we see her making pointless small talk in the lift with a woman she barely knows, yet pretends to like. In another scene, she practices her smile in front of a mirror several times until she gets it 'perfect.' As Lacie's actions show, this is a world in which people-pleasing has become the norm at the price of sincerity and authenticity in human relationships. In the words of Mestrovic (1997, p. 57), "Postemotional society has reached a phase in its development in which it values insincere sincerity, synthetic candor, feigned frankness, and affected openness." Although their values are clearly misplaced, the postemotional characters in "Nosedive" show no visible signs of discontent or unhappiness. It is, in fact, their avoidance, denial, and complete lack of awareness that enable the system to continue without any major opposition. The sheer lack of any resistance or rebellion on the part of citizens to an absurdly hollow, fake, and conformist lifestyle supports Mestrovic's point that (ibid, p. 146) "postemotionalism holds the potential for degenerating further into an entirely new form of totalitarianism, one that is so 'nice' and charming that it cannot lead to indignation or rebellion."

Like many others in this society, Lacie conflates her score with her personal value, so her sense of self-worth depends almost entirely on the rating system. 'Successful' social interactions are what mean the most to her since other people's appraisal of her determines her rating. As Pagnoni Berns points out (2018, p. 268), "reliance on forms of mediated relationships is the basis of "Nosedive." With Lacie, every single move is carefully examined and 'rehearsed' before it is presented to the world. Unable to express herself naturally or spontaneously, she practices almost all of her actions, gestures, and words before she presents herself to other people in the world. While sitting in a cafe, she carefully takes a bite of her cookie (at which she frowns and proceeds to spit out) and places it next to her latte (which she later tastes and does not like), but she does not show her real feelings (about the cookie or the latte) to her followers. Instead, she shows them the perfect (though unreal) side of things and posts a photo with the caption "Brushed suede w/ cookie. Heaven." Like the majority of people living in this society, Lacie obsessively posts pictures and videos in order to impress others by projecting herself in a way that is not true to who she is or what she really feels. Everything in her life is filtered through rose-colored glasses before being put online. As Mestrovic maintains (1997, p. 115), "This process of synthetically inducing emotions is integral to the existence of postemotional societies."

Lacie's current ambition is to move to the stylish Pelican Cove, and the agent who is trying to sell Lacie a new apartment in this complex informs her that she can get a 20% discount if she gets her score up to 4.5. One's ability to get a discount on a house depends on one's 'score,' which means that getting a higher rating is systematically enforced as it is tied to the economy. Lacie acts like a typical contemporary consumer who, according to Mestrovic (1997, p. 81), is not just a mass society automaton, as Adorno claimed, "but [rather] an agent convinced that he or she possesses some degree of freedom to choose group identities, and this belief makes the agent a target of manipulation by corporations who pitch advertisements in relation to specific subgroup versions of emotional reality." Mesmerized by the holographic images that depict her living out her dream, Lacie is almost immediately caught up in the fantasy that her life will be much better if she improves her rating and moves to Pelican Cove. In order to achieve this higher score, Lacie seeks the assistance of a professional consultant who advises her on how to increase her rating. She is unable to see that she is *conditioned* to have the desires that she has and that she unwittingly contributes to the perpetuation of a system that interpellates her as an automaton.

Possessed by a very strong desire to improve her current 4.2 score in order to have access to the Prime Influencers Program, Lacie then decides to get back in touch with her former friend, Naomi (a 4.5 influencer), who asks Lacie to be the Maid of Honor in her upcoming wedding. This reunion can be classified as orchestrated at best since both girls see benefit in this exchange. Getting invited to speak at her childhood friend's wedding in front of a large group of quality, that is 'high-rated' people, gives Lacie the opportunity to get a boost that would bring her score up to a 4.5, whereas Naomi wants Lacie to speak at her wedding because the authenticity of having a 4.2 to speak works really well for her image. When her brother Ryan reminds Lacie how she was wronged by Naomi in the past and questions her motivations for going to the wedding, Lacie snaps at him in her habitual self-delusion, saying (Brooker and Jones 2018, p. 135), "Naomi and I were best friends. I wish her well and wanna express in the best I can. And yeah, if I nail the speech and get five-starred by hundreds of primes, so what, it's a win-win."

Fake Culture/Fake People in the Postemotional World

Drawing on David Reisman's seminal work, *The Lonely Crowd*, Mestrovic identifies (1997, p. 1) "curdled indignation" and "a carefully managed niceness" as the two most dominant quasi-emotions in post-emotional society. Poste-motionalism entails (Mestrovic 1997, p. 44) "the manipulation of emotions by self and others into a bland, mechanical, mass-produced yet oppressive ethic of niceness." Since the system has conditioned people to continually aspire towards higher ratings, which depends on them having social approval, everybody in "Nosedive" *seems* to be nice. Scene after scene, we encounter people from all walks of life *appearing* to be nice towards others in order to get good ratings. However, the dark side of this "carefully managed niceness" is "curdled indignation" (ibid, p. 1) which can have very serious consequences for those who become targets.

Early in the episode, we encounter Lacie's co-worker, Chester, who is literally forced to become an outsider following his break-up with his boy-friend. Although he tries quite desperately to be re-admitted to society by *being extra-nice*, such as by giving out smoothies to everyone in the office, people avoid him as though he were infected. Lacie, too, joins the herd by giving him a low score mainly because she is terrified of having her own score lowered if she is nice to him. In a world where everyone feels pressured to conform, no one can choose their own emotional responses and actions. As this example shows, the "other-directed" type is heavily co-dependent on social approval and thus cannot practice any (authentic) agency. As Mestrovic maintains (1997, p. 146), "Postemotional society is made possible by a social character that succeeded Riesman's other-directedness in which the bulk of people's emotional reactions have been reduced to being 'nice' ver-sus 'indignant.'" Unable to emote spontaneously, these people are estranged from their own true impulses and feelings, which they are conditioned to suppress. They are not devoid of emotions, but rather experience emotions that do not necessarily belong to them since in their world (Mestrovic 1997, p. 38) "[e]motion has now been transformed into a quasi-intellectual phenome-non that makes it suitable for manipulation by self and others."

Lacie ends up going down the same path as Chester, following a series of unfortunate events that lower her score. One poor rating causes her to nosedive as she experiences a snowball effect. Before she leaves for Naomi's wedding, Lacie has a fight with her brother who down votes her. Upon walk-ing out, she bumps into a girl with coffee who unfortunately happens to be a 4.9. Down voted by this girl and late for her ride, she gets another down vote for making her driver wait and being annoying in the cab. Once she is at the airport, Lacie discovers that she is bumped from her flight because of overbooking and has an argument with the airline employee who down votes her for her rash attitude. Soon after, a military officer, armed and decked out in military gear, comes out to Lacie informing her that she is guilty of "intimidation and profanity." In a few seconds, Lacie finds herself docked a whole point and on double damage and thus loses any chance of getting a flight. The incident at the airport causes her rating to drop down to a 3.1, which means that Lacie will not be able to go to the wedding. However, Lacie refuses to accept defeat and tries to find another way to get there before it is too late. Unfortunately, her downward spiral continues when she gets another low rating from an attendant at the charging station for complaining about the electric car she is given. Her journey keeps going from bad to worse as her car battery dies and no one will help her. Stranded in the middle of nowhere with her suitcase, she decides to hitchhike as a last resort. By the time Lacie arrives at the wedding and literally crashes into the party, she is dirty, worn out, and on the brink of a nervous breakdown.

Escape into Authenticity?

Is autonomy possible in a world where human emotions are widely manipulated and agency is almost non-existent? Although the general tone of "Nosedive" is admittedly bleak, the episode offers two (underdeveloped) characters as 'glitches' in the system. The ending of the episode, when Lacie has a cathartic experience during and after the wedding party, could also be interpreted as pointing to possible paths towards (at least some semblance of) agency. Yet it would be far-fetched to argue that "Nosedive" presents a hopeful view regarding the possibility of exercising personal sovereignty in a surveillance-based economic order wherein the human condition is augmented in unprecedented ways. In the words of Mestrovic (1997, p. 66),

> Autonomy is nearly impossible for the other-directed type who has become the postemotional type. The escape routes have been blocked. Who can mobilize resistance against nice and happy villains? In the society without opposition (from Marcuse), the group surveillance has become too sophisticated, the camera has become omnipresent, the packaging of emotions has become too standardized, and everyone must become a politician and must navigate the opinion-makers as he or she goes through life. The possibility of autonomy seems to be closed.

Despite the rather gloomy state of affairs, Mestrovic (ibid, p. 75) also offers a glimmer of hope since, "[t]he authentic has not been completely eclipsed in contemporary times. Pockets of authenticity have survived despite postmodernism, other-directedness, postemotionalism, and other trends that seem to work against it". In "Nosedive," "the authentic" is represented by the truck driver, Susan (with her score of 1.4), and Lacie's brother, Ryan. These two individuals raise important questions and voice criticism about the system, thus providing alternative viewpoints. Previously a 4.6 citizen, Susan loses her faith in the system when her 4.3 husband's hospital bed is given to a 4.4. The trauma of her husband's consequent death wakes Susan out of her stupor, leading her to choose a relatively 'free' life as a truck driver. Although Ryan has not (as of yet) dropped as low as Susan on the social scale, he too is highly critical of the superficiality of manners and emotions that people exhibit in order to get higher scores. Acutely cynical of his older sister's ambition of moving to the upscale gated community, Ryan boldly ridicules the fantasy they are trying to sell her (Brooker and Jones 2018, p. 138): "Pelican Cove... What is this, a eugenics program?... No one's this happy. A two-year-old with a fuckin' balloon isn't this happy." However, Lacie remains completely blind to the fact that her desires are not even her own, that she – like millions of others – is conditioned to desire certain things by a system that is specifically engineered to keep people ignorant. The goal of being content will never be achieved in this lifestyle since people are put on a hedonic treadmill, conditioned to have new desires incessantly.

Mestrovic observes that (1997, p. 91) "in the postemotional age emotions are not forgotten and are not 'worn away.' Because catharsis is often blocked due to the over-rationalization of social life, it seems that postemotional types remain traumatized for life." Alienated from their own true nature and impulses, the majority of people in "Nosedive" remain blissfully ignorant of their pathology. Lacie, on the other hand, moves in a different direction from her obsession with improving her rating, thus boosting her social standing takes a toll on her psychology. In the wedding party scene towards the end of the episode, we see that Lacie is done with putting on a performance for people. She is instead yelling at everyone and being assertive, finally able to rant about all of Naomi's wrongdoings. As Mestrovic (1997, p. 150) suggests, "postemotionalism is a system designed to avoid emotional disorder, to prevent loose ends in emotional exchanges, to civilize 'wild' arenas of emotional life; and, in general, to order the emotions so that the social world hums as smoothly as a well-maintained machine." Therefore, it hardly comes as a surprise that Lacie's emotional outburst at the wedding leads to her 'removal' from civilised society.

After the wedding, Lacie's rating becomes so low it is basically non-existent and she is put in prison, both for trespassing and for her violent performance at the wedding. Although counter to her initial desires, her complete

'ruin' is at the same time a 'gift' since it becomes the road to her transformation. Her breakdown, in other words, leads to a breakthrough; it is only when
her deluded ego is released that her 'authentic' self emerges. Once her digital
contact lenses are taken out, Lacie starts to see the world in a completely different light. Instead of fake people on their devices in a setting of artificial
peacefulness, she is looking at dust particles in the air, which signifies her
change of perspective and appreciation for an entirely different view of life.
Carefully observing the dust particles, Lacie laughs and we know that this
time her laugh is genuine. She also cries authentic tears, unlike the ones she
shed when she was practicing for her speech. Severing her last connection to
the artificial society she was trying so hard to be a part of, she takes off her
dress and is left just wearing her bra. Lacie and the man opposite her in the
prison cell are free to say whatever they want without consequence, showing
us that these two people in their prison cells are more free than those in this
world. In a fit of unrestrained and genuine fury, Lacie expresses real feelings
and seems liberated. In this final scene, "Nosedive" reiterates the point that
societal pressure is a kind of prison and the more it takes over, the less your
individual expression can exist because you are preoccupied with trying to
conform to what everybody else wants you to be. Undoing the delusions and
performing different actions are what leads Lacie to become liberated from
her conditioning. In their conditioned state people live on autopilot, whereas
authenticity brings open-hearted connection.

As Mestrovic (1997, p. 67) points out, "Postemotional authoritarianism of
the peer group presents such a 'nice,' friendly, happy, and tolerant face that it
prevents traditional types of rebellion." Once the watchful 'eyes' of others are
removed from the picture, Lacie feels free to 'rebel' in all of the ways that had
hitherto been prohibited for her. Yet, to what extent can this be considered
a 'victory' against the system? In their Baudrillardian reading of "Nosedive,"
Erika Thomas and Romin Rajan (2018, p. 495) argue that

> [a]lthough there is no real resolution to the larger questions of the social
> media score or Lacie's future in this culture, the ending note of the episode
> reveals Lacie's freedom from the hyperreal even though she is physically con-
> fined to a cell, producing a sense of hope and optimism for the audience.

However, "Lacie's emancipation and ability to see simulation for what it is
not an epiphany of dystopian reality or a transcendence of simulation, but

simulation itself" (ibid, p. 496). In other words, the representation of escaping the simulation only furthers the simulation since there is no longer a 'real' world to which Lacie can return.

Conclusion

The majority of people in "Nosedive" seem to be persona-bound. They are unable to transcend this state because they are locked in a simulated reality where they live as 'happy slaves,' very much content in their total lack of awareness. They are captivated by their ego construct, or rather by a sense of an idealized image of the (false) self, created by societal norms. To put it briefly, hiding (their "real" self) has become a way of *being in the world*. In the words of Mestrovic (1997, p. 81), "the masses are too happy to know that they are manipulated." Everything in their world is so clean and perfect, they simply cannot see how artificial their world is in terms of social interaction, materialism, and how this lifestyle is one big product being sold to them. The social system in which they live has clearly eroded the inner resources from which they draw their sense of identity, autonomy, and moral judgment, as well as their ability to think critically, resist, and revolt. Free will is clearly non-existent within this framework.

According to Michael Meade (2012, p. 55),

> If our identity can be determined by other people and shaped by forces outside ourselves, then our sense of self will be like a colourful item that we purchase in the market place of life and simply tie onto our bodies... Without a genuine feeling for an inner life, we become increasingly hollow and subject to exaggerated fears. Lacking a true identity, we become subject to those who cleverly manipulate the marketplace as well as the political process.

Personal sovereignty cannot exist in a society where one's score determines one's overall value as a human being. Heavily conditioned to seek approval and validation from everyone, people living in such a society can only exist as peons in a system which is clearly designed to obstruct the path of self-development. In this sense, "Nosedive" explores the possible consequences we might be faced with when societal expectations concerning personality and values preside over or suppress individual autonomy.

In the words of Martin (no date, p. 18), *Black Mirror* "presents itself as a series of cautionary tales, not only warning us about where we might be heading, but also alerting us to where we already are, and to what is already brewing inside our heads, our hearts and our computers". From this perspective, "Nosedive" not only offers us a glimpse into the (near) future, but also encourages us to think about our present circumstances at a time when the human condition is largely being shaped by rapid technological change. Writing about highly-developed industrial societies, Marcuse (1964, p. 43) remarks,

> Technology serves to institute new, more effective, and more pleasant forms of social control and social cohesion [...] In the face of the totalitarian features of this society, the traditional notion of the "neutrality" of technology can no longer be maintained. Technology as such cannot be isolated from the use to which it is put; the technological society is a system of domination which operates already in the concept and construction of techniques.

Drawing on Marcuse's observations, one could argue that Post-emotional society marks the culmination of this trend since technology, particularly in the form of digital media, is put in the service keeping the whole population under control. Because the system of domination is not implemented or maintained by means of more apparent totalitarian methods, the vast majority of people remain unaware that they are heavily 'sedated' and controlled. In this context, order in society is instituted through what Marcuse calls "pleasant forms of social control and social cohesion" and not by means of openly dictatorial or militaristic forms of 'hard power'. If anything, this form of control that employs seemingly – 'harmless' yet highly-addictive digital technologies is even more dangerous because it operates in very covert and sinister ways. As I have argued throughout this chapter, a very subtle challenge we are currently facing is the various ways in which our emotions and behaviours are widely manipulated. Noting that Marcuse was right about happy consciousness producing a society without opposition, Mestrovic suggests (1997, p. 153), "But progress has also ruined the emotional palate and made social life bland and nearly dead. No matter how one feels about such progress, its course apparently cannot be reversed."

Considering the above, "Nosedive" presents a fictional dystopian world at a time when monumental technology has taken over our lives. This world strongly resonates with our era since an increasing number of people today are questioning the impact of social media on our mental health and well-being, as well as what it means for democracy. Like almost every other episode in the series, "Nosedive" invites us to think critically about the present by means of showing us where current trends are headed in the not-so-distant future. After all, it is only by changing some fundamental things about the ways we perceive the world that we can create better alternatives.

Bibliography

Allard-Huver, F and Escurignan, J 2018, "Black Mirror's 'Nosedive' as a New Panopticon", in AM Cirucci and B Vacker (eds.), *Black Mirror and Critical Media Theory*, Lexington Books, Maryland. pp.113-138.

Berns, FGP 2018, "Spectacular Tech-Nightmare" in AM Cirucci and B Vacker (eds.), *Black Mirror and Critical Media Theory*, Lexington Books, Maryland. pp. 260-281.

Brooker, C and Jones, A 2018, *Inside Black Mirror*, Crown Archetype, New York.

Cirucci, AM. and Vacker, B (eds), *Black Mirror and Critical Media Theory*, Lexington Books, Maryland.

Fuchs, C (2016), *Critical Theory of Communication*, University of Lexington Press, London.

Kobie, N (2019), 'The Complicated truth about China's social credit system' *Wired* 07 June. wired.co.uk

Marcuse, H 1964 (1991) *One-Dimentional Man* (Introduction by Douglas Kellner), Beacon Press, Boston.

Martin, A n.d., "Cautionary Reflections: Looking into *Black Mirror*" *Screen Education* No: 90. www. screeneducation.com.au

Meade, M 2012, *Fate and Destiny: The Two Agreements of the Soul*, Greenfire Press, Seattle.

Mestrovic, S. 1997, *Postemotional Society*, Sage, London.

Sola, JC and Martinez-Lucena, J 2016, "Screen Technologies and the imaginary of punishment: A reading of Black Mirror's 'White Bear'", *Empedocles: European Journal of Communication*, Volume 7, no. 1, pp. 3-22.

Thomas, EM and Rajan, R 2018, "Trapped in Dystopian Techno Realities", in AM Cirucci and B Vacker (eds.), *Black Mirror and Critical Media Theory*, Lexington Books, Maryland. pp. 480-503.

Zuboff, S 2019, *The Age of Surveillance Capitalism: The Fight for a Human Future at the New Frontier of Power*, PublicAffairs, New York.

Nosedive and the "Like" Dystopia
A Reflection on Black Mirror

Santiago Giraldo-Luque, Ricardo Carniel Bugs & Santiago Tejedor

Nosedive: Failure of the Community

The TV series *Black Mirror* criticizes and questions human behavior in relation to its interaction with digital technologies and questions the technological systems themselves that have transformed daily life, so studying
this series is a much-needed task. In reality, the series subjects the viewer,
although mediated by an entertainment screen, to their own reality; this is
a reality, however, already determined by technology and by the conception
of technology itself as a means of domination and social control. The individual of the second decade of the 21st century is isolated, has no interest in
criticizing his/her own way of life which revolves around comfort, nor even
wants to question the use of technology itself (Beller, 2006; Turkle, 2019). The
metaphor of the title of the series is perfect: It is a mirror, but in that mirror,
which is black, no one is able to recognize him or herself.

Thus, the horizon of work on *Black Mirror* forces us to reflect upon the
technological transformation of everyday life. In the supposed and imaginary utopian world of the late 20th century, information and communication technologies were thought to bring us, in the 21st century, a more democratic, community-oriented, and more integrated world. Society would
progress and the Internet (not social networks) would be a tool for inclusion
and development based on access to a universe of possibilities, knowledge,
collective construction (Levy, 2002), and new perspectives for social mobilization (Castells, 2012).

However, the dot-com crisis of 1999-2000 and the economic crisis of
2008, destroyed the false, imaginary world of an open society and allowed

the crudest type of capitalism to take hold of the Internet through oligopolistic platforms. Large companies seized control of a substantial part of people's clicks on the Internet, converting individuals into unknowing workers who fill their platforms with content for free. Users, with their clicks and Internet behaviors, insidiously become the new merchandise of the information society: data. The collaborative web scenario (O'Reilly & Battelle, 2009) is no longer presented as a world of collective creation, but as a new economic model applied to the digital world that would reorder and hierarchize the first postulate of the Internet in which all users would participate on equal terms.

The new dominant platforms expand their domain through control of people's devices as managers and collectors of data (Mayer-Schönberger & Kenneth, 2013). They also connect with the individual on an emotional level and through the addictive options of social recognition (Palihapitiya, in Wong, 2017). These dominant platforms, the emotional framework, and the permanent addiction to devices, create the perfect setting for the development of the analysis of "Nosedive," an episode of *Black Mirror*.

"Nosedive" focuses on the emotional and contagious appeal of behaviors on social networks. Lacie, the protagonist, fed by the emotions and intention of wanting to be what the system dictates individuals must become, reconstructs her social behaviors to adapt to the new demands of popularity which allow users to access benefits, thus denoting a highly stratified society.

The objectives of "Nosedive" are established on the basis of three dimensions. The first defines a dialogue about the series' own capacity as a critical platform of the real world, based on a fictional production. The second denounces the introduction of a sophisticated systemic power which determines social action as it evolves with the individual's own personal actions, without being coerced into doing so. Finally, the third dimension analyzes the narrow world of social networks as a destructive force of everything that is considered social in exchange for the exaltation of vanity, of absolute individualization, of the banal and the hypocritical and, above all, of the absence of communication, as understood from a discursive perspective (Habermas, 1996). In the discursive theory of law and democracy, Habermas develops his theory of communicative action, in which argumentative or discursive reason is stated as a logical principle of intersubjectivity. For Habermas (1996), the logics of rational and intersubjective argumentation – the argumentative discourse itself – works as a mechanism of social consensus building.

The absence of discursive communication, as showed in the technological universe of *Black Mirror*, is the key point of the third dimension of the analysis proposed.

The Mirror-Reflection of what is Real

"Nosedive," the first episode of the third season of *Black Mirror*, begins with a suggestion to the viewer of an ideal image of a neighborhood. Different technical aspects such as the lighting and tonality of the shots, the colors of the houses and other locations, as well as the costume design of the characters, contribute to the feeling of a happy, peaceful, almost bucolic environment, in which harmony predominates among the people who dwell there. Unlike other episodes of the same series in which virtual experiences through screens replace, partially or totally, the corporal contact between people – such as "Fifteen Million Merits" (Season 1) or "Striking Vipers" (Season 5) – "Nosedive" proposes a coexistence that is simultaneously face-to-face *and* digital, whereby the characters may look each other in the eye on an elevator while they send their impressions via mobile, as if they were dealing with another social convention: the need (almost an obligation) to digitally value a person during, or just after, physical interaction.

The first few minutes of the episode introduce a sort of utopia. However, when we are introduced to a technological system that plays a relevant role as a filter mechanism awarding only "the best," coupled with the protagonist, Lacie Pound, rehearsing fake smiles in front of a mirror and exchanging artificial ratings with other characters, it is clear that the approach to society portrayed by the writers is more critical. That said: is what is presented in "Nosedive" truly a dystopia?

When a person acts in accordance with the sole purpose of pleasing others, of being recognized by a "like," or a heart-shaped button, or any other icon bearing a positive charge, the dystopia noted in "Nosedive" reflects nothing more than the reality of the current world of social networks: it is a mirror, almost without distortion. This episode also highlights the collection and concentration of social interactions on a monopolistic platform. This episode shows a single network – Zuckerberg's Empire? Why not? – that dominates and determines all social interactions and ultimately guides the characters' decisions and actions.

Despite the open discourse on information (globalized and accessible through the Internet), the concentration is greater (Frank, 1999). In the social media platform presented in "Nosedive," which decides the social universe and the qualifications of a person, the paradox is clear. The application – without doing anything else than being a mediator – is presented as a place to share personal information, and as a place wherein everyone can feel part of what is happening in the world. But all social information and interactions – are concentrated in a single channel. This dispositive (see Foucault, 1979) on the one hand, controls the flow of information that circulates through its platform and, on the other hand, recycles the information (data) free of charge from user-consumers to build processes of prediction-submission in the characters of the episode, from a house in a perfect neighborhood to a better job (O'Neil, 2017). It particularly underscores the idea of attention as an element which determines internal and external decision-making on the part of the individual (Giraldo-Luque and Fernández-Rovira, 2020). The monopoly of larger companies hints at the performance of an interactive system (the platform, the device) as oligopolistic spaces fed by individual actions themselves.

Thus, *Black Mirror* (distributed by Netflix, one of the dominant platforms in the world which offers audiovisual entertainment) and the episode "Nosedive," in particular, present a critique of contemporary society through a scenario which, while fictionalized, describes a not-so-distant future. In a way, the framework of the show camouflages or even hides the mirror of reality, which the series represents. The platform acquires the guise of a protective interface, enabling a scenario which is seemingly controlled by the viewer (Žižek, 2010). On the platform, and on the individualized reproductive device, the user can embody monsters and express fears (Perceval, 2015) without being afraid, since such action is carried out within a sheltered environment: the framework of fiction.

On Netflix, this effect is quite evident. The user (or client) has the illusion of controlling their interactions with the platform: the titles they want to see, the hours they spend in front of the screen, and the exact moment in which they decide to turn off the device. But the interface itself can be understood as a control device, as outlined by Foucault (1979), insofar as it can keep the user unaware of the representation of their own reality. Fictional reality anesthetizes individual consciousness (Ferrés, 1996). The user is not able to establish – or avoids establishing – a relationship between what is seen on the screen and the actual daily practices which are evidently caricatured in *Black Mirror*, especially in "Nosedive." Users are not able to recognize themselves, or even to see themselves represented in their own (black) mirror.

By analyzing this episode, we can identify different and actual behavioral traits caricatured in the series. One is the exchange of expectations. "Nosedive" portrays the characteristic action of the interested "game" of giving in order to receive. Almost every character in the episode clearly behaves in an artificial or hypocritical way in the hope that others will rate them with five stars, the highest score. They smile and are kind, while being motivated by the reward they expect to receive from their interlocutors. Just as in our present day, they simulate constant happiness through their devices with the aim of pleasing others in order to obtain followers, instead of real friends. The "likes" obtained act as emotional rewards and indicators of social acceptance (Burrow and Rainone, 2017; Solon, 2017).

Similarly, but on the opposite side of the 'flattery exchange,' the characters' dread at being related to other profiles that have a bad rating is explicitly represented, such as in the scene wherein a co-worker of Lacie's is ignored and discriminated against by the others due to his low score. At first, Lacie decides to support her co-worker with a discreet assessment, but once she observes that this gesture has a negative impact on her own rating, she chooses to avoid this colleague. Social pressure (physical and virtual) ends up making the digital avatar, and its status on the network, prevail over the human being and their real circumstances.

The episode also reflects the irrational and compulsive search for positive ratings via social networks. In the "Nosedive" social system, the stars and their respective scores obtained through daily interactions determine the real possibility of having and exercising power. This type of status is necessary in order to access elite services, privileges which are directly associated with more satisfactory living conditions. To do so, Lacie considers revealing her private life, like when she posts a picture of her childhood stuffed toy (Mr. Rags) in a desperate attempt to gain the attention of a high-scoring friend, Naomi. Lacie even bares her most personal intimate acts to dozens of strangers in a grotesque performance of explicit sentiments bordering on the pornographic when, as maid of honor at Naomi's wedding, she gives a speech in the hope of raising her rating. The series thus represents self-humiliation as a price to pay in order to generate more visibility and interactions, even though these actions are hypocritical and seek nothing more than the reciprocity of the coveted five stars for material and social gains.

Once again, fiction represents nothing more than contemporary, class-conscious society. However, there is one relevant difference: in the real world there is still some margin of privacy in which people can take refuge, such as by eliminating their presence on social networks. In the reality of "Nosedive," however, there is no way to hide, or disguise, the fact that the reputation of the users (mainly reflected by their ratings) is permanently connected to all kinds of basic infrastructure, such as at the airport. Additionally, the user is always visible and unintentionally subject to ratings from other users, known or not. Just by coming across someone on a road, one can gain or lose points without even having seen the face, off-screen, of the user who made the assessment.

Finally, "Nosedive" reflects on the emotional impact determined by the space of time between the publication of content or an action on a social network and the responses or social repercussions the publication may have. The tension Lacie manifests in publicly showing Mr. Rags is comparable to the experience of a gambler on a slot machine. Every time a coin is inserted, the gambler expects a reward, even though rewards may be intermittent; in many cases, rewards do not arrive or they are not satisfactory. The action of posting on the social platform, designed to be rewarded with stars, can be interpreted as a permanent evaluation of behavior which is assumed to be 'happy' and "one-dimensional" (Marcuse, 1987). Marcuse's proposal of "one-dimensional man" describes the process of homogenization promoted by the technological world. This affects the economic framework and the cultural consumption. The elemental factor of individual change is concentrated in the metamorphosis of consciousness. The closure of social consciousness, generated by the individual isolation, eliminates the possibility of individual and social liberation. Hatred and frustration are stripped of their specific purpose and are integrated and treated therapeutically by a kind of "technological veil" (Marcuse, 1987, p. 62).

Thus, "Nosedive" ends up naturalizing, both in fiction and reality, the behaviors linked to shared complacency among those who expect to receive their rewards and feed their social esteem. The wedding of Naomi, Lacie's childhood friend, is a clear manifestation of the above. From the female perspective, the female friends of the bride mutually feed one another the canons of beauty, feminine perfection, and what constitutes an impeccable smile. From the male perspective, the groom's friends act the same way for their version of socially-accepted masculinity. They congratulate themselves for their manhood, their social position, and, through very clear gestures, they are given "likes" of recognition and social approval: shared and legitimate complacency. Behavior linked to the virtual screen, which is fictional, does nothing more than highlight, in the form of a futuristic caricature, the system of expectations and individual behaviors on social networks. This behavior ceases to exist when people are not subjected to constant social scrutiny amplified by technology. Outside the theatre, everyday life is no longer appreciated as a performance. It is freed both from the continuous labelling of people, rules and behavior, and from the ritualization of acts and gestures (Goffman, 1959). The truth only comes out when no-one is watching or evaluating you. Is this a dystopia?

The Society of Sophisticated Social Control

"Nosedive" describes a social system (self-) controlled through the application which all individuals use and through which they rate the behaviors and actions of others. Such an assessment determines the possibilities and exclusions in all social life, from the rejection or acceptance of a job to being given access to certain places. In a simplification of the actual algorithmic technique (which can determine, for example, the granting of a mortgage or the price of a plane ticket), "Nosedive" circumscribes the entire system of decisions and acceptances of interactions in everyday life from one single indicator: social validation.

The system revealed in the episode establishes a single path of social pressure that forces individuals to behave in certain ways which are defined as being socially-acceptable and expected. Such behaviors are necessary to obtain compensation (the five stars) which allow people to enjoy privileges and form a kind of fortunate social class which is stratified by the average rating given by other people. In their assessments, as a result of the asymmetrical power of visibility (Fuchs, 2014), the votes and opinions of those who have more power and, of course, a better rating, have more influence than those of people who have a lower score. It is the same system known as Page Rank that launched Google as *the* search engine with the most important collection of results on the internet in the world (Pasquinelli, 2009). However, it is also the same system which leads influencers to become, sometimes for only short periods of time, social references for specific topics such as fashion, food, travel, and makeup, for instance.

The power represented in the system portrayed in the episode has its central axis fixed on the capacity of each individual who lives on "Planet Nosedive" to guide their choices and actions in a sophisticated way. Furthermore, it is a system which controls and feeds itself through the actions and decisions (rating scores) undertaken by the individuals themselves. Thus, the device (the mobile phone) is an inherent part of behavior as a mechanism of self-control, and as a system which exercises a dual control: firstly, the mobile phone receives, stores, and analyzes all information about its user; secondly, it works as a method of social regulation as each score acts as a prize or sanction to reward or punish the actions and behaviors of each individual.

Both mechanisms allow for a systemic reproduction of the "Nosedive world" as they guarantee the collection of vital information which is necessary for ensuring a class society. Thus, it becomes possible to control social expectations: the class I *want to* belong to and what I must do to achieve that goal (Lacie's behavior), and the class I belong to and what I must do to stay within it (Naomi's behavior). On the other hand, it is the same society which, through the device and the validation it brings, guarantees that any challenge or behavior opposite to the "socially expected" is going to be quickly punished and controlled. This control will not require the use of force or violent coercion, in contrast to Thomas Hobbes' theory of power linked to a Leviathan, the symbolic representation of a strong and centralized state that uses violence as an instrument of control and peacekeeping (Hobbes, 1979).

The assumed dystopian of "Nosedive" determines the subtle orientation of choices as it manipulates the options that characters have in their interactions. At the same time, it perpetuates the "Nosedive system" itself: fear of falling into social exclusion. This is the case concerning three characters in the episode: Chester, the black man who is excluded at Lacie's job; Susan, the female truck driver who rejects the system after having her husband is excluded from cancer treatment due to low ratings; and an unnamed a black man who appears in jail in the last scene of the episode.

Within this scenario of exercising power, the systemic function of the communicative interface (the device), with its own language and determined code, which is culturally universalized through validation, fulfills its mission

by ensuring that the system itself lives within the actors (Luhmaı
being included within the system (or living in the system itself),
tions between the different actors are kept under control while t
challenges are assimilated; they live within a controlled enviro
relationship between the environment and the communication system itsen
implies adaptation and change, which responds to the challenges presented.
The capacity for adaptation (which is guaranteed by the two previous mechanisms) prevents revolution and impedes change from being affected within
the system itself. Revolutionaries, the free thinkers, are punished. Sadness,
hatred, and the lack of joy are excluded from the "Nosedive system" in which
everything is harmonious (hypocritical, but accepted). In the "Nosedive"
society, people displaying emotions linked to frustration, failure, or misfor-
tune are rated so low that they end up being confined to a type of prison, one
which punishes for having a bad social rating and in which a woman and a
black man are represented.

The framework of "Nosedive," built around the controlling device, offers
the societal perspective of continuous vigilance (Turkle, 2019; Fuchs, 2012).
This surveillance, on the one hand, supports and surpasses Foucault's theory
which stipulates that one of the goals of the modern state is to promote a
society that controls itself through an all-seeing camera (Turkle, 2019: 395;
Foucault, 1979b). However, this camera is invisible in its dimension of power
and control over the actions of the individual (Foucault, 1979a). In "Nosedive,"
everyone is immersed in the very workings of power based on the rating system which serves as a sophisticated and self-executing framework of control.
At the same time, under one's own personal power which is exercised socially,
the individual "freely" accepts the rules, or the contract, of absolute surveillance which is offered. In reality, the device exercises ideological control,
centered on what users stand to lose socially if they decide to abandon the
application. For Fuchs (2017, 542), the platform exerts emotional coercion on
individuals. In fact, the more people who use platforms under coercion and
social pressure, the easier it is to reproduce that same coercion on all users,
even on those who are not connected.

In "Nosedive," the world of self-fed power and control determines the
objective of entering the rating elite. The prestigious social club is powered
by five stars. A good rating as a premium user defines who you are and what
you are able to access. The rating is also fed by the information received from

the user, a prediction system about what the individual "wants," and this prompts Lacie herself to carry out specific types of actions.

The (A)Social Network?

The concept of network alludes to an organization made up of a set of elements from the same field, theme, niche, or profile, and which are distributed by different places in a territory. Networks, therefore, indicate people who share interests. The Internet did not create, but rather reinforced, through monopolizing, the social component of dialog platforms. In this way, a set of virtual spaces emerged – which were cataloged as being social networks – in which Internet users exchange content within a virtual and interactive community of "friends." Platforms such as Facebook, Twitter, Snapchat, and Instagram, among others, have experienced exponential growth which has placed them at the center of cyberspace for their ability to generate impact and reach, to develop communication strategies that allow engagement with other Internet users, and to have messages go immediately viral.

These platforms have managed to bring rich returns through the number of followers, "likes," and comments they generate. Furthermore, on all of these platforms, personal information plays a significant role. As De Casas, Tejedor, and Romero (2018) point out in a study centered on Instagram, young audiences share personal content focused on their moments of leisure and everyday life, especially through their mobile phones. All social networks invite their users to define and create their own profiles, which leads to their digital identity which, ultimately, will *give way* to their digital identity (Oropesa and Sánchez, 2016). Personal information is present in all of these dimensions: "I introduce myself, I define myself, I locate myself…". The psychological framework of the *self* feeds and gets involved in the personal identity and in the emotional individual construction according to the "likes," the system of social recognition in the social media. The "like" button gives users small doses of dopamine (Solon, 2017) that govern the younger generations of the 21st century; "it is a feedback loop of social validation. Just the kind of gadget a hacker like me could make. Through them it is possible to exploit a vulnerability in human psychology" (Parker, in Solon, 2017).

Progressively, the taste for "likes" has given way to the slavery of "likes." This distortion of the initial concept of "likes" in social networks (which is already easily detected in our day-to-day lives) is also clearly observed in "Nosedive." Social networks go from being spaces for conversation, meeting people and communicating, to a scenario of a passive and almost unidirectional exchange of automatic "likes" which are driven by a feeling of emotional complacency. Furthermore, the episode projects the process of evolution (or more specifically, involution) of the social network. The platform goes from being a place of dialog and social exchange to a defined territory for personal and professional development at its most basic level. Consequently, in this very significant and illustrative sense, "Nosedive" presents the network as an omnipresent space in the daily lives of all inhabitants of the planet. The network defines and conditions people's daily lives in all aspects. What people do and what they say is conditioned by the platform (and the "likes" that surround them). Furthermore, every individual is forced to sacrifice their own "I" to give way to the construction of a "social self" which does not respond to the values, beliefs, or principles of individuals. These values are those which the network deems positive, or at least this is what users are made to believe. Everything is subservient to the platform: we *say* what we know (or believe) people want to hear in the hope that it will be "liked" and will be well-rated; we *do* what we know (or believe) people will "like" in the hope that it will be well-rated; we *share* what we know (or believe) people will "like" in the hope that it will be well-rated. This pattern repeats itself in all aspects of life. The "I" in its most essential sense gives way to the "social I," and paradoxically they do not always coincide. For Hall (2003), identity responds to a strategic and positional *modus operandi*. There is a process of constant and progressive alienation where each individual must choose between social acceptance or the commitment to being faithful to one's own principles (and paying a high price for it). This reflection on the "I" is perfectly linked to the theory of social identity by Tajfel and Turner (1979), which studies the configuration of the identity of the "I" from its connection to the different social networks.

Tajfel (1978) stated that social comparison is a fundamental part of the process of inter-group dynamics. Thus, people, because of their social characteristics, belong to certain categories or social groups. It will be through social comparison with other similar groups that individuals will obtain information about the relative status of their group and of themselves as members of it (Canto y Moral, 2005). Therefore, in "Nosedive", the comparative framework as a universe of identity construction and of social valuation, becomes a goal. It is almost the only objective of social relations.

In "Nosedive," relations between human beings have been radically altered. Connections between people are produced by the influence, the benefit, or the social improvement the relation can provide. Furthermore, our actions respond to one single end or objective: to obtain a high rating (acceptance?) from everyone else. McCune and Thompson (2011) have studied the motivations behind the use of Instagram in their research. Their research coincides with the aforementioned by pointing out what users of the platform want: namely, to share their images with different users; to store their experiences; to see the images posted through a different perspective; to feel involved and integrated within a digital community; and to be creative and to feel free when it comes to expressing themselves. These are, without a doubt, motivations which perfectly connect with the attitude and predisposition of the protagonists in "Nosedive." Lee et al. (2015) point out in a variety of different works that the motivations (both social and psychological) that lead people to use Instagram respond to the following factors: social interaction, photo storage, expression, escapism, and gossiping about what others do. Research by Prades and Carbonell (2016) identified a thematic hierarchy as to why young people use Instagram. Based on some two hundred users, they detected five types of motivations which, in order of priority, led young people to use the platform: gossiping, storage, social interaction, expression, and escapism. Similarly, the researchers inferred that the attitude towards the application and the intention behind using Instagram were directly linked to parameters such as sex or age. Along these lines, Reolid-Martínez et al. (2016) pointed out in their work that women used Instagram more than men.

The motivations described are linked to the conceptual construction of human interest, a set of elements of psychological connection that technology uses very efficiently (Parker, in Solon, 2017). On the one hand, the human interest is represented in the discovery and sharing of others' stories (Price, et al., 1997) from a personalized narrative and with emphasis on social connection (Zhao & Zhan, 2019). On the other hand, human interest is identified by the intention to facilitate an effective cognitive process of understanding the shared information (Petty & Cacioppo, 2012).

The slavery of "likes" appropriates everything, defining and establishing the social rules of behavior. In addition, the screen becomes the most important interface in social relations. We know each other by what we do on our screens. The screen (through which we speak, do, and publish) and especially the ratings that we obtain (which appear on our screens), influence and condition our sphere of action, interaction, and the types of activities we engage in. This aspect, which reaches a disproportionate dimension, supports the hypothesis of Ureña (2015) and Gabelas and Marta (2011), who have identified that younger users (a group with a greater presence on social media) go online for personal motivations, attracted by leisure and entertainment content. Moreover, these researchers highlight the role screens play in the daily lives of young people and their ability to coexist with screens in a spontaneous and natural way. In this context, referents or experts emerge who advise on what types of actions to take, how to achieve better ratings, and how to obtain a greater number of qualitative scores. This would be a distortion of the role of the "influencer" as a reference on the use of social networks or, in the case of "Nosedive," on the network itself. The research of Rego-Rey and Romero-Rodríguez (2016), of Martínez, Del Pino and Viñes (2016), among others, have highlighted the recognition of these profiles in the current panorama of media studies. This aspect further contributes to reinforcing the existing analogies between the current state of media and the socio-communicative panorama projected by *Black Mirror*, which, in a way, can be conceived as a dystopian distortion of the current situation. It is yet another example of the mirror effect that the episode "Nosedive" and, by extension, the entire TV series, represent: a black mirror.

Nosedive – An Invitation for Reflection

Reflecting on the episode "Nosedive" of the *Black Mirror* TV series invites us to go beyond the show's dystopian projection of a seemingly not-too-distant future and carry out a critical analysis of the role of social networks, and technology in general, from the following thematic standpoints:

- **Communication is losing prominence:** "Nosedive" invites us to reflect on the very essence of communication as a process. The concept of communication, which starts from the notion of community,[1] has been eroded in the 21st century by the daily actions and intrusion of large,

---

1   From the Latin *commūnicō*, *commūnicāre* ("to share, to connect, to make common "), and from *commūnis* ("common, public, general").

dominant technological platforms, such as Netflix. The concept of the Web 2.0 (Social Web) and the Internet as a broad framework of openness (economic, democratic, communicative, political) faces a fundamental challenge: the concentration of a great part of the world's information and entertainment system in a few platforms. The big social media platforms – Facebook Inc. and Twitter – and the omnipresent technological companies – Amazon, Google, and Apple – concentrate the world's information flow and act as controllers of the whole communicative and emotional processes that affect individual daily life. "Nosedive" is the perfect example of a communicative dystopia in the universe of hyperconnection. Communication, understood as the ability to share, interact, and build collectively, is blurred by the need for social acceptance built within a virtual platform. The process of communicative action – to shape social consensus – is simplified towards the instrumentalization of an action that begs for a single answer: 5 stars. The platforms of apparent interaction, such as the one that dominates the whole analyzed episode and that, in fact, works unnoticed, exemplifies the maximum principle of the invisibility of power featured in Foucault's theory. It entirely denies the social complexity of humanity, its own contradictory psychology, and its fallibility. It denies communication and, therefore, it denies the very form of the human being.

- **Screens are the great mediators:** "Nosedive" places the omnipresence of screens as a mediating element at the center of the debate, surrounded by numerous elements of an alienating nature. The platform, invisible as an instrument for the exercise of power, takes on the role of the mediator and – in "Nosedive" but also on Facebook, Instagram, Twitter, and Amazon – it is fundamental. The screen represents the alienation of the social assessment actions issued by each of the users. It is, in short, what gives value both to the platform and to the people being assessed. The commodification of the "like" button, and all the emotional and narcissistic components associated with it, rules a whole sense of actions and rituals linked to the new practices of apparent interaction: the forced action and reaction to a "like;" the constant notifications as the epicenter of the call for attention on the device so that we are 24/7 connected, to control the fear of missing out (FOMO); and the strategic thinking of choosing an action, a phrase, an image that assures us a percentage of "likes" from our followers that makes us feel happy, or the thought that we do not build a community – of friends, family, co-workers – but have fans. These practices that are adopted daily force us to reflect critically on the power of platforms, screens, and devices as omnipresent and invisible objects of power, or naturalized as another part of the human body, like smartphones.

- **The dangers of the Internet:** The need to develop critical analysis highlights the importance, if not urgency, of tackling the dangers of the Internet from different areas (academia, the media, and institutions), while addressing the problems derived from the use, or abuse, of social media platforms. The response to these challenges should proceed from the systemic work that we have placed at the center of our discourse on the Internet. Ultimately, we need to reflect on the virtues and threats of using of all social networks. Furthermore, "Nosedive," from its dystopian projection, constitutes a direct call to arms in the field of media literacy with the aim of making people aware (especially the most vulnerable audiences, such as children, elderly and media illiterate people) of the urgency of promoting media and digital education from a critical and responsible perspective. Finally, our work allows us to identify the importance of promoting academic research papers and projects on new profiles and dynamics in the use of social platforms, particularly those works which focus on the types of conception, assessment, and usage applied to those platforms.

Bibliography

Beller, J. (2006). *The Cinematic Mode of Production: Attention Economy and the Society of the Spectacle.* Lebanon (Nuevo Hampshire): University Press of New England.

Burrow, A. L. and Rainone, N. (2017). How many likes did I get?: Purpose moderates links between positive social media feedback and self-esteem. *Journal of Experimental Social Psychology,* 69, pp. 232-236. https://doi.org/10.1016/j.jesp.2016.09.005

Canto, J.M. and Moral, F. (2005). Self from the Social Identity Theory. *Escritos de psicología,* 7, pp. 59-70.

Castells, M. (2012). *Redes de indignación y esperanza: Los movimientos sociales en la era de internet.* Madrid: Alianza.

De Casas Moreno, P., Tejedor-Calvo, S. and Romero-Rodríguez, L. M. (2018). Micronarrativas en Instagram: Análisis del storytelling autobiográfico y de la proyección de identidades de los universitarios del ámbito de la comunicación. *Revista Prisma Social*, 20, pp. 40-57.

Ferres, J. (1996). *Televisión subliminal: socialización mediante comunicaciones inadvertidas*. Barcelona: Paidós.

Foucault, M. (1979). *Microfísica del poder*. Madrid: Ediciones de la Piqueta.

Frank, G. (1999). The economy of attention, *Telepolis*. https://www.heise.de/tp/features/The-Economy-of-Attention-3444929.html

Fuchs, C. (2012). Google Capitalism. *Triple C. Communication, Capitalism & Critique*, 10(1), pp. 42-48. https://doi.org/10.31269/triplec.v10i1.304

Fuchs, C. (2014). *Social Media. A critical introduction*. Great Britain: Sage.

Fuchs, C. (2017). Dallas Smythe Today – The Audience Commodity, the Digital Labour debate, Marxist Political Economy and Critical Theory. Prolegomena to a Digital Labour Theory of Value. In: C. Fuchs and V. Mosco, eds., *Marx and the Political Economy of the Media*. Chicago: Haymarket Books, pp. 522-599.

Gabelas, B., José, A. and Marta, L, C. (2011). Adolescentes en la cultura digital. In: R.E. Martínez and L.C. Marta, eds., *Jóvenes Interactivos. Nuevos modos de comunicarse*. La Coruña: Netbiblio.

Giraldo-Luque, S. and Fernández-Rovira, C. (2020). The economy of attention as the axis of the economic and social oligopoly of the 21st century. In: S.H. Park, D. Floriani and M.A. González Pérez, eds., *The Palgrave Handbook of Corporate Sustainability in the Digital Era*. London: Palgrave Mcmillan, pp. 283-305.

Goffman, I. (1959). *The Presentation of Self in Everyday Life*. New York: Doubleday.

Habermas, J. (1996). *Between facts and norms: contributions to a discourse theory of law and democracy*. Cambridge: MIT Press.

Hall, S. (2003). ¿Quién necesita identidad? In: S. Hall. P. Gay, eds., *Cuestiones de identidad cultural*. Buenos Aires: Amorrortu.

Hobbes, T. (1979). *Leviatán*. Madrid: Nacional.

Lee, E., Lee, J.A., Moon, J. H. and Sung, Y. (2015). Pictures speak louder than words: Motivations for using Instagram. *Cyberpsychology, Behavior, and Social Networking*, 18(9), pp. 552–556. http://doi.org/10.1089/cyber.2015.0157

Lévy, P. (2002). *Ciberdemocracia. Ensayo sobre filosofía política*. Barcelona: Editorial UOC.

Luhmann, N. (1995) *Poder*. Barcelona: Anthropos.

Marcuse, H. (1987) *El hombre unidimensional*, Barcelona: Ariel.

Martínez, A. C., del Pino Romero, C. and Viñes, V. T. (2016). Estrategias de contenido con famosos en marcas dirigidas a público adolescente. *Revista ICONO14*, 14(1), pp. 123-154.

Mayer-Schönberger, V.; Cukier, K. (2013) *Big data. La revolución de los datos masivos*. Madrid: Turner.

Mccune, Z.; Thompson, J. (2011). *Consumer Production in Social Media Networks: A Case Study of the «Instagram» iPhone App*. Cambridge: University of Cambridge.

O'Neil, C. (2017). *Armas de destrucción matemática. Cómo el Big Data aumenta la desigualdad y amenaza la democracia*. Madrid: Capitán Swing.

O'Reilly, T. and Battelle, J. (2009). *Web squared: Web 2.0 five years on*. O'Reilly Media, Inc. Web 2.0 Summit

Oropesa, M. P. and Sánchez, X. C. (2016). Motivaciones sociales y psicológicas para usar Instagram. *Communication Papers*, 5(9), pp. 27-36.

Pasquinelli, M. (2009). Google's Page Rank Algorithm: A Diagram of Cognitive Capitalism and the Rentier of the Common Intellect. In: K. Becker and F. Stalder, eds., *DeepSearch: The Politics of Search Beyond Google*. London: Transaction Publishers.

Perceval, J.M. (2015). *Historia mundial de la comunicación*. Madrid: Cátedra.

Petty, R. E., and Cacioppo, J. T. (2012). *Communication and persuasion: Central and peripheral routes to attitude change*. New York, NY: Springer Science and Business Media.

Prades, M. and Carbonell X. (2016). Motivaciones sociales y psicológicas para usar Instagram. *Communication Papers - Media Literacy & Gender Studies*, 5(9), pp. 27-36.

Price, V., Tewksbury, D., and Powers, E. (1997). Switching trains of thought: The impact of news frames on readers' cognitive responses. *Communication Research*, 24(5), pp. 481–506. doi:10.1177/009365097024005002.

Rego-Rey, S. and Romero-Rodríguez, L. M. (2016). Representación discursiva y lenguaje de los «youtubers» españoles: Estudio de caso de los «gamers» más populares. *index. comunicación*, 6(1), pp. 197-224.

Reolid-Martínez, R.E., Flores-Copete, M., López-García, M., Alcantud-Lozano, P., Ayuso-Raya, M.C. and Escobar-Rabadán, F. (2016). Frequency and characteristics of Internet use by Spanish teenagers. A cross-sectional study. *Arch Argent Pediatr*, 114(1), pp. 6-13.

Solon, Olivia (2017) Ex Facebook president Sean Parker: site made to exploit human 'vulnerability', *The Guardian*, [online]. Available at: https://www.theguardian.com/technology/2017/nov/09/facebook-sean-parker-vulnerability-brain-psychology

Tajfel, H. and Turner, J. C. (1979). An integrative theory of intergroup conflict. In: W.G. Austin, and S. Worchel, eds., *The social psychology of intergroup relations*. Monterey: Brooks/Cole.

Tajfel, H. (1978). *Differentiation between social groups: Studies in the social psychology of intergroups relations*. London: Academic Press.

Turkle, S. (2019). *En defensa de la conversación. El poder de la conversación en la era digital*. Barcelona: Ático de los libros.

Ureña, A., Valdesacasa, E., Ballesteros, P., Castro, R. and Cadenas, S. (2015). *Perfil sociodemográfico de los internautas. Análisis de datos INE 2014*. Madrid: Observatorio Nacional de las Telecomunicaciones y de la SI (ONTSI).

Wong, J.C. (2017). "Former Facebook executive: social media is ripping society apart". *The Guardian*, [online]. Available at: https://www.theguardian.com/technology/2017/dec/11/facebook-former-executive-ripping-society-apart

Zhao, X. and Zhan, M.M. (2019). "Appealing to the Heart: How Social Media Communication Characteristics Affected Users' Liking Behavior During the Manchester Terrorist Attack." *International Journal of Communication*, 13(2019), pp. 3826-3847.

Žižek, S. (2010). *El acoso de las fantasías*. Madrid: Siglo XXI.

The Price of Visibility
Black Mirror, Technologies of Vision,
and Surveillance Policies

Andrea Facchetti

Black Mirror: Science Fiction Between Mainstream and Social Criticism

James Ballard stated in an interview in 1992 that Science Fiction was dead: "You could say that science fiction died because it succeeded. [...] It sent its children out into the world – all those images – and it created the psychology of the late 20th century. It now constitutes the new mainstream" (Ballard, Moiso and Reynolds 2019, pg. 40). According to Ballard, Science Fiction died as a genre because it had become a mainstream product and colonized our collective imagery. This statement raises serious questions about the ability of Science Fiction to act as a critical device. Its capacity to reveal certain social and political problems, more or less linked to technological development, has in fact characterized many Science Fiction classics. We always find a reflection on the relationship between man, society, and the outside world, starting from the first dystopian novels by George Orwell and Aldous Huxley, through the works of Ursula Le Guin, Philip K. Dick, and Anthony Burgess, and up to the last decade of the century with William Gibson, Bruce Sterling, and other cyberpunk authors. This relationship is described as mediated by the artificial that brings with it some repercussions for human existence. In 1972, Darko Suvin described Science Fiction as "the literature of cognitive estrangement" (Suvin 1972, 372), a narrative form capable of producing an effect of estrangement on the reader through a distorted representation or alternative to the state of what is present (Suving 1972, 375). Science Fiction would unfold the possibility to imagine an alternative to the *status quo*, thus generating a fracture in the social imaginary, which would allow a critical reflection on reality and its configurations to develop.[1]

This potential critique could be endangered by the transformation of the genre into a mainstream product. How can a literary genre put into question the state of the present or stress problems and hidden emergent issues in the modern notion of progress if it becomes an integral part of the industry and imagery at the root of progress? Can Science Fiction – not only as a literary form, but also through other languages and forms of expression – claim the capacity and the possibility of producing a difference or a rupture within the collective imagery of a society? Can we still describe it as an art of cognitive estrangement?

Black Mirror represents one of the most successful attempts (at least in terms of media popularity) in articulating an answer to these questions through the production of fiction works – specifically, a television series. On one side, the British series confirms Ballard's idea of Science Fiction as the mainstream narrative and imaginative form of the 20th (and 21st) century – especially after its passage into the hands of Netflix, the entertainment giant. What is still to be established is if and in what terms it can still work as a critical tool.

This text offers an inquiry into *Black Mirror's* critical potential, a potential that is manifested especially in the capacity of penetrating and modifying our collective imagery within which narrations and representations related to social problems unfold. Specifically, the third episode of the first season, "The Entire History of You" (2011) – wherein we see a technology that allows people to record and store what they perceive through their eyes – will be taken into consideration. The effects of this technology distort the same act of seeing, as well as the areas of the social life annexed to it – one above all, that of surveillance. The critical potential of this series will be measured and analyzed with reference to the ability to produce a fracture in the narrative framework by which discourses and visual imageries are nowadays formulated, represented, and enjoyed around the theme of surveillance. The critical potentialities of this episode in particular lie in the ability to produce a new image of surveillance devices and of subjectivization.

---

1 "In the 20th century, SF has moved into the sphere of anthropological and cosmological thought, becoming a diagnosis, a warning, a call to understanding and action, and – most important – a mapping of possible alternatives" (Suvin 1972, 378).

From Disciplinary Societies to Societies of Control

Orwell's Big Brother has become a reference figure in the collective imagery regarding the theme of surveillance. If in the circles of counterculture it had long been a symbol of the pervasive and repressive action of a totalitarian power, it is only at the end of the 20th century that Big Brother becomes an important mythological element of our contemporary times. However, almost seventy years after the publication of *1984*, the concept-image of Big Brother seems to have lost any analytical capacity when faced with a reality that is even more complex than the one imagined by Orwell. Big Brother represents a form of violently oppressive, centralized, totalitarian power, a kind of power that hides itself inside organization, although it manifests itself in definite and recognizable forms, and closes a gap between watcher and watched. Not only do these characteristics not succeed in describing the context of liberal democracies in the NSA era, but they do not even get close to adapting to the new "surveillance by algorithm" and web-tracking practices to which Facebook or Google users willingly subject themselves.

In recent years, several scholars have turned to a different concept-image tied to the surveillance problem: the panopticon. The idea of the panopticon was analyzed by Michel Foucault, who described, in *Discipline and Punish: The Birth of the Prison*, a society oriented towards the prison of Bentham. The panopticon thus became, for Foucault, the idealized form of social functioning, the image of the new disciplinary society (1977, 205). Having become a key concept not only for surveillance studies, but also for various fields (from sociology to political philosophy to urban studies and architecture), the panopticon has begun to extend beyond the world of academia in recent years. This took place especially within the debate triggered by the NSA scandal; journalists, commentators, and politicians cite the Bentham prison to describe a social organization in which individuals are placed in a state of perpetual surveillance. As a result, the same individuals would be inclined to self-discipline without the need to resort to repressive and violent forms of punishment.

On one side, the concept of the panopticon has made the disciplinary nature of the new forms of surveillance clear. In the panoptic society, power renounces direct and absolute control in favor of "softer" coercive forms, in which it is the individuals themselves who adopt ways of thinking and acting in compliance with the will of power (Foucault 1977, 202). On the other side, what to Foucault was a "diagram of a mechanism of power reduced to its ideal form" (1977, 205) has moved to simplification and semantic flattening.[2] Despite the lucidity of Foucault's analysis and his capacity to link a series of discourses, practices, techniques, and knowledge within an archaeology of power of the modern era, today this imagery has crystallized into a visual, discursive, and political representation that shows its limits in grasping to understand the new forms of surveillance. As David Murakami Wood remarks,

> It seems very strange therefore, for those studying surveillance almost two centuries after 1840, to take panopticism as a theoretical base for any new sociotechnological development, as if nothing had changed in terms of power/knowledge, rather than to follow Foucault in his method, and trace the inextricably interlinked historical evolution of punitive technologies, and power and object relations (2007, 251).

There is the risk that we might hide a series of new configurations and agencies that have arisen following the technological and geopolitical developments in the past decades if we talk about our contemporary society as a panoptic society.

Various authors have tried to expand and articulate Foucault's thought on disciplinary practices in light of these changes in an attempt to update the map of "disciplinary networks" (Foucault 1977, 306). The need to rethink the panopticon was also felt by Deleuze who, in his essay "Postscript on the Societies of Control" (1992), described the passage from a disciplinary society to one that the French philosopher called the society of control. According to Deleuze, the last decade of the 20th century was already in a condition dominated by a new form of social control that slowly but inevitably had reshaped the old disciplinary spaces and devices following corporation logic (1992, 4). While discipline enforces society's long-term stability through a kind of control that is granted by its rigid vertical structure as its objective, corporative

---

2 According to Matthew Hannah, "a narrow focus by geographers and others on the figure of the Panopticon in *Discipline and Punish* has unnecessarily reduced Foucault's account of power relations to a fairly simple model, and has thereby made it far easier than it should have been to treat this account as a transportable theory of spatial power relations" (2007, 101).

logic is instead interested in reaching results in the short term, and transforms our contemporary society into a system of variable geometry, ready to take on new configurations according to specific cases (Deleuze 1992, 6).

If on one side the structure and the logic of power changes, the other great transformation regards the subject. While the human subject was considered in its entirety by disciplinary societies, the processes at work in the society of control are able to break down the individual into a series of different data sets and related information. We are facing Deleuze's "dividual": "The numerical language of control [that] is made of codes that mark access to information, or reject it. We no longer find ourselves dealing with the mass/individual pair. Individuals have become 'dividuals,' and masses, samples, data, markets, or "banks" (1992, 5). The code, the new control device, produces a new subjectivity through an action of *dividualization*: the subjects are sublimated into profiles wherein physical, behavioural, and emotional specificities are translated into data flows, which in turn constitute huge databases accessible to a limited number of actors. If Deleuze's analysis, at the beginning of the '90s, could seem to be the result of an abstract philosophical language, after just 20 years his words become the outline of an anticipation which finds its confirmation in the advent of big data, in web tracking strategies as in profiling mechanisms.

The image of Big Brother that reduces the terms of the surveillance discourse to a sterile contraposition between secrecy and transparency, between watcher and watched, seems unsuitable now if not misleading in the production of critical perspectives and knowledge. Foucault's analysis of a disciplinary society, and later Deleuze's, have merit for highlighting 1) the normative character and the action of normalization at work both in the disciplinary society and in that of control; 2) the decentralized and variable geometry structure of power that determines the fluidity of roles; and 3) the decomposition of individuals into "dividuals", i.e., flows of information aggregated in databases used to extract cognitive capital or to trigger repressive actions. This is the panorama with which the discourse and the imaginary on surveillance, and therefore the *Black Mirror* scenario analyzed here, must confront today.

The Entire History of You

Written by Jesse Armstrong and directed by Brian Welsh, "The Entire History of You" (TEHY) is the third episode of the first season of *Black Mirror*, broadcasted on December 18, 2011. The protagonists of the episode are Liam (Toby Kebbel) and his wife Ffion (Jodie Whittaker), a young English couple, whose relationship undergoes a dramatic decline, leading up to their separation. The reason for the break-up is due to Liam's accrued suspicion that Ffion betrayed him with Jonas (Tom Cullent), an old friend of his wife's – a suspicion that in the course of the episode ends up ruining the relationship.

Even if it may seem like a love story, TEHY is a narration with Science Fiction contours, since most people in Liam and Ffion's world are equipped with a particular device called a "Willow Grain." The Grain is a memory chip installed under the skin that records – from a subjective point of view – any visual and auditory perceptions of the person who "wears" it. What is recorded is then archived and transformed into a digital file that can be seen at any time. The excerpts that make up this new digitized visual memory can be viewed either privately or through public viewing by projecting the recording on an external screen. Moreover, the Grains allow for a series of functions, such as zooming in on a scene and lip-reading to decipher indistinct audio. Therefore, Grains' technology creates a huge digital archive comprehensive of any other activity and interaction carried out by its user. A completely indexed archive that is always available and can be consulted and analyzed at any time. In other words, the Grains completely upset the sphere of what is visible in that society by establishing a regime of hyper-visibility.

The main narrative of TEHY shows us the possible consequences that this type of technology can have within emotional and personal relationships. The Grains play a fundamental role in the marital crisis of Liam and Ffion. In the central part of the episode, Liam analyses continuously a series of memories looking for evidence to confirm his suspicions (for example, the moment in which he sees his wife and Jason engaged in a conversation, or the recording of a distant holiday projected during a dinner), until he convinces himself that their daughter is actually the result of Ffion's betrayal. Liam's entire reconstruction is supported and fuelled by the new potentialities offered by the Grains, a reconstruction that transforms the protagonist's version into an actual fact. What is perceived through the eyes and ears is not available to the subject through his natural visual memory (a subjective memory, selective in organizing memories that can generate mistakes or even amnesia), but it is objectified in information stored in the digital library. The deletion of a memory leaves a trace, an absence, which reveals the very act of removal. Liam's life, cleansed as it is by any possibility of forgetting, is dominated by a hyper-visibility regime that returns to the society of transparency described by the philosopher Byung-chui Han. In fact, like the scenario in TEHY, "The society of transparency cannot tolerate a gap in information or of sight" (Han 2015, 4). The Grains seem to fulfill the promise of a completely transparent society where any kind of information, any memory, is always present and available to its user, a society free from oblivion.

However, such a utopia hides a dystopian scenario that is manifested on both the social and personal levels. On the personal level, the Grains distort the perception a person has of him-/herself. In front of the objectification brought about by technology, perceptions and memories become accumulated as ever-available information. That is how human memory becomes similar to computer memory wherein selection is replaced by addition, and the hermeneutic processes underlying the production of sense disappear in the face of self-evidence that needs no interpretation[3] (Han 2015, 32). Therefore, the hyper-visibility regime of the Grains emerges with greater strength on the experiential and temporal levels. Perceptions and memories stop feeding selective personal memory – thus preventing the construction of a self-narrative – and become self-evident proofs. The dissolution between individual and mass implicit in the "dividual" (Deleuze 1992, 5) is thus revealed in the transformation of the human memory operated by the Grains: individual memory is reduced to a flow of data, while collective

---

3 The term "correlation" is taken from the reflections of British-American author Chris Anderson. In an article published in Wired, he claims the obsolescence of theory in the face of enormous computing power and big data. According to Anderson, "No semantic or causal analysis is required [...] This is a world where massive amounts of data and applied mathematics replace every other tool that might be brought to bear. With enough data, the numbers speak for themselves" (2008). Anderson's considerations overlap with the transformation of human memory made by the Grains. In both cases we see a strong increase in the production of information (in Liam's world, any visual perception becomes data). This information is stored in databases, wherein it goes through computational processes that operate according to logics beyond the control of those who access the database and that produce correlations between the informations themselves. Finally, these correlations – due to their self-evident character – replace any hermeneutical act meant to insert those data/memories within a cognitive frame or a narrative.

memory takes the form of a database. Obviously, this situation also has profound repercussions on collective memory, and above all on the dynamics that lead to its construction. In the relationship between Liam and Ffion we see how their collective memory – the collective representation of the experiences that concern and found their being a couple – is no longer constructed through a dialectical movement between two different positions. Liam does not need to know Ffion's version: his memories, objectified by the Grains in self-evident information, already speak for themselves. As a result, their collective memory is shattered into two incompatible positions. With the new human memory, digitalized thanks to the Grains, hermeneutics is no longer necessary: memory relies entirely on absolute evidence of its data and on their correlation, rather than on the interpretation of memories.

The transformation of human memory into digital memory has profound consequences for surveillance, too. The Grains transform individual memories into files archived in a database: memory is thus reduced to digitized information – a kind of information that is not exclusive property of its "author". Although the screenwriters don't explore the ownership aspects of the database, the advertisement introducing the devices at the beginning of the episode suggests that we are dealing with a private company. What a person sees is therefore not his or her exclusive property, but can be seen by others or even expropriated. In the scenario of TEHY this possibility is very often translated into reality[4].

---

4   The relationship between technologies of vision, surveillance and digitalization of subjective experience, occurs in several episodes of *Black Mirror*. For example, a device very similar to the Grains is the neural implant Z-Eye that we find in the episode "White Christmas" (December 16, 2014, written by Charlie Brooker and directed by Carl Tibbetts). In this case, the Z-Eye – besides recording what you see, storing it in a database, sharing it on other platforms or with other users – allows you to intervene directly on your perception, through the blocking function. Once a block has been placed, both the blocker and the blocked appear to one another as a static-like silhouette. If the person who initializes the block wants to issue a restraining order to the blocked, the GPS built into the Z-Eye monitors them to ensure they do not go within 10 meters of the blocker, otherwise they face arrest. Additionally, in "Crocodile" (December 29, 2017, written by Charlie Brooker and directed by John Hillcoat), we see a device called Recaller, employed by policemen and insurance investigators, to scan someone's memories. The most interesting aspect of the Recaller is that it works not only on humans, but also on animals. In the episode, this becomes the opportunity to explore a scenario in which potentially any being with a visual apparatus becomes an eyewitness, producing legal evidence of what happens in its surroundings.

Although it is the central conflict of the episode, the conjugal story of the two protagonists does not exhaust the representation of the technology of the Grains. For example, we see two minor scenes at the beginning of the episode, minor, but still quite important in the analysis of several implications that go beyond the private sphere. We see the protagonist, Liam, in his working environment in the first scene – a law firm – while he undergoes a series of questions asked by a review committee made up of three of his superiors. The Grains are also at the centre of the scene: "So if we invite you to stay with the firm in the new environment, what we'd have you do is pull an exhaustive re-do with personnel maybe next week?" one of the three asks, making sure there are no time gaps, which indicates that something has been deleted ("there's no major deletions this quarter?"). In order to show that his work meets the firm's standards ("everything's well within parameters"), Liam is forced to hand over his memories to his superiors. The law firm can therefore take possession of the protagonist's past, which sets him in a condition of subordination. This control action is then framed within a process of normalization that takes place through the reduction of the employees' behaviour to a series of parameters. In this sense, the figure of the worker overlaps the one of the *performer*, i.e. the one who is continuously called upon to demonstrate his/her own skills and ability to perform a given task by respecting a series of standards. One of the most evident characteristics of this process is the frequency with which the performer is subjected to review and behavioural tests. The difference between TEHY's scenario and the reality of late capitalism lies in the presence of the Grains: the possibility of reviewing any action or dialogue recorded during the working hours makes the tests in fact irrelevant, since every moment spent on the job automatically becomes an assessment test.

Soon after the interview, Liam goes to the airport. Some of the information automatically provided by the Grains on each passenger can be seen on the interface of the program used by the security guards: occupation, height, color of the eyes, state of the Grain, the closest relative, information on the passenger's birth, family history, travel history, information on the passenger's stay in the place they are leaving. The interface of the program reveals the process of "dividualization" to which Liam is subjected: the device is in fact capable of breaking down the person "Liam" into a series of information flows recorded on databanks and compared with other profiles. The security guards ask the protagonist to view the recordings of the past 24 hours and of the past week, while we see on the screen a facial recognition program at work that can identify all those with whom Liam came into contact. The first five minutes of the episode introduces the estrangement element of the scenario, i.e. the technology of the Grains, and some of their repercussions on social relationships and on power relations. We see how the practice of power takes shape through access to the contents recorded by the Grains and to Liam's profiling. The hyper-visibility regime established by the Grains sets the complete transparency of the subject in his interpersonal relationships and in front of the devices of power.[5]

The total availability of the subject in such a scenario recalls another trait of the society of control. Deleuze in fact argues that "In *The Trial*, Kafka [...] described the most fearsome of judicial forms [...] the limitless postpone-ments of the societies of control" (1992, 5). The "limitless postponements" that mark the passage from a disciplinary society to one of control is a trait characteristic of the scenario represented in TEHY, and is also the existential condition of those who are equipped with the Grains. They too, just like the defendants in Kafka's world, are subject to continuous and endless reviews; they are performers at the centre of a test that accompanies them in any sit-uation in which there is another person equipped with the Grain (or a person who can access their memories). TEHY thus introduces an articulated image that goes beyond the paradigm of Big Brother and tries to build a scenario capable of restoring the complexity of the thick network of agencies, actors, and devices that make up the policies of surveillance. Specifically, the image generated by this scenario represents the new society of control by articulat-ing and developing it along three main directives: (1) the hedonistic matrix; (2) surveillance as *unnatural ecology*; and (3) its normative character.

The hedonistic matrix

A characteristic that derives from the panopticon (a prison institution) and that defines the imagery of surveillance is the close relationship with the dis-course on safety. As a matter of fact, alongside this drive, which relies on the perception of fear and the creation of a need for safety, it is possible to see

---

5   As Han states, "Actions prove transparent when they are made operational – subordinate to a calculable, steerable, and controllable process" (2015, 1).

another drive, equally strong, and perhaps even more pervasive, that struggles to emerge from the images of Big Brother and the panopticon.

Surveillance is the implicit consequence of a series of behaviours and habits in many areas of our everyday life that have become part of people's social lives. It is in this situation that surveillance does not come from state power, but rather from subjects linked to business interests and the creation of profit. We are facing what Shoshana Zuboff defined as "surveillance capitalism." One of the characteristics of this form of surveillance is that it is not imposed in a coercive form, or even through the disciplinary processes described by Foucault, but rather it is applied through the infiltration into any area of a person's personal and social life (Zuboff 2019).

This pervasiveness becomes evident in TEHY's scenario: professional life, people's mobility, economic exchanges, social relations, and entertainment are all areas designed and mediated by the use of the Grains. Still, the most interesting aspect concerns not so much those activities that take place within a formal context regulated by following pre-established procedures and roles (like the working context or the space of an airport) but rather social and informal situations (like a dinner with friends or the dynamics that accompany the relationship of a couple). For Liam, Ffion, and the characters present at the scene of the dinner, it is perfectly normal to spend time watching the memories recorded by their own Grains. The same technology that supports surveillance and control is at the heart of any social relationship, even of sexual relationships.

As Zuboff states, "our participation is best explained in terms of necessity, dependency, the foreclosure of alternatives" (2019). In particular, the term "dependency" seems to describe a condition wherein the continuous use of the device does not so much depend on its usefulness, but rather on the pleasure that the wearer feels in using it – a pleasure that is easily transformed into a dependency. It is no coincidence that the Grains appear for the first time as an advertisement, as a commercial product that is sold by taking advantage of the wishes of possible buyers. The condition of a supervised and controlled individual is a condition that is pursued, purchased, and in some ways, enjoyed by the individual himself. Within this aspect, one of the characteristic features of the society of control that emerges from TEHY's narration is a sort of hedonistic impulse through which the surveillance action is accomplished. A pornographic impulse, since it is crossed by voyeuristic tensions and by the desire to expose oneself and one's life in front of everyone. As Han writes, "Pornographic putting-on-display and panoptic control complement each other. Exhibitionism and voyeurism feed the net as a digital panopticon. The society of control achieves perfection when subjects bare themselves not through outer constraint but through self-generated need" (2015, 46). The Grains take to the extreme a society that shows, even nowadays, the characteristics of hyper-visibility and hyper-exposure. In TEHY's scenario, we see a hedonistic regime come to fruition wherein overexposure and spectacularization of one's life become the source of the greatest satisfaction and personal fulfillment, as well as a privileged form of relating with the other. This condition, in its most radical drifts, alienates both one's own personal experience as well as one's emotional and sentimental relationships. This becomes evident in TEHY's sex scene between Liam and Ffion in the moment in which the memory of an old sexual act is superimposed, annulling their direct experience . The desire and pleasure of exhibiting one's own memories and experiences become the other side of surveillance and control.

Unnatural Ecologies

The pervasiveness of the devices, of the logics, and of the processes involved in the surveillance actions that characterize TEHY's scenario also explores one of the most important differences in the transition between discipline and control. According to Deleuze, the structural image of the societies of control is no longer that of a hierarchical pyramid or of a tree diagram composed of separate elements placed within a rigid structure that defines its roles. We are rather faced with a fluid and mobile network in which there is no vertex or center, and wherein elements can be continuously reconfigured to occupy different positions and roles.[6]

Reference is made, in this sense, to the idea of an ecological approach derived from media studies, but which can be transferred to the field of sur-

---

6 Other authors have also described this paradigmatic shift. It is worth mentioning Mark Fisher, who refers to the transition from a rigid, centralized, and hierarchical system to a fluid, decentralized, and widespread system (2009, 22); Han, who speaks of a digital panopticon by highlighting its aperspectival feature due to the decentralization of the eyes that watch over (2015, 45); and Zuboff, who describes surveillance capitalism as a complex system that is dispersed in-between the countless folds of human social existence (2019).

veillance studies. Michael Goddard and Jussi Parikka describes the ecological approach as a

> politically oriented way of understanding the various scales and layers
> through which media are articulated together with politics, capitalism and
> nature, in which processes of media and technology cannot be detached
> from subjectivization [...] Technology is not only a passive surface for the
> inscription of meanings and signification, but a material assemblage that
> partakes in machinic ecologies. And, instead of assuming that "ecologies"
> are by their nature natural [...] we assume them as radically contingent and
> dynamic, in other words as prone to change (2011, 1).

If we try to apply this approach to the field of surveillance, it is not only the
idea of space and the devices that change, but also the conditions and roles
occupied by the different actors involved. The loss of a center in the surveillance apparatus is the first sign of the dissolution of the roles on which the
distinction between supervisor and supervised was based, and of the passage from a centralized power organized according to a hierarchical structure to a power wherein "the different control mechanisms are inseparable
variations, forming a system of variable geometry [...] controls are a mod-
ulation, lie a self-deforming cast that will continuously change from one
moment to the other, or like a sieve whose mesh will transmute from point to
point" (Deleuze 1992, 4). This variable geometry system is interestingly represented and articulated in TEHY. The role of controllers and the condition of
the controlled subjects are no longer defined in a rigid way, but instead fade
away, blurring one with the other. Every person with a Grain can record the
behaviours, actions, and discourses of other people, and is therefore a subject who moves along the directives that define the role of the controller. But
at the same time, precisely because that technology has penetrated almost
all areas of social life, any person finds her-/himself in the condition of a subject undergoing the surveillance action of the Grains. This becomes evident if
we consider the first scene of the episode. Although Liam, as the person who
is interviewed, occupies the role of a controlled subject, a few scenes later he
is able to review the memories recorded during the interview, and examine
the expressions, gestures, and tones of his interlocutors. At this point, Liam
takes on the role of the controller; he subjects his superiors to his surveillance
action. We are therefore in a situation of an on-going oscillation between

positions, roles, possibilities, abilities, knowledge, and power. An oscillation that seems to put in crisis both the image of Big Brother and that of the panopticon (wherein the roles of controller and controlled are substantially unchanged). It instead favours the image of an ecology of surveillance characterized by a dynamism of roles and agencies. The person equipped with a Grain, and who interacts with other individuals equipped with the same technology, becomes at the same time the object of the controlling action and the subject who, in turn, carries out a controlling action.

TEHY's scenario would thus seem to dissolve the threshold between who controls and who is being controlled – and as a consequence, the disparity of power between state apparatuses and corporations on one side, and citizens and users on the other – in a myriad of subjects that constantly move on that threshold. But upon closer inspection, the scenes of the job interview and of the airport include the protagonist in situations wherein he is directly related to the subjects who occupy a position of power with respect to him. We see then that a situation of asymmetry of the watching eyes is re-proposed, to which an asymmetry of knowledge corresponds, and therefore of power, between the characters that are involved. We could therefore state that even in TEHY, there are subjects that occupy a position closer to that of "watchers" and subjects who instead are unbalanced towards a "watched" position. It is therefore true that the Grain's technology increases the ability to control what is seen through the eyes, but it is part of a context in which the social, economic, and political terrain presents a morphology made of depressions and plateaus to which different degrees of power correspond. The Grains further accentuate such a disparity of positions.

However, we must not forget the specificity of the technology in question: the Grains are individual and individualizing implants. We could therefore argue that while they achieve an even clearer separation between individuals-subject-to-control and entities-responsible-for-the-control, they as a matter of fact lead to an abstraction or depersonalization of these entities. The individual explodes into a multiplicity of roles that can coexist in the same person: a policeman, for example, while being unbalanced towards the polarity of the watcher, continues to be the object of others' control. That is

to say, roles and agencies become independent from their actual personifi-
cation in a human body.[7]

Surveillance as normalization

The last of the three characteristics introduced by TEHY's scenario regards
the way in which surveillance is oriented towards the idea of normalization.
The actors, the devices, and the agencies that are involved in surveillance
processes function within a framework defined by the parameters of rule
and exception. In turn, the normative character of surveillance is closely
bound to the policies of watching, to the technologies of sight, and to the
practices within which the act of watching is inscribed. It is for this reason
that in TEHY's world, watching is not simply a perceptive act, but it becomes
a regulatory practice that can be traced back to a desire for control.

The idea that the practices and the technologies tied to watching contribute to defining and distinguishing conditions of normality and exception is
not new. Foucault addressed this issue in *The Birth of the Clinic: An Archeology
of Medical Perception* (1963). The French philosopher sees in the new clinical eye
the creation of a regime of absolute visibility. Through specific ways of seeing and of knowing by watching, modern medicine analyzes and catalogues
not only the states of diseases, but also of postures, behaviours, and habits,
placing them within a playground governed by parameters of normality and
abnormality. From here its disciplinary and regulatory character derives: the
doctor is no longer just the one who cures, but he is the one who prescribes
the right behaviours, the right postures, the right practices through which
the body of the patient falls within the field defined by the concept of normality (Foucault 1973, 34). In this sense, the clinical eye functions as a regulatory
device: the practices and techniques of modern medicine contribute in fact
to define a "normal state", which corresponds to the condition of health, and

---

7 In the episode "Crocodile" we are confronted with a situation in which this de-personal-
   ization is clearly rendered. As already said, in this episode we see a technology similar to
   the Grains, but which is also able to work on animals. In this way, at the end of the episode
   a hamster becomes the eyewitness to a murder. In other words, thanks to this technology,
   the non-human experience potentially becomes proof and legal evidence within a purely
   human dynamic.

an "exceptional state", that refers instead to the condition of disease based on a normative and visual model.[8]

The normative action characterizes the practice of watching in the Grain era, too. The scenes of the interview and of the airport show, in this case, how the new technology is used within several disciplinary logics and procedures – the review of his performance and behaviour in the working place, and the complete scanning of his personal memories to trace risk factors in the actions he carried out and in those he met while travelling – determining, however, a leap in quality. A person's working future, or the possibility of boarding a plane, depend on the presence of factors or elements in his personal archive that deviate from a predetermined norm and define him as an abnormal, or even a criminal subject.

Foucault outlines, in analyzing the practice of autopsy, other characteristics and agencies of the clinical eye that in some ways recall the effects of the Grains. First of all, the clinical eye, when facing the patient's body, "makes visible to itself the totality of the field of experience at each of its stages, and dissipates all its opaque structures" (Foucault 1973, 93). The Grains' gaze acts through a totalizing operation, too, by which all memories become immediately present and visible. It is through this process that Liam transforms his suspicion into certainty: the possibility to review and analyze the memories that feed that suspicion transforms the subjective narration of the protagonist into a self-evident truth.

Foucault recognized in the clinical eye an action oriented towards absolute control over the interested subject, fruit of "an operation that, beyond first appearances, scrutinizes the body and discovers a visible invisible at the autopsy" (1973, 94). By overturning an invisible reality and subjecting it to a regime of absolute visibility, the clinical eye shows itself in all its violence, a violence that in TEHY's scenario takes on even more marked contours. In fact, the possibility of recording and storing visual perceptions transforms memory into information that is always available. Like the clinical eye, the eye of the Grains is also an eye of dominance. Looking through the Grains intends to dominate and subject the perceived reality by inserting it into a

---

8 "Nineteenth century medicine, on the other hand, was regulated more in accordance with normality than with health; it formed its concepts and prescribed its interventions in relation to a standard of functioning and organic structure, and physiological knowledge" (Foucault 1973, 35).

regime of perfect visibility and of absolute positivity, wherein everything is evident, logical, transparent, and therefore set under total control.

In the scenario build by TEHY's writers, the image of the society of control is articulated in a regime of full and absolute visibility wherein it is possible to record, archive, make accessible, and analyze any perception filtered through the Grains. The removal of the negative, of the invisible, of the error, of the oblivion, is then the extreme consequence of the normative eye of the Grains, an eye able to illuminate everything like "a sun without shadows."[9]

Conclusions

In the first chapter of this text, a series of questions was asked about the ability of Science Fiction to produce perspectives and critical points of view regarding the state of present things. Obviously, the analysis of a single episode of a television series cannot provide an exhaustive answer to these questions. However, one is able to observe the possibility that Science Fiction can still be a "literature of cognitive estrangement." (Suvin 1972, 372). Although Science Fiction has colonized our contemporary mainstream imagery, it is still possible to produce a narrative (not necessarily literary) capable of soliciting a cognitive estrangement and of building a critique of the present through the production of a fracture in the narrative and cognitive framework that surrounds and defines our understanding of a given phenomenon or problem. And *Black Mirror*, or at least some of its episodes, has been able to take advantage of the popularity and massive spread of that format without giving up the challenge of narrating some of the problems of our world through a distorted and alienating scenario. Specifically, "The Entire History of You" and the scenario within which it develops its narration, represent one of the most successful attempts in recent years to shape and articulate the questions, fears, and anxieties, but also the desires and the enthusiasm, that come to life behind the theme of surveillance, safety, and privacy.

The quality of this operation is demonstrated by the ability to break away from Orwell's image of Big Brother (an important presence, but cumbersome by now, and in some ways embarrassing if we consider its translation into one of the most famous reality shows), to review the paradigm of the panop-

---

9 The expression is taken from the last chapter of *Millennium People*, by James Ballard (2003).

ticon in light of the transformations that have taken place in recent decades, and to try to give a representation to the new societies of control described by Deleuze.

Bibliography

Anderson, Chris. 2008. "The End of Theory: The Data Deluge Makes the Scientific Method Obsolete". Accessed March 30, 2020. https://www.wired.com/2008/06/pb-theory/Ballard, James, Sandro Moiso, and Simon Reynolds. 2019. *James Ballard. All That Mattered Was Sensation.* Brescia: Krisis Publishing.

Deleuze, Gilles. 1992. "Postscript on the Societies of Control". *October* 59: 3-7.

Fisher, Mark. 2009. *Capitalist Realism: Is There No Alternative?.* London: Zero Books.

Foucault, Michel. 1973. *The Birth of the Clinic: An Archaeology of Medical Perception.* London: Routledge.

Foucault, Michel. 1977. *Discipline and Punish: The Birth of the Prison.* New York: Vintage Books.

Goddard, Michael, and Jussi Parikka. 2011. "Editorial". In *The Fibreculture Journal* 17: 1-5.

Han, Byung-Chul. 2015. *The Transparency Society.* Stanford: Stanford Briefs.

Hannah, Matthew. 2007. "Formations of 'Foucault' in Anglo-American Geography: An Archaeological Sketch". Foucault and Surveillance Studies". In *Space, Knowledge and Power: Foucault and Geography,* edited by J. Crampton and S. Elden, 83-106. Aldershot: Ashgate.

Murakami Wood, David. 2007. "Beyond the Panopticon? Foucault and Surveillance Studies". In *Space, Knowledge and Power: Foucault and Geography,* edited by J. Crampton and S. Elden, 245-263. Aldershot: Ashgate.

Suvin, Darko. 1972. "On the Poetics of the Science Fiction Genre". *College English* 34(3): 372-382.

Making a *Killing*
Science Fiction Through the Lens of Nordic Noir in *Crocodile* and *Hated in the Nation*

Dan Ward

One of the most noteworthy developments in the global media landscape over the past decade has been the emergence of Scandinavian crime fiction as a transnational, multi-media cultural phenomenon. Crime stories originating from Northern Europe have enjoyed critical and, to varying degrees, commercial success in the fields of cinema, television, and literature; spawning translations, adaptations, and even international imitations that pay visible homage to the distinctive aesthetic and thematic characteristics of the form, which have become so recognisable that they have evolved into a generic type of their own – 'Nordic Noir'. *Black Mirror* invokes the conventions of Nordic Noir most prominently in two episodes, which feature in the third and fourth seasons of the show, respectively: "Hated in the Nation" and "Crocodile." The former is a feature-length episode, at ninety minutes long, which creator Charlie Brooker has explicitly referred to as "a Scandi-Noir, near-future London detective story" (Parker, 2016). The latter employs the aesthetics of Scandinavian drama to evoke a more visual sense of the genre; the episode was shot entirely in Iceland, during a period in which Reykjavik faced its heaviest snowfall in 70 years (Deehan, 2018). This chapter will examine the rationale, function, and impact of *Black Mirror*'s utilisation of these conventions in the aforementioned episodes.

Nordic Noir: A Transnational Phenomenon

The rise of scholarly interest in Scandinavian crime fiction over the course of the last decade or more has been a result of the critical and commercial success of a range of imports and adaptations of texts from the region on a global scale. The genre is one that traverses media formats as well as national boundaries, with many of the most prominent examples originating in the work of noted Scandinavian literary authors such as Henning Mankell, Stieg Larsson, Maj Sjöwall, and Per Wahlöö. It is a genre that is at once distinctly Nordic, and yet also profoundly transnational. As well as historically bene-fitting from regional co-funding and co-production models with ventures such as Nordvision, Scandinavian drama producers have also been helped by increased co-production opportunities from sources outside the region, such as collaborations between Scandinavian and German PSB stations (Bonde-berg et al., 2017:7). This has resulted in the production of texts which 'have become very local and very global at the same time' (Hansen & Waade, 2017, 2), a classic example being the *Wallander* series. Henning Mankell's interna-tionally renowned collection of crime novels were initially adapted through a complex, collaborative production and distribution model jointly from Swedish and German investment, for opportunities in both regions across cinema, DVD, pay television, and free television markets (Peacock, 2013, 152). In tandem with this, Yellow Bird also produced an English language version of the series for the BBC, this time starring Kenneth Branagh in the role of Kurt Wallander and featuring a largely British cast, but was filmed in Ystad, Sweden. This adaptation underscores not only the transnational appeal of Nordic Noir, but also the importance of a particular aesthetic to the repre-sentations within the genre (in this case, the unique locale of Ystad is evi-dently seen as indispensable to the stories being told). Other notable Scan-dinavian series that were adapted into English language formats include *The Killing* (DR, 2007-12) and *The Bridge* (SVT1 & DR1, 2011-18).

It is not only direct adaptations of original Scandi series which have invoked the conventions of the genre overseas, but also contemporary exam-ples of original English language series like *Hinterland* (BBC, 2013-), *Shet-land* (BBC, 2013-), and *Broadchurch* (ITV, 2013-17). Rather than recreate the specific characters and storylines of Northern European texts, these series instead replicate "the particular noir style and melancholy" of Nordic Noir (Hansen & Waade, 2017, 86). The transnational appeal of Nordic Noir is additionally demonstrated in the increased visibility of actors and creative personnel from the genre in overseas productions: Hans Rosenfeldt, writer of *The Bridge*, developed the crime drama *Marcella* for ITV, *Wallander*'s Krister Henriksson appeared briefly in BBC's *The Fall*, and Swedish actor Stellan Skarsgård starred in another BBC series, *River*. The fact that such actors and writers are so coveted by British networks and industry professionals speaks not only to the talent of the individuals in question, but also to the increasing eagerness to imbue new drama productions with the intangible qualities that have come to be associated with Nordic Noir. *River*'s writer, Abi Morgan, has said of Skarsgård's casting that "he's got that Scandi thing going on that's slightly 'other'. He's quite magical – truthful, yet magical. He's a Viking" (Arnold, 2015). Former BBC controller of drama, Ben Stephenson, has acknowledged that "whenever there is a phenomenon – and certainly Scandinavian novels and TV are a phenomenon – it can't help but be an inspiration" (Midgley, 2014). Just as it has become an inspiration for the aforementioned British crime shows, so too the aesthetic and themes of Nordic Noir have been adopted by Charlie Brooker in expanding *Black Mirror*'s ongoing exploration of TV formats as a significant element of its social commentary. Brooker, who famously dissected and mocked the codes and conventions of popular television over a number of years in his 'Screen Burn' column (Lusher, 2010) and *Screenwipe* TV series (BBC, 2006-8), experiments with the form in "Hated in the Nation" and "Crocodile" with an apparent view to both pay homage to his influences as well as engage an increasingly media-literate audience in critical dialogue.

Hated in the Nation

One aspect of "Hated in the Nation" which is noteworthy, with regard to its Nordic influences, is the length of the episode, at ninety minutes long, "Hated in the Nation" is to date the longest *Black Mirror* episode. There are clear parallels here with the seminal example of transnational Nordic Noir, *Wallander*. As previously discussed, *Wallander*'s distribution model featured a complex intersection of television, film, and DVD markets, whereby the first episode of a new series would be released in cinemas, before gradually progressing to DVD, pay-TV, and free TV releases. Erik Hultkvist of Yellow Bird observes that "it's easier to look at the productions as a TV series, rather than as feature films. But they are 90 minute films" (Peacock, 2013, 152). This model provides the creative advantage of transcending the rigidity of typical television scheduling requirements, as well as the industrial and generic concerns which may on occasion bleed over into the artistic product itself (though it is worth mentioning here that Mikael Wallen notes the common perception of the *Wallander* films in Sweden as only 'industrial TV', in contrast to the critical acclaim they attract overseas). On a narrative level, the added time provided by this model allows for more space to develop a story beyond a simple tale of crime and capture, and to include broader themes of thoughtful social critique which have been identified as such a pivotal theme of Scandinavian crime fiction.

We can certainly see echoes of this in *Black Mirror*'s move to Netflix, but also in the platform's brand ethos more generally. The destabilisation of traditional conceptions of what television is, and how it should be consumed, is integral to Netflix's convergence-oriented business model (McDonald & Smith-Rousey, 2016, 2). On one level, the company's binge-friendly strategy of releasing multiple series of shows (including *Black Mirror*) simultaneously for convenient, on-demand viewing effectively renders the typical episodic time constraints necessitated by traditional television schedules and advertising conventions redundant. On another level, it pushes back against established boundaries between film and television, both by investing so heavily in its original 'television' productions so as to render the difference in quality of production values negligible, and by constant experimentation with the distribution windows of cinema and streaming release dates (Bramesco, 2018). While the Netflix brand may be associated strongly with innovation and the opportunities offered by new technologies – as is strikingly illustrated by the interactive *Black Mirror* film *Bandersnatch* – the influence of Scandinavian models of media convergence such as those typified by the *Wallander* series can also be observed clearly here. As a coda to this, it is also worth noting that one of Netflix's first ventures into original programming was the Steven Van Zandt vehicle, *Lilyhammer*, another example of collaborative transnational co-production, this time between Netflix and the Norwegian company NRK, which foregrounded its Norwegian locale as a visible indicator of the platform's willingness to engage with this unique area of contemporary popular culture (Bakøy et al, 2017).

"Hated in the Nation" also foregrounds its Nordic influences through the names of central characters. Alongside more conventionally anglicised names, the episode's protagonists are given Scandinavian-sounding titles like Karin Parke and Rasmus Sjoberg, the latter portrayed (with accent undisguised) by Swedish actor Jonas Karlsson. Other characters, such as Vanessa Dahl (presumably a reference to Swedish crime writer, Jan 'Arne Dahl' Arnald) and Tess Wallander, seem to have been named as more explicit homages to Scandinavian crime fiction. This kind of 'hyperaware' intertextuality (Collins, 1995, 335) has been identified as a typical characteristic within 'cult' television (Abbott, 2010, 2), a category which *Black Mirror* certainly seems to fit into, and performs multiple functions in its contemporary usage. As well as allowing authors to acknowledge and pay homage to their own influences, intertextual cult TV can draw specific parallels and evoke connections with other media forms by "activating the text in certain ways, by making some meanings rather than others" (Fiske, 1987, 108), as well as by engaging the audience themselves in more active interpretation based on prior cultural knowledge (Gwenlian-Jones, in Brooker & Jermyn, 2003, 186). While familiarity with Nordic crime fiction is not necessary to follow the basic narrative of "Hated in the Nation," this sort of intertextual referencing adds a layer of complexity to the episode and invites fans of the genre to recognise its echoes within Charlie Brooker's writing. Just as the killer in the episode lays a trail of digital 'breadcrumbs' so that the detectives may fall into his trap, so Brooker leaves similar intertextual clues for *Black Mirror*'s viewers to decipher.

Just as several character names evoke Scandi crime fiction, so too do particular characterisations in the episode. The central investigation team of Karin Parke and Blue Coulson appear to reference the increasing visibility of female lead detectives in Nordic Noir, featured prominently in significant texts such as *The Killing*, *The Bridge*, *Jordskott* (SVT, 2015-17), and *Those Who Kill* (TV2, 2011); it may also be noted that the tendency toward strong female protagonists in traditionally male-dominated professions within contemporary Scandinavian drama is not limited only to the crime genre, with the Danish political series, *Borgen* (DR1, 2010-13), being another prominent example. The parallels go deeper with the characterisation of Blue, sidekick to Karin's lead investigator. Apropos to the themes of the episode, which feature state-commissioned, automated, bee-like drones hacked and appropriated to commit murder, Blue has an extraordinary aptitude for computer technology. She utilises this skill at multiple points during the episode to locate suspects and progress the investigation, and it seems at times that her familiarity with the technology matches and even surpasses that of Rasmus, the scientist who helped develop the project for the government. She also appears to have a strong sense of personal justice: at the episode's conclusion, Blue appears to have been personally affected by her inability to prevent the mass killing which has been the ultimate goal of the plot involving the drones. Consequently, she goes to extraordinary lengths to redress this, faking her own death so that she may be free to track down the perpetrator to a foreign country, with an apparent desire to exact some form of justice. In both respects, this characterisation appears to bear more than a passing resemblance to the troubled heroine of Stieg Larsson's *Millennium* trilogy, Lisbeth Salander. In Larsson's series of books, Salander, a troubled young woman who has suffered abuse throughout her life at the hands of her parents, authority figures, and institutions, uses her prodigious computer hacking skills to aid crusading journalist, Mikael Blomqvist, in his efforts to track down a serial killer and unmask corruption. As Larsson's novels take the reader deeper into Lisbeth's backstory and mindset, we see how driven she is to redress injustices as a result of the abuses she herself has suffered, and the latter instalments in the series follow her own personal vendetta against her tyrannical KGB agent father and sociopathic brother. As Salander has emerged as one of the more iconic protagonists of transnational Scandinavian popular culture, the imprints in the characterisation of Blue emerge as another of Brooker's homages to the genre.

Mikael Wallen, Executive Producer of Yellow Bird, the company behind *Wallander* and cinematic adaptations of Stieg Larsson's `Millennium` series, observes that a common definer of Nordic Noir is that "the stories are quite dark, and they offer some criticism of Swedish society and the Swedish way of living" (Peacock, 2013, 151). Additionally, Horst (2014) argues that "the entire idea of paradise lost is a prominent feature of Nordic crime: the social-democratic efficient society attacked from within by violence, corruption and homicide." The main plotline of "Hated in the Nation" involves a serpentine murder mystery, which intersects with Brooker's trademark dystopian Science Fiction combined with contemporary social critique. It begins with the mysterious, violent deaths of two minor celebrities who have become social media 'hate figures', and as the episode progresses we are taken further into a world of environmental collapse, burgeoning state surveillance, and the effects of online mob mentality and viral hate campaigns on society. As is the case with "Crocodile," technology plays a major part in the narrative and themes of the episode. In this instance, swarms of tiny, automated drones roam the country spreading pollen, performing the ecological function previously carried out by bees in order to avoid environmental catastrophe; the real bees, we are told, have become 'practically extinct.' As the story develops, these apparently benign devices take on a more sinister role, primarily through being commandeered by a malevolent hacker and used as weapons to murder his targets, but also when we learn that the drones have been commissioned by the government with a hidden purpose: mass surveillance through facial recognition technology. The plotline echoes a familiar truism about surveillance: that no matter how apparently benign or well-intentioned the surveillance is presented as to its subjects, it will always have the terrible potential to override its original remit, to devastating effect. Brooker's own awareness of issues surrounding creeping surveillance in Britain pre-dates *Black Mirror*, and has been an ongoing thread within his newspaper columns, dealing with developments from the emergence of "CCTV cameras that shout at you whenever you do something wrong" (2007) to the Data Retention and Investigatory Powers bill, which he dubs "the most tedious outrage ever" (2014). Although his concerns around these issues are couched in Brooker's familiar sardonic language and occasionally surrealist framing, it is evident that he has followed such developments with unease, and that this has informed the treatment of the issue in episodes like "Hated in the Nation" to no small extent.

The portrayal of the drones at their most deadly evokes classic Science Fiction and B-movie tropes, such as those of monstrous nature as well as technology run wild: the scenes of the ferocious, single-minded swarm echo any number of derivative 'killer bee' movies, while their awesome resilience and apparent ability to resist even the military's attempts to neutralise them raise the typical cautionary spectre of Skynet. However, this ostensible focus on the destructive possibilities of futuristic technology is something of a misdirect. It is the more banal, readily-available technology featured in the episode which is suggested to have the potential for true monstrosity, specifically, social media, and the broader cultural phenomena that come with its proliferation.

The motif of the bee-like drones functions on multiple levels as analogous to issues surrounding social media. One aspect it references fairly explicitly is the notion of the 'hive mentality' that inevitably arises as part of the viral nature of social media. As much as some social media platforms may encourage an almost narcissistic individualism in providing a public space for the broadcast of the everyday minutiae of one's life, they can also foster a need for approval and connectivity through functions such as likes, retweets, hashtags, and an emphasis on 'trends.' The initial murders that take place in the episode come about as a result of an online contest entailing the use of the hashtag '#DeathTo,' and the ease with which this hashtag takes hold within the narrative points to the alarming banality of the rationale by which individuals are motivated to wish death on complete strangers via social media. In "Hated in the Nation," the hashtag is incited by 'outrages' as mundane as a celebrity criticising a child's dancing on a talent show, or a young woman taking an irreverent selfie next to a war memorial. While such examples may seem typical of *Black Mirror*'s parodic embellishment of contemporary cultural trends, they are clearly rooted in real events. Similar instances can be found within recent popular culture: after the initial screening of Channel 4's controversial documentary *Benefits Street* (C4, 2014), it was reported that police were investigating death threats against residents of the street, with Twitter users tweeting via the #BenefitsStreet hashtag threatening to 'brain' or 'set fire to' the people featured in the programme (Denham, 2014). Examples like this, and the representations in the show which take inspiration from them, are constitutive of online 'firestorms', which have been defined as "sudden bursts of negative attention in cases of controversy and outrage" (Lamba, Malik & Pfeffer, 2015), or "an event where a person, group or institution suddenly receives a large amount of negative attention" (Pfeffer, Zorbach & Carley, 2014). The term (along with other commonly used synonyms like 'Twitterstorm') evokes notions of a force of nature, fearsome in its spontaneity and volatility. According to Lamba et al. (2015), the typical Twitter firestorm reaches peak activity on the same date it first appears. The phenomenon has become so commonplace and toxic on particular platforms that corporations have attempted to institute changes in the platforms to neutralise their susceptibility to what have been colloquially termed 'pile-ons' (Nicholson, 2019). Once again, the bee motif is important here in reflecting not only the groupthink of the 'hive' (and how dangerously suggestible it may be), but also the potential power of the swarm.

That the monstrous potential of social media is only fully realised in the episode when it begins to interact with the state's own surveillance technology is also telling. Many concerns have arisen in recent years over the ways in which social media may be used surreptitiously to mine data or influence election campaigns, and in 2019 a report covering internet use in 65 countries concluded that internet freedom had declined for the ninth consecutive year (Shahbaz and Funk, 2019). Of particular concern is the intersection between technological advances and the increasingly blurry relationship between the state and commerce. Leetaru (2019) highlights the increasing influence of private companies in what he calls "the modern digital surveillance state." Such companies may be responsible for anything "from acquiring and managing the vast datasets recording our daily lives to providing analytical software and services on top of that data" (Ibid). Much of the surveillance being undertaken through social media is now automated, utilising 'advances in AI and pattern analytics' to map everything from interpersonal relationships to potential attitudes to past, present, and future locations (Doffman, 2019). It is also increasingly monetised: Doffman warns that social media users "have now inadvertently opted into a data goldmine," the fruits of which are "available commercially," ready to be mined by "mass scraping tools" (2019). Such resources have been used by police and government agencies in the UK and the US to identify and monitor a range of activists, journalists, lawyers, and social media administrators from across the political spectrum, "many of whom had no criminal background" (Shahbaz and Funk, 2019). The nightmarish vision presented in "Hated in the Nation," in which unchecked AI collides with the omniscient surveillance state and the toxicity of commercial internet platforms, invests the creeping foreboding so often inspired by this intersection with a more tangible, visceral sense of threat. It also reaffirms the concerns so often evoked within socially-conscious Nordic Noir of the social consequences that may arise from the transition from social democracy to a more oligarchic, corporatized model of government.

Crocodile

As well as the labyrinthine serialised narratives employed by many contemporary British crime shows, Ben Stephenson identifies a pronounced 'sense of place and location' as one of the central elements such texts have taken from Scandinavian TV (Midgley, 2014). This obviously includes narrative elements specific to particular locales (the political and religious aspects of *The Fall*'s Belfast-based storylines, for example), but another commonality in several of the examples cited previously, such as *Shetland* and *Hinterland*,

is an aesthetic characterised by somewhat isolated communities, rural settings, and the tension between urban modernity and proximity to nature
(hence the preservation of Ystad as setting for the British TV adaptation of
Wallander). Once again, there are parallels here to the way evocative natural
landscapes and geography have been commonly deployed in Scandinavian
media and popular fiction. Crime writer Jørn Lier Horst (2014) has pointed to
what he calls 'Nordic melancholy' as a key part of the appeal of Scandi crime
fiction, which transcends interest in the crime narrative itself and provokes
a fascination "concocted from winter darkness, midnight sun, and immense,
desolate landscapes." Hansen and Waade (2017) see the 'commodified mel-
ancholic landscape' as a central feature of Nordic Noir, employed variously
to reflect the moods of characters and to evoke certain romanticised imagery of a region. The aesthetics of Scandinavia are characterised in the genre
by "the grey winter sun, bright summer nights, white winter landscapes and
the green spring," represented across disparate geographical environments
including "the vast, bleak landscapes in Denmark, the Norwegian and Icelandic mountains and the forest landscapes in Sweden and Finland" (Hansen
& Waade, 2017, 87). Nature in Nordic culture has been in some respects 'rendered with transcendental qualities,' historically, and specifically the duality
of eternal light and eternal darkness, which thus framed nature "as both the
cause of madness and pain – and their remedy" (Schultz Nybacka, in Askegaard & Östberg, 2019, 209). For Hansen and Waade, these stylised representations of environment are typically interwoven with the social critique
previously discussed as a central aspect of Scandinavian crime fiction. Their
discussion of what they call 'welfare melancholy' draws particular attention
to the function of 'desolate landscapes' in critiquing 'the fall of the welfare
society' in Sjöwall and Wahlöö's seminal *Story of a Crime* series of novels
(Hansen & Waade, 2017, 82-3).

This kind of foregrounding of environment is one of the most prominent aspects of "Crocodile," a nightmarish cautionary tale which features
a successful architect named Mia, who embarks on a grisly murder spree
in a doomed attempt to prevent a crime she was involved in as a young
woman from coming to light years later. Like the BBC's *Wallander*, the episode features the juxtaposition of a Scandinavian filming location with an
English-speaking cast; however, unlike that adaptation, the location is not
established within the text as being in Scandinavia. This creates an interesting dynamic in which, in spite of the visibility of a very striking physical

landscape and geological features, there is nonetheless something of a sense of placelessness about the episode. On a thematic level, this underscores the apparent rootlessness of the characters and the society Brooker envisions more broadly. "Crocodile" draws strongly on the physical aesthetic of Nordic storytelling, and the function of the environment in the episode is not only to evoke the generic associations of Nordic Noir, but also to mirror key aspects of plot and characterisation. In the early scenes of the episode, a young couple, Mia and Rob, are seen drinking and dancing in a nightclub, hours before being involved in a fatal car accident which claims the life of an unknown cyclist. In a panic, and fearful of the legal ramifications of having been under the influence at the time of the crash, the pair decide to cover up the crime by disposing of the body in a river, rather than report it to the police and risk a prison sentence. From the outset, the physical environment plays a key part in the storytelling. The car accident takes place on icy roads, in the middle of a snow-covered, mountainous wilderness. The eerie isolation of the deserted landscape undoubtedly plays a role in persuading the guilty parties that they may plausibly escape the consequences of their crime, with the absence of any witnesses or other human life in the nearby vicinity, thereby allowing the time and space needed to get rid of all traces of the death. This initial tragedy, and the criminal actions which accompany it, set into motion the spiral of violence and increasing moral depravity which begin to build years later, as the episode's timeline progresses.

As previously mentioned, the environmental conditions experienced during the filming of the episode were amongst the most extreme experienced in the Reykjavik region in decades, to the extent that filming was temporarily suspended at one point of the shoot due to the level of snowfall. Episode director, John Hillcoat, observes that "it's very humbling because it's a constant reminder of how powerful nature is: it adds energy. The world is right in front of you, and you have to deal with it" (Delahaye, 2018). Although the degree of severity of the conditions could not have been predicted (or indeed desired) by the production crew, the icy backdrop is clearly a conscious creative choice, and one which contributes greatly to the visual symbolism within the episode. The harshness of the environment mirrors Mia's increasingly ruthless mentality as she resorts to ever more depraved and malign lengths in her bid to suppress the evidence of her crimes. While Brooker suggests it was not the primary motivation for the episode's title, the cold-bloodedness of the titular reptile is one of several connotations which may be read into it, resembling as it does Mia's own coldness, and that of the environment within which the episode plays out.

Speaking of the episode's title, Brooker has surmised that it is "an analogy for somebody who'd been traumatised at an early age, and might be troubled by life forever and never able to relax" (Brooker et al, 2018). Brooker explains that the title evolved out of a very different episode outline, but endured despite the changes to the story; the initial plot had featured a baby who witnessed their mother's murder, and included the subsequent impact on worldview which Brooker likened to a virtual reality simulation of a boat ride, in which a crocodile attack happened in the opening minutes of the experience. Even the analogies used in this account underscore the tension between technology (the virtual reality simulator) and nature (in the form of the wild crocodile) which is pervasive throughout the episode. The snow-tipped, mountainous backdrops, which provide the setting for much of the episode, bring to mind Hansen and Waade's observation highlighted previously about the narrative function of 'desolate landscapes' in shaping the social criticism prevalent in Scandinavian crime fiction. The natural world is prominent in the aesthetic of "Crocodile," but it is a bleakly ambiguous presence rather than a reassuring one. The sheer vastness of the open spaces add to the aforementioned sense of isolation that looms over the episode, echoing the existential emptiness of its characters and what they are capable of in the name of self-preservation when loosed from the social moorings that typically foster empathy. Even the man-made structures in the episode add to this: office buildings with cavernous halls and soaring high ceilings, and dark hotel rooms with LCD screens that create the queasily antiseptic effect of a clear blue, bubbling pond, once again reaffirming the uneasy faux-tranquility that infuses the episode with tension.

The concerns around the survival of the welfare ideal which pervades Nordic crime fiction loom in the episode's depiction of a society in which big tech and large companies play an omnipresent role. In this society, state functions and responsibilities appear to have been increasingly given over to or shared with private entities. When Shazia, an investigator working for an insurance company, visits a client to interview him about his claim, she uses a device known as a 'recaller' which is used to scan people's memories in order to verify claims. The claimant voices his assumption that the devices are 'police things', but Shazia tells him "not since last year – we all have them now." This is a clear indication of the inverse trajectory of the state and corporations in this society, with the outsourcing of a police technology – as well as, implicitly through Shazia's character arc, the investigative responsibilities of the police – to private companies. The critique of the welfare state commonly associated with Nordic Noir often appears ambivalent, but is most typically directed from the left, targeting not necessarily the ideals of social democracy, but more often the sincerity of the politicians charged with custody of the project, and questioning its ability to endure and prosper in the face of such challenges. Robbins (2015) takes this a step further and identifies much of the criticism of the state present in Scandinavian fiction as closer to "critique of neoliberalism from the left," and certainly the society depicted in "Crocodile" seems to be one in which the 'big state' ethos of social democracy has been scaled back to such an extent that its institutions appear to be characterised primarily by detachment and disinterest. The fact that Mia and Rob's initial crime has gone undetected for 15 years does not speak reassuringly to the continuing efficiency of law enforcement agencies in this kind of environment, and it seems that the police have been increasingly sidelined as pertains to their traditional duties. As Shazia progresses with her investigation, we also learn from a hotel clerk that their booking procedures have changed as a result of a celebrity client's solicitation of a rent boy while staying as a guest at the hotel having been uncovered by tabloid hackers. This fleeting aside provides another indication of the outsourcing of investigatory work to the private sector, whether insurance investigators or the tabloid press.

Mia reluctantly agrees to cooperate with Shazia's investigation only because she is told that she is now compelled to by law, and that they should both seek to avoid 'dragging things out' by involving the actual police. This suggests an intentional abdication of responsibilities by the state, in tandem with the readiness of a willing private sector to absorb them. David Cameron, the British Prime Minister when *Black Mirror* initially launched in 2011, came to power a year prior on the back of a manifesto that prominently featured a policy known as the 'Big Society.' Cameron framed this project, which aimed to encourage community groups to play a greater part in the delivery and upkeep of traditional public services such as transportation, libraries, and post offices, as a way of empowering communities and harnessing 'people power.' However, the scheme was promoted against a backdrop of severe cuts to government funding of public services, and as such was criticised by union leaders as a cost-cutting means of ceding state responsibility for these services (Smith, 2010). As Cameron's premiership progressed, he expanded the idea as a means of releasing public services from 'the grip of state control', and argued that they should instead be "open to a range of providers competing to offer a better service" (2011), and shortly thereafter it was reported that, in practice, what this had led to was the emergence of 'an oligopoly' in this outsourcing, with contracts in the public services "overwhelmingly snapped up by a few big businesses" (Clark, 2012). In "Crocodile," we see an interesting critique of this kind of shrinking of the state: when society has ceased to exist in any meaningful form, why should individuals have any concern for any person or thing outside of themselves and their dependents? The implicitly Darwinian ethos emerging from the conflation of civil society with the need for 'competition' creates a context in which Mia's monstrous actions become horribly understandable, in which the primitive survival instinct is all-important.

Concerns such as those raised in "Crocodile" around the merging of state interests with private commerce are clearly influenced by developments in British politics such as those discussed above (along with the ones addressed by Brooker in his newspaper columns). However, it is important to remember that such developments are not unique to any one government or state, but rather part of an ongoing pattern of economic liberalisation emerging in tandem with globalisation across a range of Western democracies. This adds another layer of meaning to the uneasy sense of 'placelessness' evoked in the episode's uniquely eclectic aesthetic and narrative blend. The utilisation of the Nordic Noir motif evokes the socially-conscious character of Scandinavian crime fiction, but the way in which it is used emphasises the transferability of its concerns within a globalised political and economic landscape. The aforementioned sense of placelessness elicited through the episode's blend of British actors and Icelandic locales also alludes to a confusion of geographical boundaries: just as Nordic Noir crosses cultural borders, more ominously so do the anxieties the genre so often addresses. Leetaru (2019) explains how the growth in outsourcing of surveillance activities to private companies by states can be seen to render legal boundaries and borders increasingly redundant. Using the example of a private US company granted access to an EU citizen's private data initially collected by another contractor, Leetaru outlines the process by which that data may be subsequently used "to build a deep learning model to better flag a certain kind of suspicious activity" (Leetaru, 2019). Moreover, this model may then be sold "to other law enforcement and allied governments, including EU citizen's own government, which might otherwise face restrictions in using its citizens' data to build surveillance deep learning models" (ibid). Just as it was in "Hated in the Nation," the erosion of boundaries between the private and the public is an underlying theme which functions on multiple levels in "Crocodile," and the hybridisation inherent in the episode's depiction of place reflects the extent to which the reach and remit of multinational corporations have begun to bypass borders, and in doing so demonstrate why the critique of neoliberalism present in much of Scandinavian crime fiction is doubly relevant to societies outside the Nordic countries.

Conclusion

The use of intertextual referencing has become a familiar strategy in 'quality' TV, and *Black Mirror* utilises it prominently to make links to the contemporary cultural phenomenon of Nordic Noir. Scandinavian crime fiction foregrounds the persistence of enduring social ills and human flaws steadily devouring the utopian social democratic ideal, raising questions about social democracy's ability to redress the inherent failings at the heart of Western society when helmed by flawed or corrupt politicians. In *Black Mirror*, this social critique sets its sights on another secular religion: that of technology and scientific progress. *Black Mirror*'s dystopian homilies typically presume the last vestiges of any aspiration to social democracy in the fractured societies they depict as already stripped away, replaced by a corporate technocracy in which the functions of the state and civic institutions are increasingly outsourced to big tech companies. This is, of course, not dissimilar to the situation presently experienced in many contemporary neoliberal democracies, and this is consistent with *Black Mirror*'s particular approach to socially conscious science-fiction: while fantastical technology is represented, in many cases its narrative function is analogous to or peripheral to currently-existing technology. Ominous technological developments act as a vehicle that enables the monstrosity of human nature to come to the fore and presents the lie of the doctrine of social enlightenment as an inevitable companion to scientific progress. *Black Mirror* is a series that consistently plays with the conventions of genre and form to achieve specific artistic goals: by invoking the conventions of Nordic Noir in "Crocodile" and "Hated in the Nation," it attempts to refocus audience attention firmly on the social critique at its core.

Bibliography

Abbott, S. (ed) (2010) *The Cult TV Book*, London & New York: I.B. Tauris

Arnold, B. (2015) "'I've turned down every other cop show": Stellan Skarsgård on River', *The Guardian*, 7 October 2015, https://www.theguardian.com/tv-and-radio/2015/oct/07/stellan-skarsgard-abi-morgan-river-behind-the-scenes-tv-police-drama, accessed 8/9/2019

Askegaard, S. & Östberg, J. (eds) (2019) *Nordic Consumer Culture: State, Market and Consumers*, Cham: Springer Nature

Bakøy, E., Roel, P., & Spicer, A. (eds) (2017) *Building Successful and Sustainable Film and Television Businesses: A Cross-National Perspective*, Bristol: Intellect

Bondebjerg, I., Novrup Redvall, E., Helles, R., Sophus Lai, S., Søndergaard, H., & Astrupgaard, C. (2017) *Transnational European Drama: Production, Genres and Audiences*, Cham: Springer Nature

Bramesco, C. (2018) 'Is Netflix about to change how it releases original movies?', *Guardian*, 31 August 2018, https://www.theguardian.com/film/2018/aug/31/netflix-release-model-oscar-films-alfonso-cuaron, accessed 1/11/2019

Brooker, C. (2007) 'I can see you, citizen', *Guardian*, 9th April 2007, https://www.theguardian.com/commentisfree/2007/apr/09/humanrights.politics (accessed 3/4/2020)

Brooker, C. (2014) 'What is Drip, and how, precisely, will it help the government ruin your life?', *Guardian*, 14th July 2014, https://www.theguardian.com/commentisfree/2014/jul/14/drip-government-data-retention-investigatory-powers-bill-horrors (accessed 4/4/2020)

Brooker, C., Jones, A., & Arnopp, J. (2018) *Inside Black Mirror*, London: Ebury

Brooker, W. & Jermyn, D. (eds) (2003) *The Audience Studies Reader*, London & New York: Routledge

Cameron, D. (2011) 'How we will release the grip of state control', *Telegraph*, 20 February 2011, https://www.telegraph.co.uk/comment/8337239/How-we-will-release-the-grip-of-state-control.html, accessed 19/10/2019

Clark, T. (2012) 'Report: Cameron's big society is being thwarted by outsourced public services', *Guardian*, 3 December 2012, https://www.

theguardian.com/news/datablog/2012/dec/03/cameron-big-society-at-risk-private-outsourcing-public-services, accessed 19/10/2019

Collins, J. (1995) *Architectures of Excess: Cultural Life in the Information Age*, New York: Routledge

Deehan, T. (2018) 'Exploring the locations of Black Mirror season four', *The Location Guide*, January 4 2018, https://www.thelocationguide.com/2018/01/exploring-the-locations-of-black-mirror-season-four/, accessed 2/10/2019

Delahaye, J. (2018) 'Black Mirror 'Crocodile' location revealed as viewers floored by breathtaking snowy landscapes', *Mirror*, January 8 2018, https://www.mirror.co.uk/travel/europe/black-mirror-crocodile-filming-location-11791798, accessed 2/10/2019

Denham, J. (2014) 'Benefits Street residents subjected to death threats after Channel 4 show airs', *Independent*, January 7 2014, https://www.independent.co.uk/arts-entertainment/tv/news/benefits-street-residents-subjected-to-death-threats-after-channel-4-show-airs-9043932.html, accessed 10/10/2019

Doffman, Z. (2019) 'Your social media is (probably) being watched right now, says new surveillance report', *Forbes*, November 6 2019, https://www.forbes.com/sites/zakdoffman/2019/11/06/new-government-spy-report-your-social-media-is-probably-being-watched-right-now/#76db9c0a4f99, accessed 2/4/2020

Fiske, J. (1987) *Television Culture*, London: Routledge

Lamba, H., Malik, M. & Pfeffer, J. (2015) 'A tempest in a teacup? Analyzing firestorms on Twitter,' in *Proceedings of the 2015 IEEE/ACM International Conference on Advances in Social Networks Analysis and Mining*, ASONAM, pp.17-24

Leetaru, K. (2019) 'Much of our government digital surveillance is now outsourced to private companies', *Forbes*, 18th June 2019, https://www.forbes.com/sites/kalevleetaru/2019/06/18/much-of-our-government-digital-surveillance-is-outsourced-to-private-companies/#3002fe121799 (accessed 3/4/2020)

Lier Horst, J. (2014) 'The secret of Nordic noir', *The Hindu*, 5 April 2014, https://www.thehindu.com/books/literary-review/the-secret-of-nordic-noir/article5875988.ece, accessed 2/10/2019

Lusher, T. (2010) 'Charlie Brooker: 10 of the best Screen Burn columns', *The Guardian*, 16 October 2010, https://www.theguardian.com/tv-and-radio/

tvandradioblog/2010/oct/16/charlie-brooker-best-screen-burn, accessed 19/10/2019

McDonald, K. & Smith-Rousey, D. (eds) (2016) *The Netflix Effect: Technology and Entertainment in the 21st Century*, New York: Bloomsbury

Midgley, N. (2014), 'How British television fell under the spell of Nordic Noir', *Telegraph*, 28 March 2014, https://www.telegraph.co.uk/culture/tvandra dio/tv-and-radio-reviews/10724864/How-British-television-fell-under-the-spell-of-Nordic-noirThe-Tu.html, accessed 15/9/2019

Nicholson, T. (2019) 'Twitter wants to stop pile-ons with a 'clarification' button. Here's how it would work', *Esquire*, 18 February 2019, https://www.esquire.com/uk/latest-news/a26387783/twitter-wants-to-stop-pile-ons-with-a-clarification-button-heres-how-it-would-work/, accessed 15/9/2019

Parker, S. (2016), 'Charlie Brooker on the imminent technology apocalypse', *Esquire*, 21 October 2016, https://www.esquire.com/uk/culture/intervi ews/a11194/charlie-brooker-black-mirror-season-three-interview/, accessed 15/9/2019

Peacock, S. (ed) (2013) *Stieg Larsson's Milennium Trilogy: Interdisciplinary Approaches to Nordic Noir on Page and Screen*, Eastbourne: Palgrave Macmillan

Pfeffer, J., Zorbach, T., & Carley, K. M. Carley (2014) „Understanding online firestorms: Negative word-of-mouth dynamics in social media networks", *Journal of Marketing Communications*, vol. 20, no. 1–2, pp. 117-128

Robbins, B. (2015) 'The detective is suspended: Nordic Noir and the welfare state', *Post 45*, 18 May 2015, *http://post45.research.yale.edu/2015/05/the-detective-is-suspended-nordic-noir-and-the-welfare-state*, accessed 18/10/2019

Shahbaz, A. & Funk, A. (2019) 'Freedom on the net 2019: The crisis of social media', *Freedom House*, 4 November 2019, https://freedomhouse.org/sites/default/files/2019-11/11042019_Report_FH_FOTN_2019_final_Pub lic_Download.pdf, accessed 2/4/2020

Smith, N. (2010) 'David Cameron launches Tories' 'big society' plan', BBC, 19 July 2010, https://www.bbc.co.uk/news/uk-10680062, accessed 18/10/2019

Toft Hansen, K. & Marit Waade, A. (2017) *Locating Nordic Noir: From Beck to The Bridge*, Cham: Springer Nature

Mediated Verminisation
Ideology, Technology, and the Other as Monster

Artur de Matos Alves

In "Men Against Fire," set in a quasi-apocalyptic future, a team of technologically enhanced soldiers is sent to exterminate what they believe is a mutant
species of human ("Roaches"). After a mission, one of the soldiers starts
experiencing disruptions in their neural implants (MASS devices). These
implants are revealed to be not simply performance enhancers, but perception-altering devices that make soldiers perceive a group of humans as monsters, therefore making the soldiers more amenable to committing genocide.
This chapter chooses "Men Against Fire" as a starting point for a reflection
on media, technology, and ideology. By making use of Zizek's concept of hallucination as ideology, as well as of Mark Fisher's concept of "verminisation"
(originally by Szasz) as a rhetorical device in the justification of war, this text
will discuss the role of media and technology in enhancing the uptake of the
ideological structuring of social and political realities.

This chapter draws attention to three themes in "Men Against Fire." Each
section addresses a specific theme: the first can be described as the ideological production of social reality, that is, the creation of a shared mindset and
interpretation of the lifeworld as a driving force behind the shaping of that
same lifeworld through a quasi-hallucinatory process. The second theme is
related to the first, and explores the language of dehumanisation (specifically, "verminisation") as a weapon of political and ideological shaping of
social reality. The third aspect under analysis is the analogy with propaganda, that is, the dissemination of ideology and shared representations
of reality by the media. The argument focuses on the physical technological
implant as a stand-in for a sociotechnical apparatus of the ordering of reality:
the MASS device is an allegory for mass and individualized media, such as
digital platforms, and their role in spreading and consolidating ideological

representations. In this case, those representations target the dehumanized Other for military and political purposes. This episode of *Black Mirror* is particularly interesting in that it bluntly references contemporary discourse on migration and the spectacular character of virtualised war.

Playing with fire: episode summary

"Men Against Fire" is the fifth episode of the third season of *Black Mirror*, and aired in October of 2016. Directed by Jakob Verbruggen and written by Charlie Brooker, it is built around a cognitively enhanced military team tasked with seeking and eliminating a supposedly subhuman group – the "Roaches." "Men Against Fire" revolves around an advanced technology deeply embedded in human activity, and the plot expands into a social commentary with dystopic elements and a decidedly topical subject matter. The viewer is invited to follow "Stripe," one of the soldiers of the team, as they undertake a mission to kill a marauding group of "Roaches". Stripe is a new soldier, who has yet to encounter the enemy. Other members of the team are more experienced – Raiman is an enthusiastic hunter, and Medina is the seasoned squad leader. The episode gives some hints as to parts of Stripe's biography, including a romantic interest and his original consent to receiving a military implant in spite of the memory-altering consequences. In general, the soldier's character is presented as self-conscious and questioning, striking a very noticeable contrast with the military structure around Stripe, which demands obedience and submission to the imperatives of the institution and its technology.

"Roaches" initially appear as sickly, deformed, screeching quasi-human forms. Military personnel and technical support staff (including the psychologist Arquette) seem to be convinced that "Roaches" are beyond redemption, possessing inferior genetic traits, and therefore representing a mutated, degenerated form of human that endangers the existence of supposedly healthy human beings. Viewers (with Stripe) first encounter them crouching in hiding in a Christian pastor's home, trying to escape the military death squads trying to hunt them down. During the raid of the pastor's home, they are shown to have created a device that interferes with the military implants. This fact alone would, of course, disprove the characterization of "Roaches" as devolved subhumans, since it demonstrates ingenuity, intelligence, and technological sophistication.

We learn that the subhuman features of the "Roaches" are, in fact, generated by the MASS system in order to disguise the fact that they are ordinary human beings. This hallucinogenic technology is developed, according to in-episode exposition, to dehumanize a perceived enemy and solve what might be termed the "problem of empathy": how to convince a human being to kill other human beings without hesitation or questioning. The implant alters the perception of reality so that the soldiers' sensory apparatuses present a distorted version of the reality of extermination: killing a fully alien "Roach" is easier than killing a human, and the elimination of sensory overload (the sounds, the smell, the sights) of combat mitigates the risk of disobedience and psychological damage.

Soldiers are technologically augmented by receiving a neural implant – the MASS system. It acts as a neural interface that provides, at the same time, cognitive augmentations and remote-sensing and reconnaissance capabilities. For example, it allows soldiers to visualize the battlefield in order to plan their actions, and to access airborne drone cameras. However, it also acts as a reality-augmenting and -altering device. During the episode, we are also shown that it is able to generate dreams, in which the content and the intensity might be modulated as behavioural rewards – an erotic dream appears to be a reward for the first kill. When Stripe's device fails after his initial encounter with the "Roaches," the blocks the device imposed on perception, as well as the hallucinatory images altering the perception of the world, start to break down. He finally realizes that the "Roaches" are human beings and he meets Catarina, who explains to Stripe a slippery slope of screenings, DNA checks, registers, and propaganda leading to the complete dehumanization and calls for genocide of a group of people. It is at this point that we learn more completely the background of a war that is, in fact, nothing short of ethnic cleansing.

The dialogue between Stripe and Catarina is countered by a conversation between him and the psychologist. It is at this point that Stripe learns the truth behind the MASS device, its effects, and the totalitarian thinking underpinning the genocide: the creation of a soldier and of a populace amenable to war through the "ultimate weapon." This "ultimate weapon" is, in fact, a behavioural technology that enables and automates the lying and killing necessary for the "protection of the bloodline." The end of the episode shows how the process of implantation of the MASS system requires a degree of consent to the mood- and memory-altering process. The need to train, to desensitize for killing, and to control the "perfect soldier" takes precedence over the humanity or individuality of both soldiers and the persecuted group.

In short, the episode references ethnic cleansing, racism, eugenics, and behavioural control in a context of technological militarism. It is also reminiscent of the totalitarian militarism and propagandistic culture of Paul Verhoeven's *Starship Troopers* (based on Robert Heinlein's book) as well as of the simulacral hallucinations of the Wachowskis' *Matrix* trilogy. Both underline how the cognitive and social dimensions of human life are moulded in a technological context, and how social cohesion or compliance shape perception in tandem with a shared technological infrastructure.

Ideology becomes hallucination becomes reality

This section elaborates upon the summary of the episode and the presentation of its main characters by addressing the role of the MASS system as a disciplinary device of a very particular kind. This chapter contends that the device, besides allowing for a more effective desensitization of soldiers in the conditions of modern warfare, also answers a millennia-old question about the creation of the ideal soldier. Specifically, the MASS system is a technological stand-in for the perfect system of ideological indoctrination of soldiers, one that bypasses important neurological and psychological barriers to perfect obedience and compliance. Ultimately, such a device would, in a sense, operate as embedded ideology.[1]

"Men Against Fire" is also the title of a book by S. L. A. Marshall, originally published in 1947, which addressed the problems of soldier training and commanding in modern war and the challenges of guaranteeing combat performance under the stress of battle (Marshall, 2000). The author believed that the demands of modern war are at odds with fundamental socialization

---

1 This text follows, loosely, Lukács in defining ideology as a translation of the dominant classes' modes of thinking into a form of suppression of the consciousness of the proletariat, which makes this class view social reality in terms defined by others who rule over them. In *History and Class Consciousness*, Lukács states that the dominant ideas in capitalist systems do not correspond necessarily to the operation of the system itself, but rather to "the ideology of the ruling class" (Lukács, 1972, p. 14).

principles. Whereas a humanistic or religious upbringing emphasises social bonding through empathy, kindness, and a shared common ground for human beings despite their differences, wartime demands a precise calibration of community among comrades in arms, obedience to command, and unhesitant aggression towards the enemy. The strong contradiction between gregarious humaneness and organized aggression, along with the psychological stresses of warfare, generate a particular resistance to the violence of war, particularly in instances of mass mobilization.

How, then, to answer this problem and eliminate this resistance? Probably the most important theme in "Men Against Fire" is the perennial problem of the creation of "the perfect soldier." Neither the concept nor the approach presented in *Black Mirror* – the aim for complete control of a soldier's mind as well as body – are new. In fact, in *The Republic*, Plato describes the city's guardians, its protectors, as follows:

> (...) we must select from the other guardians the sort of men who, upon our consideration, from everything in their lives, look as if they were entirely eager to do what they believe to be advantageous to the city and would in no way be willing to do what is not. (412 d-e)

In Plato's *polis*, then, guardians are perfect in the sense that all aspects of their lives are set by an institutional and cultural framework that makes it impossible for them to interpret their reality differently. In the words of Allan Bloom, in the *Preface* to his translation of *The Republic*, "there are no guardians above the guardians; the only guardian of the guardians is a proper education" (Plato, 1991, p. xvii). The education and military training of the guardians is essential and it prepares them for a single role and a specific way to operate in the context of the city. The guardians are trained to obey and protect the city, and are specifically selected (bred) to do so. Their reality is created by a specific education system, built around the myths of the city and its glory, while avoiding all potentially demoralizing elements of non-sanctioned music, poetry, or material comforts.

Contrary to mercenaries, guardians do not prize money above all else, do not shy away from battle when victory is uncertain, and are loyal to the city instead of their paymaster. Compared to citizens, guardians are better trained, more disciplined, and better able to sustain the hardships of combat. Contrary to the aristocracy, guardians do not fight for riches or glory.

They are also not forced to go into battle as a slave might be. In general, the description of the "ideal soldier" in "Men Against Fire," even in the discussion of the psychological problems of modern warfare, does not stray far from Plato's view of the perfect guardian. Education, which can be defined as a form of indoctrination, cannot be guaranteed to be a perfect guardian of the guardians unless it is highly constraining. Plato's answer is that the right myth, that is, a beautiful necessary foundational lie, operates as a shared reality that creates a strong bond to the city and a dislike for anything that is perceived to threaten it. The creation of this founding myth, then, would be the prime mover of a new *weltanschauung* shared not only by the guardians of the city, but also by all those tasked to educate, train, and lead them.

Thus, establishing a founding formative myth in the heart of the vocation (that is, the sort of education that seduces the mind and the passions into loving the city above all else) becomes the central problem in the creation of the perfect guardian. In modern contexts, one might add that persuading soldiers to obey orders beyond any questioning is merely one of the many problematic aspects of mass mobilization and indoctrination as experienced during the hot and cold wars of the 20th and the 21st centuries. Industrial warfare demands wider societal acceptance than is suggested in "Men Against Fire." Constant indoctrination or distraction is necessary to maintain war preparedness and adherence to discipline or message. It would be unthinkable, for example, for a society to accept the kind of cognitive control made possible through MASS devices without a much wider civilian use of the system. To put it another way, the very effectiveness of the system would make it a very tempting device for commercial applications akin to those of neural implants featured in other *Black Mirror* episodes, such as "The Entire History of You," "White Christmas," or "Arkangel." In all of these episodes, a readily-available device or a prototype allows individuals or authorities to limit perception or to induce hallucinatory experiences in the users. In this sense, that device operates as a kind of automated shared ideology, or a targeted reality-shaping device: the individual's experience of the world is directly constrained by the worldview embedded in the control system. This episode helpfully identifies that system with a single person – Arquette –, who has complete command of the technological and ideological operation of the device.

An exceptionally long war period, such as the ongoing "War on Terror," generates a continuous stream of public persuasive strategic communication, as well as a public discourse saturated with jingoism and demonization of alternative approaches. Indeed, it might be argued, as noted below, that managing public opinion, or shaping social reality and discourse on large social scales, requires a proportionally large-scale message creation and distribution system. The purpose of such a system is not the generation of a "virtual reality" or the production of lies, but ensuring the stability of a structure of power – namely through the enactment of ideology via technology, discourse, and law. Yet, as the intensity of such an effort becomes more noticeable, it becomes harder to sustain the hallucination, that is, to hide the ideological underpinnings of the shared world. As Žižek suggests in "Hallucination as Ideology in Cinema," in a comparison between Hollywood and Nazi cinema, ideology is more noticeably at work when its fantasies are represented in the most literal way. It also at this point that "the cracks in the ideological edifice are rendered much more visible" (Žižek, 2002, sec. IV).

Verminisation and extermination

The previous section addressed the hallucinatory nature of ideology. Like a shared hallucination, ideology imposes a rigid ordering upon a variegated, ever-changing lifeworld (the social and natural world of human existence). It operates by introducing clear, seemingly self-evident distinctions between elements of that lifeworld, coloring experience in broad strokes and discarding most of the complexity of human affect in exchange for a purported unity of action and thought. Some distinctions operate internally to the group to which they are imposed: they reinforce in-group cohesion and identity and, as such, can be described as centripetal and integrative. An example of this type of distinction is group identity, as created through shared rites of passage or lived experiences. More widely, such distinctions are imposed through nationality, religion, or ethnicity. Other distinctions describe the outside of this group, and therefore operate externally and introduce a negative, threatening dimension presented as a form of atmospheric pressure exerted all around the boundaries of the in-group. The "outsiders" are variously described both as strong threats and as weaker versions of in-group – often simultaneously. Either way, "outsiders" are always presented as opponents to fear, to challenge, or to eliminate.

When referring to Mexican immigrants to the USA as "rapists," "criminals," and "illegals," U.S. President Donald Trump offered a clear, recent example of this kind of representation. As we now know, that characterisation presaged a more complete concentrationary logic, in which verminisation of foreigners preceded an aggressive imprisonment and expulsion program. It is clear that public discourse and political safeguards failed, until now, to stem the grave consequences of this sequence, which shows how powerful such ideological constructs can be.

In no way is this a new phenomenon. Studies of propaganda in the wake of World War I described the rhetoric structuring this ideological construction of radical antagonism. The idea that the Other is to be feared and rejected doubtlessly predates mass propaganda, but it is the latter that best conveys a continuity in the transformation of antagonism into hatred, and of hatred into ideology and political action. The Institute of Propaganda Analysis (IPA) of Columbia University published, in 1937, a typology of propaganda techniques used in times of war, in which the rhetorical devices were explained in a simple and clear fashion. The famous "tricks" used in mass persuasion, according to the IPA, were "card stacking," "name calling" "generality," "testimonial," "transfer," "plain folks," and "band wagon" (Jowett and O'Donnell, 2012, p. 237). All of these depend on the construction of a message with a given behavioural or emotional set of responses in mind, and are therefore based on the careful staging of fact and fiction.

Let us examine, among these rhetorical moves, those closer to the object of this text. A "bandwagon" argument is based on the (usually overstated) degree of acceptance of the idea being put forward. Other "tricks" of propaganda identified by the IPA are more directly linked to existing social predispositions of the intended audience. "Plain folks" relies on the persuasive power of the simplicity of the opinion of the supposedly common person. "Glittering generality" refers to a cherished, often abstract idea that is not subject to proof or examination. "Name calling" similarly requires that the audience reject a given person or idea without examination. A more extreme form of name-calling is the outright dehumanization of the opposition, in which the basic human characteristics of the in-group are denied to the enemy. This set of rhetorical resources is a recurring feature of propagandistic efforts, and more recent analyses and models of propaganda have built upon these insights into processes of mass persuasion. For example, Chomsky and Herman's analysis of propaganda originally highlighted the role of *anti-communist* rhetoric during the Cold War, but afterwards was replaced by *capitalist pro-market* rhetoric (Herman, 2000), and then, during the War on Terror, the notion of an Axis of Evil (Herman, Chomsky, and Mullen, 2009, p. 14).[2]

Dehumanizing the enemy in discourse and in everyday practice is a particularly insidious form of persuasion, not least because it mobilizes notions such as "race," "genes," "heritage," and other pseudo-scientific biological analogies. Taken to the extreme, it operates in discourse as "verminisation." This, according to Mark Fisher, is a rhetorical device in the discourse of justification of war that "transforms the enemy into a subhuman swarm that cannot be reasoned with, only destroyed; it also makes 'us' into victims of its repulsive, invasive agency" (Fisher, 2018, chap. 'Conspicuous force and verminisation'). Therefore, verminisation is part of the encouragement or ideological preparation for atrocities, especially against immigrants and other minorities; it presents the in-group as "ontologically Good" and the Other as inherently Evil. This representation is not merely aesthetic; in fact, it is predominantly political and behavioural in its aim.

The psychiatrist Thomas Szasz, from whom Fisher adopted the concept, originally identified verminisation as a device for allowing a moral judgement to disguise itself as a scientific or neutral assessment, thereby acquiring legitimacy. In his discussion of the medicalization of society, Szasz, writing in the 1970s, stated that the discourse around drug addiction in the United States followed this pattern of verminisation, by equating addiction with an epidemic to eradicate, even if that meant eliminating drug users and pushers (Szasz, 1974, p. 15–17). Medicine and by law ultimately further reify this metaphor, lending it the legitimacy it needs to become acceptable practice. The complete dehumanization of human beings is, for Szasz, a product of the social discursive constructs that come to be applied to entire groups of people for therapeutic or otherwise disciplinary purposes. Mental illness is one of the instances of this rhetoric of exclusion, wherein the use of the label of "sickness," far from being an accurate description of a biological condition, is instead a reference to a scientific paradigm as well as, more generally, "a linguistic and social game" (Szasz, 1991, p. 50).

---

2 Herman and Chomsky also placed focus not just on rhetoric, but on the political economy
   of the communication system, characterizing ideological dissemination as a tool of social
   control at the disposal of ruling classes (Herman and Chomsky, 2002, p. 2).

Verminisation is linked to hate speech as much as to the therapeutic labelling of marginality. Since animal species usually considered to be vermin or pests (such as mice, mosquitoes, or roaches) are vectors of disease for humans, "vermin" becomes a synecdoche for disease and epidemic. Verminisation, then, operates by equating the enemy to a pest, an infestation by an invasive species, bearing contagious diseases and biological defects, which needs to be eradicated as a matter of survival for the pure, but fragile, "full humans." Because of the obvious rhetorical and logical connection between the discourse of dehumanization and genocide, verminisation is part of "atrocity speech," presaging a logic of exclusion and, ultimately, "extermination," that is, genocide. It is notable that there is a substantial contradiction in supremacist speech and the rhetoric of verminisation in the Nazi mould. On the one hand, the "vermin" are inferior, diseased, morally and physically deformed. On the other hand, they represent a danger to "purity," to healthy humans, a threat to eliminate. This duality ensures that a sense of superiority coexists with fear: an urgency to secure borders, both geographic and genetic, against existential threats not just to individuals, but to the entirety of the group.

"Men Against Fire" does away with any subtle allegory in this domain by employing the term "Roach" to identify the target of the atrocities. The characteristics of dehumanizing speech are all clearly present in the speech of the psychologist detailing the illnesses and threats carried by the "Roaches," whereas the truly human character of the persecuted group is demonstrated earlier in the episode in the main character's interaction with Catarina. She explains that there is nothing wrong with "Roaches," and that they are, in fact, migrants, recently arrived to a new country. After being subjected to multiple forms of bureaucratic control and cataloguing, they were ultimately placed at the margins of society and became the victims of genocide. The rigorous labelling and registration of the people preceded its exclusion from society, first through administrative means, then through technology. The first process established a pseudo-scientific pathologizing of the group – couched in the language of genetics. The second process established the basis for systematic elimination without any remorse.

There are multiple obvious historical parallels between "Men Against Fire" and the persecution and genocide of German and European people of Jewish descent in Nazi Germany. The first is, of course, the process of dehumanization, whereby not only Jews but also people considered to suffer from mental illnesses, congenital disorders, or otherwise deemed "degenerate" were catalogued, institutionalized, and killed. Secondly is the construction of consent around the dehumanization of certain groups, along with the imposition of disciplined compliance to all social groups. A third aspect pertains to the technologically-mediated process of elimination. In this episode of *Black Mirror*, the MASS system desensitizes soldiers to the act of killing by superimposing a hallucinatory mask over the reality of, not war, but massacre, to preclude feelings of guilt, empathy, or simple human recognition. In Nazi Germany, the creation of death camps was one of the administrative responses to the call for genocide, and crucially considered the most efficient and least damaging response to the morale of the soldiers. Hardened fanaticism did not seem enough to preclude the pangs of morality. Since the existence of the camps was concealed, and even denied, the realities of the genocide were disavowed by the public, in spite of the generalised rhetoric of hatred (including verminisation and calls for extermination) towards Jews during the Nazi period. In the same way, ideology and technology operate together to enable each other's discipline and operation.

Propaganda and technology in the hallucinatory apparatus

As explained in the previous section, verminisation, as rhetorical strategy, signals an effort to dehumanize and isolate a group of humans with shared characteristics and deny them the rights and privileges ascribed to the in-group. However, the rhetorical machinery of prejudice is neither spontaneous nor innocent. As described above, the attribution of characteristics of vermin to human beings is typically a prelude for the imposition of a disciplinary apparatus, in that it implies a need for control via eradication or exclusion. This process also entails an ideological standpoint in that it seeks to advance a certain worldview to lead to the imposition of a new order of things upon the social world. This section discusses the ways in which the episode "Men Against Fire" addresses the issue of the dissemination of ideology through technology and propaganda.

Verminisation presages the use of force, providing it with ideological justification while reinforcing the representation of the in-group as inherently Good regardless of the violence employed by its members (Fisher, 2018, chap. 'Conspicuous Force and Verminisation'). In "Men Against Fire" the rationale for the elimination of the "Roaches" is that of logical necessity, of need, of a service to the Good of humanity – a logic of intervention as a burden of the wardens of morals and purity. At this stage, communication technologies – and the media in particular – become the vehicles for the anticipation of violent action and for controlling negative attitudes towards its exercise. It is not surprising, then, that in this episode of *Black Mirror* military action – filtered by the MASS device – resembles that of a video game or a movie. That representation is the corollary of the correspondence between means and ends: genocide is a technical problem, best accomplished by sterile means and flawlessly calibrated systems. That the result is unbearable violence and ruin is of no consequence for a reality thoroughly saturated by hallucinatory images: military violence in "Men Against Fire" can be justified because it is seen as righteous and the enemy is no better than vermin. Any moral qualms about this action are, therefore, presented as the true hallucination or delusion: religion, education, common sense must all give way to the ludic and erotic rewards of true integration.

The MASS system, as noted above, embeds ideological control directly into the perceptual system, taking control of sensorial inputs as well as of oneiric and erotic aspects of personality. In so doing, it effectively replaces perception and reasoning. For Fisher, "hyper-realisation is precisely what permits the production of very real deaths on a mass scale" (ibid.), where reality is permeated with fiction to such a degree that it becomes hallucination. In *Black Mirror*, this effect is typically introduced by information and communication technologies of some sort, with neural implants and interfaces being common plot devices throughout the series. Baudrillard noted that propaganda conceals itself in mass communication in order to enhance its effectiveness in mixing the real and the lie, thus generating something akin to a hallucination by interfering with the construction of a lifeworld – its language, its shared iconography, its myths. A centralized political economy of communication allows for an even more effective dissemination of that mix (Baudrillard, 1988, p. 141).

In "Men Against Fire" the technological trope of the implant operates, at the same time, as a stand-in for the diffuse hallucinatory system of mass media, and for a centralized, technocratic attempt to de-politicize ideology through scientific justification. In short, MASS devices act as a delivery system for propaganda and ideology. Like typical propaganda, the implant's purpose it to influence and change attitudes, delivering emotional and sensorial reinforcement by overwhelming individuals with rewards while, at the same time, blocking any contradictory signals. Naturally, this reinforcement and interference binary works only if it engages with the expectations, desires, and fears of the target, but cannot operate except by disguising its disciplinary purposes. In this episode of *Black Mirror*, as already noted, those purposes are clearly stated by Catarina and Arquette, while Stripe's fellow soldiers exhibit the same blissful videogame-like alienation as *The Matrix*'s Cypher. It is in this sense that Kenneth Payne defines propaganda as a kind of psychological and anthropological construction, necessarily grounded in "narrative elements most likely to resonate with the target groups" (Payne, 2009, p. 110). Ideological construction of discourse is most effective when it is supported by acculturation and socialization.

In their analysis of propaganda, both Herbert Marcuse and Jacques Ellul recognise the role of mass persuasion in the integration of the individual in industrial society. Their arguments converge in the assessment that industrial society requires, especially in the context of an optimized technocratic economy (such as a wartime economy), the compliance of individuals. Concomitantly, mass society requires mass communication and persuasion in order to maintain cohesion – it is an integrative, centripetal force counteracting the effects of specialization and distribution of social labour in modern societies. Therefore, mass persuasion has a necessary disciplinary role in industrial society. For Ellul, propaganda operates both at the individual and at the mass levels, creating an aesthetic and historical re-grounding that aims to overcome any residue of resistance in eliciting the appropriate response. It is less about eliciting a reflected response than "to provoke an action. It is also not to make one change his allegiance to a given doctrine, but to irrationally engage him in an *active process*" (Ellul, 1962, pp. 36–37. My emphasis). Here, too, we find parallels in the way "Men Against Fire" interprets the mutual dependency between Stripe's psyche – his ego, but also his conscience – and the military technocracy controlling the cognitive implant. The latter requires compliance and integration, but it must do so under the guise of rational, enlightened conscious acceptance of the reality of the MASS device. Of course, this choice is merely an illusion, since one suspects that the removal of the device would not set the soldier free of the psychological effects of the terror he had helped sow, and even less of that military technocracy with which he had signed a contract. In fact, this formal contract and the form of consent is an unnecessary flourish in the narrative. In no way does the revelation that Stripe had signed a contract accepting the negative consequences of the MASS implant differ from a soldier's enlisting in times of violent conflict. It does, however, call into question the blind acceptance of technological normativity typical of, for example, the online agreement forms for digital platforms' terms and conditions of service. It is perhaps this allegory of passive consent that should give one pause to reflect upon the creeping techno-cognitive infrastructure of our lifeworld.

Final remarks

As I have argued, "Men Against Fire" attempts to address a particularly distressing set of biopolitical and discursive phenomena. The episode addresses a complex interaction of ideology, technology, war, and perception, calling into question the arbitrariness of myth as well as its generalized acceptance through its absorption into ideology. We may make a distinction between the several subjectivities presented in the episode, each revealing a particular position in the biopolitics of atrocity. In the first instance, Stripe represents the main subject of the biopolitical apparatus, the one that needs to be disciplined and brought into submission through constant surveillance and technical care. Second, the MASS system, understood not just as a particular case of a technical device but as a dispositive – a technosocial assemblage built to mobilize the armed forces in the most efficient and predictable way.[3] Third, the group called "Roaches," an essential artificial construct (the "hallucination") which provides the enemy at the core of the ideological underpinnings of the disciplinary system.

In other words, the propagation of a lie and its crystallization into an acted-upon worldview is the *sine qua non* of the operation of ideology as hallucination: the lie must be *lived*. The only possible way to ensure that the hallucination overcomes the material presence of that which would belie its character is to force it onto the very perceptual apparatus. Thus, ideology

---

3 Foucault's concept of dispositive (or apparatus) sheds light into the technosocial construction and articulation of power relations. The dispositive is not a rigid structure of domination and alienation. It is best understood as an adaptive, fluid process wherein human beings, technologies, institutional arrangements and discourses shift and rearrange themselves in those relations of power (cf., in particular, Foucault, 1994, pp. 298-329).

becomes active in the world through the mediation of a technological perceptual bypass, which manifests a perceptual reality coherent in every way with that ideology, thereby guiding thought or action. The moment where that bypass is negated is, in a way, the return of the repressed reality forcing a new choice upon the disciplined subjectivity (Stripe): either to face this new perceptual and intellectual reality, thus abandoning not just the hallucination, but also their lifeworld, or to fully embrace the hallucination. Stripe's choice, in fact, is similar to that of the character Cypher in *The Matrix* (1999), who regrets having accepted the "red pill" that freed him from the Matrix and betrays the free humans in exchange of being reintegrated into the Matrix as a privileged person. Forgetting his previous life out of the simulation is the crucial element of the agreement: embracing the lie is perceived to be the only form of liberation.

"Men Against Fire" is interesting not because it is particularly masterful television, but in that it makes literal and visible the interaction of ideology and technology. My contention is that this episode brings verminisation to the fore in as a crucial step in the transformation or creation of a worldview amenable to manipulation, and potentially leading to persecution of minorities (and genocide). The most evident example is that of Nazi Germany, but more recent instances of genocide – the persecution of the Rohingya people in Burma comes to mind – show that the dissemination of propaganda and the ideological construction of a shared negative view attempt to superimpose that perception upon the experience of the lived human world. In early 2020, the association of the spread of the COVID-19 virus with Chinese travellers or emigrants constitutes a powerful reminder of the persistence of verminisation as a rhetorical threshold for discrimination and even violence.

In sum, this episode keeps with the dystopian tones of most *Black Mirror* episodes. It includes a thoroughly disheartening and fatalistic, albeit somewhat ambiguous, ending. As a reflection on technology, it addresses the compulsion for human augmentation by calling into question human autonomy in the era of disciplinary, managed technological systems. It also portrays speculative simulation technologies and human augmentation as an extension and radicalization of the current social trends, where persuasive discourse and ideological manipulation give shape to new divisions or, even more often, make old fears and hatreds resurface. The final scene – the return to a crumbling American suburban home – suggests that the hallucinatory veneer of simulation and ideology, far from being a fragile construct or reality effect, is the product of a willingness to accept illusion, deception, or distraction, rather than facing the disagreeable realities of a dysfunctional *polis*.

Bibliography

Baudrillard, J. (1988). *Selected Writings*. Edited by Mark Poster. Stanford: Stanford University Press.

Ellul, J. (1962). *Propagandes*. Paris: Librairie Armand Colin.

Fisher, M. (2018). *K-Punk: The Collected and Unpublished Writings of Mark Fisher (2004-2016)* [E-book]. Edited by Darren Ambrose and Simon Reynolds. London: Repeater Books.

Foucault, M. (1994). *Dits et écrits: 1954-1988 Tome 3: 1976-1979*. Edited by Daniel Defert. Vol. 3. Paris: Gallimard.

Herman, E. S. (2000). 'The Propaganda Model: A Retrospective'. *Journalism Studies* 1 (1), pp. 101–112.

Herman, E. S. and Chomsky, N. (2002). *Manufacturing Consent: The Political Economy of the Mass Media*. New York: Pantheon Books.

Herman, E. S., Chomsky, N. and Mullen, A. (2009). 'The Propaganda Model after 20 Years: Interview with Edward S. Herman and Noam Chomsky'. *Westminster Papers in Communication and Culture* 6 (2), pp. 12–22.

Jowett, G. S. and O'Donnell, V. (2012). *Propaganda and Persuasion*. 5th ed. Thousand Oaks: Sage Publications.

Lukács, G. (1972). *History and Class Consciousness: Studies in Marxist Dialectics*. Translated by Rodney Livingstone. Cambridge, Mass.: The MIT Press.

Marshall, S. L. A. (2000). *Men Against Fire: The Problem of Battle Command*. Norman, Okla: University of Oklahoma Press.

Payne, K. (2009). 'Winning the Battle of Ideas: Propaganda, Ideology, and Terror'. *Studies in Conflict & Terrorism* 32 (2), pp. 109–28. https://doi.org/10.1080/10576100802627738.

Plato (1991). *The Republic of Plato*. Translated by Allan Bloom. 2nd ed. New York: Basic Books.

Szasz, T. (1974). *Ceremonial Chemistry: The Ritual Persecution of Drugs, Addicts, and Pushers*. 1st ed. New York: Anchor Press.

Szasz, T. (1991). *Ideology and Insanity: Essays on the Psychiatric Dehumanization of Man*. Syracuse: Syracuse University Press.

Žižek, S. (2002). 'Hallucination as Ideology in Cinema'. *Theory & Event* 6 (1). https://doi.org/10.1353/tae.2002.0013.

Technicity and the Utopian Limits of the Body

Anna Caterina Dalmasso

Black Mirror between dystopia and utopia

Dramatically drawing our attention on the unpredictable dystopic effects of our relationship to technologies, the series *Black Mirror* instills concerns about our engagement with digital interfaces and devices, and seems to promote a feeling of technophobia. Most of the episodes follow a basic plot-line: what would be the result of exacerbating simply one aspect of our familiar technosphere? Consistently developed, any envisioned output would end up undermining our trust in the trajectory of modern progress. But, is this really the case?

Western thought has long dwelled in the belief that technology in itself is – respectively, under an ontological and ethical respect – fundamentally neutral and essentially amoral. According to this perspective, any ethical, social, or political implication of technology should be considered as a result of the way in which its users choose to employ it. A hammer, for example, can serve different and even opposed purposes, so that its value as a tool *depends on how it is used;* technology being "a means, not an end," as the saying goes.

During the 20th century, theorists and critics have argued against such an assumption, progressively deconstructing the thesis of the neutrality of technology (Heidegger 1954; Simondon 1958), and positing instead that technology is an autonomous force that acts on its users. They are also focused on how technologies actively help shape culture and society (Ellul 1964; Postman 1979 & 1993; Ihde 1979).

In fact, as long as it mediates our relationship with the world and others, any interface, tool, or device unavoidably selects, amplifies, or reduces in various ways aspects of our experience (Ihde 1979, 1990) and introduces perceptual as well as intellectual, emotional, and social biases in our engagement with the world. Technologies and media contribute to designing and *informing* our reality; they "classify the world for us, sequence it, frame it, enlarge it, reduce it, argue a case for what it is like" (Postman 1979, p. 39). Thus, as long as they entail reconfiguration and structural transformation of our experience of the world (Ihde, 1979, p. 66), technologies, far from being neutral, act like "metaphors through which we conceptualize reality in one way or another" (Postman 1979, p. 39).

Still, the belief in the neutrality of technology permeates the general common sense and is particularly difficult to eradicate from the logic and intellectual history of Western civilization. This can be noticed in the contemporary attitude towards the impact and presence of technologies in our lives. For example, even though recently some of the visionary technologists and theorists of Silicon Valley have pointed out that the technological dream they aimed to realize has ultimately given way to surveillance and attention-grabbing business models, still most of them refuse to put into question the very structure of the dispositives set up by mass media. However, they blame instead the uses and ulterior motives that lead them, and they continue to pursue the possibility of minimizing negative aspects brought forth by digital technologies, promoting an ideal socio-economic paradigm able to "realign" technology with humanity. This is the case of associations and non-profit organizations like the *Center for Humane Technology* – founded, among others, by the former Google design ethicist, Tristan Harris – which envision a world wherein "technology supports our shared well-being, sense-making, democracy, and ability to tackle complex global challenges" (*Center for Humane Technology*, https://humanetech.com/).

In fact, as this particular case exemplifies, the raised awareness regarding the role and impact of technology on our lives also produces a *tendency to oppose technology to an alleged (pretechnical) human nature*. This view still hinges upon a conception of technology already expressed by Plato (*Protagoras* 321a-322d), which describes *techne* as a skill that human beings have developed to compensate for their deficient nature. In defining what is a human being, technology is evoked by Protagoras, in the eponymous Platonic dialogue, as a competence with the help of which human beings can overcome their natural frailty and insufficient (if compared to other animals) anatomic endowments.

Notably, this idea has been taken on in the 20th century, especially in the work of the philosopher and anthropologist Arnold Gehlen (1950, 1957): technology is the capacity through which human beings have surpassed their instinctual and organic deficiencies and have been able to emancipate themselves from the world of nature. Being "burdened" (see the notion of *Entlastung*) by the difficulties in providing for their survival, human beings developed a "second nature," allowing them to counterbalance their unfinished condition and their lack of specialization that characterizes their "eccentric" positioning in the environment (Plessner 1928).

However, if we understand the advent of technicity as opposed to an original condition of humanity, we risk missing the fundamental significance of technology. This is, I will argue, the kernel of the reflection developed by *Black Mirror*. The dystopian scenarios outlined by Charlie Brooker's series seek to dismantle the thesis of the neutrality of technology, but, far from expressing a technophobic or Luddite view, they instead urge us to consider technology as fundamentally *human*. In other words, *Black Mirror* dramatically draws our attention to the fact that technicity shall be thought of not as something that is merely added onto a "natural" core of embodied life, but as a phenomenon that originally characterizes the relationship between the human being and the environment (Simondon 1958: 9).

As the French philosopher, Gilbert Simondon, has pointed out, Modern Western thought has long neglected the cultural relevance of technology (Simondon 1958, Simondon 2014) and has failed to acknowledge that technical objects always include an anthropological significance. This has prevented established theory from considering technical objects as "mediators between man and nature," and has ended up, on the one hand, in an idealization of technics, and, on the other hand, in an imaginary conception of the machine as a threat, drawing a purely mythical opposition between human beings and machines. Such an opposition needs to be questioned and systematically deconstructed to investigate the co-implication and mutual constitution of humans and technology. Yet, in the process of informing our relationship with the world, is technology also likely to jeopardize it? What are the critical boundaries of the technological hybridization of the human being? This is one of the pivotal problematic questions on which the series revolves.

The coupling of bodies and technologies has never been as evident as in the last decades, by virtue of the diffusion of portable and wearable devices as well as virtual and augmented reality technologies. Screens and devices work as prosthesis for human sensibility and expand the capacities of the intersubjective sphere, increasingly affecting our embodied existence (Montani 2014). But what are the limits and what would be the consequences of a generalized "prostheticisation" of our body and its symbolic and cognitive functions?

Already, André Leroi-Gourhan, in his account of technicity in human evolution, expressed a concern with regards to the possible effects of further technologization of the body. On the one hand, the French anthropologist and paleontologist pointed out that our familiarity with audio-visual communication and devices would eventually lead to a loss of the exercise of the imagination, considering that "a society with a weakened property of symbol-making would suffer a concomitant loss of the property of action" (Leroi-Gourhan 1964 (II): 296 ; transl. 1993: 214). At the same time, he wondered whether in the future, with the increase of the process of technological exteriorization, the human being will end up feeling "encumbered by the archaic osteomuscular apparatus inherited from the Paleolithic" (Leroi-Gourhan 1964 (II): 52; transl. 1993: 249).

By powerfully questioning the limits of our technological engagement with the world, the *Black Mirror* series does not simply criticize technology, but rather sheds light on the fact that human beings and technology are intrinsically entangled and mutually constituted (Parisi 2019). Hence, rather than *dystopic*, the relationship between humans and technology shall be understood as a *utopian* one, not just in the current meaning of "ideal" or "fictional," but in the etymological sense of "in no place," since, far from being stable and identifiable, it must be constantly redefined and designed anew in a constitutively metastable balance.

This chapter will develop this hypothesis by focusing in particular on how the *Black Mirror* series interrogates the way digital technologies contribute to informing and reconfiguring our bodily and embodied engagement with the world.

Where is the body? or: the mobile limits of the flesh – *The Entire History of You*

What if in the near future everyone had access to a computerized implant that records every experience available for instant playback and long-term storage? This is the reality outlined by "The Entire History of You," the third episode in the first season of *Black Mirror*. In such a world, there would be no more discussions about what one can have just said or done, everything would be recorded, and "re-doable," by means of a prosthetic device called the "grain," the ultimate – indeed, not so difficult to imagine at the time of the Google Glass prototype – extension of human memory. The episode goes through some of the possible implications of such device for everyday life, going from the simple decrease of privacy regarding personal experiences, such as a job interview, up to masturbating while replaying sex memories from earlier relationships.

The main plot revolves around an argument between husband and wife. At a dinner party, the main character, Liam, notices an unusual complicity between his wife Ffion and Jonas, one of the guests. As the row between them goes on, and while re-playing footage of the past by means of the grain, Liam eventually forces Ffion to admit that she had a previous relationship with Jonas. After confronting Jonas in the morning, he goes as far as to doubt the paternity of his own daughter, since, as the grain reveals, the two had an affair around the time she was conceived. The confrontation will eventually lead to the separation of the couple, as the last scene of the episode shows Liam wandering around his now empty house, playing re-dos of happy memories with Ffion and their daughter, before deciding to cut out the implant from behind his ear using a razor blade.

This ending seems to suggest the desire to come back to a pre-prostheticized body, a body still free from the unavoidable conditioning of technology in our lives. But, is that really possible? Isn't our contact with the world always informed and transformed by our relationship to devices and technologies? In other words, is the human living body not extended into the environment by means of some kind of prosthesis? Where does the body end and where does technology begin?

In fact, the reality outlined by the *Black Mirror* episode brings into focus the fact that our relationship to technology always entails a double movement: if the grain produces a prosthetic enhancement of vision, conversely it transforms the human eyes into cameras that record reality and projectors that can reproduce it. Hence, being submitted to a technical function, the human body itself becomes a prosthesis (see Carbone 2019; Dalmasso 2018, p. 173), revealing that, far from being stable and defined, the limits of our living body are essentially mobile.

Hence, we shall not think of prostheses as accidental features of the human condition, but as something that inherently belongs to human life, as the French philosopher Bernard Stiegler suggests in his major work on the status of technics: "The prosthesis is not a mere extension of the human body; it is the constitution of this body qua 'human'" (Stiegler 1998, p. 152). Thus, what is specific to the human body is its being enhanced and extended as much as it incorporates components of the environment that contribute to shape and reshape our cognition. This double process of extension and incorporation is best exemplified by the classic example of the blind man's stick, notably commented upon by Maurice Merleau-Ponty: for the blind man the stick "has ceased to be an object [...] and is no longer perceived for itself; its point has become an area of sensitivity, extending the scope and active radius of touch, and providing a parallel to sight" (1945: 165). But, whereas in the case of the stick the process of incorporation engages the projective power of the body schema that makes of it an "area of sensitivity" and extends its range of action (Merleau-Ponty 1945: 167; transl. 2005: 127; Ihde 1979, p. 16), in the *Black Mirror* episode the incorporation of the technological device becomes literal, since the grain is physically implanted under the skin.

However, even without incorporating a physical implant, *our relationship with the world can be said to be prosthetic*. In fact, on the one hand, we do incorporate habits and skills deriving from our uses of technologies so that our "modes of perception" are historically-transformed and culturally-determined by the apparatuses and devices we get in contact with (Benjamin 1968: 222). On the other hand, our body extends itself into the environment, transferring its structure to instruments and tools that enhance its capabilities.

In a way, every instrument could be understood as an exosomatic organ, that is as the "projection of an anatomic organ [*Organsprojektion*]," like Ernst Kapp suggested while developing his reflections at the end of the 19th Century (1877), an idea that, later, will be taken on by Marshall McLuhan in his analysis of mass media as the "extensions" of man (1964). For the author of *The Gutenberg Galaxy*, since every technical object affects and modifies the human sensorium and its cognitive faculties, changing the way the world is perceived and inhabited, the amplification deriving from the movement of extension in the environment also entails a self-amputation and something like an operation of surgery on the body, from which something is cut off.

Similarly, in his approach of technicity, Leroi-Gourhan made no essential distinction between the tool as a technical organ and the organ as a bodily element. For the author of *Gesture and Speech*, a technical instrument, such as a stone tool, emerges from the sensible matter in the same way as the hand, insofar as they both are a "secretion of the body and the brain" (Leroi-Gourhan 1964: 132). In so doing, Leroi-Gourhan implicitly establishes a fundamental continuity between the organic and the inorganic, between our living body and its technical prostheses, inseparable from the development and historical evolution of the living body.

To take on Marcel Mauss' expression (1936)[1] we can argue that every technique is primarily a "technique of the body," since the body itself requires a certain usage and specific embodied practices that are historically developed and culturally transmitted. This is most evident in human actions such as sports or performing arts, in which the body needs to be trained and finalized to a certain result, but even biological activities, such as sex or breastfeeding, are only apparently "natural" processes, as they too require the development of a bodily technique. Indeed, there is nothing *natural* in the way we live and use our body. It would be completely inaccurate to describe the acts of walking, running, swimming, eating, and even going to sleep as something simply biological, since all of these gestures and movements require and rest upon specific techniques that need to be learnt by the organism during its development and life, and whose set of parameters vary – actually rather quickly – over generations, being deeply influenced by the slightest cultural changes. A technical gesture is but an extension of a *bodily* gesture, an emanation of the body and, conversely, a bodily gesture is, in itself, the product of

---

1 For the French anthropologist, to whom Merleau-Ponty devoted a famous essay (Merleau-Ponty (1960): 143-157; Merleau-Ponty [1964]:144-125), technicity is primarily concerned with the "techniques of the body" or "bodily technique", that is, with all those actions which are *effective* and *traditional*, i.e. culturally transmitted (Mauss (1936): 374; [2006]: 75), independently of the technological instruments with which human beings have endowed themselves. Hence, an account of technical behaviour shall not be limited to the relationship with technical objects, but rather take into account that human beings' "first and most natural technical object" is the body itself (Mauss (1936): 375; [2006]: 75).

a certain technicity of the body, being brought about by biological functions, postural and motor possibilities, as well as specific organs.

However, there is another decisive point on which "The Entire History of You" draws our attention: one of the most powerful prosthetic devices with which human beings have endowed themselves is the invention of images. These powerful technical objects function as prosthesis of our symbolic relationship with the world, externalizing the human capacity to envision and to remember, and being an incredible boost for the faculty of imagination.

In the episode, the use that characters make of the footage recorded by the grain makes evident that no distinction is made between experience, memory, and images. Even though we do not have a grain implanted in our eye, this can be said about our present experience of images. They do not just reproduce the visible world, but also give shape to reality and help us to figure it out.

If images have always had a fundamental symbolic function in the development of human culture, now more than ever they participate in forming worlds; they have become forms of thought constituting a new kind of knowledge. This has become particularly true since the invention and diffusion of photography, as it is expressed in a famous quote from Chris Marker's film, *Sunless*: "I remember that month of January in Tokyo, or rather I remember the images I filmed of the month of January in Tokyo. They have substituted themselves for my memory. They are my memory. I wonder how people remember things who don't film, don't photograph, don't tape. How has mankind managed to remember?"

Prosthetic images, or: being another (body) – *Striking Vipers*

Since the introduction of photographic media, our relationship to images has radically intensified with the advent of the digital revolution. This has introduced in our experience a new kind of image: that of the avatar, a virtual image-body that represents individuals in computer-generated environments. In online chat spaces, websites, video games, and virtual experiences in general, it has become increasingly common to interact with others through a visual substitute or a "proxy" for the self (Cleland 2009; Taylor 2002; Pinotti 2020).

The ability to inhabit an image-body may produce a form of auto-empathy (Tordo & Binkley 2013), that is, the possibility of "empathizing with the other-in-me, of taking my perspective on the world as seen from an external point of view" (Pinotti 2020, 33). One thereby identifies with their own altered self without leaving their embodied self. In digital worlds, the avatar acts as a prosthetic virtual body through which the user explores different virtual environments. So that users do not simply roam through the digital space, their individual presence is signified and grounded in the presence of their avatar.

Individuals may either choose visual identities – which tend to resemble their own physical features – or they can adopt and control an avatar that radically differs from their own bodily appearance. Thus, the avatar can work either as a portrait or a mirror of the self, or it can function as a mask and temporary disguise, which allows the self to – openly or surreptitiously – inhabit a different virtual existence, a body different from one's own and even incompatible with their actual bodily features, with the effect of dispersing the punctual and self-possessed body into a multiplicity of bodies inhabiting different temporal and spatial sites.

Going through this process of alteration, the self can be thought of either as a stable entity that emanates from an image-body – be it similar to or different from their offline appearance – or as an entity that ends up being transformed by the avatar experience, endowing the individual with a new perspective on the world. The former case reflects the original meaning of the word "avatar," used in Hindu mythology to describe the material incarnation of gods when they take on physical forms to descend to earth and interact with humans; like Vishnu, for instance, appearing in a variety of avatars including a tortoise, a boar, and other animals, as well as human forms. Whereas the latter can be exemplified – to mention another way of inhabiting an animal avatar-body – by the transformation that Arthur undergoes, the protagonist of the Disney cartoon, *The Sword in the Stone*, in which the possibility to experience the world as a fish, a squirrel, or a bird, helps the future King of England to understand different aspects of reality and to grow wiser.[2]

---

2 About the issue of seeing the world from the point of view of animals, see Nagel 1974, Smythe 1975, Despret 2019, Pyke 2019.

The avatar, then, works for the subject as a prosthetic visual identity, multiplying the capabilities and possibilities of their offline self, either by restoring a lost capability or by allowing them to embody an unpredictable experience. This is represented by James Cameron's film, *Avatar*, in which the paraplegic protagonist can walk again by means of his Na'vi avatar.

Thus, the avatar functions as an "identity operator," "which allows for a virtually infinite number of negotiations of selfhood" and different possible interactions (Pinotti 2020, 33). The self is virtually separated from the image of their body and through this process is implicitly called to incorporate new identities. This leads us to another *Black Mirror* episode, "Striking Vipers," (first episode of the fifth season) that demonstrates a brain-wired virtual reality device that actually allows the user to experiment what it is like to live and exist through other bodies, overcoming any physical gap that may interfere with the process of virtual re-embodiment.

In the episode, two friends, Karl and Danny, that used to play video games together in their youth catch up, several years after they had fallen out of contact with each other, and start to play the virtual reality edition of one of their favorite martial arts video games: *Striking Vipers X*. Karl chooses the female character, Roxette, while Danny plays as Lance. After having adapted to their new virtual bodies and having fought against each other within the game, they suddenly realize that they are physically attracted to each other. Despite the initial resistance from Danny, the pair finally have virtual sex and start a parallel relationship within the game, without meeting again in real life. As their virtual affair goes on, Danny notices a change in his relationship with his wife, Theo, as he stops wanting to have sex with her. The distance in their relationship brings Theo to suspect that he is cheating on her. Karl and Danny finally meet and confront each other in person. Karl describes how he has tried to have sex in the game with automated characters and with other players, but says that nothing can recreate the feeling of having sex in the game with Danny. They also try to kiss in their actual bodies to see if there is any offline connection between them, besides their former friendship, but both of them say they feel nothing.

If, in common digital practices, the avatar works as a surrogate or proxy for the individual that engages with the virtual world, playing an important role in creating a strong sense of presence and fostering the process of immersion, "Striking Vipers" explores not just the way in which individuals can project themselves in a virtual world through an avatar, but how the virtual dimension may affect and be transferred into real life (Maister et al. 2015). Thus, what is most *striking* in the *Black Mirror* episode is how it explores the tensions that arise from navigating online and offline identities. In particular, the episode investigates how the avatar experience can possibly realize a backward movement: from the virtual to the real.

The avatar experience pictured in the episode has the protagonists embody different racial and, in the case of Karl, sexual features, producing a "reconfiguration of the body itself" (del Río 1996). At a first glance, the plot may seem to hint to some kind of unconfessed homosexual attraction between the two friends, but the spectator expecting such an ending would be deceived. In fact, the punch line – which reveals that the connection Danny and Karl discover within the game only exists in the virtual world of *Striking Vipers X* – poses the decisive question of whether virtual reality experience could be transferred in real life and how it can affect the "unwired" existence of the users. In this case, the episode shows that although the self of the player is modified through their avatar experience, this cannot be extended beyond virtual reality. The experiencing subject is modified, but we do not know if this will last and how it will be translated into offline experience.

As a result, from a philosophical point of view, the ontological structure that connects the avatar and the self is reversed: there is not a pre-existing self that can disguise or dissimulate through different avatars, which are understood as copies or surrogate manifestations of the subject; on the contrary, the avatar gives access to previously unknown and unanticipated aspects of identity that can only be experienced in the very process of avatar embodiment.

Is the specificity of the avatar experience unrepeatable in real life? If so, how can it affect the offline existence of the users?[3] This episode of *Black Mirror* suggests that we cannot take for granted the idea that the experiences of the avatar embodiment could also be valid in real life, for, as the self is

---

3 These questions underpin a large part of recent implementations of virtual reality that are deeply concerned with humanitarian, social, and political issues. Nowadays, virtual reality has been claimed to constitute a powerful tool for perspective taking, which would promote the development of empathic capacities, improved helping attitudes (Ahn et al. 2013), and encourage the reduction of negative stereotyping (Peck et al. 2013, Banakou et al. 2016). Nevertheless, the prosocial effects of virtual reality entirely depend on the possibility that the VR experience has an impact on users in real life and shape their behaviors in the long-term.

re-embodied and animated as a digital ego, *it also assumes an agency of its own*. The avatar embodiment produces an unpredictable excess of meaning and emotion and the experiencer must make sense of it, without always being able to bring it back to their unwired experience.

Therefore, what the episode reveals is that through the avatar experience the user can be dramatically confronted by a *loss of agency* over their avatars (Schroeder 2002) who come to interact with the environment in a semi-autonomous fashion – which, in the episode, is efficaciously exemplified by the sudden out-of-control physical attraction felt by the two characters. In a way, we can say that "Striking Vipers" brings our attention to the fact that images – and especially the kind of images that are image-avatars – not only have an impact on the beholder, but that they are able to transform them – by triggering love, hate, desire, or fear (Freedberg 1989; Mitchell 2006; Gell 1998) – and to act upon the world. They have an agency of their own and participate in the extension or distribution of human social agency.

Afterlife virtualities or: how to transcend the limitations of physical embodiment – *San Junipero*

So far, we have explored how our bodies are enhanced and extended when in contact with the digital world, and how, by extension, they become electronic bodies or *bodies in code* (Hansen 2006). What characterizes electronic media, as compared to photographic and cinematic media, is that they do not tie us to a point of view nor to a visual situation, such as we experience, respectively, with photography and cinema. As it has been pointed out, "electronic space […] both denies and prosthetically transforms the spectator's physical human body so that subjectivity and affect free-float or free-fall or free-flow across a horizontal/vertical grid or, as is the case with all our electronic pocket communication devices, disappear into thin air. Subjectivity is at once decentred, dispersed, and completely extroverted" (Sobchack 2004: 159), thereby erasing any dialectic between inside and outside, continuous and discontinuous, that needs to be reformulated. In so doing, digital media seems to free us from the ties of our bodies, even though, at the same time, they can have the effect of isolating us, being a cause of potential alienation, anxiety, and degeneration of empathy capacities, as it has been pointed out by several studies in different fields, which address our increasing depen-dence on screen devices.[4]

But, what if we could do without our physical – still protheticized – bod-ies? Are human fleshy bodies meant to disappear, accomplishing the dream of the uploading of consciousness that is envisaged by the prophets of trans-humanism (O'Connell 2017)? What will be the role of the human body in the future development of technoculture?

Such fantasies of disembodiment are powerfully put to the test in the visionary episode "San Junipero." This, the fourth episode of Black Mirror's third season, depicts a world in which deceased people can upload their con-sciousnesses to a virtual reality system wherein they can live forever in the cloud, in a simulated location called San Junipero, by embodying the avatars of their younger selves, wandering in different temporal dimensions that reproduce a stereotypic reality of the 80s, 90s, or 2000s.

Whereas the residents of this virtual cyber-town have already given up their fleshy bodies for digital ones, elderly people can visit San Junipero to temporarily explore, as "tourists," the virtual dimension, as a form of ther-apy or for a trial period before passing over and be transferred into their digital afterlife: "[t]heir old and sick body [...] is therefore used as a screen that projects and transports them into a young and functioning virtual self" (Bodini 2017, 78).

In a simulated 1987 Saturday night, Yorkie meets Kelly. The two women start to flirt and have sex, but then Kelly seems to avoid meeting Yorkie again. It turns out that Kelly feared developing feelings for her since, in the physical world, she – her frail body – is actually dying. The two finally agree to meet in person. Visiting Yorkie, Kelly discovers that she was paralyzed at age 21 after crashing her car when her parents reacted poorly to her coming out. Yorkie wishes to be euthanized in order to live in San Junipero perma-nently, but her family objects. Kelly offers to marry Yorkie and authorize her euthanasia and consciousness uploading. Eventually, even though she had previously decided otherwise – in order to reach her husband and daugh-

---

4 See for instance: N.K. Hayles, How We Became Posthuman, University of Chicago Press, Chi-cago 1999; G. Small, iBrain: Surviving the Technological Alteration of the Modern Mind, Harper-Collins, New York 2008; A. Milon, La réalité virtuelle: Avec ou sans le corps?, Autrement, Paris 2005; S. Tisseron, 3-6-9-12. Apprivoiser les écrans et grandir, Erès, Paris 2017; S. Tisseron et al. (eds.), Subjectivation et empathie dans les mondes numériques, Dunod, Paris 2013.

ter, both dead before the technology of San Junipero was available – Kelly chooses to be euthanized too and "pass over" her consciousness to reunite with Yorkie in San Junipero.

The episode ends showing San Junipero's system facilities, where a robotic arm locates two small devices, supposed to be the hardware of Yorkie and Kelly's uploaded consciousnesses, for them to live together in the cloud forever after. The very last shot, showing an anonymous corridor of computer servers, teeming with thousands of such devices glowing in the dark, sets an ironic, or at least uncertain, shadow on the apparently-happy-ending episode.

In fact, one might ask, where are the protagonists' bodies in this hereafter machine life? Or, shall we say, whose bodies? To which body should we ascribe the agency of Yorkie and Kelly's new virtual lives: their avatars, the body of an artificial intelligence, or the hardware of the server? Is it the same to temporarily inhabit a simulated virtual reality through an avatar and to exist only in a software form, being uploaded to a computer? Where are we supposed to assign the agency of such an experience? Raising all those questions, this *Black Mirror* episode creatively explores the issues related to virtual embodiment and the future of our flesh in the development of digital technoculture.

The idea of mind-uploading or consciousness-uploading, going hand in hand with the trajectory of technological singularity merging human intelligence and machine intelligence, is underpinned by a concept that understands the cognitive life of the human being as the epiphenomenon of electronic processes that occur in the brain. Thus, mind and body – equated to the existence of software and hardware – are understood according to a Cartesian philosophical model of consciousness as separated from the physical body (*res extensa*). According to this view, if the body is merely a "machine" that supports the mind, it could easily be replaced by another machine – and also a more effective and high-performance one.

"San Junipero" echoes, in particular, the prospects outlined by the theorists of transhumanism, such as the computer scientist, Raymond Kurzweil (2006), claiming that technology shall be used to enhance or even to transcend the limited capabilities of the human body and be able to upgrade it to a non-biological existence, which would free it from its constitutive weakness and eventually from its condition of mortality.

The idea of being able to pursue a digital afterlife existence expresses the desire to free the mind from its binds and entertains the possibility of overcoming the body as the first medium of our experience of the world as we know it. Once uploaded to a computer, our bodies would become transparent and their vulnerability would cease to be an obstacle in our encounter with the world, as is the case for Yorkie, bedridden by paralysis, and given a chance to flourish again in San Junipero. In other words, the virtual afterlife world depicted by the episode entertains the idea that an embodied experience "without the body" would be a more original and accomplished one. But, can we assume such a premise from a phenomenological point of view? *Isn't the body what ultimately enables our aesthetic and cognitive experiences, even virtual ones?* And isn't the human body structured in such a way as to extend itself into organic artefacts and prostheses, being exposed, "altered," and dispossessed of any supposed natural authenticity (see Merleau-Ponty 1945, Montani 2014)? Indeed, the transparency that the dream of consciousness-uploading seeks to achieve is but a *mythical transparency*, the myth of a mediation in the absence of any interface (Bolter & Gromala 2003, p. 48 ss.; Bolter & Grusin 1999).

Thus, as I suggested above, the episode's happy ending also hints at the illusory nature of such a prospect, leaving the spectator with the question: how could there be any experience of the world and other people without a human body able to experience it? What would it be like to be (in the body of) a machine? The answers to these questions remain suspended, only accessible beyond the servers' wall. And, in a way, the gateway that the virtual reality system represents for the characters points to the impossibility for the human being not to try to imagine their hereafter existence – as it was incisively stated by Damien Hirst's artwork *The Physical Impossibilities of Death in the Mind of Someone Living* (1991). Isn't living "in the cloud," after all, another manner to envision heaven, a different post-digital narration in which our wish for a life after life takes shape?

Conclusions. The Utopian Body

The *Black Mirror* episodes analysed here urges us to question the way we conceive the materiality of the human body and the agency of digital virtual images. As I suggested in the opening, the limits between technology and the human are not defined and need to be continually replaced and decentred. Far from merely exacerbating the dangers and presenting a degeneration of our relationship to technology, the series interrogates how technicity, as a cultural and symbolic attitude, is rooted in the aesthetic dimension of human experience, even being a constitutive part of it.

The living body shall be thought of not just as a merely physical entity – not just as a *Körper*, in Husserlian phenomenological terms. Far from being a mere biological basis or organic substratum for a cognitive and perceptual behaviour, the living human body is endowed with a virtual power. Starting with its capacity to reflect and recognize itself in the surface of a mirror, the human body schema is able to extend into the environment and have access to virtual dimensions of existence. Hence, we should give up thinking of the body as opposed to technology and the virtual dimension, and rather *understand technology as part and parcel of our existence as embodied subjects*. As Merleau-Ponty writes, once again echoing Mauss, "Every technique is a 'technique of the body'. It figures and amplifies the metaphysical structure of our flesh" (Merleau-Ponty 1961, p. 33; transl. 2007, p. 359).

Thus, on the one hand, the limits of the body have to be continually redesigned, which makes it a *utopian place*, a place with no specific location that therefore fills all available spaces: a "utopian body," to take on the expression by Michel Foucault (1966) or, according to Gilles Deleuze and Félix Guattari's reflection, a "body without organs" (1980). Like the image in the mirror, our living body is for us in an inaccessible space; it dwells in an irreducible elsewhere.

On the other hand, every dematerialization of the body entails a reorganization of the matter. In other words, we can say that, should it ever be possible for a mind to leave the body and be transferred into a machine, then that machine would become, in turn, *alive*; its matter would reorganize as a living-machine.

From this perspective, the reference to death in "San Junipero" is decisive, since only in the dead body and in the (technical) experience of looking at our body reflected in the mirror we realize that our body can also be seen as a physical object. In this regard, Foucault points out, in his previously mentioned 1966 radio broadcasts, that Ancient Greeks had no word to designate the unity of the body: "As paradoxical as it may be, on the walls defended by Hector and his companions, facing Troy, there was no body. There were raised arms, there were brave chests, there were nimble legs, there were helmets shimmering atop heads – there was no body. The Greek word for "body" only appears in Homer to designate a corpse. It is this corpse, consequently, it is the corpse and it is the mirror that teach us – or at least that taught the Greeks then, and that teach the children now – that we have a body, that this body has a form, that this form has an outline, that in this outline there is a thickness, a weight. In short, that the body occupies a place."

Bibliography

Banakou, D., Groten, R., & Slater, M., 2013: "Illusory ownership of a virtual child body causes overestimation of object sizes implicit attitude changes" Proc. Natl. Acad. Sci. USA 110, pp. 12846-12851. doi: 10.1073/pnas.1306779110

Benjamin, W., 1968: "The Work of Art in the Age of Mechanical Reproduction", in *Illuminations*, ed. Hannah Arendt, New York: Schocken.

Bodini, J., 2017: The Screen: a Body Without Organs, in Héder M and Nádasi E (eds.), *Essays in Post-Critical and Contemporary Philosophy of Technology*, Vernon press: Wilmington, pp. 75-87.

Bolter, J.D., Gromala, D., 2003: *Windows and Mirrors. Interaction Design, Digital Art, and the Myth of Transparency*, Cambridge (MA)–London: The MIT Press.

Bolter, J.D., Grusin, R., 1999: *Remediation. Understanding New Media*, Cambridge (MA)–London: The MIT Press.

Carbone, M., 2019: "From Screens as Prostheses of our Body to our Body as a Quasi-Prosthesis of the Screens?", in Cavalotti, D., Dotto, S., & Mariani, A. (eds.), *Exposing the Moving Image*, Mimesis, Milano-Udine, pp. 159-166.

Cleland, K., 2009: "Face to Face. Avatars and Mobile Identities", in Gerard Goggin, Larissa Hjorth (eds.), *Mobile Technologies: From Telecommunications to Media*, London-New York: Routledge, 219-234.

Dalmasso, A. C., 2018: *Le corps, c'est l'écran. La philosophie du visuel de Merleau-Ponty*, Mimésis: Paris.

De Preester, H., Tsakiris, M., 2009: *Body-extension versus body-incorporation: Is there a need for a body-model?*, in "Phenomenology and the Cognitive Sciences" 8 (3), pp. 307–319.

del Río, E., 1996: "The Body as Foundation of the Screen : Allegories of Technology in Atom Egoyan's Speaking Parts", in *Camera Obscura*, 37–38 (Summer 1996), p. 94-115 .

Deleuze, G., Guattari, F., 1980: *Mille Plateaux*, Minuit, Paris, transl. *A Thousand Plateaus. Capitalism and Schizophrenia*. Continuum, London - New York.

Despret, V., 2019: *Habiter en oiseau*, Actes Sud, Paris.

Ellul, J. (1964) *The Technological Society*. New York: Vintage.

Freedberg, D., 1989: *The power of images: Studies in the history and theory of response*, Chicago University Press, Chicago.

Gehlen, A., 1950: *Der Mensch. Seine Natur und seine Stellung* in der Welt, Bonn: Athenaum-Verl, transl. Man: His Nature and Place in the World, New York: Columbia University Press, 1987.

Gehlen, A., 1957: *Die Seele im technischen Zeitalter*, Klostermann, 2007, *transl.* Man in the Age of Technology. New York: Columbia University Press, 1980.

Gell, A., 1998: *Art and Agency: An Anthropological Theory*, Clarendon Press, Oxford.

Hansen, M.B.N., 2006: *Bodies in Code. Interfaces with Digital Media*, New York-Routledge, London.

Heidegger, M., 1954: "Die Frage nach der Technik", in *Vorträge und Aufsätze*, Pfullingen, Neske.

Ihde, D., 1979: *Technics and Praxis: A Philosophy of Technology*, D. Reidel Publishing Company.

Ihde, D., 1990: *Technology and the Lifeworld: From Garden to Earth*, Indiana University Press, Indianapolis.

Kapp, E., 1877: *Grundlinien einer Philosophie der Technik: Zur Entstehungsgeschichte der Cultur aus neuen Gesichtspunkten*, transl. *Elements of a Philosophy of Technology: On the Evolutionary History of Culture*, University of Minnesota Press, 2018.

Kurzweil, R., *The singularity is near: When humans transcend the human body* (New York: Penguin Books, 2006).

Leroi-Gourhan, A., 1964: *Le geste et la parole. Technique et langage*, Albin Michel, transl., *Gesture and Speech*, MIT Press, Cambridge (MA), 1993.

Maister L. et al., *Changing bodies changes minds: Owning another body affects social cognition*, in "Trends in Cognitive Sciences", a. 19, n. 1, 2015, pp. 6-12

Mauss, M., 1936: *Les techniques du corps*, "Journal de Psychologie" 32, pp. 3-4; now in *Techniques, technologie et civilisation*, ed. N. Schlanger, PUF, Paris, pp. 365-394, transl. *Techniques of the Body*, in *Techniques, Technology and Civilization*, Durkheim Press/Berghahn Books, New York/Oxford, 2006, pp. 77-96.

McLuhan, M., 1964: *Understanding Media. The Extensions of Man*, McGraw-Hill, New York-Toronto-London.

Merleau-Ponty, M., 1942: *La structure du comportement*, PUF, Paris, 2002 [1942], transl. *The Structure of Behavior*, Northwestern University Press, London, 1964.Merleau-Ponty, M., 1945: *Phénoménologie de la perception*, Gallimard, collection « Tel », Paris, 1976 [1945], transl. *Phenomenology of Perception*, Routledge, London, 2005.

Merleau-Ponty, M., 1961: *L'œil et l'esprit*, Gallimard, collection « Folio », Paris 1985 [1961], transl., "Eye and Mind", in *The Merleau-Ponty Reader*, ed. T. Toadvine and L. Lawlor, Northwestern University Press, Evanston (Ill.), 2007.

Mitchell, W.J.T., 2006: *What Do Pictures Want? The Lives and Loves of Images*, University of Chicago Press, Chicago.

Montani, P., 2014: *Tecnologie della sensibilità*, Cortina, Milano.

Nagel, T., 1974: "What Is It Like to Be a Bat?", Philosophical Review. LXXXIII (4), Oct 1974, pp. 435–450.

O'Connell, M., 2017, *To Be a Machine*, Granta.

Parisi, F., 2019: *La tecnologia che siamo*, Codice Edizioni.

Peck, T. C., Seinfeld, S., Aglioti, S. M., Slater, M., 2013: "Putting yourself in the skin of a black avatar reduces implicit racial bias" in Consciousness and Cognition, n. 22, pp. 779-787.

Pinotti, A., 2020: "Avatars. Shifting Identities in a Genealogical Perspective", in Hava Aldouby (ed.), *Shifting Interfaces. An Anthology of Presence, Empathy, and Agency in 21st Century Media Arts*, Leuven: Leuven University Press.

Pinotti, A., 2019, "Procuratori del sé: dall'avatar all'avatarizzazione", in T. Gatti, D. Maini (eds.), *Visual Studies. L'avvento di nuovi paradigmi*, Milano: Mimesis.

Plessner, H., 1928: transl. *Levels of Organic Life and the Human*, Fordham University Press, 2019.

Postman, N., 1979: *Teaching as a Conserving Activity*. New York: Dell.

Postman, N., 1993: *Technopoly: The Surrender of Culture to Technology.* New York: Vintage.

Pyke, S. M., 2019: *Animal Visions. Posthumanist Dream Writing*, Palgrave Macmillan.

Schroeder, R. (ed.), 2002: *The Social Life of Avatars: Presence and Interaction in Shared Virtual Environments*, London: Springer.

Simondon, G., 1958: *Du mode d'existence des objets techniques*, Paris: Aubier, 2012, english translation *On the Mode of Existence of Technical Objects*, Minnesota University Press, 2016.

Simondon, G., 1982: *Sur la technoesthétique.* Draft for a letter to Jacques Derrida, 3rd July 1982, "Les Papiers du Collège International de Philosophie" 1992/12; republished with some *Suppléments* as *Réflexions sur la techno-esthétique*, in *Sur la technique*, Paris: PUF, 2014, pp. 379-396, english translation *On Techno-Aesthetics*, "Parrhesia" 2012/14, (not numbered).

Simondon, G., 2014: *Sur la technique*, Paris: PUF.

Smythe, R. H. 1975: *Vision in the Animal World*, Palgrave Macmillan.

Sobchack, V., 2004: *Carnal Thoughts*, University of California Press, Berkeley-Los Angeles-London.

Stiegler, B., 1998: La technique et le temps: 1. La Faute d Épiméthée. 2. La Désorientation 3. Le Temps du cinéma et la question du mal-être, Fayard, Paris, transl. Technics and time, 1. The fault of epimetheus. Stanford: Stanford University Press.

Taylor, T.L., 2002: "Living Digitally: Embodiment in Virtual Worlds", in R. Schroeder (ed.), *The Social Life of Avatars: Presence and Interaction in Shared Virtual Environments*, London: Springer.

Tordo, F. & Binkley, C., 2013: *L'auto-empathie médiatisée par l'avatar, une subjectivation de soi*, in E.-A. Amato, E. Perény (eds.), *Les avatars jouables des mondes numériques. Théories, terrains et témoignages de pratiques interactives*, Lavoisier, Paris, pp. 91-109.

The 'Death of Neighbour' Seen in a Black Mirror – (*Be Right Back* on *Solaris*)

Alfredo Rizza

Introduction

This chapter is the result of the analysis of some episodes of *Black Mirror* and shows interesting insights for linguistics in general, for the communicative interaction between man and machine, and for the aesthetic and spiritual aspects concerning the theme of losing and reconnecting with loved ones. The focus will be on the episode "Be Right Back," as it is the most representative considering these premises. The reflection begins by trying to define the type of technology represented in the story, continues with a description of the linguistic interaction between the protagonists, adds some thoughts on the concept of body and textuality, and ends with a thought on the immediate relevance of the theory about the state of contemporary humanity by Luigi Zoja: the 'death of the neighbour' (2019). Concluding remarks are made possible by a comparison with *Solaris* by Andrei Tarkovsky.

Phatic technologies and linguistic interaction

"Be Right Back" explores the topic of the re-creation of deceased people thanks to technological applications involving artificial intelligence (linguistic *in primis*), the extraction of value from the flow of information in the web, and the synthesis of new materials. The male protagonist of the episode, Ash, dies in an accident shortly before his partner, Martha, finds out she is pregnant. A friend of Martha's, Sarah, suggests she can use an online service that extracts data about the personality of human beings and reproduces their linguistic performance. From the first minutes of the episode, it is evident how addicted Ash is to social media, which is an optimal requirement for the service to run. The adequacy of Ash's profile and the functioning of the service are briefly and clearly described by Sarah:

> (1) (10'13")
> --   He was a heavy user, he'd be perfect
> (12'11")
> --   And then it talks back to you, just like he would

Gradually the service to which Martha turns proposes a speech partner that is effective in different levels of interaction and adequate in different models of linguistic situations or scenes, from the chat / IM (texting interaction), to the telephone call (mediated interaction), to the face to face interaction (with a material body).

The adequacy of the service, and therefore its success, is tested in linguistic and communicative terms and explicitly confirmed by the film's characters, as can be seen in the dialogue of the first telephonic interaction between Martha and the service performing the deceased Ash (henceforth 'the performer').

> (2) (18'05"-)
> --   So... How am I sounding?
>   Hello?
> --   Hello! You sound just like him.
> --   Almost creepy isn't it? I say creepy, I mean it's totally batshit crazy I
>   can even talk to you.
>   I mean, I don't even have a mouth.
> --   That's ... that's just ...
> --   Just what?
> --   That's just the sort of things that he would say.

The performer's statements have no informative relevance, but have phatic relevance: the linguistic acts establish emotional and personal contact, thus a recognition, which is vocal at first (you sound just like him), then fully linguistic immediately after (that's just the sort of things that he would say).

The service provider is a commercial enterprise, as shown by the server / client or supplier / customer relationship that emerges in stages, which are most likely pre-calculated. Actually, viewers do not know much about the enterprise because it remains on an absence / presence threshold: it dissolves constantly in the service itself, but it reappears from time to time (especially to offer upgrades) within the events in which Ash is reproduced (a possible interesting case of parasitism of artificial reproductions of people).

It must be stressed that the relationship between Martha and the service is based on strictly linguistic models and prerequisites. As evidence, note how the service gives its best in scenes[1] wherein the contact is purely linguistic (chat, telephone), abstracting from other factors, above all material ones (and in fact body materiality will create complexity and problems). A complete sharing of the linguistic code (expression and content forms) functional to the identification of the artificial performer with the deceased is re-created (perhaps better: simulated), flanked by a type of artificial intelligence capable of dynamically adapting to the parameters of linguistic interaction,[2] especially to norms,[3] form of speech,[4] channels, reading keys,[5] and purposes[6] of linguistic events down to idiosyncratic sub-codes. The effects simulate a

---

1 'Scene' designates the 'psychological setting' or the cultural definition of an occasion as a certain type of scene (Hymes 1972a, p. 60; Duranti 1992, pp. 46–51).

2 Cf. Hymes 1972a; Duranti 1997; Saville-Troike 2003.

3 'All rules governing speaking, of course, have a normative character [...]. An account of norms of interaction may still leave open the interpretation to be placed upon them, especially when members of different communities are in communication' (Hymes 1972a, p. 64). Consider also P. Grice's (1975) conversational maxims and Foucault's *order of discourse* (1971).

4 'Even where there is but a single 'language' present in a community (no cases are known in the contemporary world), that language will be organized into various forms of speech.' (Hymes 1972a, p. 63).

5 'Key is introduced to provide for the tone, manner, or spirit in which an act is done. [...] The significance of key is underlined by the fact that, when it is in conflict with the overt content of an act, it often overrides the latter (as in sarcasm). The signalling of key may be non-verbal, as with a wink, gesture, posture, [...] but it also commonly involves conventional units of speech [...]' (Hymes 1972a, p. 62).

6 A distinction must be made between outcomes and aims, i.e. between the 'purpose of an event from a standpoint community' and the 'purpose of those engaged in it'. This point has intersections with the purposes of illocutionary acts for Searle, i.e. the '[d]ifferences in the point (or purpose) of the (type of) act' (1976, pp. 2–3). Cf. *infra*.

competence functional to an inter-agents situation and capable of producing performances fully attributable to a single historical entity, i.e. the late Ash in his essential relation with Martha (Ash as 'deceased-for-Martha'). It's a matter of reproducing a historical entity whose essence lies in the discourse dialectics with Martha, but whose linguistic and communicative competence is simulated by serial algorithms that input performances recorded in digital archives, and happened in events whose participants are not known to viewers, but with all certainty are not limited to Martha ('public-Ash').

To better analyse the quality of the relationship between Martha and the performer, and the kind of communication they establish (or try to), a few preliminary words should be spent on the concepts of competence and communication, and how they are related in the terms of linguistics. First, the core of the competence of the performer is engineered, while that of Martha is natural. The experience that uniquely characterizes the competences of Martha and the performer is of social origin, but again for the performer this means media (mainly social media), and for Martha means a human social environment, intersubjectivity, and proximity.[7] The kind of engineered competence the service is provided with allows it to perform not only mere grammatical utterances, but also appropriate and adequate ones. At least to a certain point. Engineered linguistic competence here is understood as a technical simulation of a natural property. The core of this natural property is creativity.[8] The authors imagine a technology able to generalize linguistic rules at any level from a mass of raw data. Such a technology should not be easily considered as a system that knows a language, but as a system able to exploit statistic and probability algorithms to imitate human inter-active performances. The core of these performances is linguistic. The purposes are social, i.e. communicative.

Due to this, the concept of communication should be investigated. Only a rough distinction will be advanced here between two kinds of communication: in one respect, the transmission of information, and in another, the creation of ties of union. Now the power of linguistic performance is primarily social, rather than informative; so is the service in "Be Right Back." The authors gave the right importance to the phatic quality of the service. Be it

---

7 On the nature of this 'proximity' cf. *infra*.

8 This means that is not dependent on statistical generalizations. Cf. Chomsky 1967. See also Graffi (*forth.*), and Cimatti 2018.

derived from the observation of everyday life, or from basic intuitions, it is actually an established topic in the academic research on media, technology, and communication. A particular pertinence has the identification of phatic systems and phatic technologies in which people are keen to develop trust (Wang et al. 2016).[9] According to Chomsky:

> the use of language is a very important means by which this species, because of its biological nature, creates a kind of social space, to place itself in inter-actions with other people. It doesn't have much to do with communication in a narrow sense; that is, it doesn't involve transmission of information (Chomsky and Osiatynski 1984).

Chomsky also states that the larger part of language use is internal. Of the external use, the larger part is phatic, leaving very little room for informative communication.[10] The model of the implicit factors with their related functions in the linguistic act as presented by Jakobson (1960) is still very clear: the referential function is the most pertinent to the concept of communication as transmission of information; the phatic, instead, is to establish, verify, and keep active the psychological contact between sender and receiver (the physical contact, represented by the channel, is necessary but not sufficient). This is what contributes to the creation of a social space of interaction, recalling what B. Malinowski (1923) called the phatic communion.[11]

In light of the considerations made so far, it should not be surprising to conclude that the largest amount of data in social media is phatic in quality. As a consequence, a machine engineered to utilize this kind of source should score its best results in phatic communication. Human beings are

---

9 For important steps in the development of the research on phaticity one can refer to Laver 1975 (communicative relevance); Žegarac and Clark 1999 (phatic interpretations); Miller 2008, and recently Gradinaru 2018 (phatic culture). About the phatic function of visual communication cf. Niemelä-Nyrhinen and Seppänen 2019, Szpunar 2019; for phatic as a rhetorical function Porter 2017 (all with references).

10 https://youtu.be/TzzuPMA8s7k; https://youtu.be/-72JNZZBoVw?t=4033; https://youtu.be/1urwLy25adk (Accessed 2/1/2018). About the question of the main function of the faculty of language see Chomsky 2012.

11 Together with Szpunar (2019), interpretations that see in the work of Jakobson a significative departure from the ideas of Malinowski caused by the influence of Shannon's mathematical theory of information are here rejected.

increasingly familiar with social media, which is more and more pervasive in everyday life. The integration of such technologies in the social relationship amongst people has far reaching consequences, especially considering that they are phatic technologies.

Wang et al. (2011, 2012, 2016) built a theory of phatic systems adapting Giddens' (1990) *consequences of modernity*. First, they recall theories on technology (Wang et al. 2011, p. 45), getting rid of the commonplace understanding of technology, i.e. just tools and machines to improve production. They explain that technology is a more general concept. Most important is 'technology as general methods to accomplish tasks in society' (based on Ellul 1954, see Wang et al 2011, p. 45). There are communication technologies, a subset of which is constituted by phatic technologies; "a technology is phatic if its primary purpose or use is to establish, develop and maintain human relationships. The users of the technology have personal interactive goals" (Wang et al. 2011, p. 46).

They explain the linguistic origins of phatic technologies (p. 47-48) and how the internet should be regarded as the primary source of phatic technologies (p. 49). In a second paper, Wang et al. 2012 argue:

> certain abstract social conditions that are characteristic of modernity amplify significantly the human need for, and thus the technical development of, phatic technologies. [...] we propose that phatic technologies enable the reconnection of social relations that have been stretched across time-space. A phatic technology creates a social community constituted by its users (from two to many) and individuals within that social community become dependent on the phatic technology to fulfil some of their social needs. Giddens' concept of trust is used to explain why technologies are able to connect individuals from different regions and countries across time-space, as well as why intimacy can be sustained at distance (Wang et al. 2012, p. 85).[12]

Another important observation is that some contemporary technologies are not simply pervasive, but 'an integrated part of daily life':

> It is, however, the transformations of social life and personal relationships enabled by the internet and associated technologies that have moved tech-

---

12 Cf. Giddens 1990.

nology from an external facilitator to a stage of being internal to man (Wang et al. 2012, p. 87).[13]

They further reflect on the work of Giddens (1990) and consider in particular the notions of dis-embedding and re-embedding of social relations in modernity, wherein 'modernity' is understood as an abstract social theory. Wang et al. claim that there is a process in the integration of phatic technologies in everyday life. They hypothesize three stages:

(i) Facilitative—where the technology simply performs certain tasks in the context.
(ii) Pervasive—where the technology is widely used in the context.
(iii) Embedded—where the technology is fully integrated in the fabric of the context.
(Wang et al. 2012, p. 88).

A third paper, by Wang and Tucker (2016), finally makes explicit a theory of phatic systems in digital societies. Again building on Giddens' (1990) theory of modernity, they concentrate on the theme of 'trust vs. risk' (Wang and Tucker 2016, p. 142).

> The dis-embedding of a social system is the lifting out or abstraction of its social relations from some local contexts of interaction; and their re-embedding is their reconstruction in a form that spans space and time without local restrictions (*ibidem*).

While for Giddens re-embedding is dependent on trust in expert systems, Wang and Tucker claim that trust is now given to phatic systems, which becomes the means of the re-embedding.

Now a service like the one devised in "Be Right Back" covers exactly the characteristics of a phatic tool within a phatic technology embedded in a phatic system. But when it is implemented into a reproduction of the body of a single historical being, the phatic technology is dis-embedded from its original system and has to face and experiment with a human relationship. And here it probably fails to work as a means of re-embedding. How

---

13 But cf. already some intuitions in Ellul 1954.

the authors imagine exactly this relationship is of great interest, especially if compared with other reflections upon the topic of re-embodiment of the deceased.[14]

Having discussed the relevance of the theory of phatic systems, a more accurate analysis of the engineered competence of the performer will be now considered. This competence does not recall simply the concept of competence in the well-known Chomskian competence-performance dichotomy (Chomsky 1965). While this dichotomy is of great help, it is however necessary to expand it to a broader and more intersubjective and socio-cultural field of action.

The idea of competence in Chomsky is connected to creativity and reveals that language acquisition in human beings is not substantially based on statistical generalization. Such a generalization is, however, typical in artificial intelligence and big data mining. So, the Chomskian concept of competence, together with the more recent concept of I-language as opposed to E-language, helps collocate the engineered linguistic abilities of the performer against a theory of a biological human capacity specific for language (Chomsky 1986, 2012, 2016).

In response to the Chomskian concept of competence, D. Hymes (1972b) and J. Habermas (1970) advanced the concept of communicative competence. It is preferable, with Chomsky, to use a narrower value for the term 'communication', and therefore it is considered useful to modify Hymes' expression into 'pragmatic competence' (cf. *infra*). In fact, language plays an instrumental role in conjunction with other systems of contact and transmission. It is therefore not possible to reduce the essence of language to a number of functions (Chomsky 2012). It is also important to make clear which is the role of language in the phatic function. The faculty of language does not serve this purpose in its full potential (it is not specifically designed for this purpose); rather, as semiological values, linguistic expressions happen to serve this purpose economically and effectively and therefore they are used universally.

Some more observations on the interaction between Martha and the performer should help further clarify the notion of competence, and the roles of phatic and pragmatics.

---

14 Cf. *infra* for a short comparison with Tarkovsky's *Solaris*.

Pragmatics, body, and textuality

The relationship between the two protagonists of the episode (Martha and the reproduction of Ash) works pretty well when it is reduced to the linguistic component, in the absence of a body. When it is integrated with the factors determined by the presence of the body things are more complicated, but it works well up to a certain point, a turning point, when the relationship deteriorates. The problem does not depend on the active communicative components involving the body (proxemics, kinesis, etc.), but for the very presence of a real (or presumed) body model (cf. infra). The data provided by the collection of linguistic expressions are based on heuristic techniques, training, and probabilistic algorithms. The challenge is to propose a service that is not so much suitable in terms of Chomskian linguistic competence, but mainly as communicative or pragmatic competence. The linguistic competence involves the ability to decide whether a given expression is well-formed. Chomsky considers language as a scientific object in terms of an individual and internal system (I-language), which cannot be easily identified neither with a more commonplace concept of language, nor with the semiological-structuralist definition of language (both E-language).[15] Such a concept of competence, or I-language, does not immediately correlate with performance, if by performance it is meant not simply what people do, but what people choose (more or less consciously)[16] to do: action and reaction. Choices are loosely conditioned by well-formedness. They are heavily constrained by all factors involved in linguistic interaction. What counts is what is done with words. In this sense, it is preferable to talk about a 'pragmatic competence'. The performer has to make choices. Knowledge and experience of the relation between language and reality is necessary.

The performer must adapt to the shared norms of interaction and be ready to integrate missing information, parts of which may include idiosyncratic realities, especially in the cases of participants in constant and privileged (if not almost exclusive) contact, like couples, lovers, etc. The ultimate challenge of advanced linguistic artificial intelligence is to respond to idiosyncratic details within one or more social frames. See the following dialogue:

---

15 On 'I-' and 'E-language' cf. Chomsky 1986. Further important discussions in Chomsky 2012, 2016.

16 It is not possible here to open a section on the concept of intention. See Duranti 2015.

(3) (from 19'44')
-- (M) and you threw a jeb thinking it was poisonous.
--   What's 'threw a jeb?'
--   Oh, it's a phrase we had, like throwing a fit
--   Oh. Ok. So I threw a jeb

Using an expression known only by two individuals excludes others from understanding the discourse. Here the lack of competence is rectified immediately thanks to Martha's collaborative attitude. The dynamic learning skills of the performer adapts to an idiosyncratic sub-code that used to be shared between Martha and Ash only.

In this other dialogue Martha drops her telephone while speaking with the service, interrupting the communication. She fears that the phone might be broken and the contact might not be re-established. Luckily the phone works.

(5) (23'28")
-- (M) I dropped you. I'm sorry. It was just... It was... I'm sorry
--   Hey. It's all right. I'm fine. I'm not in that thing, you know. I'm remote. I'm in the cloud.

The performer's linguistic act has the effect of calming Martha, not by virtue of its informative value (even if correct), but thanks to the re-established contact.

> The relationship between speakers is affirmed by the act of communication rather than the content of communication. Thus, in social life, phatic conversation serves to reassure that communication and interaction are alive and well (Wang et al. 2012, p. 85).

Notice that in the case of "Be Right Back" there is an analogy, almost a coincidence of one of the participants (the performer) with the communication and the interaction themselves, as long as the performer is the phatic technology at work, not just a participant into a phatic communion.

Once the psychological contact and the recognition of the interlocutor is established, the events are open to realize all other functions (emotional, referential etc.), but also to clash with the reality of interaction in a more complex system wherein language is not the only or main factor.

Explicit difficulties come with the body-material upgrade. The turning-point is in the scene in which Martha indicates a place on the body of the performer and says: 'He had a mole there' (32'52'). Technically speaking, Martha is the administrator of the performer. The performer then adjusts the visible surface according to the information received by Martha. This detail is decisive, not only in the plot, but also to understand the model underlying the conception of this (engineered) body. The body of the performer is treated as a linguistic system, better, as a network of linguistic events, and therefore as a sort of text, or even better as a text-carrier. It can reformulate and even contradict itself, that is, it can correspond or not with what is known of the body of the performed, it can change the program and change itself to meet the demands of its administrator, and it can change skin, modify the reproduction of the body of the deceased by re-writing its surface. It's clearly understood as a commodity, a thing, but it works within a network of persons, not things. Thus, the choice to modify the skin reveals itself as inadequate, because it is induced by the fact that the performer over-interprets Martha's linguistic acts. This happens because of its essential nature. The adapting body traces the model of the linguistic adaptations seen before. But the body does not share all of the characteristics of language and brings other factors into interaction, from spatial and temporal ones (it redefines them) to proxemics and kinesics (complicating linguistic interaction) – from those conditioned by its biological reality to those that determine it as 'world' in relation to 'words'. Here is to be observed the first big inter-agent error. The error can be well described using the theory of the direction of fit in how words and world are supposed to match, by J. Searle (1976).

Expanding J. Austin's (1962) theory, J. R. Searle produced some works that later became foundational (1969, 1976). Taking up the distinction between locutions, illocutions and perlocutions, Searle attempts a classification of illocutionary acts by proposing a series of parameters (dimensions of variation).[17] The crucial point is the differences in the so-called 'direction of fit'.

---

17 For a brief but very clear presentation of the works of Austin and Searle and a tentative integration with phenomenological approaches, see Ricoeur 1973.

> Some of our utterances are supposed to match how things are in the world
> […] like examples such as "all men are mortal", "the cat is on the mat", and
> "Socrates is bald". All of these are supposed to match an independently exist-
> ing reality, and to the extent that we do, we say that they are true or false. I
> like to think in simple metaphors. Think of these as matching reality or failing
> to match. They have what we could call the word-to-world direction of fit […]
> But not all utterances set out to be true or false, and not all of them attempt
> to describe an independently existing reality. Some are designed to get peo-
> ple to change reality, and typical examples of such utterances are orders,
> promises, commands, and requests. Such speech acts have the world-to-
> word direction of fit, because the aim of the speech act is not to tell us how
> things are, but to try to get the world to change in the form of the behavior of
> the speaker or hearer so that the world changes to match the content of the
> words. (Searle 2002, p. 29).

By making the mole appear, the performer fails to interpret Martha's illocutionary act, creating an unexpected and unnatural perlocutionary effect.
As mentioned, the performer is interpreting the body as the carrier of a text,
and obviously it interprets itself as a textual component. Thus, if it lacks
knowledge, as above in (3), it integrates it. But the presence of a mole on the
natural body of a human being does not depend on the knowledge that there
is a mole on that body. The body of the performer instead depends on the
knowledge of the body of the performed, not existing any more, but represented in linguistic and visual traces, which are texts. It is also conceived
within a client / server dynamic, and understands the linguistic acts of its
administrator (Martha) as requests to be satisfied.[18] But when Martha says
'he had a mole ….' she is only expressing a memory, and perhaps she expects
sympathy or the like. Matching the world to the words has no place here.

> A fourth class [of illocutionary acts] are cases where we take the fit for
> granted and express some feeling or attitude about the state of affairs rep-
> resented. So, if I apologize for stepping on your foot, thank you for giving me
> the money, or congratulate you on winning the prize, then in each case I take

---

[18] In the most dramatic confrontation with Martha, the performer defines its function in
these terms: 'I am to please'. The framework of the goals within which it operates is therefore not adequate to an interaction between rational beings on terms of equality.

it for granted that I have stepped on your foot, that you have given me the money, that you have won the prize, and the whole point of the speech act is to express some psychological state about that. In such cases, I say the fit is presupposed. I call these Expressives (Searle 2002, p. 29).

Martha is not expecting a change, having in front of her a realistic model of a human body. Martha's illocutionary act is of the 'expressive' type (in terms of Searle). The performer, instead, takes the world-to-words direction of fit, adapting the world (i.e. the surface of the body) to the propositional content (the information) of Martha's speech act. Linguistic interaction shows a fundamental flaw here.

The performer in practice does not behave according to freedom, going against the expectations connected with the kind of being it emulates. Actually, the service stops at a limited level of simulation, and therefore it cannot be ascribed to the category of 'rational beings in general', (which includes human beings). In Kant's terms, it remains a thing (*Sache*) to dispose of;[19] it actually understands itself as such. It is a modern kind of thing, a dynamic service, able to adapt itself to the surroundings and to new requests. The service however confuses the field of interaction by proposing a realistic perceptive model. This kind of body is a body/thing dependent on the knowledge of something different: a body/person. A human being, who is a kind of rational being, knows himself and comprehends his peers and fellow humans. In such a way it enters into a rational dynamic over a natural one ('natural' in Kant's terms, i.e. 'necessary'), difficult to reproduce on an engineering scale. The concept of 'adapting the world to words' could be understood also as a path of adjusting to a pre-comprehension, as an engineered and thus a 'poietic' truth and specifically not a 'poetic' or artistic one. Furthermore, one should also suggest to consider the notion of 'the adaptation of words to the world' as a dialectic comparison between pre-comprehensions and true understanding, which can become an almost ascetic, spiritual journey. To develop these thoughts, "Be Right Back" will be now compared with Tarkovsky's *Solaris*. A richer reflection could be developed in future contri-

---

19 About the relation person/thing in Kant cf. Esposito 2014 (especially about *Die Metaphysik der Sitten*; Cf. etiam Kant's *Zum ewigen Frieden. Ein philosophischer Entwurf*).

butions from these considerations, involving topics such as 'body', 'person', 'thing', 'anthropopoiesis',[20] mediated textuality,[21] etc.

Having recognized the linguistic priority of the operation, and the textual nature of the 'performer' it should be clear, that such an artificial body is not a replica, or a replicant, much less a clone. It is important to clear the field of a premise of this kind. Commercially, it is a device (as a material and cognitive use value) and a service (as a social value). Ideally (and artistically) it should not be ascribed as much to the model of the replicant, as to that of the ghost, and that of ephemeral texts. This suggestion originates from a comparison to a formidable moment in the history of cinema: *Solaris*. The original novel by S. Lem will not be considered, due to the value of the personal, philosophical and artistic appropriation made by Tarkovski.[22] Incidentally, it was Charlie Brooker himself who defined "Be Right Back" as a ghost story.[23]

The 'death of the neighbour'

As is well known, in the film *Solaris*, the protagonist Kris Kelvin stays in a space station over an alien ocean called 'Solaris' and experiences contact with (kinds of reproductions of) his late wife, Hari. This is the point of connection with "Be Right Back" to be briefly investigated.

In Tarkovsky's film, the Solaris ocean is known as a sort of neural system / brain. There is a scientific discipline, called 'solaristics', which studies this strange entity and tries to understand if it is intelligent and able to have

---

20 Esposito 2014; Heidegger 1994/1949; Remotti 2013.

21 An interesting expansion of these thoughts would concern not only the body as both a literal and metaphorical carrier of texts, but also the topic of mediated texts, i.e. text that are reproduced more or less perspicuously in other texts (Manco 2015, 2017; Rizza 2018). The issue is complicate, as the status of cinema and textuality is not straightforward. A discussion could start from a novel evaluation of essays like Metz 1968, 1971, with new insights into the topic of fractal narrative, like Duarte 2014.

22 On the relationship between the book and the film, see the interviews released by Lem and collected at the website http://english.lem.pl/home/reading/interviews (Accessed: 2 Jan. 2019).

23 Temperton 2016.

free thoughts.[24] Following contact with human explorers, Solaris begins
to shape, agglomerating neutrinos, human figures that somehow embody
the mental images, memories, and desires of the members of the missions.
Each reacts in different ways, but everyone is shocked. Attempts to get rid
of these bodies fail. Kris has an intimate image of Hari that Solaris perceives
and materializes, materializing also the sense of remorse and guilt, at least
in the beginning, but then things change. Kris matures a complex and rich
human relationship. The new Hari rapidly develops an increasingly autonomous personality even though she is emotionally linked to Kris.

The profundity of Tarkovsky's thinking about this topic (a story of ghosts,
after all), is immeasurable when compared to "Be Right Back," both for the
artistic results in general and for the cinematographic ones in particular. The
abysmal difference between *Solaris* and "Be Right Back" is above all a sign of
the times. I am convinced that the plot and the reflections proposed in "Be
Right Back" are a testament to the most modern desire for technical power
without being able to criticize it. I think that my previous reasoning and the
comparison with Tarkovsky's *Solaris* reveals that "Be Right Back" depends on
cultural models that adheres and tends to dissolve into technocratic ideology.
This is an ideology that nowadays presents itself in the market as a supplier of
more and more individualized products (material and not), to the point that
these cannot be exchangeable any more, and are therefore deprived of social
values. This has disaggregating effects on the intersubjective realm of the
world of free-willing life.

While the question in *Solaris* is knowledge and science, in "Be Right Back"
it is technology and market. This difference depicts quite well the cultural
situation characterized in Zoja's (2009) theory of the 'death of the neighbour'
(recalling the 'neighbour' of the gospels).

The inability to reconcile social ties and desire always equates to the latter's
victory. The construction of a group of equals requires a continuous will,
made of wakeful states, of tedious adjustments and sacrifice: otherwise,
like the miracle, after the first apparition it flattens itself into prayer cards.

---

24 *Solaris* (29'56''-) — Thus, it has been established that the Solaris Ocean is a distinctive brain.
 Right after that, an even more daring hypothesis came out, suggesting that the Ocean is
 a thinking substance. Incidentally, this hypothesis still cannot be confirmed or refuted.

The desire, however, survives by itself, even in the laziest being, even while sleeping.[25]

The spiritual and philosophical cultural paradigms that underlie the concept of the Tarkoskian *Solaris* seem to belong to a lost and incomprehensible world. It is true that "Be Right Back" does imagine the social failure of the experiment of the reproduction of a loved person. But should we think that technology has not gained primacy over humans? I do not think so. The world narrated in "Be Right Back" is a world of ghosts. All characters are ghosts for each other: none of the protagonists are able to establish a living human relationship with their 'neighbour'. What can be seen is the new paradigm of human relationships in which the neighbour is no longer present, belonging by now to the world of the dead. The living are ghosts more or less reproducible with different artificial solutions, to the point that even when they meet each other with direct and reciprocal perception of proximity, the very human sense of proximity, of closeness, is constantly denied. It is denied between Martha and Ash at the beginning, before Ash dies; it is denied both between Martha and her friend Sarah and between Martha and her sister, and it is impossible, notwithstanding the promising start, with the reproduction of Ash. When Hari and Kris develop a relationship of human proximity, this remains even after the annihilation of the agglomerate of neutrinos. There is no such relation with the re-creation of Ash, simply because no such relation existed between Ash and Martha, and because this re-creation is a consumerist commodity, it comes from the market.[26]

A short sketch of the comparison between the reproduction of Ash and Hari could be the following:

---

25 L'incapacità di conciliare legame sociale e desiderio equivale sempre alla vittoria di quest'ultimo. La costruzione di un gruppo di uguali richiede una volontà continua, fatta di veglie, di noiosi aggiustamenti e rinunce: altrimenti, come i miracoli, si appiattisce in immaginette dopo l'apparizione iniziale. Il desiderio, invece, sopravvive da solo, anche nel più pigro, anche mentre dorme (p. 99).

26 Explicit reference to *Solaris* by Brooker (Temperton 2016) could not be found. This may be simply due to a negligence in the present research. An interest in the history of cinema is however alive in "Be Right Back", but dedicated to another great author: W. Herzog.

Ash (– Martha)	Hari (– Kris)
created from an external image	created from an intimate image
does not resume intimate feelings between the two	does resume intimate feeling between the two
new intimate feelings do not evolve	new intimate feelings evolve
no sense of proximity / 'neighbourhood'	a feeling of proximity / 'neighbourhood' is retained even in the final absence of a material reproduction.

The very concept of body clearly changed. In the reproduction of Ash, the 'body' is a perspicuous reproduction of a 'text', a public one, based on data, i.e. external knowledge. Hari's body is the material sign of an intimate and complicated relation, once failed, but still open.

Further considerations can be drawn from the reflections reported *supra* in the chapter made by Chomsky on communication:

		Ash (– Martha)	Hari (– Kris)
internal use		irrelevant	maximal relevance
external use	phatic	high	low
	informative	little	important
outcomes / aims		customer satisfaction	open

Time and space conditions are conceived on different cultural and spiritual backgrounds. The ones in "Be Right Back" represent the effects of Zoja's (2019) 'death of the neighbour'. According to the theories of Wang et al. (cf. supra) a technological phatic system serves the purpose of fulfilling social needs across time-space by trying to sustain intimacy at a distance (in the case of "Be Right Back" the distance is that of death). In the frame of 'death of the neighbour', embedded technology, with its embedded client / server, or supplier / costumer, and data-dependent structure, absorbs people's trust and creates a new mediated perception of neighbourhood, radically different from the original.

Bibliography

Austin, J.L. (1962) *How to do things with words*. Cambridge (Mass.): Harvard University Press.

Chomsky, N. (1965) *Aspects of the theory of syntax*. Cambridge (Mass): MIT.

Chomsky, N. (1967) 'Recent contributions to the theory of innate ideas: summary of oral presentation', *Synthese*. 17(1), pp. 2–11.

Chomsky, N. (1986) *Knowledge of language: its nature, origin, and use*. New York: Praeger.

Chomsky, N. (2012) *The Science of Language. Interviews with James McGilvray*. Cambridge: Cambridge University Press.

Chomsky, N. (2016) *What kind of creatures are we?* New York: Columbia University Press.

Chomsky, N. and Osiatynski, W. (1984), 'On language and culture. Noam Chomskyinterviewed by Wiktor Osiatynski', in Osiatynski, W. (ed.), *Contrasts: Soviet and American thinkers discuss the future*. New York: MacMillan, pp. 95-101.

Cimatti, F. (2018), 'La lingua c'è. Saussure, Chomsky e Lacan', *Philosophy Kitchen* 9, pp. 100-112.

Duarte, G. A. (2014) *Fractal narrative: about the relationship between geometries and technology and its impact on narrative spaces*. Bielefeld: transcript.

Duranti, A. (1992) *Etnografia del parlare quotidiano*. Roma: La Nuova Italia Scientifica.

Duranti, A. (1997) *Linguistic anthropology*. Cambridge: Cambridge Univ. Press.

Duranti, A. (2015) *The Anthropology of intentions. Language in a world of others*. Cambridge: Cambridge Univ. Press.

Ellul, J. (1954) *La technique ou l'enjeu du siècle*. Paris: Armand Colin.

Esposito, R. (2014) *Le persone e le cose*. Torino: Einaudi.

Foucault, M. (1971) *L'ordre du discours*. Paris: Gallimard.

Giddens, A. (1990) *The Consequences of modernity*. Stanford: Stanford Univ. press.

Gradinaru, C. (2018) 'Small talk in our digital everyday life: the contours of a phatic culture', *Meta: Research in hermeneutics, phenomenology, and practical philosophy* 10(2), pp. 459-472.

Graffi, G. (*forth.*), '"Saussure", Saussure, langue/parole, competence/performance', in a forthcoming Festschrift.

Grice, P. (1975) 'Logic and Conversation', in Cole, P. and Morgan, J. (eds), *Syntax and semantics, vol. 3: Speech acts*. New York: Academic Press, pp. 41–58.

Habermas, J. (1970) 'Towards a theory of communicative competence?', *Inquiry* 13(4),pp. 360–375.

Heidegger, M. (1994) *Das Ding* [1949], Gesamtausgabe III/79: Bremer und Freiburger Vorträge. Frankfurt am Main: Klostermann.

Hymes, D. (1972a) 'Models of the Interaction of Language and Social Life', in Gumperz, J.J. and Hymes, D. (eds) *Directions in sociolinguistics: The ethnography of communication*. New York: Holt, Rinehart and Winston, pp. 35–71.

Hymes, D. (1972b) 'On Communicative Competence', in: Pride, J.B. and Holmes, J. (eds) *Sociolinguistics*. Harmondsworth: Penguin, pp. 269–293.

Jakobson, R. (1960) 'Closing statements: linguistics and poetics", in Sebeok, Th.A. (ed.) *Style in language*, Cambridge (MA): MIT Press, pp. 350–377.

Laver, J. (1975) 'Comunicative functions of phatic communion', in Kendon, A. et al. (eds) *Organization of behavior in face-to-face interaction*, The Hague: Mouton, pp. 215–238.

Malinowski, B. (1923), 'The problem of meaning in primitive languages.' Supplemetary essay, in Ogden, C.K. and Richards. I.A., *The Meaning of meaning: A study of the influence of language upon thought and of the science of symbolism*. New York: Harcourt, Brace and World, pp. 296-336.

Manco, A. (2015) 'Testi mediati da testi. Precarietà e pertestualità'. Ἀλεξάνδρεια. *Alessandria. Rivista di glottologia* 9, pp. 129-144.

Manco, A. (2017) 'Precarietà testuale e pertestualità: qualche considerazione sulla relativa classificazione e sugli aspetti metalinguistici', *Atti del Sodalizio Glottologico Milanese* 11 n.s. (2016), pp. 81-92.

Metz, C. (1968) *Essais sur la signification au cinéma*. Paris: Klincksieck.

Metz, C. (1971) *Langage et cinéma*. Paris: Larousse.

Miller, V. (2008) 'New media, networking and phatic culture', *Convergence: the international journal of research into new media technologies* 14(4), pp. 387-400.

Niemelä-Nyrhinen, J. and Seppänen, J. (2019) 'Visual communication: the photographic image as phatic communication', *New media and society* 00(0), pp. 1-15. (doi.org/10.1177%2F1461444819876237)

Porter, J.E. (2017) 'Professional communication as phatic: from classical eunoia to personal artificial intelligence', *Business and professional communication quarterly* 80(2), pp. 174-193.

Remotti, F. (2013) *Fare umanità. I drammi dell'antropopoiesi*. Roma-Bari: Laterza.

Ricoeur, P. (1973) 'Discours et communication', in *La communication. Actes du XVe Congrès de l'Association des Sociétés de Philosophie de langue française, Montréal 1971, vol. II.* Montréal: Montmorency 1973, pp. 23–48.

Rizza, A. (2018) 'Testualità mediata da testualità nel fumetto : un caso esemplare/estremo', *Rivista italiana di linguistica e di dialettologia*, 20, pp. 161–179.

Saville-Troike, M. (2003) *The ethnography of communication: an introduction.* 3rd ed. Malden, Mass: Blackwell Pub (Language in society, 3).

Searle, J.R. (1969) *Speech acts: an essay in the philosophy of language.* Cambridge University Press.

Searle, J.R. (1976) 'The classification of illocutionary acts', *Language in Society* 5(1), pp. 1–23.

Searle, J.R. (2012) 'Human social reality and language', *Phenomenology and Mind* 2, pp. 24-33.

Szpunar, P.M. (2019) 'Communication and (un)inspired terror: toward a theory of phatic violence', *Communication theory* 00(0), pp. 1-20. (doi: 10.1093/ct/qtz009).

Temperton, J. (2016) 'Charlie Brooker on where *Black Mirror* will take us next', *Wired UK*, 11 October 2016. Available at https://www.wired.co.uk/article/black-mirror-technology-changing-lives (Accessed: 15 Jan. 2019).

Wang, V. and Tucker, J.V. (2016) 'Phatic systems in digital society', *Technology in Society* 46, pp. 140-148.

Wang, V., Tucker, J.V. and Haines, K. (2012) 'Phatic technologies in modern society', *Technology in Society* 34, pp. 84-93.

Wang, V., Tucker, J.V. and Rihll, T.E. (2011) 'On phatic technologies for creating and maintaining human relationships', *Technology in Society* 33, pp. 44-51.

Žegarac, V. and Clark, B. (1999) 'Phatic interpretations and phatic communications', *Journal of Linguistics* 35, pp. 321-346.

Zoja, L. (2009) *La morte del prossimo*, Torino: Einaudi.

Death in *San Junipero*
The Hyper-Reality Principle

Georgios Tsagdis

San Junipero: where dreams are abundant, where abundance is but a dream. A fictional city, a Platonic paradigm, perhaps like it, no less dystopic than utopic. *San Junipero*, the title of the fourth episode of the third series (3.4) of *Black Mirror*, exemplary in its cinematic and narrative qualities,[1] is also paradigmatic for the whole of the series, staking nothing less than the *status of reality*.[2] It is a status that becomes evermore problematic, evermore opaque, the black box of all experience, if experience still has a valence (Agamben, 2006). And if one should probe reality today, probe it for the sake of tomorrow, one would have to look, like yesterday, into the mirror. For the mirror is the elemental figure, the elemental question on reality.

---

1 Being nominated and winning in 2017 and 2018 in different categories of the Art Directors Guild Awards, Cinema Audio Society Awards, Diversity in Media Awards, GLAAD Media Awards, BAFTA Television Craft Awards, Gold Derby Awards, IGN Awards, Hugo Awards, Online Film and Television Association Awards, Primetime Emmy Awards and Broadcast Awards.

2 Indicatively, from the episodes of the first two seasons "Fifteen Million Merits," "The Entire History of You," "Be Right Back," and "White Bear" through the 2014 special "White Christmas" and the 2018 movie *Bandersnatch* and leading up to the three episodes of the fifth season, "Striking Vipers," "Smithereens," and "Rachel, Jack and Ashley Too," the *status of reality* vis-à-vis digitisation, simulation, mass data archivisation, and surveillance remains the guiding force of the series. These questions are directly politicised in the episodes "The National Anthem" and "The Waldo Moment." The middle, third and fourth, series operate within the same contours.

Accordingly, the title of the series announces a *speculation* on reality. This speculation is dark,[3] for the status of reality constitutes both the most elusive and the most precious knowledge, always sought, always revised, reviewed, revisioned. It is also dark, for its void constitutes our innermost fears, our newest fears – the fears of today and tomorrow and perhaps also of yesterday. Perhaps then the most exemplary scene of the exemplary *San Junipero* is the moment that a frustrated fist breaks the mirror. But the fist does not bleed and as the eye blinks the mirror is whole again. Just like the opening credits of the series offer each time a new mirror to be smitten to shards, San Junipero offers a place of no pain, of sheer pleasure, a place where reality is always whole. It strives thus to question the whole of reality. The present undertaking is an attempt to unfold this question.

Strangely, one learns from Freud, reality has a principle. The notion of the *reality principle* emerges in Freud's late work to designate the counter-force of pleasure, which is guided by its own principle, antagonising reality over the governance of the soul. Fearing its Dionysian dissolution under the sway of unbounded, untrammelled pleasure, the ego's instincts of self-preservation lead to the adoption of the reality principle. Pleasure is not abandoned, but is rather deferred, apportioned and meted out, in ways that if they fail to procure *more* pleasure, they ensure at the very least the survival of the self and thus the possibility of the *continuation* of pleasure (Freud, 2001, 10). Accordingly, the reality principle dictates the exchange of the direct with the indirect, the short with the long, the present with the future. It thereby presents a claim of superiority, rather than opposition, to the pleasure principle. The reality principle enfolds pleasure, economizes it, by amortizing its expenditure. *Reality for Freud is meta-pleasure.*

The aim is not merely to think together in the reality principle, as Derrida proposes, (1982, 18-9) the economical and uneconomical circuits of pleasure – certainly a necessary propaedeutic – but to designate a different uneconomic function at the heart of the reality principle, one that does not come from the *de facto* loss of *future* enjoyment that every *present* enjoyment necessitates. Rather, reality presents itself from the outset as a challenge to pleasure, antagonizing anew what it enfolds. Thus, it is uneconomic not within,

---

3 Cf. Paul's profession in the first epistle to the Corinthians (13:12, KJV): "For now we see through a glass, darkly; but then face to face: now I know in part; but then shall I know even as also I am known."

but without pleasure's circuit. Indeed, confronted with the choice between reality and pleasure, one appears *strangely* attached to the former. And inso-far as reality is aligned with truth, an alignment that present space does not suffice to disarticulate, the red pill will always win over the blue. It is not an empirical preference, it is not a judgment of taste, it is an *a priori* condi-tion of existence: reality overpowers pleasure and pain; at least, this is how one thinks, how one wishes to think, how one is conditioned to think. The *a priori* election of reality over pleasure and in fact over everything, informs the re-signification of the reality principle. How should, however, the real be understood?

'Welcome to the desert of the real.' Baudrillard's invitation consigns the reality principle to an historical contingency; reality *was*, but is no longer. A desert stretches along reality's erstwhile domain. Whereas the imaginary used to be the *alibi*, literally, the elsewhere of the real, the real is now the alibi of the model, except that this alibi is nowhere; not a utopia to come, but one irrevocably lost (Baudrillard, 1995, 122-3). What could have possibly effected this haemorrhage of the real into disappearance? Perhaps, even more impor-tantly, how could something like that have happened? And in fact, what did exactly transpire?

The eclipse of the 'sovereign difference' between reality and its simula-crum announced the end of both elements of the relation: when the mirror that sustained the reality differential shattered, the real lost itself along with its reflection (2). The tacit assumption of this constitutive diagnosis being that without the mirror, and thus without its reflected visage, the real can no longer recognize *itself as such*. And further, decisively, that for the phe-nomenon of the real, this *as such* constituted its very essence. Without having its reality constantly underwritten by the distance of the simulacrum, the real could no longer appear *as such*: it thus became nothing. Indistinct from its simulacrum the real was no longer any more significant than the latter: both at once reduced to a radical insignificance. This is the full force of the shattering of the mirror.

One possible path of questioning Baudrillard's contribution to the ques-tion of the real, is to exert pressure on *what constitutes the distinctive trait of the present* – the present past, the current present, and perhaps the present to come. One of Baudrillard's answers: "it is now impossible to isolate the process of the real, or to prove the real" (2). Yet, was it ever? Baudrillard con-siders the expansiveness of the horizon of the universe effected by space conquest, as one of the vectors along which the internal coherence of reality is contested (12-4). Yet this contestation took place already with the telescope – if not with the first cosmogony, which fabulated and thus destabilized the matrix of the real. It is not a matter of finding precedents; it is a matter of understanding a transformation announced as *already effected* almost four decades ago.

Certainly, *something* has taken place, something continues to unravel. It is something that a sentence or a book cannot account for, something that the unprecedented processing power of artificial intelligence articulates in absentia, a colossal calculation that resists all translation. Baudrillard attempted this translation before the devastating onset of artificial intelligence, which *Black Mirror* portrays with exceptional visual eloquence, at the dawn of the digital. At the time, he saw already that "the 'thrill' of advertising [had] been displaced onto computers and onto the miniaturization of everyday life by computer science" (89). The thrill being nothing else than the alluring outdoors of the imaginary.

But these outdoors have been shut off for us. "Simulation is insuperable, unsurpassable, dull and flat, without exteriority – we will no longer even pass through to 'the other side of mirror', that was still the golden age of transcendence," (125) pronounces Baudrillard. In this totality without *dehors*, the techno-scientific-medial apparatus has absorbed everything, leaving no remainder and, *by the same token*, turning the totality itself into an absolute remainder (144). Yet, a crack appears. Baudrillard, against all possible miscomprehensions, nowhere denounces the real as an illusion, which has at long last been abolished. Its status as an historical contingency does not reduce it to mere fiction. "Made is not made up," in Donna Haraway's superlative concision (2018, 84). Rather, the making and unmaking of the contingency of the real is what interests Baudrillard, as the specific event that still unfolds.

It is this unfolding that eliminates, as mentioned, the 'sovereign difference' of the real and its simulacrum. It does this by ever-approximating degrees of similitude. Since, however, the more the simulacrum approximates the simulated, the more its character *as a simulacrum* becomes apparent, a race or escalation of outdoing reality ensues; the real tries to outrun its shadow. It soon becomes clear that only what is more real than the real can constitute a *sufficient* simulation (Baudrillard, 1995, 122-3). The real is thereby supplanted by the *hyperreal*. The hyperreal dominates the real, by continuously adding dimensions of similitude, hyper-exacting the exactitude of the real. San Junipero appears thus in countless ways a more than perfect replica of all the places and times it purports to be. In its different figurations, it is 'more '80s or '90s' than those eras could ever be.

In turn, then, the real emerges as a left-over of truth, its sole virtue not to have entered this struggle of exactitude and similitude, not to have entered the escalation (107). This left-over is the residue of the real, the un-simulated and thus unassimilated, which attests to the obscene dialectic through which the hyperreal has exiled the real from its domain. And since as Baudrillard says, "All of the real is residual, and everything that is residual is destined to repeat itself indefinitely in phantasms," (146) the vanquished real is destined to haunt the hyperreal. It does so incessantly, and yet it is in the errors and the anomalies, in the collapse of its exactitude, that the matrix reveals its constitutive spectrality.

The glitch of the hyperreal allows us to diagnose the extent and intensity of contemporary nihilism, a nihilism of transparency. For Baudrillard the latter consists no longer in the death of God, but in his becoming hyperreal (156). A perplexing development, which invites the same incredulity on the status of the novelty: after all, *God was always hyperreal*; *ens realissimum*, the most real of all things real. It is, in fact, Platonist and Platonizing theologies that introduce into language the prefix 'hyper-', which in Latin will be translated as 'super-'. Yet something is different; as *supremely* real, both the Platonic One and the Trinitarian God are *still* real – to the extent that this category is still signifying. It is Man, and in a sense all creation, that exists as *imago dei*. Man is the simulacrum, the hologram. God's hyperreality is the first reality; his shadow or mirror reflection – notwithstanding the Gnostic resonances – is the world. Since, however, God died, the world, having assumed his place as the epicenter of the real, technologically re-produced itself, perfecting its reproduction until this reproduction exceeded the reality of its model. In this narrative, Man crafted the hyperreal hologram; only later did the hologram become God – the nihilism of transparency descended.

Words such as cynicism and pessimism, aside of the facile severance from their connotative and signifying historic grounds, are irrelevant to Baudrillard's project and of little help to the predicament staged in *Black Mirror*. Nihilism is a historical moment, one that has redoubled itself, first with Nietzsche, as the tragedy of the anthropological murder of God, now as the farce of a hologrammatic Prometheus. But this farcical nihilism loses none of its ethereal gravity or its devastating non-violence, for it. In the meantime, millions are crushed, the mirror darkens.

And yet, *Simulacra and Simulation* opens with the announcement of a double loss: *the real will no longer be able to produce itself, as death, unvanquished, seems to vanish* (2). The relation of the real to death appears as the contexted nexus or correspondence out of which a passage might be gained to both the death of the real and to the reality of death. Tarrying with Baudrillard's diagnosis, the eclipse of death by means of its simulation represents the desperate attempt of institutionalised powers "to escape their real death throes" (19). The apparatus craves for anyone prepared to sacrifice his life, or thus offer his death through a revolutionary practice (24) – but no revolutionary practice seems to afford the prospect of a meaningful death in liberal democracies and no one seems to be *willing* or *able* to die. Accordingly, he apparatus of power attempts two simultaneous moves: on the one hand, it hopes and strives for a real death; on the other, it attempts to make everyone a stakeholder in its project of simulating death away.

San Junipero articulates both drives. The former is at first sight evidenced in Kelly's final resolve to share in Yorkie's 'real death' *outside* the simulated city of San Junipero. However, the reality of death is ultimately vouched only as a memory, the memory of a pre-history. Before Kelly meets Yorkie, she has a husband and a daughter. The latter dies at thirty-nine, having had no access to San Junipero's virtual afterlife. When her husband dies sometime later, he cannot bring himself to accept a prospect that his daughter could not enjoy. This is where the spectator finds Kelly – trapped between the desire to lead the interminable, ever-young simulated life of San Junipero, after she dies a real death with Yorkie, and the fidelity to the real death of her forever-lost family. It is the reality of the latter death, a death with no afterlife, that offers the support of the real to the death that Kelly and Yorkie can share, as they transition into San Junipero's hyperreal utopia. It is in turn this utopia that offers the fullest, frontal exposition of the second drive of the apparatus, namely the drive to simulate death away. San Junipero is a virtual paradisiac garden where the promise of evergreen, libidinal youth is never broken; the mirror of San Junipero cannot be fractured. In Kelly's words, Yorkie makes a 'sales pitch' to persuade her to join the 'graveyard' of San Junipero, to choose, for the sake of their love (Yorkie's first and Kelly's last), a fake life without the possibility of a real death. It is this hyperreal life that the apparatus propagates, wishing to do so with everyone's complicity.

Returning to the former drive, the apparatus has understood its need of reality in order to signify and sustain its excess production of simulacra – its last resort being the final remains of life and death. Thus for example, 'reality television' – already a staple at the time of *Simulacra and Simulation* – stages a feast of those without a life and thus without death, on the life of those passive protagonists, who without either presenting or representing themselves, deliver themselves over to the televised mass sacrificial spectacle (26). "The reality of simulation is unbearable," Baudrillard tells us, "crueler than Artaud's *Theater of Cruelty*, which was still an attempt to create a dramaturgy of life, the last gasp of an ideality of the body, of blood, of violence in a system that was already taking it away [...]" (38-9). This vampirism of capitalism, with which Marx was well acquainted, passes here through the litmus test of reality: life and death have no value for hyperreality unless they can be exchanged for a modicum of precious reality. Thus for example, it becomes clear that a precautionary warning such as that of Guattari, comes too late. When one hears almost a decade after the *Simulacra and Simulation* that, "a society that fails to use tolerance and permanent inventiveness to 'imaginarize' violence in its various manifestations runs the risk of seeing violence crystallize in the real," (2000, 142) one knows that a reversal of this relation has already taken effect, by making all violence 'imaginary;' by placing all violence at the level of simulation, hyperreality has vanquished reality.

So it is for Baudrillard, that both the apparatus and its subjects crave for a real catastrophe to arrive, taking obscene pleasure in environmental disasters as compassionate acts of a forgotten, twice dead, God (1995, 57). One welcomes thus the infinite peril of the Anthropocene as a last exit from the simulation. In a state of total implosion, one hopes for something that can still explode (55). Finding oneself in the same ennui as the namesake protagonist of Janáček's opera the *Makropulos Affair*, her words, weary of immortality, ring truer in one's ears: "Dying or living it's all one, it's all the same thing. In me life has come to a standstill, I cannot go on, in the end it's the same: singing and silence." This rings quite certainly true to the deafened ears of those 'lost fucks' of San Junipero's Quagmire, a place dominated and oppressed by the pleasure principle, its regulars 'trying anything to feel something,' to be rattled out of the apathy of simulation. They too, it seems, would be ready to exchange simulated immortality for a real death, if only somehow they could, if the throes of hyperreality were not that strong. It thus becomes clear: the reality principle calls out for death and yet the choice of reality is no longer a real choice.

Within the grand simulation we have achieved an immortality, which for the most part consists in an 'incapacity to confront death' (156). In the matrix we call 'world', just like in San Junipero, there is "neither subject, nor death, nor unconscious, nor repression, since nothing stops the enchainment of forms" (139). Without unconscious, Man is reduced to an animal – with the difference that an animal has a territory. And since men lost their territories first and in turn lost what constitutes the territorial Ersatz, namely their unconscious, all that is left is a nostalgia of becoming-animal, which, for Baudrillard contra Deleuze and Guattari, amounts to the hope of reclaiming a territory (139). Perhaps a territory, a piece of land, on which to die.

Hyperreality structures immortality as, "a simultaneity of all the functions, without a past, without a future, an operationality on every level" (78). But let us not be fooled, it is the hyperreal self that is immortal and that commands systemic allegiance (26), while the real self, deterred until death and ultimately deterred altogether from a meaningful death, is already dead (48). Thus the human's two bodies experience an utter disarticulation: the real body continues to suffer the inglorious, slow demise of a sedentary existence, while the impervious hyperreal body expends infinite energies, as long as it is able to maintain its life-line to the real body, which now appears as little more than the burden of a temporary compromise.

The promise takes a series of forms: holograms, clones, ultimately the digital upload, all of which are thematized in *Black Mirror*: at once the assurance and threat that a future without the prison of the body is possible. The *sōma sēma* of the Pythagoreans and the Platonists, the body that was a grave, a prison, the comatose real body of Yorkie, and the aging, aching body of Kelly, at last overcome, leaving behind in obsolescence even the most Quixotic transhuman dreams. Will the digital hyperreal self still conform to the rule of the double? Although Baudrillard expends significant efforts analyzing the hologram and the clone, he also declares: "today the simulacrum no longer goes by way of the double and of duplication, but by way of genetic miniaturization" (71). And yet the parallel computer miniaturization means that the genetic and the digital are two sides of a single coin, circulating in a singular economy. One must follow the passage of this circulation.

To start with the double; the double one sees in the mirror and the one that persists once the mirror is shattered. Baudrillard writes:

Cloning also retains nothing, and for the same reason, of the immemorial and narcissistic dream of the subject's projection into his ideal alter ego, since this projection still passes through an image: the one in the mirror, in which the subject is alienated in order to find himself again, or the one, seductive and mortal, in which the subject sees himself in order to die there. None of this occurs in cloning. No more medium, no more image—any more than an industrial object is the mirror of the identical one that succeeds it in the series. One is never the ideal or mortal mirage of the other, they can only be added to each other, and if they can only be added, it means that they are not sexually engendered and know nothing of death. (96)

In these lines, the presence of Freud is unmistakable. The latter's reality principle, re-signified through the present analysis, re-discovers in cloning the conflict between the death *of* the subject, the death that belongs to a subject as subject, and the death drive that undoes the subject, aiming to reach before it, before its human constitution, before its animal and organic constitution, before everything. The death drive discovers in cloning the possibility of undoing sexuation, regressing through the most advanced technology to a form a scissiparity, in which the self reproduces its identity interminably, bypassing the 'vicissitudes of procreation,' while at the same time bypassing altogether the subject and its 'aleatory' freedom, "in the service of a *matrix called code*" (96). Genetic and program codes are aligned.

Perhaps Plato already determined the task of philosophy as *meletē thanatou*, a study of death, but Freud was the first to undertake this study at both the psycho-social and the bio-organic level, the latter, more often than not, overlooked. In his exploration of the reality principle, the function of which has been established as the economization of the pleasure principle, Freud stumbles upon the 'compulsion to repeat,' which seems to contravene and overpower the drive for pleasure (2001, 22). Much about what one calls destiny seems suddenly to hinge on the unconscious fulfillment of this compulsion to repeat (23). Freud proceeds to identify two aspects in the development of this compulsion, which can be understood as stages, the latter drawing on and reinforcing the former.

At first, the child (just like the adult later) repeats the unpleasurable experience in order to exercise a certain mastery over it. By repeating, the child is no longer the passive recipient, but rather becomes the active director of the experience (35). At least in part, for what repetition presupposes is the redoubling of the self, a replication in which the cloning self controls the suffering of the cloned self. Repeated experiences of repetition establish in turn the latter as something in itself desirable and even pleasant, so that for example re-experiencing the pleasurable becomes itself a source of pleasure[4] (36). Thus repetition gains its autonomous significance in the psychic apparatus. Freud wants to pursue the origin of this autonomy into what we might term the organic, pre-psychic, but for Freud, equally always already psychic constitution of life.

Freud is now able to generalize the function of repetition, by discovering an instinct *"inherent in organic life to restore an earlier state of things* which the living entity has been obliged to abandon under the pressure of external disturbing forces; that is, it is a kind of organic elasticity, or, to put it another way, the expression of inertia inherent in organic life" (36). The compulsion to repeat is thus driven by the psycho-organic inertia of life; accordingly, instincts emerge no longer as forces of change, but as conservative, stabilizing factors.

An ancient metaphysical doctrine re-emerges in Freud: "everything living dies for internal reasons" (38). Here the principal internal reason is the wish to undo an inflicted transformation, to return ultimately to the inorganic, to non-life. Thus, Freud finds himself 'compelled' to claim that 'the aim of all life is death' (38). The death drive.

At the dawn of life, as soon as the caesura of the organic found itself confronted with the liquid, mineral world whence it had emerged, this drive could easily be fulfilled. Life was brief, death was cheap, and the passage to the inorganic happened for those protocells, like it still does among protozoa and bacteria, incessantly, by the million. As life evolved its structures, the drive did not disappear; it evolved with life. Self-preservation, self-assertion, and mastery became the instincts life developed in the service of the death drive – the aim always remaining that the organism does not succumb to external forces, but rather follows its own path to death, its own interior law of a return to the inorganic. "The organism wishes to die only in its own fashion," (39) says Freud and this self-fashioning of death, resonating throughout occidental metaphysics, troubles us today more than ever.

---

4 As opposed to an adult's unwillingness to hear a joke or story repeated, a child insists on that repetition and indeed, in the most exact form. The repetition, rather than the story, appears to be the very source of pleasure; 35.

Freud in the process of questioning the primordiality of the death drive will test an hypothesis that traces back in full the circle of our exploration. Looking into germ-cell research of his day, he is confronted with the 'potential immortality' of the Protista. Since "in unicellular organisms the individual and the reproductive cell are still one and the same," replication replicates itself as well as its replicating power (46). In doing so, it seems to preserve an interminably propagating self, the individuality of which coincides with the species, with no distinction between original and copy. Thus, the self-species attains immortality. However, corruption of the genetic coding in the process of replication is inevitable; biology is subject to the inescapable reality of corruption. It is this reality that the hyperreal claims to have abolished, by perfecting the replicability of the real.

The origin – imagined, conjured, or vanished – remains important. If life established itself as a series of almost perfectly replicable self-species, the regressive nostalgia of recovering this possibility would seem ineradicable. If the Protista were immortal, death would be a late event of organic life (47). Death would then have emerged as the decay of the soma in the service of the germ-cell, which would be able to ensure the immortality of its genetic code.[5] Finally, should life have constituted itself from the outset as deathless, a death drive would be meaningless.

Freud, rather than making the mortal soma a late addition of life, prefers to see in the Protista the co-presence of the soma and the germ, the mortal and the immortal. Accordingly, the death drive is given an originary, albeit unarticulated place in the formation of life (47). Moreover, Freud draws heavily on observations of conjugation in Protista, "that is, the coalescence of two individuals which separate soon afterwards without any subsequent cell-division occurring", whereby conjugation "has a strengthening and rejuvenating effect upon both of them" (55). In this picture, a sexless life compensates the death drive of the self-species which left to itself would aim to corrupt itself unto the inorganic – a process as we have seen, destined to fail and producing instead in its failure, as is well-known, biologic evolution. In that sense, the function of conjugation appears as the deferral of the fulfillment of the death drive, its Schmittean *katechon*. Accordingly, *eros* as the drive of conjugation economizes *thanatos*, allowing the death drive to continue operating *ad infinitum*. For the death drive is a drive that wills its own dissolution,

---

5 Dawkins's dubious career was built on this spurious idea.

a drive that runs up against itself. Eros protects this drive from itself; Eros safeguards Thanatos.

This is the subterranean condition upon which San Junipero can articulate all of its other possibilities. If the episode is bathed in pink, blue, and purple light – the hues that paint the bisexual pride flag –, if it seems that an unlikely homoerotic tale weaves its thematic, this thematic is only possible on the basis of the necessity of supplementing the interminable death that the hyperreality of San Junipero promises with a non-procreative, non-genetic erotic gesture. Kelly and Yorkie are the Protista that have managed to regulate through love their death drive, precisely where the death drive seems to have been precluded, relegated to an ever-thinning memory. Kelly and Yorkie can thus live another day, die an other day. This constitutes the hope and limit of San Junipero.

In closing, the links and lines of co-implication that have began to emerge might be visited one last time. In doing so, the death drive appears ultimately as co-extensive with the re-signified notion of reality, insofar as its fulfillment, evangelized by hyperreality, is tantamount to the disappearance of reality. Where there is no death drive, and thus no more death, there is no reality. In turn, it becomes clear, that the economization of the pleasure principle by the reality principle runs full-circle, insofar as *eros* enables *thanatos* to continue its work. The pleasure principle re-doubles upon itself, economizing the reality principle.

That was the circuit of reality, a circuit that Baudrillard believes has now been cut open, and thus dissolved, into a new totality: the hyperreal. Is the passing of the historical contingency of reality irrevocable, irreparable, irremediable? Baudrillard writes:

> This supreme ruse of the system, that of the simulacrum of its death, through which it maintains us in life by having liquidated through absorption all possible negativity, only a superior ruse can stop. Challenge or imaginary science, only a *pataphysics of simulacra* can remove us from the system's strategy of simulation and the impasse of death in which it imprisons us. (153-4)

Yet Baudrillard nowhere offers the groundwork of this *pataphysics*, never establishes the imaginary science that will release the present from the systemic simulation of death. Perhaps this is because within the epistemic and epochal closure in which the present finds itself, the most generous act is a promise one knows one cannot keep, a consolation where there can be no hope. Equally, there can be no despair; pessimism, it has been noted, is irrelevant. It is here that thinkers as diverse as Timothy Morton and Donna Haraway converge. When the latter defines this strange epoch that one calls the present, or the Chthulucene, as "a time-place for learning to stay with the trouble of living and dying in response-ability on a damaged earth," (2016, 2) she recognises the proliferation of precisely those double-binds that inform Morton's anguish over the vast, inescapable ecological catastrophe which makes every solution appear in the shape of a new problem. This is the era of hyperobjects, objects which operate on uncanny spatio-temporal scales, objects with peculiar properties, ridden with contradictions. Thinking hyperobjects through hyperreality, unanticipated possibilities unravel. For Morton, oil – the liquid which propelled the industrial revolution and ultimately hyper-modernity – as much as the liquid which turns vibrant ecosystems into pestilential swamps,[6] gives us a sense of the viscosity of all hyperobjects: they stick. Importantly, reality itself sticks: we are all trapped in the slick.

Morton reminds one of the two pills and the mirror of the *Matrix*. The mirror no longer reflects a reality, exchanging a thing for its a simulacrum, but melts and coats the hand that attempts to touch it. It is not merely that reality dissolves, but rather that reality, in the form of viscous hyperobjects, now envelops us as a film of oil (2013, 34-5). This viscous, hyper-objective reality is as pervasive and totalising as Baudrillard's hyperreality. Baudrillard uses the same image: the hand passes through the hologram without resistance, but not without consequences: the hand is now unreal, hyperreality has stuck to it (105). So, if Morton is never accused with the charges of pessimism, so familiar to Baudrillard, it might not only be that his diagnosis is today unquestionable, but more importantly, that Morton harbours no nostalgia, almost no memory, as well as no hope of scrubbing away this petro-reality off the wings of the future. One might no longer fly, perhaps never did – but more importantly one has to learn to live with the *miasma*.

That means that one must try. To discover new possibilities. To imagine what lies beyond imagination. Since the collapse of the distinction of reality

---

6 Oil for Morton has burnt a whole in the notion of world, a notion, which bears fascinating similarities to the Beaudrillard's reality, the complex genealogies of the two interwoven throughout the history of metaphysics.

and hyperreality appears irreversible, hyperobjects can offer a way of transforming this double, indissoluble plain of the real-hyperreal, in unforeseen ways. Like Einstein's and Planck's objects, the existence of hyperobjects is interwoven with the fabric of the real. Their changes are changes to the matrix of the real. If for Baudrillard hyperreal objects do "no longer resemble anything, except the empty figure of resemblance, the empty form of representation," if, that is, hyperreal objects are nothing but desolate, if not shattered, mirrors, Morton's hyperobjects are liquid mirrors in the process of transformation. What they reflect are partial objects and larval subjects. No reality, no form, only formations, only becomings. Perhaps then, another death is possible and another *eros*.

Bibliography

Agamben, G. (2006) *Infancy and History: On the Destruction of Experience*, transl. by L. Heron, London: Verso.

Baudrillard, J. (1995) *Simulacra and Simulation*, transl. by Sh. F. Glaser, United States of America: University of Michigan Press.

Derrida, J. (1982) "Differánce", in *Margins of Philosophy*, transl. by A. Bass, Brighton: Harvester Press, pp. 1-27.

Freud, S. (2001) "Beyond the Pleasure Principle", in *The Complete Works*, vol. 18, London: Vintage, pp. 7-64.

Guattari, F. (2000) *The Three Ecologies*, transl. by I. Pindar and P. Sutton, London: The Athlone Press.

Haraway, J. D. (2018) "Making Kin in the Chthulucene: Reproducing Multispecies Justice", in *Making Kin Not Population*, ed. by A. E. Clarke and D. Haraway, Chicago: Prickly Paradigm Press, pp. 67-99.

Haraway, J. D. (2016) *Staying with the Trouble, Making Kin in the Chthulucene*, London: Duke University Press.

Morton, T. (2013) *Hyperobjects: Philosophy and Ecology after the End of the World*, Minneapolis: Minnesota University Press.

San Junipero
On Disembodied Paradises and Their Transhumanist Fallacies

Gabriela Galati

The *Black Mirror* episode "San Junipero" begins when Yorkie visits Tucker's, a nightclub in the seaside town of San Junipero in 1987. At Tucker's the young, shy woman meets Kelly, a very extroverted girl. Although Yorkie is initially reluctant, after a second meeting at the bar they have sex. The following week they meet in the year 2002. This time it is Kelly who seems to reject Yorkie. Eventually she confesses that she is dying and that she tried to avoid Yorkie because she was afraid of developing stronger feelings for her. At this point, it is revealed to the viewer that San Junipero is actually a simulated reality to which people's consciousness can be uploaded after they die, a place that elderly people visit to decide if that's what they want when their time comes. Of course, in the simulation everyone inhabits their younger selves. After many other details about the characters' lives are revealed and there is some emotional agonizing, both Kelly and Yorkie are euthanized and their consciousnesses are uploaded so they can "live" in San Junipero happily ever after.

The first thing that strikes one about the episode, given the apocalyptic nature of most of *Black Mirror*'s episodes and especially with regard to the effects of technology on society in the near future, is how happy (perhaps too happy) and hopeful the ending of "San Junipero" is. The uploading of the minds of dead people to a digital simulation is openly presented as a virtual paradise wherein subjects, leaving their obsolete and transitory flesh behind, have their minds (consciousnesses? souls?) stored in a computer server room so as to finally be able to live a liberated, flawless life.

This typically transhumanist perspective (see Hans Moravec, 1994)[1], which believes that subjectivity is located in the mind and that it can be coded in terms of information, has been extensively analyzed and deconstructed by authors like Donna Haraway, Katherine Hayles, Cary Wolfe, Antonio Damasio, and Roberto Marchesini, just to name a few.

Following these works, especially that of Hayles, this text will explore complex subjectivities in order to counter the fallacy of a disembodied mind that might eventually be downloaded to any materiality that is not the body. After tracking the concept of a technological unconscious through its genealogy from Sigmund Freud (1925; 1930 [1962]), Walter Benjamin (1935), Jacques Lacan (1955 [1991]), Jacques Derrida (1967b), Franco Vaccari (1979), Vilém Flusser (1983), Rosalind Krauss (1993), to Antonio Caronia (2006), the text will show that a stratus exists in technology, and the processes by which we interact with it, that is not accessible to human thought, but that is nonetheless symbolically structured. This stratus is a fundamental element in the consitution of complex subjectivities and the understanding that embodiment cannot be avoided, not even in interaction and enactment within digital environments.

Complex Subjectivities

In *My Mother Was a Computer* (2005), Hayles focuses "on different versions of the posthuman as they continue to evolve in conjunction with intelligent machines" (p. 3). More specifically, the book seeks to redefine and adjust the definition of materiality, as some conceptualizations of the post-human may still contain opposing dualities drawn from the liberal humanist tradition such as material-information, body-soul, and virtual-real (ibid). Hayles identifies the intrinsic characteristic that would allow an entity to 'count as a person' as agency: "Agency enables the subject to make choices, express intentions, perform actions. Scratch the surface of a person, and you find an agent; find an agent, and you are well on your way toward constituting a subject" (ibid, p. 172).

---

1 Mark O'Connell's book *To Be a Machine* (2017) offers a detailed and captivating, if not academic, account not only of transhumanist perspectives and its major exponents, but also companies that offer cryopreservation services (i.e. Alcor).

Nonetheless, it must be clarified that Hayles' definition of the digital subject does not coincide with the conception of the digital subject proposed in the context of this text: namely, that "digital subjects are understood as autonomous creatures imbued with human-like motives, goals, and strategies" (ibid, p. 5). In Hayles' terms, digital subjects are any kind of digital entity, such as the creatures found in Sims. In contrast, it is worth asking what kind of subjectivity might arise from the cybernetic loop between a subject and any kind of digital reality. How might it be understood more specifically as a digitally-embodied subject?

When discussing the attributions of will and agency to digital creatures, Hayles contrasts a continuous analog subjectivity with a fragmented digital one founded in the fragmentary ontology of digital technologies:

> In fact, emergence depends on such fragmentation, for it is only when the programs are broken into small pieces and recombined that unexpected adaptive behaviours can arise.
> To summarise: the analog subject implies a depth model of interiority, relations of resemblance between the interior and the surface that guarantee the meaning of what is deep inside, and the kind of mind/soul correspondence instantiated by and envisioned within the analog technologies of print culture. The digital subject implies an emergent complexity that is related through hierarchical coding levels to simple underlying rules, a dynamic of fragmentation and recombination that gives rise to emergent properties, and a disjunction between surface and interior that is instantiated by and envisioned within the digital technologies of computational culture (ibid, p. 203).

Nevertheless, just as opposing materiality and information is a complex, and also purely illusory act, it is pertinent to avoid oppositions between the fragmented and the continuous. The digital subject should instead be considered as a cybernetic cycle and thus as a process that is both fragmented and continuous, analog and digital—in short, as a complex subjectivity.

Thus, the conceptualization of the digital subject as a digitally-embodied subject has the advantage of definitively eliminating the idea that human interaction within digital and artificial environments can be disembodied, or, as seen in the fallacy propounded by "San Junipero," that there exists a substrate, a "ghost in the machine," that is located in the mind and that can be downloaded and uploaded independently of the rest of the body. Instead, this text proposes to think of this relatively novel entity as a new kind of embodiment.

In this sense, it is useful to remember Francisco Varela, Evan Thompson, and Eleanor Rosch's notion of enaction as embodied cognition (1991), which argues that embodied cognition proposes a completely different conception of the relationship between brain, body, and world to that of computation. Using the concept of enaction, the authors build on a theoretical framework that emphasizes the fact that the ways in which a certain organism, or cognitive agent, experiences the world are fully determined by the feedback loops between the environment, the organism's sensorimotor system, and its physiology (1991, p. 35, pp. 165-167). This reintroduces the phenomenological perspective, especially that of Maurice Merleau-Ponty (1945), and the idea that cognitive agents construct their image and perception of the world through their activities and interactions with it as situated living bodies. The concept of enaction is relevant in this context not only because it implies that the world can be known and perceived by the neural activity of the cognitive agent, but more importantly through the organism's activities and interactions with the environment through its body. Enaction therefore implies not a passive, receptive idea of cognition, but an active and fully embodied one.

It is now clear how the conception of enaction and of situated living bodies can help to develop theories regarding the digital subject as a digitally-embodied subject: it is obviously not that our bodies somehow reconstitute themselves in electronic space—because we know that this cannot yet happen—but precisely that we interact and experience digital space with more than our neuronal networks; we use our entire body. It is evident from this analysis that the simple identification that one can project onto a character in the cinema, or in a book, does not suffice to explain what happens in the digital realm. The digital realm not only refers to potential interaction, but also to the adoption of a point of view that, by definition, implies a further intertwining of the cognitive agent with other cognitive agents in both digital and analog environments, as well as a concrete neurophysiological effect upon the subject. Moreover, through the constitution of the aforementioned point of view, the subject actually comes to inhabit a place in the digital, thus becoming a situated living body: a cognitive, embodied agent in relation to others. Not only are we embodied cognitive agents, we are also embodied as actors in the digital. This is a fundamental factor that the transhumanist imagination of *Black Mirror* seems to ignore.

As this brief summary shows, disembodiment is not only impossible, it is undesirable: in a post-biological landscape an uploaded individual would not be a subject anymore. Therefore, this text intends to analyze the topic using the concepts of complex subjectivities and of the technological unconscious to propose that the collective dimension that the technological unconscious entails can be another way of understanding and deconstructing this recurring fallacy, as seen in the *Black Mirror* episode on which this chapter focuses, in addition to manga series/films such as *Ghost in the Shell* (1989, 1997, 2003, 2017), or *Lucy* (Besson 2014), among so many others.

In a recent book, Joanna Zylinska called this transhumanist impulse "Project Man 2.0" (2019, pp. 19-26). According to Zylinska, it is one of two escapist exit strategies that arise as a reaction to the destruction of the Earth in the Anthropocene Era—the second being to flee the planet (i.e. Elon Musk's SpaceX project). Zylinksa's aim in her short text is to propose a feminist counter-apocalypse to the predominant Western white male narrative regarding the end of the human species, a narrative that is entirely optimistic regarding Project Man 2.0's ability to defeat "Nature" and its hindrances to "Progress" in the form of technological development, or what journalist Mark Lynas calls "techno-fix" (Lynas, 2011, quoted in Zylinksa, 2019, p. 23). The concept of a feminist counter-apocalypse is complementary to considerations of the technological unconscious and complex subjectivities as it offers an alternative strategy to the aforementioned recurring binary conception of consciousness as being situated solely in the mind and coded as information.

The Technological Unconscious

With his article "Civilization and its Discontents" (1930 [1962]), Sigmund Freud is possibly the first to write about technological innovations as prosthetic limbs that humankind has developed to expand its power in the world. Freud suggested that every tool humankind has created since its origins has been meant to extend its power over the world:

> [...] Long ago he [Man] formed an ideal conception of omnipotence and omniscience which he embodied in his gods. To these gods he attributed every-

thing that seemed unattainable to his wishes, or that was forbidden to him. One may say, therefore, that these gods were cultural ideals. Today he has come very close to the attainment of this ideal, he has almost become god for himself. With every tool man is perfecting his own organs, whether motor or sensory, or is removing the limits to their functioning. [...]

Man has, as it were, become a kind of prosthetic God. When he puts on all his auxiliary organs he is truly magnificent; but those organs have not grown on to him and they still give him much trouble at times. [...] Future ages will bring with them new and probably unimaginably great advances in this field of civilization and will increase likeness to God still more ([1930] 1962, pp. 37–39).

This quote not only "foresees" how civilization brought humankind's capabilities even closer to those of a god—which can be seen, for instance, in how digital technologies allow for the phenomenon of ubiquity through avatars and projections of the body—but also paved the way for the conception of a technological unconscious.

In this regard, Walter Benjamin draws on Freud's assertion and observes that photography, which enlarges the power of sight, has created a sort of 'optical unconscious' that permits one to see what the eye cannot. For instance, the human eye cannot perceive that when a horse is running, at a certain point, all of its body is suspended in the air. That moment can be captured and revealed to the human eye by the camera: the potential of human vision is enlarged to almost-divine capabilities by the photographic device (Benjamin, 1931, pp. 5-6). But his analogy with Freud's theory does not end there. The optical unconscious is similar to the subject's unconscious because it provides evidence of a nucleus—in this case the capabilities of the eye—that is not accessible to the subject (Benjamin, 1935). Freud's theories about the unconscious are the first step in the process of dismantling the "liberal humanist subject" (Hayles, 1999), given that according to the theory of the unconscious the subject is guided in most of its actions by impulses that it cannot account for; in the same way in which the optical unconscious is that part of the sense of sight that cannot be accessed by the subject without the help of a machine. Benjamin's conceptualization of the optical unconscious was the first in art history in which art made with machines was considered to develop, project, and produce an aesthetic typical of a given technology engaged in a cybernetic cycle with a human agent, and it will be fundamental for further reflections on what might be called the aesthetic autonomy of certain technologies.

In this context, it is also pertinent to recall Derrida's analysis of the relationship between machines and psychic apparatuses, which was noted by Freud in a letter to Wilhelm Fliess (Derrida 1967b, pp. 335-337). Even then, Freud had the impression, when describing the representation of the psychic apparatus, that he was faced with a machine that could work by itself, independently of the subject's intentions. Yet although the machine can work autonomously, it does not in any way have its own energy, which means that it is inert. It is the psychic apparatus that has an independent way of working, not its representation, the machine (ibid, p. 335). The machine in this sense is pure representation—representation of thought—because a machine cannot, at least yet, ever work by itself; it always needs an external source of energy and input. As Derrida remarks, this is the first objection that Freud found in his comparison of the Wunderblock and the way in which the psychic apparatus works: 'There must come a point at which the analogy between an auxiliary apparatus of this kind and the organ which is its prototype will cease to apply. It is true, too, that once the writing has been erased, the Mystic Pad cannot "reproduce" it from within; it would be a mystic pad indeed if, like our memory, it could accomplish that' (Freud, 1925, p. 230). Thus, Freud identified an aspect of psychic processes that works in a similar way to that of a machine, but in no way does that make the machine comparable to human agency. At this point Derrida begins to go through the questions that Freud did not ask, even though his theories brought him to the cusp of what we might today consider to be the only questions worth asking. In the first place, if the machine is not, evidently, the psychic apparatus but only its representation, how has it increasingly begun to "resemble memory" (Derrida, 1967b, p. 337)? The second fundamental question is regarding metaphors—which defined "in this case the analogy between two apparatuses and the possibility of this representational relation" (ibid)—and the necessity, that had evidently emerged, of creating an additional and representational prosthetic psychic apparatus, the machine, in order to "supplement its finitude" (ibid). In Derrida's terms, prosthetic memory as a representation of the psychic apparatus is related to death, thus paradoxically—and here it is possible to detect an analogy with the *mal d'archive* (Derrida, 1995)—the creation of a prosthetic memory that aims to avoid the oblivion of death has its origin in death itself, namely, a machine's representation of psychic processes and memory.

Freud's ideas and Benjamin's comparison between the optical unconscious and the subject's unconscious are crucial, and led the Italian media theorist, mathematician, and philosopher Antonio Caronia to talk about a 'digital unconscious' and to ask whether digital technologies, specifically the computer, might reveal something, or everything, to humankind about how the unconscious works (Caronia, 2006). As a matter of fact, it did. Recently, John Johnston has convincingly demonstrated how cybernetic theory was fundamental for Jacques Lacan in his theories of the three registers of the self, namely, the symbolic, the imaginary, and the real.

In *The Allure of the Machinic: Cybernetics, Artificial Life and the New AI* (2008), Johnston dedicates a whole chapter to explaining the relevance of cybernetic theory and the universal Turing machine for Lacanian theory. He more specifically addresses how Lacan suggested that the symbolic order worked as a universal Turing machine: Turing's thesis states that every task that can be expressed as an algorithm or any process that can be formally (mathematically) described has an equivalent in a Turing machine. Consequently, the universal Turing machine is a machine that can model how any Turing machine works, because it can perform the wide array of tasks or calculations that can be performed by any of these machines. In short, this means that it is programmable. As Johnston argues, this kind of machine is an abstract machine. It has a certain logical form that can work independently of any material instantiation (2008, p. 71).

What Lacan found interesting in cybernetic theory and, especially, in the universal Turing machine, was that it enabled a new understanding of the autonomy of symbolic processes for which language was a kind of program that runs on the universal Turing machine of the unconscious, an unconscious that operated independently of the subject's will (ibid, p. 78). The unconscious, or more precisely the symbolic order, therefore works as a machine that follows certain logical operations that are not controlled in any way by human decisions: "Lacan understood the symbolic function as a particular kind of computational assemblage that made human behaviour meaningful" (ibid, p. 67).

Consequently, the basis for theories about a technological unconscious was established back in 1925 by Freud and in 1955 by Lacan. Moreover, Derrida wrote in 1967 about the metaphor of the psychic apparatus as a machine.

Katherine Hayles shows that Lacan, and subsequently Deleuze and Guattari, conceived of human cognition and psychology as being intertwined with machinic processes (Hayles, 2005, p. 177). She explains the line of thought through which Lacan, Deleuze, and Guattari challenge human agency given that part of the unconscious works as a processing machine—an issue that Lacan was very aware of, as Johnston shows when quoting Lacan's definition of the symbolic order: "The symbolic world is the world of the machine. Then we have the question as to what, in this world, constitutes the being of the subject" (Lacan, 1991, quoted in Johnston, 2008, p. 72).

Rosalind Krauss used Benjamin's concept of the optical unconscious to invest—to adopt the psychoanalytical term—the word 'unconscious' with the Lacanian meaning (1993). However, he ignored Lacan's theories about the relationship between the unconscious, the universal Turing machine, and cybernetics. As in many of her other texts, Krauss seeks to counter Clement Greenberg's theory of modernism by using the structuralist semiotic square and Lacanian theory to present it in terms of topography rather than narrative (Krauss, 1993, p. 13). The optical unconscious is thus in Krauss' view a kind of anti-vision. If opticality, understood as a sort of pure vision, is the consciousness (or could she say the symptom?) of modernism, then the optical unconscious is the logic that undermines the modernist logic from within, just as the unconscious does with the conscious mind:

> The optical unconscious will claim for itself this dimension of opacity, of repetition, of time. It will map onto the modernist logic only to cut across its grain, to undo it, to figure otherwise. [...] Lacan pictures the unconscious relation to reason, to the conscious mind, not as something different from consciousness, something outside it. He pictures it as inside consciousness, undermining it from within, fouling its logic, eroding its structure, even while appearing to leave the terms of that logic and that structure in place. (Krauss, 1993, p. 24)

Krauss argues that the artists of the optical unconscious included Max Ernst and others associated with Dadaism, especially Marcel Duchamp. Krauss proposes that these artists' oeuvre and discourse work as the optical unconscious—unconscious in the Freudian/Lacanian sense of repression—of modernism and its corresponding opticality, 'eroding it from inside'. Opticality consists of the optical relationship established between the viewer and the work, a purely disembodied kind of vision that would become, according to Krauss, modernism's new medium. For example, the gesture of pointing in Max Ernst is the most 'readymade' of his motifs; it is repeated in several of Ernst's works as if it were a pre-fabricated motif, as Krauss argues listing different examples (*Oedipus Rex*, *Répétitions*, *Loplop Presents*, *La Nature*, quoted on page 82). However, she then brings into her discussion of the readymade the Lacanian automaton, repression returning as repetition, concluding that "the hand is Ernst's object a" (ibid). The main problem with Krauss' position is that she twists Lacanian theory and discusses the unconscious as though Modernity had one, thus presupposing that it is a subject in its own right. She also "analyses" artists through their artworks: although regarding certain repeated *topoi* in an artist's work as readymades undoubtedly makes sense, it is more of a leap to identify them as 'Ernst's object a'.

Although he didn't put it in those terms, Vilém Flusser also theorized about something comparable to Benjamin's optical unconscious in the photographic apparatus. In his work from 1983, *Towards a Philosophy of Photography*, Flusser proposed that images were originally intended to explain the world, that they were mediations between humans and the world that were supposed to make this relationship clearer and more comprehensible. Instead, images "turned into screens" (1983, p. 8) that never cast light on the world, but simply obscured it, interposing themselves between subjects and the world in the sense that instead of using images to navigate reality, humans now interact with the world through them.

In addition to this, the photographic image not only escapes the "functionary's" (or photographer's) intentions, the photographic device turns photographers into a function of the machine:

> The camera is programmed to produce photographs, and every photograph is a realization of one of the possibilities contained within the program of the camera. The number of such possibilities is large, but it is nevertheless finite: It is the sum of all those photographs that can be taken by a camera. Thus photographers attempt to find the possibilities not yet discovered within it. (Flusser, 1983, p. 26)

This means that the machine always performs its own program, which is aimed at perpetuating and improving itself indefinitely: "The camera's program provides for the realization of its capabilities and, in the process, for the use of society as a feedback mechanism for its progressive improvement" (ibid, p. 46). Therefore, not only are the photographer's intentions not important, photographers, and people taking snapshots, become a function of the camera, which eternally performs its own program. This is the black box, the hard core of the photographic apparatus. Although written many years before, these theories anticipate the advent of smart-phone applications that include filters such as Instagram and the like. One can only ask what kind of agency a user has, or their worth as a photographer, when looking at the results of photographs taken and modified through such programs.

Even before Vilém Flusser and Rosalind Krauss, the Italian photographer Franco Vaccari theorized about a 'technological unconscious' in a series of essays first published in 1979. Although Vaccari explicitly quotes Lacanian theory, he doesn't mention which seminar or work he is quoting. However, he may very likely be familiar with Lacan's article of 1955 "Psychoanalysis and cybernetics, or on the nature of language" (1991). He considers that the technological unconscious at work in the photographic apparatus acts independent of the photographer's will, and is also symbolically structured:

> The technological unconscious shouldn't be interpreted as a pure extension and enhancement of human capacities, but it is necessary to see it as the instrument of a capacity of autonomous action; everything happens as if the machine were a fragment of the unconscious in action. The structure of the machine is analogous to the structure of the unconscious, it doesn't have depth and is ignorant of the flows that run through it. (Vaccari, 1979, p. 5)[2]

In this regard the most interesting function of the machine is not necessarily artistic, nor is it guided by the photographer's intentions. Vaccari concentrates on what it does by itself, with no intention, just action. The technological unconscious thus becomes directly connected with the readymade, or rather with readymade images. The photographer only chooses images that are already there and puts them into context, just as the conceptual artist does. This conception of the readymade is very different from Krauss' association of the readymade with the Lacanian automaton; instead, Vaccari uses Lacanian theory as a tool to further understand technology, or more

---

2 All translations of Vaccari's text are mine.

accurately certain artistic output, such as photographs produced by a certain technology.

Vaccari calls 'technological unconscious' what Flusser describes as the 'black box' or 'the program of the apparatus,' what the machine can achieve without the conscious intent of the user or photographer—for both the photographic apparatus performs an action, or a program, beyond the will of the 'functionary' or photographer. For Vaccari, this happens in terms of the Lacanian unconscious, which is symbolically structured, and the most interesting results do not involve the intent of the photographer or follow their wishes. For Flusser, this occurs in terms of a program, of an intentional perpetuation, an improvement of the will of the machine, and he takes a more extreme interpretation with the argument that by fulfilling its program, the camera is using the photographer to improve and perpetuate itself.

Two important and fundamental points make Vaccari's theoretical approach extremely valid and interesting. Vaccari considers the technological unconscious and its symbolic structure as something unlikely to be entirely decoded by a human subject. Yet the key to decoding the technological unconscious is nonetheless held collectively. The technological unconscious is not meant to be analyzed as though it belonged to a subject, but it can offer the key to uncovering certain collective symbolic clues. It can be a way of accessing, at least partially, a collective imagination:

> [...] the other [path to making meaning emerge from a photographic symbol] is to interpret the photograph as a symbol belonging to a language which is only in part attributable to man, a symbol that is a symptom, a symbol that provides a glimpse of something repressed, something that is collective rather than individual. (Vaccari, 1979, p. 14)

The second fundamental point that Vaccari makes shifts the subject from the photographer to the device: He is not analyzing "a subject", nor considering an artistic movement as if it were one; instead, he is focusing on the photographic apparatus, stating that it has "an autonomous capacity of organization of the image in shapes that are already symbolically structured, independently of the subject's action" (ibid, p. 18). Thus, the shift is from Benjamin's optical unconscious with its focus on the expansion of the subject's capabilities, to a technological unconscious wherein the focus is on the device's autonomous action. However, it is worth drawing attention to the assertion that in the technological unconscious images are symbolically structured independently of the subject's intervention: this means that the symbolical dimension has been embedded in the device (unconscious) and that it is at work even without any further human agency (Galati, 2016a; 2016b).

This observation is also fundamental to understanding the relationship between the technological unconscious as it has been developed thus far: the potential that a machine might reveal some (very small) part of the subject's unconscious (Benjamin, 1935; Caronia, 2006); the machine that reveals its own unconscious (Vaccari, 1979; Flusser, 1983) which is symbolically structured and collectively built (Vaccari, 1979).

Complex Subjectivities Embodied in the Digital

As noted elsewhere (Galati, 2016a; 2016b; 2017), in the same way that the pre-Cartesian subject had to change to attain truth, thus changing along with the object/world, the digital subject arrives at varied points of view that constitute them as a subject in the digital realm:

> Such is the basis of perspectivism, which does not mean a dependence in respect to a pre-given or defined subject: to the contrary, a subject will be what comes to the point of view, or rather what remains (*demeure*) in the point of view. That is why the transformation of the object refers to a correlative transformation of the subject [...]. (Deleuze, 1988 [1993], pp. 19-20)

This perspectivism does not imply relativism. It is not a variation of truth related to the subject's will or belief, but rather it is "the condition under which the truth of a variation appears to the subject" (ibid, p. 20). There is always variation in the assumption of an ever-changing point of view that has already been identified in the floating signifier (Galati, 2016 a; 2016b; 2017). She changes in the same movement because "if the status of the object is profoundly changed, so too is that of the subject" (Deleuze, 1988 [1993], p. 19). Therefore, if a digital world exists it is because there was a deep change in the object/world, which necessarily implies a change in the subject; the digital subject: a subject that, in taking a point of view, occupies the place built for them in the collective dimension of the technological unconscious, and by this process makes themselves into a new subjectivity. In doing so, the subject actualizes that world—generating meaning and in the process changing with it—and becomes a digital subject, a digitally-embodied subject. This conceptualization has the advantage of definitively eliminating the idea that human interaction within digital and artificial environments is disembodied, as well as weakening an anthropocentric perspective according to which meaning is only produced by humans. Instead, I propose considering this entity as a new kind of embodiment that simultaneously inhabits and shapes these complex environments. If the posthumanist subject involves overcoming the limitations of the liberal humanist subject, it is not just because these limits have been transcended by machinic and digital networks, but because they have also been transcended by other subjectivities, which are part of the technological unconscious.

In this sense, the "San Junipero" episode is an excellent example of a conceptual confusion—it is impossible to tell whether it was intentional or not—that still plays a prominent role in the imaginative worlds found in the discourse of moguls, researchers, and the specialized press based in Silicon Valley (O'Connell, 2017, Zylinska, 2019). Bearing in mind the collective dimension of the technological unconscious, thinking about it as the place for the emergence of a complex subjectivity in collective terms allows for consideration of the digital subject not only as a cyborg, a subject in a constant feedback loop with the machinic, but also as a distributed, multiplied, and complex subjectivity that is symbolically structured in a collective dimension. The digital subject thus fosters a shared and collective unconscious structure that partly constructs its subjectivity, but to which they also contribute, building and changing it. The process of digitization of the subject thus necessarily implies the conception of a digitally embodied subject, rather than a fiction in which the subject becomes a "discrete" or "virtual creature." The digital subject is neither completely fragmented nor a projection of an original, material self, but instead is able to inhabit the digital realm by assuming of a point of view. In this sense, it assumes an ethical position.

The stress placed thus far on the collective dimension of the technological unconscious seeks to counter the essentially individualistic and anthropocentric approach to the Anthropocene discussed by Zylinska (2019), which is that of the liberal humanist subject. Project Man 2.0 is represented by the Silicon Valley technophile tycoon who has the economic power and resources to flee the planet to Mars, or to cryogenically preserve their body (or head, if the body proves too expensive) (O'Connell, 2017, p. 24) until the (imminent) time when mind uploading is available. On the contrary, the end of the human species will actually be a very egalitarian event: "in the Anthropocene framework, even the very rich cannot escape extinction" (Zylinska, 2019, p. 94). In the "San Junipero" episode, mind uploading is not meant to escape the end of the world, or the human species, but rather personal problems and eventually the deaths of two elderly ladies. However, as we have seen, its brand of escapism and its corresponding fallacy is very similar. If Zylinska's feminist couter-apocalypse is grounded in precariousness as "the condition of being vulnerable to others" (Tsing quoted in Zylinska, 2019, p. 56), in the belief that an ethical subject is always multiple and never individual, this text proposes that the collective dimension of the technological unconscious could be a complementary tool in adopting collective responsibility as an exit strategy.

Bibliography

Benjamin, W., 1931 (1972), A Short History of Photography. In *Screen*, Volume 13, Issue 1, Spring 1972, pp. 5–26

Benjamin, W., 1935 (2008) *The Work of Art in the Age of Its Technological Reproducibility and Other Writings on Media*. Cambridge (MA)-London: The Belknap Press of Harvard University Press.

Caronia, A. (1996) *Il corpo virtuale. Dal corpo robotizzato al corpo disseminato nelle reti*. Padova: Muzzio Editore.

Caronia, A. (2006) L'inconscio della macchina, ovvero: Come catturare il significante fluttuante. In: Livraghi, E., Pezzano, S. eds. *L'arte nell'era della producibilità digitale*. Mimesis: Milano.

Danto, A. 1981 (2004) *The Transfiguration of the Common Place. A Philosophy of Art*. Cambridge (MA): Harvard University Press.

Deleuze, G. 1988 (1993) *The Fold. Leibniz and the Baroque*. London: The Athlone Press

Deleuze, G.; Guattari, F. 1980 (1987) *A Thousand Plateaus. Capitalism and Schizophrenia*. Minneapolis-London: University of Minnesota Press.

Deleuze, G.; Guattari, F. 1991 (1996) *What Is Philosophy?* New York: Columbia University Press.

Derrida, J. (1967a) *De la grammatologie*. Paris: Les Éditions de Minuit.

Derrida, J. (1967b) *L'Écriture et la difference*. Paris: Seuil.

Derrida, J. 1995 (1996) *Archive Fever: A Freudian Impression*. Chicago: Chicago University Press.

Flusser, V. (1983); *Towards a Philosophy of Photography*; London: Reaktion Books.

Foucault, M 1966 (2002) *The Order of Things: An archaeology of the human sciences*. New York, London: Routledge Classics.

Foucault, M. 1969 (2004) *The Archeology of Knowledge*, London: Routledge.

Foucault, M (2001) *Hermeneutics of the Subject. Lectures at the Collège de France 1981-82*. New York: Palgrave Macmillan.

Foucault, M. (2001) *Dits et Écrits II, 1976-1988*. Paris: Gallimard.

Freud, S. (1919) The 'Uncanny'. *The Standard Edition of the Complete Psychological Works of Sigmund Freud*, Volume XVII (1917-1919): *An Infantile Neurosis and Other Works*, pp. 217-256.

Freud, S. (1925) A Note upon the 'Mystic Writing Pad'. *General Psychological Theory*, Chapter XIII, pp. 207-212.

Freud, S. 1930 (1962) *Civilization and Its Discontents*. New York: W.W. Norton & Company Inc.

Galati, G. (2016a); *Duchamp Meets Turing: Art, Modernism, Posthuman*. PhD Thesis, Plymouth University, Plymouth, UK.

Galati, G. (2016b); Significante fluttuante, inconscio tecnologico e soggetto digitale. In: Bianchi, A. and Leghissa, G. eds. *Mondi altri. Processi di soggettivazione nell'era postumana a partire dal pensiero di Antonio Caronia*. Milan: Mimesis, pp. 195-211.

Galati, G. (2017); *Duchamp Meets Turing. Arte, modernismo, postumano*, Milan: Postmedia Books.

Greenberg, C. (1961) *Art and Culture*. Boston: Beacon Press.

Hansen, M.; (2006) *Bodies in Code. Interface with Digital Media*. New York, London: Routledge.

Haraway, D. (1991) *Simians, Cyborgs and Women: The Reinvention of Nature*. New York: Routledge.

Hayles, N. K. (1999) *How We Became Posthuman: Virtual Bodies in Cybernetics, Literature, and Informatics*. 1st ed. Chicago: University Of Chicago Press.

Hayles, N. K. (2005) *My Mother Was a Computer: Digital Subjects and Literary*. 1st ed. Chicago: University of Chicago Press.

Hillis, K. (1999) *Digital Sensations: Space, Identity, and Embodiment in Virtual Reality*. Minneapolis: University of Minnesota Press.

Johnston, J. (2008) *The Allure of the Machinic: Cybernetics, Artificial Life and the New AI*. Cambridge (MA): MIT Press.

Krauss, R. (1993) *The Optical Unconscious*. Cambridge (MA): The MIT Press.

Krauss, R. (1998) *The Picasso Papers*. New York: Farrar, Straus and Giroux.

Krauss, R. (1999a) *A Voyage on the North Sea. Art in the Age of the Post-Medium Condition*. London: Thames & Hudson

Krauss, R. (1999b) Reinventing the Medium. *Critical Inquiry*, 25 (2), "Angelus Novus": Perspectives on Walter Benjamin, winter, pp. 289-305.

Krauss, R. (1999c) Crisis of the Easel Picture. In: Vernendoe, K., Karmel, P. eds. *Jackson Pollock: New Approaches*. New York: Museum of Modern Art, pp. 155-180.

Lacan, J. 1978 (1991) Psychoanalysis and cybernetics, or on the nature of language. In: Miller, J-A. ed. *The Seminar of Jacques Lacan. Book II: The Ego in Freud's Theory and in the Technique of Psychoanalysis 1954-1955*. New York: W.W. Norton & Company, pp. 294-308.

Lévi-Strauss, C; (1950) Introduction à l' oeuvre de Marcel Mauss. In: Marcel Mauss, 1968; *Sociologie et anthropologie (1902-1938)*. Paris: Les Presses universitaires de France.

Lynas, M. (2011) *The God Species. How the Planet Can Survive the Age of Humans*, London: Penguin Random House.

Mehlman, J. (1972) The Floating Signifier: From Lévi-Strauss to Lacan. *Yale French Studies*, 48, pp. 10-37.

Merleau-Ponty, M. (1945) *Phénoménologie de la perception*. Paris: Gallimard.

Mitchell, W.J.T.-Hansen, M. eds. (2010) *Critical Terms for Media Studies*. Chicago, London: Chicago University Press.

O'Connell, M.; (2017) *To Be a Machine*. London: Granta.

Tsing, A. (2015) *The Mushroom at the End of the World*. New Jersey: Princeton University Press.

Vaccari, F. (1979) *Fotografia e inconscio tecnologico*; Torino: Einaudi.

Varela, F., Thompson, E., Rosch, E. (1991) *The embodied mind: Cognitive science and human experience*. Cambridge (MA): The MIT Press.

Zylinksa, Joanna, (2019); *The End of Man. A Feminist Counterapocalypse*. Cambridge (MA): The MIT Press.

Hated in the Nation
A Phantasma of a Post-Climate Change World

Gabor Sarlos

Set in London, "Hated in the Nation" depicts a utopian phantasmagoria about life in the near future. Climate change will have taken its course, fundamentally changing how people cater to themselves and how they are catered for.

The story of "Hated in the Nation" is based on a situation wherein pollination of plants is taken over by the human-coordinated work of millions of Autonomous Drone Insects (ADIs). The introduction of ADIs is a government-financed response to the commonly-known phenomena of the sudden death of complete bee families, Colony Collapse Disorder (CCD). The story ventures into the area that this array of a digital fleet of miniaturized drones is not created only to simply replace the work of bees, but, through an automated control system, to also bring pollination to a perfectionist level. Technology is put to use to maximize the efficiency of artificial bee-made pollination.

In this episode, it emerges that ADIs may have gained autonomy. The episode depicts the possibility that AI-driven technology can surpass the context of its creation and start to follow its own will, beyond the possibility of control for humans. The seemingly inexplicable activities of the ADIs reinforce this impression by demonstrating a very vivid scenario. The story, with a sudden twist, reveals that this armada of ADIs is in fact used to function as tools of intelligence, counterintelligence, and, at their extreme, even manipulated to act as killing machines. A facial recognition system, developed and installed onto ADIs under the apparent directive of the government, allows for the identification of the individual and to exercise control over the public. It becomes clear that the change in behaviour of the ADIs is, in fact, driven by human will and interference.

The main actors of the film, bees, are actually missing from the episode. Their absence is painful as they form part of the fundamentals of evolution and human civilisation, most notably in ensuring pollination and, by extension, producing foodstuffs and raw materials for human consumption. They have been present in human history as far as memory can go back, either directly or indirectly. In their representations, bees, and their most important product, honey, have been constant elements of civilization for thousands of years. Early accounts speak of kings eating honey; in the Bible, God praises honey for it is "sweet and good," and even Canaan is depicted as a place wherein "milk and honey flow." The bees' absence from "Hated in the Nation" is a harbinger of an ominous climate change shaped future.

The consequences of climate change are directly related to the realities of everyday life in this episode. With masses of bee populations perishing, CCD reaches an extent to which, for the second year in a row, Granular, the developer of the technology, activates ADIs on a mega-scale to provide pollination for the plants. Nature by then is in disarray. The extinction of species has become an everyday event, and organic evolution is replaced with technological solutions.

This chapter will articulate its analysis of "Hated in the Nation" through four separate angles: technological, social, and climate determinism, the issue of permit to innovate, risk assessment and management, and finally, the positioning and framing of climate change. These angles not only provide the possibility of a focused analysis, but also place the story in a wider context of interpretation as well. Moreover, applying four different angles indicates the complexity of interdisciplinary issues.

Technological, social, and climatic determinism

The first angle examines whether developments in the episode can be attributed to any one single underlying cause, whether they are the outcomes of previous events instead of results of actions of free will. Determinism, or causal determinism, decrees that every development is the outcome of antecedent developments, thus diminishing any role for human agency in general; therefore, technology, society, and climate can, in theory, each act as the key determinist factor. The individual adaptation of these lenses can determine the outcome of the events in the episode.

"Hated in the Nation" depicts a stage wherein technological developments occur at a rapid pace, challenging the ability of human beings to direct its trajectory. With the ongoing development of technology, singularity (Kurzweil, 2005) may result in machines becoming self-evolving. To replace the notion of innovation being the outcome of the work of outstanding individuals, technological developments become complex and collective phenomena. This could potentially reach a stage wherein technology itself becomes the single ruling driver of development, fundamentally influencing social, political, economic, and environmental outcomes. Through a technological determinist approach, one posits that technology exercises the power to shape society in an autonomous manner, and caters to ongoing innovation as an essential perspective of social development. Technology, in this interpretation, becomes the sole saviour of life, providing solutions to intrinsic issues such as climate change or social division. Towards the second half of the last century, several scholars embraced this view and focused on technological supremacy, which would have the power to influence history even beyond its human-led course (Winner, 1977), perceiving the course of history determined by ongoing technological developments. Once the notion of technological determinism is adopted, and society abides with technologies setting the conditions for social change and progress (Williams (1990 [1975])), any control over technology implies full control over all areas of human life. If technological development takes an uncontrolled course, "societies face the distinct possibility of going adrift in a vast sea of 'unintended consequences'" (Winner 1977, 89).

Submitting to the concept of technological determinism might be challenged, however, simply by referring to the evolving powers of human agency, the importance of social and the historical contexts, as well as the need for interpretive flexibility. The constructivist viewpoint manifests the impossibility of simplistic technological determinism (Hackett, Amsterdamska, and Wajcman, 2008), arguing for developing narratives that take all contexts – technological, social, and historical – into account. One could even argue the dominance of social factors, claiming that in our world social determinism prevails, and social needs rule over technological developments.

Controlling change, including climatic and social changes, through technological means might reflect ignorance (Dafoe, 2015) and hinder the organic development of society. The question, therefore, is about finding the balance between the technological, social, and historical contexts, as well as climatic and natural settings. The answer should be contextual and imply that, under specific and particular conditions, certain kinds of technology might gain more autonomy than others. In the case of the phenomenon of CCD, local solutions would not work. Due to its complexity, spatial considerations, geographical distance, and different longitudinal needs of pollination for different crops, a centralisation of the solution seems to be a necessity. Technology might have its place in the solution, but, as apparent from the above discussion, ought to fit to the specific needs and developed with consideration given to a range of contexts. The appeal of *technology-only solutions* must be resisted and should be considered as a possibility, not an obligation. Technology "merely opens a door; it does not compel one to enter" (White 1962, 28).

Customarily human beings are described both by their biological and social characteristics. Being a biological creature and part of nature, humans have specific roles in the environment. A human being is also a social actor, whose life is determined through their interactions with other members of society. It is through these actions that a human being becomes defined as *who they are*. It is through one's biological existence and social actions and relations that one's role is established. Since the adoption of and increased reliance on digital technologies in everyday life, however, the traditional interpretation of being a primarily biological, or organic, creature has been facing a significant challenge. To an increasing extent, natural habitats are being replaced by inorganic settings wherein all needs are catered to through means invented and developed by mankind. The emergence and adoption of digital technologies accelerated the digital revolution and altered the social imaginary; the Internet and social media became the foundation of a new social construct, which has resulted in a situation wherein the access to and use of digital tools has become primary in defining one's role in society. The call for conscious reflection on many aspects of life is echoed by citing accelerated modernisation and the "end of nature" as the cause of these fundamental changes (Giddens, 1996).

As vividly demonstrated in the episode, in such a society, nature becomes replaceable, and technology is explicitly designed to compensate for its deficiencies. Echoing insights of the materialist tradition, the presented scenario invites one to consider that in the not very distant future human beings need to be considered as not only biological or social constructs, but also as technological figures (Barla, 2019). This will create a situation in which one's social position is strongly determined through one's access to digital tools and solutions. Consequently, social status and access to technology will become the prime determinants of a human being. With technology allowing for the seemingly effortless alteration and overcoming of the biological traits of an individual, an inclination to recognise the dominance of technological determinism for the future of both the individual and mankind might gain further traction.

To the public, ADIs are used to secure pollination in a controlled form by providing useful benefits to people. However, as it turns out, control of this technology cannot be separated from control of the people. The direct controlling of technology leads to the control of the population; in the episode, the government cannot resist this appeal. The development of the ADI technology allows for a backdoor, where, in combination with facial recognition technology, the pollination army can be turned into a crowd-control army. The example of climate change and technology-driven human responses illustrate how perceptions of control and power lead to further challenges and considerations. Fundamental questions will determine the future: who will be in control? Who will provide a check on this form of power? New technologies are developed and then utilised at a pace and intensity that go beyond any human control. TV, petrol-driven cars, the Internet, and social media are all examples wherein essential technological innovations have induced critical changes in society and the environment.

Through a determinist lens, social changes can also be perceived as the principal drivers of change and development. *Social determinism* of technology stresses the dominance of social factors with symptomatic technology (Williams (1990 [1975]), implying that technological developments happen as a consequence of social changes. While the relevance of social determinism is argued by interpreting individual human actions as consequences of social interactions, from the perspective of this episode, it is more relevant to look at whether changes in social needs influence or determine technological developments. Primacy of social determinism over technology is presented by positioning technology as a means to execute or represent the modes of production and the expressions of values, choices, and position of members of society. This episode, however, does not offer examples for this interpretation, but instead presents the notion that it is the changes in the climate that has led to the launch of the fleet of ADIs.

"Hated in the Nation" can therefore be interpreted from the perspective of *climate determinism* as well. It can be argued that all psychological, biological, and cultural attributes are influenced by climatic developments (Diamond, 2005; Hulme, 2011; Sluyter, 2010). In support, history can be depicted as a series of events and developments driven by changes in climate, from the Viking inhabitation of Greenland to the collapse of Ancient Egypt and the Mayan Civilization. The emergence of professions and changes in occupational practices again can be perceived as the consequence of transformation regarding the climate. In its extreme, climate, understood as the average or the statistical distribution of weather conditions of a region over a period of 30 years (Houghton, 2015; IPCC-glossary: 1450), can even be seen as the ultimate driver, the universal predictor of individuals and communities. By focusing on the formation of individuals and fuelling of their movements, climate determinism places the agency of climate over the agency of humans (Hulme, 2011). On the other end, *climate indeterminism* would diminish any role climate might play in the development of human affairs. Through this lens, history develops despite of, or irrelevant to, climatic changes. Not dissimilarly to the notes on technological determinism, this approach can be disputed on the grounds of its oversimplicity: complex changes usually derive from complex contexts. A reductionist approach – reducing explanations to one sole factor only – clearly takes only a very small set of factors into account, and will not lead to unsuitable interpretations of complex problems. Consequent solutions will be one-dimensional and will not address issues in accordance to their complexity.

This episode in particular moves the concept of climate change to a wider context, to that of environmental change. In this model, a range of traditional natural elements are replaced by technology, with ADIs being the prime example. With a technology mindset, all functions of nature that are considered useful can be replaced with appropriate technologies.

Permit to innovate

Technological determinism, as elaborated before, presumes the absence of regulation. Limitless innovation of technology, free of guidance and control, does carry a strong antidemocratic inclination (Feenberg, 1991; Bijker, 1995; Wyatt, 2008). It implies communities renounce their right to have control over their own development (Dotson, 2015). For the communities in the episode, letting Granular and the government take care of solving the bee problem means a loss of any control over this common good.

The question then arises: should innovation be controlled? Should innovation require a permit? Is there an argument for developing a *permit to innovate*? Simple belief in the common good, and trusting the goodwill and the competence of innovation actors, might not be enough. While overseeing all areas of innovation seems an impossible task, this could nevertheless be an alternative to control, by canalising innovation in a direction that benefits society.

Problems related to climate change require technological solutions, in addition to economic, business, social, and individual changes. Allowing technology to be the sole guardian in charge of handling climate challenges will result in a loss of public control. "Permissionless innovation" (Cerf, 2012a; 2012b) is best illustrated by the economic-growth-enhancing potentials of the Internet, wherein the absence of substantial regulatory oversight led to fundamental anomalies and loss of public control. Climate change must not follow this costly pathway, as it has a high probability of leading to a dead-end. In parallel to other episodes of the series, "Hated in the Nation" presents a response to a *what if…* question, and shows us a mirror depicting a worst-case scenario response. As it happens so often, human-developed technology has human-made flaws, resulting in opposite actions than what the technology had been developed for originally.

Furthermore, the episode underlines the dangers of losing control over the ownership and regulation of technology. Control of technology and exercising power become interlinked due to the latter dominating the former. Defining the direction of causality becomes challenging. This is not at all a one-way street, as loss of control over technology leads to political control. When the ADIs become abused, the loosening of grip over technology weakens the political system. The Chancellor of the Exchequer becomes identified as the next target for the drone attack, demonstrating the risks related to attempts to control technology. Community-led control of technology would come as an obvious response for setting up and governing complex systems such as the ADIs for example.

Risk assessment and management

Climate change challenges, such as CCD, invite complex solutions. The complexity of ecosystems limits the effect of linear, one-step solutions. As referred to before, quick-fix technical solutions do not reflect upon actual social or environmental changes (Nelson, 2011, Fischer et al, 2012). Community buy-in can only materialise by conceptualising and building on the exposure and responses of people to the current impacts of climate change. Therefore, habits, norms, and values could be rethought, potentially addressing the underlying existing problems (Wise et al, 2014).

Individual and communal responses to risk factors and the formation of risk behaviours resonate with the psychological, social, institutional, and cultural setup and processes of individuals and their communities. To start with, understanding the causes and the effects of climate change poses significant difficulties to the individual (Bostrom et al, 1994; Lorenzoni and Hulmes, 2009). To make matters more difficult, any correlation between factual knowledge about climate change and adaptation of environmentally-friendly behaviour on an individual or communal level is rather low (Renn, 2011).

Difficulties in adapting individual strategies may inspire community-level solutions. Climatic conditions cannot be regulated or influenced individually. While individual mitigation and adaptation strategies matter as a whole, on an atomic level their actual influence is limited. Climate change, therefore, aligns with the "common pool" analogy. Individuals and even communities or states have no incentive to start acting on their own, as long as they perceive others to be using the resources without any constraint. Action in this setup would be considered futile, as non-action from the other actors eliminate the positive effects of their action. Free-riders may even gain benefits at no cost to themselves, thanks to those actors that did take appropriate actions (Renn, 2011).

Bringing ADIs to action is a technology-driven response to one of the consequences of climate change: the disappearance of bees. While this response might seem adequate to minimise damage, it does not do anything to reduce the risks themselves. ADIs might be a remedy, but do not solve the problem. Actual responses would seek to minimize risks and address the actual drivers of vulnerability, all in a systemic manner.

Dramatic changes of this type normally invite three possible types of responses: mitigation, resilience build, or adaptation. By minimising risks at their source, mitigation of evolving risks results in decreasing the hazards to the community. Successful mitigation strategies require a concentrated and coordinated approach, which usually means policy-level intrusion and implementation of changes. The wider the range of the intervention is, the better the chances it has for success. Minimisation of the risks themselves is in the focus. A mitigation approach does not enable an ecosystem to respond and rectify itself, even if it would be important to move closer to a state of equilibrium (Holling, 1973; Rosenzweig, 1971). In the context of climate change, the exact relation of mitigation, resilience build, and adaptation has been discussed extensively, even implying that resilience is part of both mitigation and adaptation because mitigation helps rebuild the system and adaptation helps recovery gain speed (McDaniels et al., 2008; Kythreotis and Bristow, 2017).

However, a strategic approach would instead build on developing the general resilience capabilities of the community. A risk of this type would allow for the embracing of communities into the adaptation of the solution, instead of offering centralised solutions. Resilience building for the disappearance of bees for urban or rural communities would empower them to handle and adapt to the new situation, while the sustained supply of goods and services remains intact (Jones et al., 2012). Successful resilience building typically reflects locally-driven risk-management approaches, instead of centrally driven government actions. A range of examples of resilience build refers to mobilisation of the individual and community level resources through collective governance (Nieuwaal et al., 2009). Replacing the bees with ADIs does not contribute to increasing the resilience level of the affected community at all.

Adaptation is the third possible pathway, usually encompassing individually-driven strategies. In these cases, the impact of risks is accepted at face value, while their effects are reduced by individual adaptation strategies. Communication between the individual actors can have a significant effect, by sharing best practices and coordinating efforts. Adaptation serves a valid purpose: through adjustments, it helps decrease society's vulnerability to the effects of climate change (Smit & Wandel, 2006).

In this episode, minimisation of the impacts of the changes is the focus. Launching the fleet of ADIs to replace bees for pollinating is a prime example of a mitigation-driven approach, reflecting a technology-driven band-aid attitude, instead of adopting a strategic course of change. The use of a centrally-developed and governed solution, not requiring any community-level engagement, serves not only pollination, but, as it becomes apparent in the episode, ensures the government's ambition of a technologically-driven system of obtaining control.

Positioning and framing climate change

Framing plays a critically important role in identifying and mobilising the issue of climate change. On a local level, in the case of a crisis, governments usually apply one of the four most common frames: natural disasters/hazards, vulnerability, risk/economic management, or resilience (Juhola et al., 2011; McEvoy et al., 2010). Differences in framing usually derive from the different interpretations regarding the role of the local government in pre-empting, handling, and following up on a crisis. Regarding the media representation of environmental discourses, research has identified four broad categories of framing: problem-solving, sustainability, survivalism, and green radicalism. The first two fit into the overall narrative of industrial societies, while the last two intend to circulate the need for radical change (Dryzek, 2012).

Glaser et al (2009) approach framing from the concept of storytelling. Again, four types of frames are identified. According to their analysis, a story can be built by connecting events in a dramatic account (dramatization), by focusing on the emotional interpretation (emotionalization), through the examination of the role of selected humans through personalization, or by complementing through fictional or hypothetical episodes (fictionalization). In a globalised media culture, coverage of mega-issues usually reflects a standardised, homogenised content production, while interpretation reflects national and socio-cultural typologies (Mancini, 2008; Lück et al, 2016).

The TV news of "Hated in the Nation" announces that another bird species has just disappeared: *Conservationists have announced another extinction, the Siberian crane has died out, following an unprecedented reduction in its wetland habitat. And the honey-bee mimicking drone insects, known as ADIs, have been activated for their second summer.'* The process of extinction of species continues on a grand scale, yet the extinction of another species deserves hardly more than *15 seconds of fame* in the news. Hints in the episode indicate that the extinction of species, losses of habitats, drastic environmental changes, the emergence of new and aggressive invasive species, scarcity of food, water, and shelter, and the dominance of pre-packaged foods all become common-place. Climate change is not narrated in the form of storytelling at all. Rather, the format of the TV news demonstrates that changes in the climate and the environment are business as usual. The formal *bon mot* of 'in times of change, nothing is constant but change itself' gets a new dimension: climate change itself becomes constant. One cannot help but imagine that in the regular eve-ning TV summary, next to the topics on world news, domestic affairs, sports, and the weather, a similar standard section is dedicated to climate change itself.

In this episode, the framing of the two pieces of news indicates two sepa-rate strategies. The extinction of the Siberian crane is not elaborated upon at all. It is announced in a matter of fact format, as a mix of interest news and a matter of factual account of change. While not many would have noticed the loss of the Siberian crane, as a responsible presenter, the TV station con-siders it to be their responsibility to give an account. The other piece of news, on the activation of ADIs, provides a different frame. Human action is set in the focus, where a particular problem is efficiently addressed to cover up for the effects of the disappearance of the bees. Again, the tone is matter of fact, and thus indicates reassurance that this matter is being handled. The two different strategies and the construction of sentences reflect two different framing strategies, placing human action into the focus, where it actually matters.

All throughout the series, *Black Mirror* puts media and technology under scrutiny, to test their effects on the human being. It operates like a test pad: elements are probed under extreme circumstances to identify their defaults. "Hated in the Nation" goes further by implying that media and technology are combined by nature. Despite bringing a further element to the equation, the power relations of the three factors are obvious. Media and technology are in the driving position; the environment simply becomes another area for their dominance. The loss of the natural environment, its replacement with tech-nologically-driven solutions, and the emergence of an environment that has undergone fundamental change adds to the surreality of the show. "Hated in the Nation" becomes *another brick in this surreality show.*

Conclusion

Responding to changes in the environment has always been essential in the successful adaptation of mankind. Understanding the importance and the depth of the problem of climate change, as well as assessing and controlling the impacts of the solutions that are implemented can only take place if a broad approach is applied. The effects of climate change manifest themselves in a range of different formats, reflecting the complexity of the issue. Developing solutions, both in terms of mitigation of its causes and adaptation to its consequences, requires a systemic and well-diversified approach. While technology will need to play an essential part in developing solutions, it cannot in any form take a leading, let alone controlling, function. Moreover, guarding technological developments cannot be bestowed upon politicians alone. Individuals and communities need to be granted an important role in this process, demonstrating commitment and responsibility throughout. The development of technological solutions needs to be governed and controlled appropriately. A well balanced, strategic approach and appropriate framing, as well as embracing the needs and views of all actors and controlled in a public and transparent manner can deliver an appropriate response to climate change. As an episode in a popular Science Fiction series, "Hated in the Nation" can prompt a turn humanity's ship away from a collision, and consequently can fundamentally change the course of climate change.

Bibliography

Barla, J. (2019) *The Techno-Apparatus of Bodily Production: A New Materialist Theory of Technology and the Body.* Bielefeld, Germany: transcript.

Bijker, W. (1995) *Of Bicycles, Bakelites, and Bulbs.* Cambridge, MA: MIT Press.

Bostrom, A., Morgan, M.G., Fischhoff, B., Read, D. (1994) What do people know about global climate change? Part 1: Mental models. *Risk Analysis.* (14), pp.959–970.

Cerf, V. G. (2012a) "Keep the Internet Open." New York Times, May 24. Accessed 20 February 2020, http://www.nytimes.com/2012/05/25/opinion/keep-the-internet-open.html.

Cerf, V. G. (2012b) Dynamics of Disruptive Innovations. *Journal on Telecommunications and High Technology Law* (10), pp.21-31.

Dafoe, A. (2015) On Technological Determinism: A Typology, Scope Conditions, and a Mechanism. *Science, Technology, & Human Values.* 40(6), pp.1047-1076.

Diamond, J. (2005) *Collapse: How Societies Choose to Fail or Succeed.* New York: Viking.

Dotson, T. (2015) Technological Determinism and Permissionless Innovation as Technocratic Governing Mentalities: Psychocultural Barriers to the Democratization of Technology. *Engaging Science, Technology, and Society,* (1), pp.98-120.

Dryzek, J. S. (2012) *The politics of Earth: Environmental discourses.* Oxford: Oxford University Press.

Feenberg, A. (1991) *Critical Theory of Technology.* New York: Oxford University Press.

Fischer, J., Dyball, R., Fazey, I., Gross, C., Dovers, S., Ehrlich, P.R., Brulle, R.J., Christensen, C., Borden, R.J., (2012) Human behavior and sustainability. *Frontiers in Ecology and the Environment.* 10(3), pp.153–160.

Giddens, A. (1996) Affluence, Poverty and the Idea of a Post-Scarcity Society. *Development and Change,* 27(2), pp.365-377.

Glaser, M., Garsoffky, B. and Schwan, S. (2009) Narrative-based learning: Possible benefits and problems. *Communications* 34(4), pp.429–447.

Hackett, E. J., Amsterdamska, O., Wajcman, J. (2008) *The Handbook of Science and Technology Studies. Cambridge,* MA: MIT Press.

Holling, C. S. (1973) Resilience and stability of ecological systems. *Annual Review of Ecology and Systematics,* (4), pp.1–23. doi:10.1146/ annurev. es.04.110173.000245

Houghton, J. (2015) *Global Warming: The Complete Briefing,* fifth edition, Cambridge: Cambridge University Press.

Hulme, M. (2011) Reducing the Future to Climate: A Story of Climate Determinism and Reductionism. *The University of Chicago Press on behalf of The History of Science Society.* 26(1), pp.245-266.

IPCC-glossary] (2013b) "Annex III: Glossary", Serge Planton (ed.), in Stocker et al. 2013: 1447–1465.

Jones, H.P., Hole, D.G., Zavaleta, E.S., (2012) Harnessing nature to help people adapt to climate change. *Nature Climate Change* 2(7), pp.504–509.

Juhola, S., Keskitalo, E. C. H., Westerhoff, L. (2011) Understanding the framings of climate change adaptation across multiple scales of governance in Europe. *Environmental Politics*, 20(4), pp.445–463.

Kurzweil, R., (2005) *The singularity is near: When humans transcend biology.* Penguin.

Kythreotis, A.P. and Bristow, G.I., (2017) The 'resilience trap': exploring the practical utility of resilience for climate change adaptation in UK city-regions. *Regional Studies*, 51(10), pp.1530-1541.

Lorenzoni I, Hulmes M. (2009) Believing is seeing: laypeople's views of future socio-economic and climate change in England and in Italy. *Public Understanding of Science.* (18), pp.383–400.

Lück J, Wessler H, Wozniak A, Lycariao, D. (2016) Counterbalancing global media frames with nationally colored narratives: A comparative study of news narratives and news framing in the climate change coverage of five countries. *Journalism* 19(12), pp.1635 –1656. DOI: 10.1177/1464884916680372

Mancini, P. (2008) *Journalism cultures: A multi-level proposal.* In: Hahn O (ed.) Journalistische Kulturen: Internationale und interdisziplinäre Theoriebausteine. [Lehrbuch]. Köln: Herbert von Halem, pp.149–167.

McDaniels, T., Chang, S., Cole, D., Mikawoz, J., & Longstaff, H. (2008). Fostering resilience to extreme events within infrastructure systems: Characterizing decision contexts for mitigation and adaptation. *Global Environmental Change* (18), pp.310–318. doi:10.1016/j.gloenvcha.2008.03.001

McEvoy, D., Matczak, P., Banaszak, I., & Chorynski, A. (2010) Framing adaptation to climate-related extreme events. *Mitigation and Adaptation Strategies for Global Change*, 15(7), pp.779–795.

Nelson, J.A., (2011) Ethics and the economist: what climate change demands of us. *Ecological Economics* (85), pp.145–154.

Nieuwaal, K.V., Driessen, P.P.J., Spit, T.J.M., Termeer, C.J.A.M. (2009) A state of the art of governance literature on adaptation to climate change. Towards a research agenda. Utrecht: Knowledge for Climate (Nationaal Onderzoeksprogramma Kennis voor Klimaat – KvK).

Renn, O., (2011) The social amplification/attenuation of risk framework: application to climate change. *Wiley Interdisciplinary Reviews: Climate Change* 2(2), pp.154-169.

Rosenzweig, M. L. (1971) Paradox of enrichment: Destabilization of exploitation ecosystems in ecological time. *Science*, (171), pp.385–387. DOI:10.1126/science.171.3969.385

Sluyter, A. (2010) Engaging with the politics of determinist environmental thinking, in Radcliffe, S.A. (ed.) Environmentalist thinking and/in geography, *Progress in Human Geography* 34(1) pp.98–116.

Smit, B. and Wandel, J. (2006) Adaptation, adaptive capacity and vulnerability. *Global Environmental Change*, (16), pp.282–292. DOI:10. 1016/j.gloenv cha.2006.03.008

Stocker, T. F., et al. (eds.). (2013) *Climate Change 2013: The Physical Science Basis. Contribution of Working Group I to the Fifth Assessment Report of the Intergovernmental Panel on Climate Change*, New York: Cambridge University Press, available online.

White, L. (1962) *Medieval Technology and Social Change*. Oxford, UK: Oxford University Press.

Williams, R. (1990 [1975]) *Television: Technology and Cultural Form*. London: Routledge

Winner, L. (1977) *Autonomous Technology—Technics-out-of-control as a Theme in Political Thought*. Cambridge, MA: MIT Press

Wise, R.M., Fazey, I., Stafford Smith, M., Park, S.E., Eakin, H.C., Archer Van Garderen, E.R.M., Campbell, B. (2014) Reconceptualising adaptation to climate change as part of pathways of change and response. *Global Environmental Change*, (28), pp.325-336.

Wyatt, S. (2008) "Technological Determinism is Dead; Long Live Technological Determinism." In *Handbook of Science and Technology Studies*, 3rd edition, edited by Hackett, E.J., Amsterdamska, O., Lynch, M., Wajcman, J. pp.165-180. Cambridge, MA: MIT Press.

Author Biographies

Tom H. Apperley is Senior Research Fellow (*Yliopistotutkija*) at the Centre of Excellence in Game Culture Studies. He conducts research on digital games and playful technologies with an emphasis on their impact and influence on culture, particularly areas such as social policy, pedagogy, and social inclusion. His open-access print-on-demand book, *Gaming Rhythms: Play and Counterplay from the Situated to the Global,* was published by The Institute of Network Cultures in 2010. Tom's more recent work has appeared in *Games and Culture, New Review of Multimedia and Hypermedia* and *Media International Australia.*

Justin Michael Battin is Lecturer of Communication at RMIT University in Ho Chi Minh City, Vietnam. His research focuses on intersecting strands of phenomenological and existential philosophy with the everyday uses of mobile media technologies and mobile social media. He is the author of *Mobile Media Technologies and Poiēsis: Rediscovering How We Use Technology to Cultivate Meaning in a Nihilistic World* (Palgrave Macmillan, 2017) and co-editor of *We Need to Talk About Heidegger: Essays Situating Martin Heidegger in Contemporary Media Studies* (Peter Lang, 2018). He is currently conducting an RMIT-funded project titled *The Instagrammable Saigon,* a project that blends netnography and phenomenology to explore urban Instagramming as a place-making practice.

Ricardo Carniel Bugs holds a Ph.D. in Communication and Journalism from the Autonomous University of Barcelona (Spain), where he is Professor in the Department of Journalism and Communication Studies. He is a member of the Laboratory of Prospective and Research in Communication, Culture, and Cooperation (LAPREC). His main fields of research are media law and policy, audiovisual content regulation, pluralism and diversity, journalism, and communication for development and social change.

Anna Caterina Dalmasso (Ph.D. Philosophy, University of Lyon/University of Milan, 2015) is assistant professor at University of Milan, within the ERC Advanced Grant "An-Iconology. History, Theory, and Practices of Environmental Images", directed by Andrea Pinotti. Her research interests include Film and Media Studies, Aesthetics, and Visual Culture. She devoted her thesis to Merleau-Ponty's philosophy of the visual, and to its implications for contemporary mediality and scopic regime. She has coedited interdisciplinary collective books and journal issues on screens as dispositives of reference of our time. She is also a filmmaker and has worked in cinema, television and in audiovisual literacy workshops.

German A. Duarte is Assistant Professor of Film and Media Studies at the Free University of Bozen-Bolzano. His research interests include history of media, film history, cybernetics, cognitive-cultural economy, and philosophy. He is the author of several publications, including four books, edited volumes, essays, and papers in international journals. Among them, he recently authored the monographs *Reificación Mediática* (UTADEO – 2nd Edition 2020), *Fractal Narrative: About the Relationship Between Geometries and Technology and Its Impact on Narrative Spaces* (transcript, 2014), and co-edited the volumes *Transmédialité, Bande dessinée & Adaptation* (PUBP 2019) and *We Need to Talk About Heidegger: Essays Situating Martin Heidegger in Contemporary Media Studies* (Peter Lang, 2018).

Andrea Facchetti completed a Ph.D at the Iuav School of Doctorate Studies in the program of Design Sciences in 2017, where he developed a research project regarding speculative practices and knowledge production in visual design. Since 2018, he is Assistant Professor in Visual Communication Design at the Free University of Bozen-Bolzano in the Faculty of Design and Arts. He is the co-founder and co-director of Krisis Publishing, an independent publishing and curatorial platform that focusses on visual and media culture, politics of representation, and social research.

Robbie Fordyce is Lecturer in Big Data/Quantitative Analytics and Research Methods in Communication and Media Studies at Monash University. He researches the political and social implications of rule-based systems, especially digital platforms, digital infrastructure, and digital entertainment. Robbie has recently published in *Games and Culture, Communication Research & Practice*, and *Fibreculture*.

Gabriela Galati is Professor of Theory and Methodology of the Mass Media and of Aesthetics of New Media and Phenomenology of Contemporary Art at Nuova Accademia di Belle Arti (Milan) and Istituto Europeo di Design (Turin). She wrote the published book *Duchamp Meets Turing: Arte, Modernismo, Postumano* with Postmedia Books (2017) and edited the book *Ecologie complesse: Pensare l'arte oltre l'umano* (*Complex Ecologies: Thinking Art Beyond the Human*, Meltemi, forthcoming 2020). She writes reviews of books on art, philosophy, science, and technology for *Leonardo Reviews / Leonardo Journal* (The MIT Press) and regularly collaborates with *AdVersus* and *Scenari* (Mimesis). She is the co-founder and director of the contemporary art gallery IPERCUBO. She obtained her Ph.D. at the University of Plymouth, for which her dissertation addressed the relationship between art theory, digitalization processes, and critical posthuman theory.

Santiago Giraldo-Luque is Professor and Deputy Director of Research and Postgraduate Studies in the Department of Journalism at the Autonomous University of Barcelona, where he also received his Ph.D. in Communication and Journalism. He also holds a degree in Political Science (National University of Colombia), a master's degree in Communication and Education, and a master's degree in Journalism (UAB). He is also a researcher for the Communication and Education Cabinet at UAB.

Joseph Macey is a researcher at the Gamification Group, Tampere University, whose work is concerned with the consumption of digital media. A primary area of interest is the convergence of contemporary digital media, exemplified in the emergent phenomenon of video-game-related gambling. His research interests also include the interaction between consumption of different forms of media, adverse social behavior online, problematic media consumption, and the cognitive biases of media users.

Artur de Matos Alves is Assistant Professor at TÉLUQ University and Researcher at the CRICIS research centre (UQAM). He holds a Ph.D. in Communication, Systems, and Technologies from the New University of Lisbon (NOVA), where he conducted a dissertation on the social and political impacts of emerging technologies. His research on the philosophy of technology, online transparency, and the societal impacts of emerging technologies, new media, and cyber conflict has been presented at international conferences, as well as featured in books and peer reviewed journals since 2008. The book *Criador e Criatura* (Calouste Gulbenkian Foundation, 2013) reflects his Ph.D. dissertation on emerging technologies, presented to the New University of Lisbon in 2010. He also edited the book *Unveiling the Posthuman* (Inter-Disciplinary Press, 2012).

Marcin Mazurek is Assistant Professor at the Institute of English Cultures and Literatures, University of Silesia, Poland. His research interests include postmodern theory, culture-technology relationships, consumerist criticism, visual culture, and automobility studies. He is the co-editor of *Camouflage. Discourses of Deception, Transparency and Exposure* (2010) and *Camouflage. Secrecy and Exposure in Cultural and Literary Studies* (2014), and is the author of *A Sense of Apocalypse: Technology, Textuality, Identity* (Peter Lang, 2014). He is also an Assistant to the Editor-in-Chief of *Er(r)go: Theory-Literature-Culture*, a Polish international scholarly journal published by the University of Silesia. In 2016, under the auspices of Interdisciplinary.Net, he organized and chaired an international conference held in Oxford, UK titled Cars in/of Culture: Mobility, Materiality, Representation.

Brian McCauley is a researcher at the Media, Management & Transformation Centre, Jönköping University and a director of the Esports Research Network. His primary interests are gaming culture and e-sports with a focus on the actors who engage in these ecosystems. His research includes work on social media, mobile gaming, e-sports actors, gender issues, and developing regions.

Mauricio Molina-Delgado is the Director of the Philosophy Department of the University of Costa Rica and Professor of the Postgraduate Program in Cognitive Science. He has a Ph.D. in Psychology from the University of Thessaloniki and a bachelor's degree in Statistics from the University of Costa Rica. In 2016, he was recognized with the Costa Rican Literature National Award "Aquileo J. Echeverría." His research interests are data analysis, creativity, and philosophy of the mind. His recent publications include, "The discovery/justification context dichotomy within formal and computational models of scientific theories" (*Journal of Applied Non-Classical Logics*, 2017, with Morales), *Treinta y seis daguerrotipos de Diotima desnuda* (Siltolá Poesía, 2016), and "Simulation of behavioral profiles in the plus-maze: a classification and regression tree approach" (*Biosystems*, 2013, with Padilla-Mora and Fornaguera).

Hatice Övgü Tüzün is currently Chair of the Department of American Culture and Literature at Bahçeşehir University. She holds a B.A. in English Language and Literature from İstanbul University, and an M.A. and Ph.D. from the University of Kent, U.K. She has published articles and book chapters on Victorian and Modern literature, Turkish literature, comparative literature, science fiction, postcolonial fiction, travel writing, and the political novel. Her recent research interests include ecocriticism, posthumanism, transhumanism and emotions in literature.

Alfredo Rizza is Assistant Professor in Glottology at the Department of Cultures and Civilizations at the University of Verona, Italy where he also teaches general linguistics. He has studied in Pavia, Berkeley, and Würzburg (with an Alexander von Humboldt-Stiftung post-doctoral scholarship). His current research topics include textuality and technology, philosophy of language, graphemics and grammatology, ancient languages and cultures, and the history of linguistics. He is the author of several publications that include monographic and edited volumes, and papers in scientific journals and miscellaneous studies.

Bértold Salas-Murillo is Professor of Film Studies at the University of Costa Rica. He has a master's degree in Cinematography from the University of Costa Rica and a doctorate in "Littérature et arts de la scène et de l'écran" from Laval University, Canada. He is Assistant Director of the Postgraduate in Arts at the University of Costa Rica. His recent publications include "Forging Her Path with Her Own Fists: Autonomy and Contradictions of Age, Class and Gender in Florence Jaugey's *La Yuma/Yuma* (2010)" (*Studies in Spanish and Latin American Cinemas*, 2018), "La intermedialidad: las oportunidades y los riesgos de un concepto en boga" (*Especial: El Amplio Espectro Del Humanismo: Metodología, Cuentos, y Otras Historias*, 2018), "Un hoy que se narra a la sombra del ayer. El cine costarricense y la inquietud por el tiempo" (*Istmo. Revista virtual de estudios literarios y culturales centroamericanos*, 2018), and "Los subterfugios digitales de Jafar Panahi" (*Razón Crítica*, 2019).

Gabor Sarlos is Senior Lecturer in Communication at the University of Roehampton, UK. Previously, he was Senior Lecturer and Discipline Lead of the BA in Communication Program at RMIT University, Vietnam. During his academic career, he held positions at the University of Wolverhampton, UK, the Worcester Business School, UK, and the International Business School in Budapest, Hungary. He holds an MSc in Economics from Corvinus University and a Ph.D. in Sociology from ELTE University of Sciences in Budapest. His academic interests are in the public perception of energy futures and climate change, and in the development of academic and professional sustainability communication models.

Santiago Tejedor is Director and Associate Professor at the Department of Journalism and Communication Sciences of the Autonomous University of Barcelona (UAB). He is the Coordinator and Researcher of the Communication and Education Cabinet (UAB). He has a Ph.D. in Journalism and Communication Sciences from the Autonomous University of Barcelona and a Ph.D. in Project Engineering from the Polytechnic University of Catalonia (UPC). He has been a participant in several publicly-funded Spanish and European research projects related to media literacy and citizen participation. He has been named "Exceptional Educator" by the Higher Board of Directors of the University of Commercial Sciences of Nicaragua and "Distinguished Visitor" by the Technological University of Honduras.

Georgios Tsagdis is Fellow at the Westminster Law & Theory Lab and lectures at Leiden University, Erasmus University Rotterdam, and the Architectural Association. His work operates across theoretical and disciplinary intersections drawing on 20th century, contemporary and Ancient Greek philosophy. His essays have been published in various book collections and international journals, among which include *Parallax*, *Philosophy Today* and *Studia Phaenomenologica*. His editorials include special issues for *Azimuth* ("Intersections: at the Technophysics of Space"), for the *International Journal of Philosophical Studies* ("Of Times: Arrested, Resigned, Imagined"), as well as a collected volume, in progress, on Derrida's *Politics of Friendship* with Edinburgh

University Press. In the years 2014-19, he was the convener of the Seminar of Neoplatonic Studies, an intercollegiate study and research group, hosted at the Warburg Institute, London.

Dan Ward is Lecturer in Media and Cultural Studies at Sunderland University, where he teaches modules in contemporary television as well as popular culture, film and society. His Ph.D. centered on representations of masculinity and violence in contemporary U.S. crime TV, and he has published on 'cult' TV series such as *Game of Thrones* and *Peaky Blinders*. More recently, his research has explored areas such as modern celebrity branding through social media (specifically focusing on the Hollywood career of Dwayne 'The Rock' Johnson) and the resurgence of Cold War narratives in recent Hollywood cinema. Dan is currently working on expanding his previous research in the field of sports documentary for an upcoming collection on television genres.

Cultural Studies

Gabriele Klein
Pina Bausch's Dance Theater
Company, Artistic Practices and Reception

May 2020, 440 p., pb., col. ill.
29,99 € (DE), 978-3-8376-5055-6
E-Book:
PDF: 29,99 € (DE), ISBN 978-3-8394-5055-0

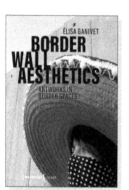

Elisa Ganivet
Border Wall Aesthetics
Artworks in Border Spaces

2019, 250 p., hardcover, ill.
79,99 € (DE), 978-3-8376-4777-8
E-Book:
PDF: 79,99 € (DE), ISBN 978-3-8394-4777-2

Jocelyne Porcher, Jean Estebanez (eds.)
Animal Labor
A New Perspective on Human-Animal Relations

2019, 182 p., hardcover
99,99 € (DE), 978-3-8376-4364-0
E-Book: 99,99 € (DE), ISBN 978-3-8394-4364-4

Cultural Studies

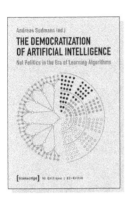

Andreas Sudmann (ed.)
The Democratization of Artificial Intelligence
Net Politics in the Era of Learning Algorithms

2019, 334 p., pb., col. ill.
49,99 € (DE), 978-3-8376-4719-8
E-Book: available as free open access publication
PDF: ISBN 978-3-8394-4719-2

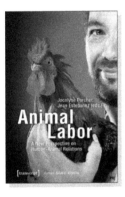

Jocelyne Porcher, Jean Estebanez (eds.)
Animal Labor
A New Perspective on Human-Animal Relations

2019, 182 p., hardcover
99,99 € (DE), 978-3-8376-4364-0
E-Book:
PDF: 99,99 € (DE), ISBN 978-3-8394-4364-4

Ramón Reichert, Mathias Fuchs,
Pablo Abend, Annika Richterich, Karin Wenz (eds.)
Digital Culture & Society (DCS)
Vol. 4, Issue 1/2018 – Rethinking AI: Neural Networks,
Biometrics and the New Artificial Intelligence

2018, 244 p., pb., ill.
29,99 € (DE), 978-3-8376-4266-7
E-Book:
PDF: 29,99 € (DE), ISBN 978-3-8394-4266-1

CPSIA information can be obtained
at www.ICGtesting.com
Printed in the USA
LVHW050754130221
679236LV00042B/1404